CW01652510

Essential
IMPRESSIONISTS

Front cover: *Woman Doing her Washing by* Camille Pissarro. Courtesy of Christie's Images
Back cover: *The Japanese Bridge* by Claude Monet.
Courtesy of Christie's Images

This is a Parragon Book
This edition published in 2003

Parragon
Queen Street House
4 Queen Street
Bath BA1 1HE, UK

Copyright © Parragon 2000

ISBN: 1-40542-322-6

All rights reserved. No part of this publication may be reproduced, stored in a retrieval system, or transmitted in any form or by any means, without the prior written permission of the copyright holder.

A copy of the CIP data for this book is available from the British Library upon request.

The right of Antonia Cunningham to be identified as the author of this work have been asserted in accordance with Section 77 of the Copyright, Designs and Patents Act of 1988.

The right of Karen Hurrell to be identified as the author of the introduction to this book has been asserted in accordance with Section 77 of the Copyright, Designs and Patents Act of 1988.

Printed and bound in China

Essential IMPRESSIONISTS

ANTONIA CUNNINGHAM

Introduction by Karen Hurrell

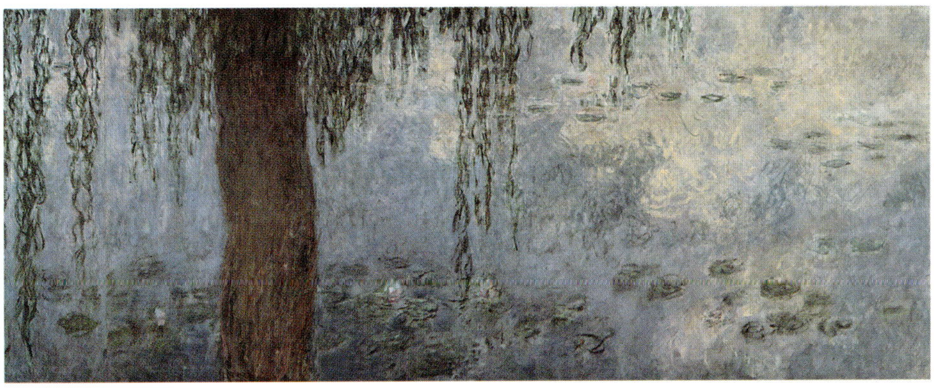

Contents

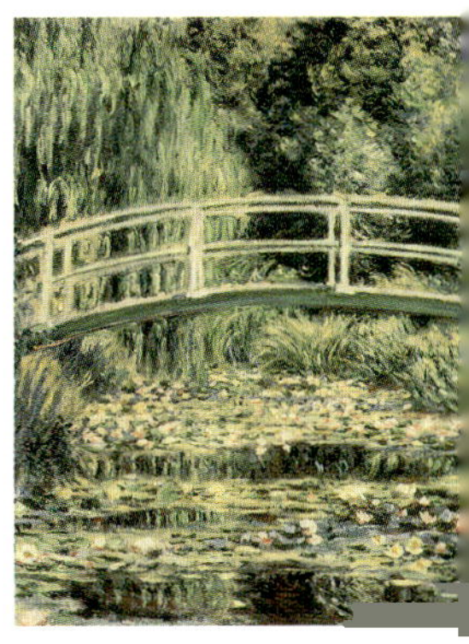

INTRODUCTION

THE Impressionists filled the hallowed halls of the French art establishment with light. As a group, they were critically derided, professionally shunned and considered to be the most outrageous and untalented artists of the 19th century. But they were revolutionary, changing the course of art for ever. Today, less than 150 years later, the paintings of the Impressionists are some of the best-known and most loved works in the entire history of art.

Paris was in the throes of the *belle époque* when 19-year-old Claude Monet (1840–1926) arrived from Le Havre in 1859. The economic recession that had been a catalyst for the 1848 revolution was over by 1851, and Napoleon Bonaparte instigated a refurbishment of the city to reflect the prosperity and splendour of the times. Life in Paris changed dramatically, and its streets became a mecca for bright young things, who brought a sense of euphoria into a new café society. In such a climate of change, Impressionism should have flourished, but the French people, and the art establishment in particular, were reluctant to embrace its vivacity and refreshing approach to art.

Paintings were expected to be refined and conservative, calling upon Classical traditions and vested with moral rectitude. Art during this time was considered to be a reflection of the spiritual health of the nation. In a time when France was just pulling itself from the depths of spiritual and economic depression, it became all the more important that art was morally upright, honest and based on a solid foundation of the acceptable and the patriotic.

Like the contemporaries who form the Impressionists, Claude Monet was a man of vision. When he was 18 he met Eugène Boudin (1824–98), and this was reputedly the determining factor in his decision to become a painter. Boudin was a landscape painter, and he painted out-of-doors, documenting with precision and originality the movement of water, air, clouds, trees. He was extraordinarily influential in Monet's life, and he is accorded the honour of being the Impressionists' first real inspiration.

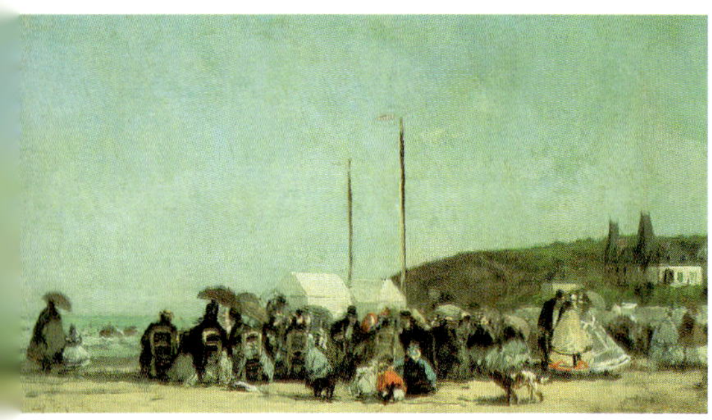

The academic tradition was strong in the French art world. Success was defined by acceptance at the Paris Salon, a biennial exhibition, as was a good education at a reputable institution such as the Académie des Beaux-Arts, which also controlled and organised the Salon. The Beaux-Arts was dominated by the great Neo-Classical painter Jean-Auguste-Dominique Ingres (1780–1867), who insisted that everyone must follow his style, with a strong emphasis on formal organisation and traditional draughtsmanship, copying the Old Masters and drawing with a clear, defined line. Monet grudgingly attended the Académie Suisse, a small, private art school where he met Camille Pissarro (1830–1903), and then entered the studio of Charles Gleyre, a respected master who encouraged individuality. Pierre-Auguste Renoir (1841–1919), Alfred Sisley (1839–99), Frédéric Bazille (1841–70) and Monet were drawn to Gleyre's studio; the four became friends.

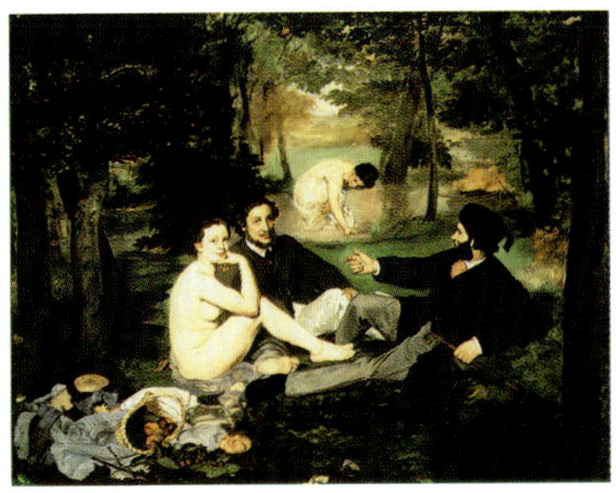

Edouard Manet (1832–83), the precursor of Impressionism, came from a prosperous Paris family and sought success in a conventional way, attaining Salon success in 1861 with *The Spanish Singer*. Pissarro also enrolled at the Beaux-Arts and studied there under landscapist Jean-Baptiste-Camille Corot (1796–1875). Edgar Degas (1834–1917), a close friend of Manet, enrolled at the Beaux-Arts in 1855.

In 1863 the Salon rejected so many submissions that the outcry led Napoleon III (1808–1873) to create the Salon des Refusés, an alternative exhibition where work refused by the Salon could be hung. The exhibition was placed alongside the official show and met with a varied critical response. Manet stole the show with *The Lunch on the Grass* (1862–63), a summer picnic set in the woods, in which two businessmen are entertaining two nude women of questionable virtue. The painting caused such a stir that it brought him instant notoriety. He became the *enfant terrible* of the art world, a title that would remain with him for most his career.

In 1865 the Salon opened its doors to the budding Impressionists, showing Degas, Manet, Pissarro, Renoir, Berthe Morisot (1841–95) (who married Manet's brother) and even Monet, whose landscapes were favourably received. The next six Salon exhibitions marked a period for the artists in which their work was alternatively acclaimed and then cast aside to be exhibited in the Salon des Refusés.

From 1866, Manet began to frequent the Café Guerbois. Many of the painters who came to be associated with Impressionism met here, such as Renoir, Sisley, Gustav Caillebotte (1848–94) and Monet, and they were known as the Batignolles group, since the café was situated in that region of Paris. Manet was the centre of evening gatherings at the café, where animated discussions on art and literature took place. He was friendly with controversial writers such as Émile Zola (1840–1902). Until his death in the Franco-Prussian War, Bazille attended the café almost daily, while Degas, Henri Fantin-Latour (1836–1904), Paul Cézanne (1839–1906) and Pissarro all made visits when they were in Paris. While never a political group, these young artists shared an ideology that was expounded in their regular meetings. When the Franco-Prussian War broke out in 1870, they dispersed. Their return, two years later, brought together a group hardened by their experiences during the war and were more ambitious than ever.

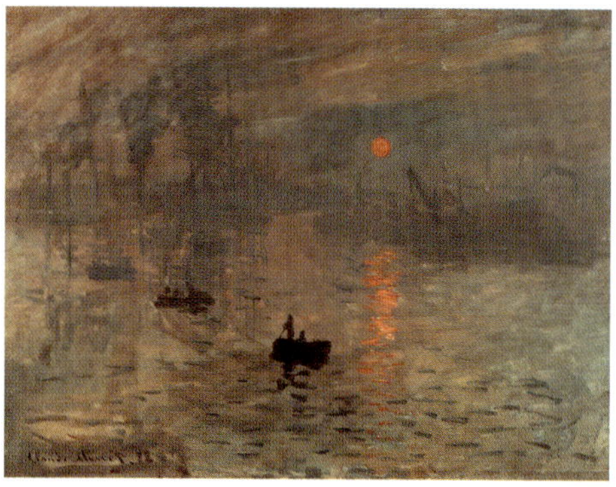

Impressionism was a reaction against both the academic tradition and Romanticism, and its painters shared a common approach to the rendering of outdoor subjects. In historical terms, the word refers to the work of artists who participated in a series of group exhibitions in Paris, the first of which was held from April to May 1874 at the studio of the photographer Nadar. The artists represented at this, and succeeding exhibitions held by the group between 1876 and 1886, included Cézanne, Degas, Armand Guillaumin (1841–1927), Morisot and, after 1879, Paul Gauguin (1848–1903) and the American artist Mary Cassatt (1845–1926).

The term Impressionism was derived from a painting by Claude Monet, *Impression: Sunrise* (1872), a view of the port of Le Havre in the mist, and was coined for the group by unfriendly critic Louis Leroy. The term was however quickly taken up by more sympathetic critics, who used it in an alternative sense to mean the impression stamped on the senses by a visual experience that is rapid and transitory. Monet, Renoir, Pissarro and Sisley were Impressionists in the latter sense; beginning in the later 1860s and culminating in 1872–75, they chose to paint out-of-doors (*en plein air*), recording the changing conditions of light and atmosphere as well as their individual sensations before nature. They used high-key colour palettes and a variety of brushstrokes, which allowed them to be responsive both to the character and texture of the object in nature and to the impact of light on its surfaces.

Degas was a new convert to the Impressionist dogma, vigorously defending the group's right to present their ideas to the public although not undertaking much of the technique himself. What drove Degas to support and help to organise the first Impressionist exhibitions was the implied challenge to establishment-led art. It was Degas who single-handedly convinced a large number of established artists to submit works to the first independent exhibition. Degas himself showed *Carriage at the Races* (1870–73).

Among paintings exhibited by Monet at the first exhibition were his version of *The Lunch on the Grass* (1865), which had been rejected for inclusion in the Salon exhibition of 1870 for being too subversive. He also included *Boulevard des Capucines* (1873), which was undertaken from the window of Nadar's studio and represents one of his most spectacular views of Paris. The critics labelled it crude and unfinished. Again, the critic Leroy had his say: 'Are you telling me that that is what I look like when I stroll along the Boulevard des Capucines ... Are you kidding?'

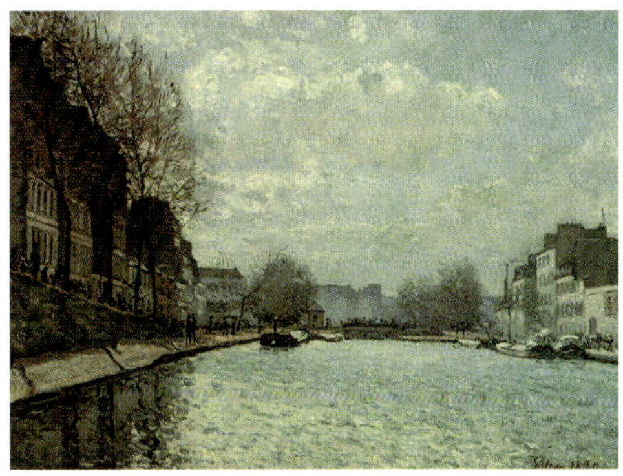

Renoir submitted *Dancer*, which was appreciated by some critics, but Leroy again said that although the artist was deemed to have an appreciation of colour, he lacked the ability to draw. He had also chosen *La Loge* (1874), *The Parisienne*, *Harvesters* and three other works to exhibit, and they were surprisingly well received, in contrast to the critical attention paid to some of his colleagues. Pissarro showed five works, including *Hoar Frost* (1873), which was considered by Leroy to have 'neither head nor tail, top nor bottom, front nor back'. Cézanne was also represented with two paintings and Sisley supplied five. In general, the few good reviews that were received were written by journalists who were sympathetic to the aims and ideals of the painters; the remainder scorned the exhibition. The animosity of the critics was unanticipated. While the term Impressionism became accepted among most critics, there was a faction who called the group 'The Intransigents', an expression which took its name from the radical political party that had attempted to take over the constitutional monarchy in Spain. The Impressionists were seen by some as anarchic, threatening the very existence of the artistic tradition in France.

Many of the artists failed to sell anything at the first independent exhibition; these paintings were then auctioned the following year at disappointing prices. Another exhibition was not planned, but, in 1876, when the Salon once again rejected the their work, another show was launched in the gallery of Paul Durand-Ruel.

This exhibition was disastrous. The Impressionists had gained a reputation for being seditious, and many of the critics made no attempt to disguise their antagonism. This time Renoir was singled out for *Nude in the Sunlight*, painted in 1876. Critic Albert Wolff wrote: 'Try to explain to M. Renoir that a woman's torso is not a mass of flesh in the process of decomposition with green and violet spots which denote the state of complete putrefaction of a corpse!' The painting was in fact a precursor to the classic Renoir nudes, an elegant, sensual work which embodied the Impressionist fascination with light.

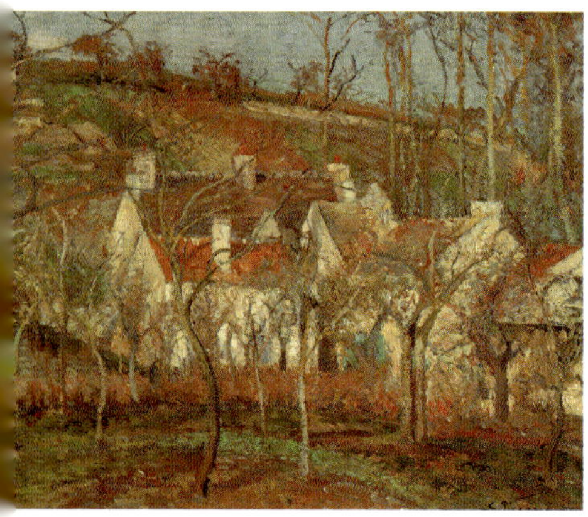

Meanwhile Monet's technique had matured and he captured the natural world around him at his home on the Seine at Argenteuil with unrestrained enthusiasm. *The Basin at Argenteuil* and *Regatta at Argenteuil*, both of which he painted in 1872, represent the decreasing emphasis on reality in his work; he sought more and more to capture the essence of a scene rather than to document it accurately. The result of this work was a stunning new vocabulary of painting, where every syllable and impression was represented with another dash of colour; a flamboyant and confident expression of what Monet actually felt about an scene rather than saw.

Renoir's painting evolved to incorporate many of the elements which would eventually guarantee his success. At the Durand-Ruel exhibition he showed 15 paintings, and there had been some quiet interest from the public, despite the almost universal damning. In 1876 he rented a studio in the Rue Cortot in Montmartre, where he produced some of his most famous works, such as *Moulin de la Galette* (1876) and *The Swing*, which were painted simultaneously in the garden of his studio; *The Swing* in the mornings and *Moulin* in the afternoons. Both emphasize the fact of Renoir's grasp on Impressionism; the effect of light on his scenes is redolent with the charm that would make his work so accessible and popular. The subject-matter of both paintings was modern, a foray away from the staid Salon-type paintings that he was accustomed to painting.

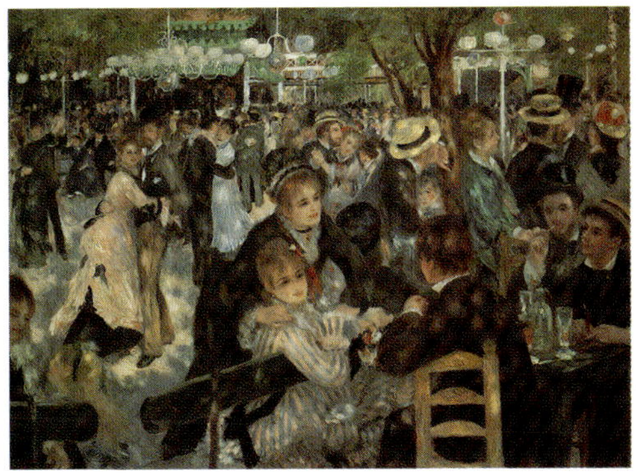

Many of the Impressionists left Paris in search of the nature they longed to paint. Pissarro moved to Pontoise and then Eragney. Monet and Caillebotte found solace in their gardens at Giverny and Petit-Gennevilliers respectively. Renoir alone chose to remain in Paris, but he had found a stunning and overgrown sanctuary in his garden at Montmartre. The 1870s was a decade of growing success for him. His studio at Montmartre was a hive of activity, becoming the central meeting place for many of his growing circle of acquaintances. He was one of the few artists in this circle to have achieved some financial success, and because he had not yet married and had no dependants, he had no responsibilities and was able to live on what he earned.

Renoir remained friends with Degas, for whom support within the group was diminishing. Until his final days, Degas insisted that he was not an Impressionist. There are, however, arguments that his work adopted at the very least the emphasis on light that permeated the works of Monet, Renoir and Pissarro. But Degas remained firmly involved with the movement. His appealing paintings of ballet dancers were painted in the 1870s, and the light reflecting on their tulles, the shimmer of net contrasting with satin bows and shadows marked in by colour and not contours all betray the growing influence of the Impressionists. The subtle effects of the tone and the contrast between the indistinct background and the exquisitely detailed ballerinas make these some of Degas's most popular works. His sketches were made from life, and although the paintings were completed in the studio, their immediacy was not diminished. He introduced Mary Cassatt, a friend and admirer of his work, to the group. An American, born in Philadelphia, Cassatt arrived in Paris the year of the first alternative exhibition. She saw a Degas pastel in a picture-dealer's window and immediately recognised a kindred approach to art. Degas saw her work at the Salon that same year, and said, 'here is one who feels as I do'.

Cassatt's work was rejected by the Salon in 1875 and 1877 and Degas suggested then that she join the Impressionists. She was delighted saying: 'I hated conventional art. Now I began to live.' She adopted the Impressionist's use of colour, lightening her palette and using sharp, broken brushstrokes. Like Morisot, her themes were predominantly feminine, but she was never sentimental or cloying. She came to personify the Impressionist movement almost as soon as she joined it, with works like *In the Cornfield at Gennevilliers (1875)* and *In the Loge* (1879), which emphasised all the qualities that eventually made the movement so successful.

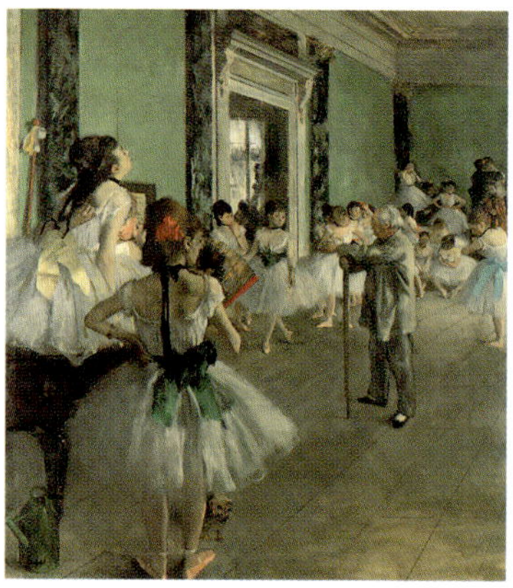

Berthe Morisot, who painted with much less definition and emphasis on line than Manet, for example, became increasingly Impressionist, revelling in the freedom that the technique offered her. Her work has the same innate charm as Renoir's; the pleasure with which she painted enlivened her subjects. She had a gift for painting upper-class women in domestic situations in an unsentimental manner.

Alfred Sisley had become dependent on the dealer Durand-Ruel to support his work, and when it became clear that his mentor had over-extended himself, he was left with virtually no means of survival. But his painting was developing in a unique manner – he had begun to focus on the use of motif in many of the works. The tree-lined road became a central theme, and it appeared in countless paintings. He painted in England, at Hampton Court on the Thames and at Charing Cross – scenes which had been undertaken by Turner, Monet and indeed Pissarro over the years. He also painted at Argenteuil with Monet, revelling in the other artist's astonishing eye for colour. Sisley remained loyal to the artistic vision of the Impressionists; he seemed to accept that fame was simply late in coming.

By 1877, the fortunes of the group were diminishing. Some of the artists had become disheartened enough to release themselves from the associations of Impressionism, but for the most part, they had great faith in their art. At the third Impressionist exhibition, held in that year, a body of grudging admirers began to emerge. The Impressionists were out in full force: Monet showed 30 paintings, Degas 25, Morisot 12, Renoir 21, Sisley 17, Cézanne 16 and Pissarro 22. But the new interest in the group was not reflected in sales and, despite some encouraging reviews, prices were low and for the most part they struggled.

By 1880, the tide had turned for the Impressionists, and the post-war economy had begun to pick up. Monet alienated himself from his peers by organizing his own show at *La Vie Moderne* in June 1880. On Renoir's advice, he also submitted two works to the Salon, one of which was accepted. Degas called Monet a traitor for denying everything the Impressionists stood for by showing at the Salon, but Monet was distancing himself from a group that had begun to expand beyond their original precepts into something quite different.

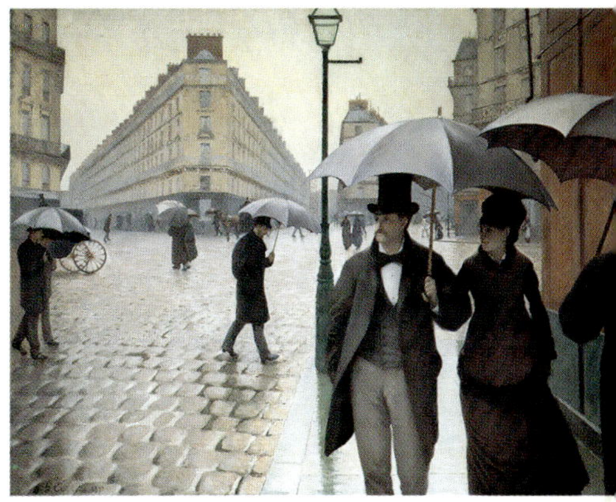

Renoir likewise became unhappy with the labels he and his colleagues were receiving, and in 1878 he also detached himself from the group, trying his luck again at the Salon. That year, one of his paintings was accepted, and the following year two were chosen. His work was celebrated by the art world, but the public still failed to come to grips with his vision.

Renoir's absence from the fourth Impressionist exhibition made his colleagues nervous. Pissarro said to Caillebotte, who was organising the show, '... if the best artists slip away, what will become of our artistic union?' The only Impressionist to exhibit at all eight of their shows, Pissarro had a large family to support and eventually they returned to his family in England, where they settled in South London, near Dulwich. Some of his most alluring landscapes were painted there.

Pissarro was firm friends with Cézanne. They worked together to develop a new, intellectual approach to their landscapes. Like Monet and Renoir in the previous decade, they sat next to one another, painting the same motifs over and over again. An onlooker remarked

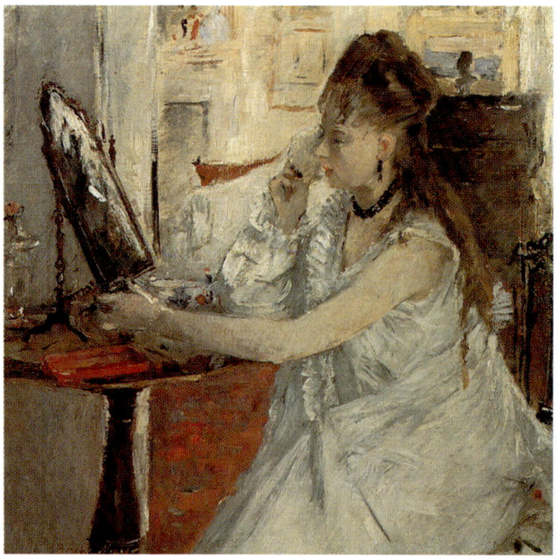

that 'Cézanne plastered and Pissarro dabbed', making the distinction between Pissarro, who fulfilled his Impressionist promise, and Cézanne, who worked in his characteristic broad, heavy brushstrokes.

Cézanne met Renoir, Pissarro, Sisley and Monet in the early 1860s, and he entered the first Impressionist exhibition, showing *The House of the Hanged Man, Auvers* (c. 1873), which was met with enormous hostility from both the public and the critics. The reception of his work did not improve with time, and by the third Impressionist exhibition he had lost interest and faith in the aims of the group, resigning in 1887.

Sisley also left the group, doubting the possibility of any future unity and concerned about the 'Intransigence' label. He had, despite growing poverty, clung to his vision for the group of painters, and had remained loyal to their aims. He waited patiently for recognition, which, sadly, did not come until after his death. In a desperate bid to draw attention to his work, he presented it to the Salon again in 1879. It was not accepted, and he entered the 1880s with a resigned attitude, wanting the luxury of exhibiting solely with the Impressionists but understanding the reality of his situation. He moved around France constantly, and was obliged to call upon the generosity of patrons and friends in order to keep his family together.

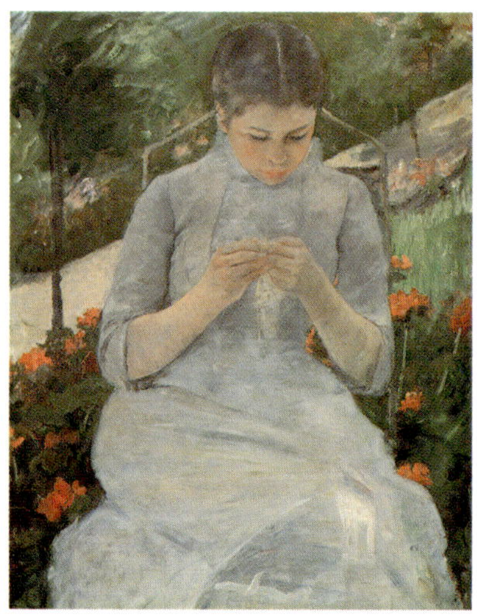

By the early 1880s, the feeling of cohesiveness that had originally brought the Impressionists together began to dissolve under the pressure of emerging factions and rivalries. The sense of a shared approach to nature among the landscape painters had also dissolved, so that each artist increasingly took individual directions. Renoir focussed on nudes and portraits, feeling that 'he had gone to the end of Impressionism'. Pissarro began to look for a way forward from Impressionism. In 1885, he met Georges Seurat (1859–91), who developed a theory called Divisionism; this, combined with a Pointillist technique, offered what seemed to Pissarro to be the antidote to the 'unpolished and rough execution' that had plagued the Impressionists. He worked with Seurat until the final Impressionist exhibition, but abandoned the technique in 1890 and returned to a further exploration of Impressionism.

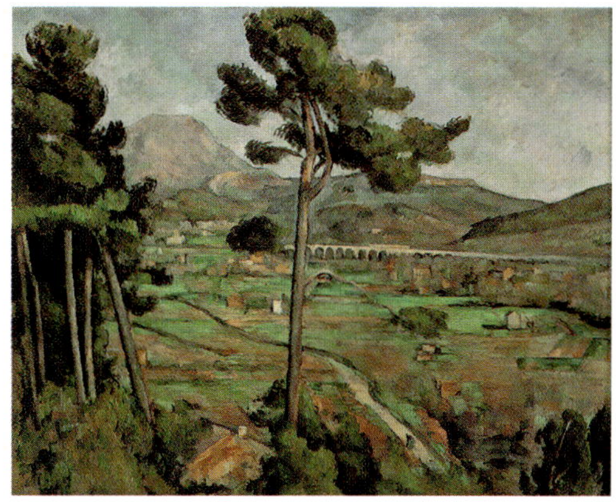

Monet, too, was deeply dissatisfied with his work, but unlike Renoir and Pissarro, he never wavered in his belief that Impressionism was the right path. Even his latest paintings developed with a single-minded logic lacking in other artists' work. In his search for the instant impression, he, paradoxically, had to abandon some of the dogmas of Impressionism. The selection of the right motif for his series paintings took on great importance: his poplars by the river, Rouen Cathedral, London, Venice and, above all, his water-garden, became the focus of his search for 'instantaneity', or the impression of an instant, and they were to absorb his interest until his death.

Ironically, as the group fell apart, Impressionism began to have a tremendous impact both on French painting generally and on the art of other countries; this continued well into the 20th century. Either directly or through developments after the 1880s, such as Neo-Impressionism and Post-Impressionism, Impressionism influenced modern art in such fundamental features as a loosening up of brushwork, which abolished the traditional distinction between the finished painting and the preliminary sketch or study; a concern for the two-dimensional surface of a painting, which is defined by the patterns and feeling of movement of the paint on the ground; and a use of pure, bright colours.

KAREN HURRELL

Eugène Boudin (1824–98)
The Beach at Trouville, 1864

Musée du Louvre, Paris. Courtesy of AKG London

AN older artist and a follower of Jean-Baptiste-Camille Corot (1796–1875), Eugène Boudin was a landscape artist who painted mainly along the coast of northern France. He was one of the first people to advocate painting in the open air, rather than sketching outside and producing a finished composition in the studio. This had become more viable from the 1840s when oil paints in tubes replaced the pigs' bladders that had been used before. Tubes meant that the paints did not dry out so quickly as the cap could be put on, making it easier to paint outdoors.

Even so, many artists did not see why they should adapt their palettes according to the natural light around them, or indeed paint landscapes under natural light conditions.

Boudin's influence on Impressionism came through his meeting with Claude Monet (1840–1926) in 1858. Monet soon came under his influence and remarked in later life: 'if I became a painter, it was thanks to Boudin'.

Boudin also painted the French at play, usually by the sea, an idea that was not especially prevalent at the time and was quickly taken up by the young, modern group of artists who came to be known as the Impressionists.

His paintings are frequently loose and sketchy and rarely have a central subject but rather small figures under a large, bright sky. In his old age, Corot referred to these renditions as 'meteorological beauties', and dubbed Boudin 'king of the skies'.

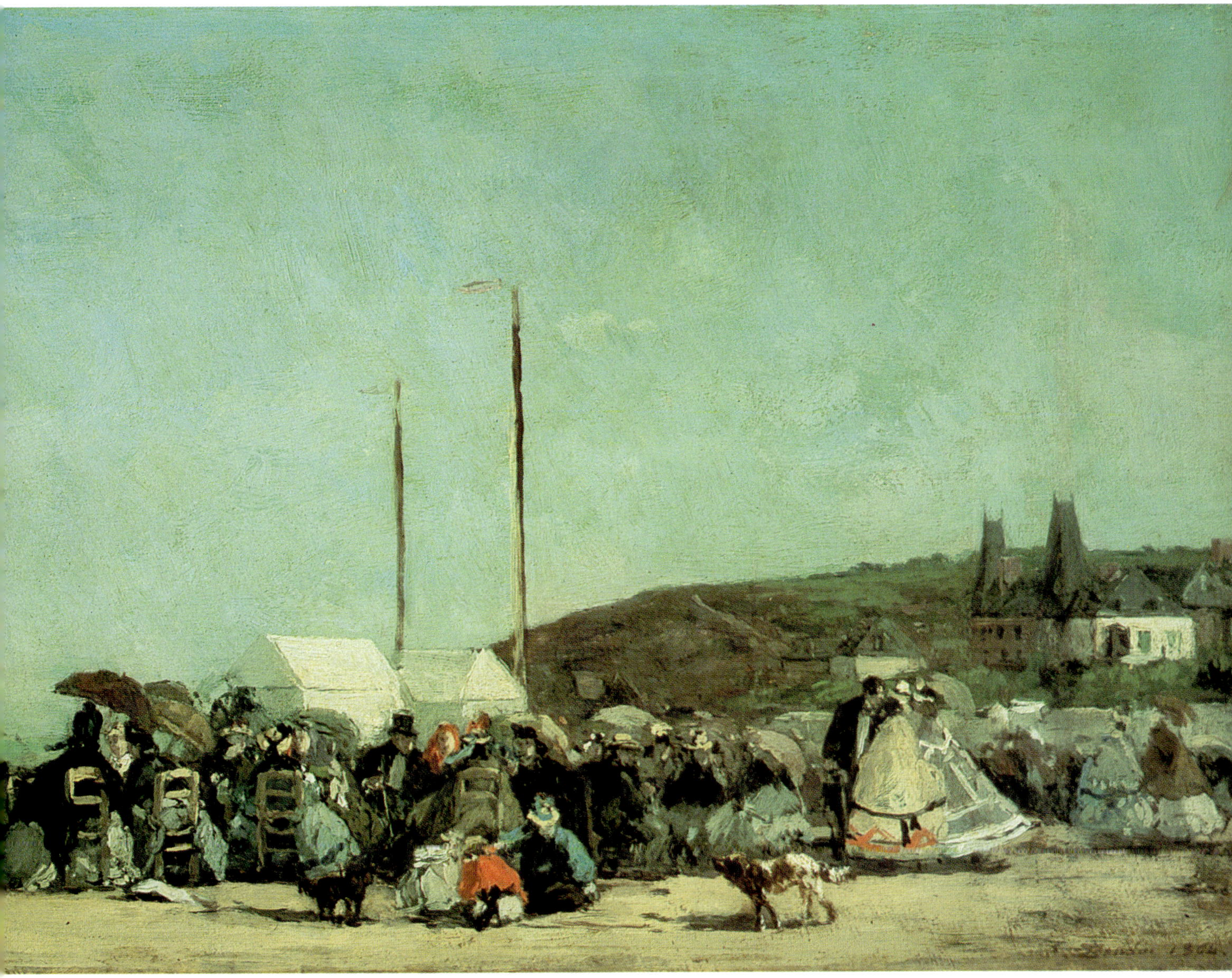

EDOUARD MANET (1832–83)
The Spanish Ballet, 1862

Phillips Collection, Washington D. C.. Courtesy of AKG London

EDOUARD Manet came from a wealthy family and trained in the traditional manner in Paris between 1849 and 1857. He copied the Old Masters at the Louvre and studied under the history painter Thomas Couture (1815–79).

His first large work, *The Absinthe Drinker* (1859), was rejected at the Salon of 1859, but two years' later a portrait of his parents, which was visibly influenced by Dutch 17th-century painters such as Frans Hals (1581–1666), and *The Spanish Singer* (1861), which received an honourable mention, were both accepted.

Thereafter, he painted many 'Spanish' subjects, including this painting of 1862. The dark palette, the figures on a flat background, the shades of white punctuated by flashes of brilliant colour, and a studio light source are typical of his paintings up to the mid 1880s. The four central figures are posed formally and their arms, legs and faces are precisely painted, in contrast with the 'sketchiness' of some of the costumes and the figures to the left and right.

Manet did not actually visit Spain until 1865 and, perhaps surprisingly, he ceased to paint Spanish subjects after this visit.

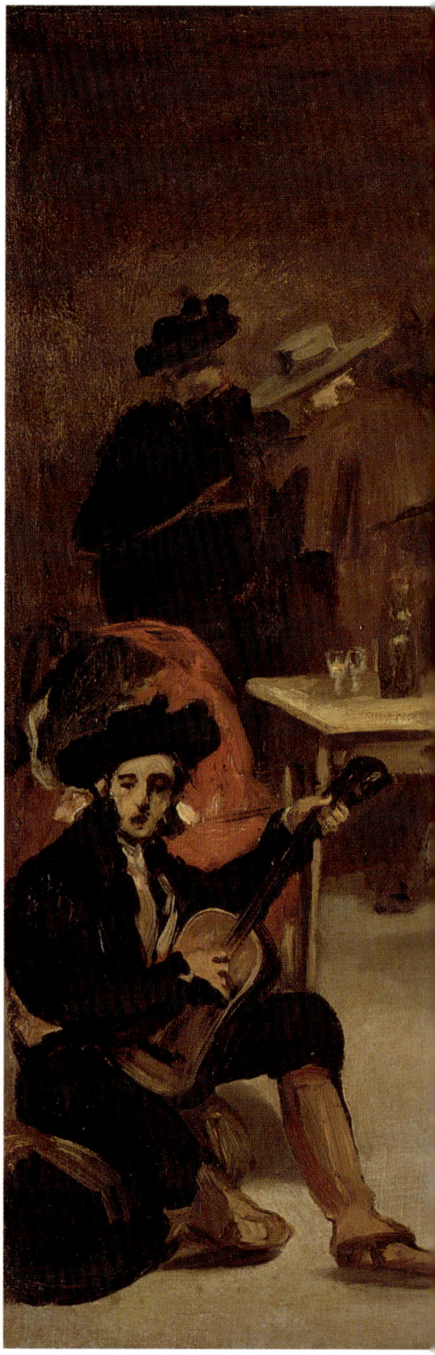

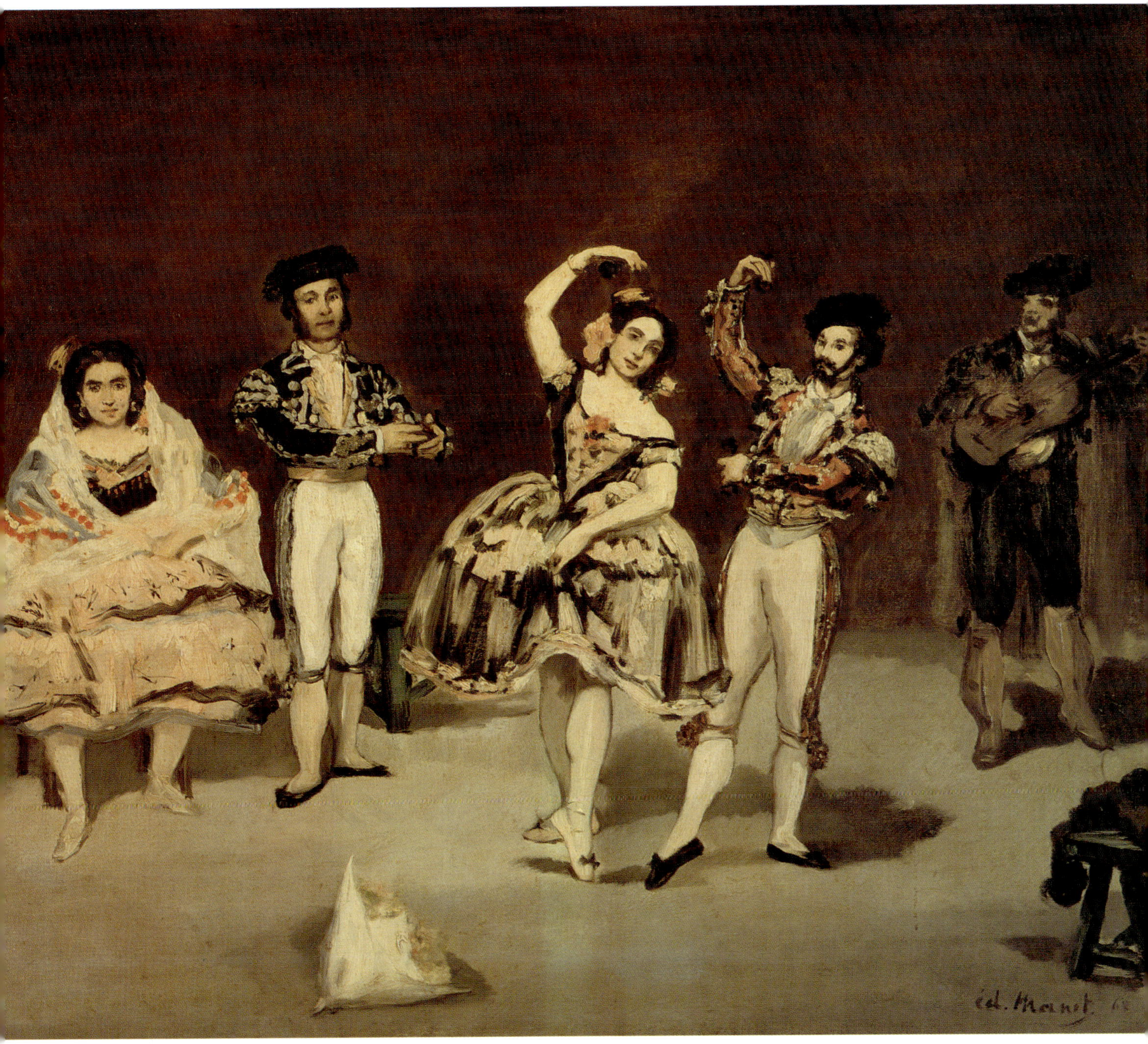

Edouard Manet
The Lunch on the Grass, 1862–63

Musée du Louvre, Paris. Courtesy of AKG London/Erich Lessing

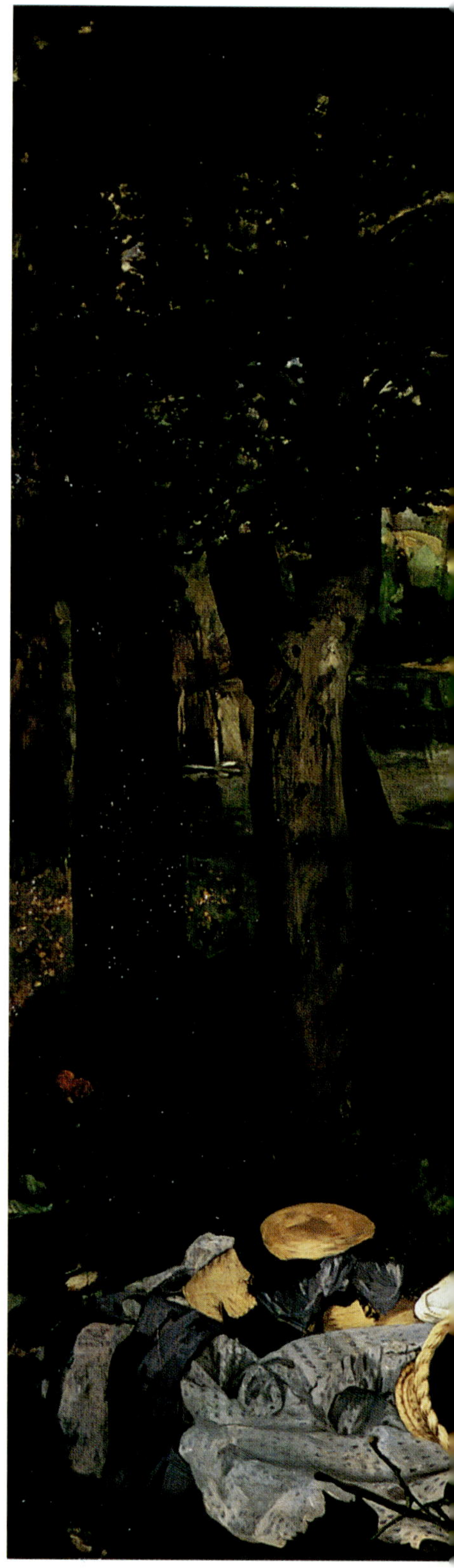

MANET revealed his revolutionary nature when he presented *The Lunch on the Grass*, under the title *The Bath*, to the Salon in 1863. Inevitably, it was rejected and when it was shown at the Salon des Refusés, an alternative exhibition inaugurated by Napoleon III (1808–1873), it caused great scandal and controversy. The public and critics alike were outraged at what they perceived to be a mockery of the Great Masters. Although the juxtaposition of dressed men and undressed women was acceptable in the 17th-century *Pastoral Symphony* (c. 1510) by artist Giorgione (Giorgio Barberelli) (c. 1477–c. 1510) in the Louvre, a modern interpretation was considered indecent.

Many Classical paintings showed nudes in a landscape, but to turn the nude (Victorine Meurent, Manet's favourite model) to face the viewer squarely, placing a scattered picnic, a pile of clothing and two fully dressed men (one of Manet's brothers and Rodolphe Leenhoff, Manet's future brother-in-law) beside her, was considered offensive.

Even the critic Théophile Thoré (1807–69), a friend of the controversial poet Charles Pierre Baudelaire (1821–1867), dismissed it as an 'absurd composition', only mentioning in passing 'the qualities of light and colour in the landscape and indeed [the] very true bits of modelling in the torso of the woman'.

The younger artists, who came to be known as the Impressionists in the 1870s, regarded the spirited Manet as their figurehead and leader, although he always distanced himself from them professionally and never exhibited in any of the group exhibitions.

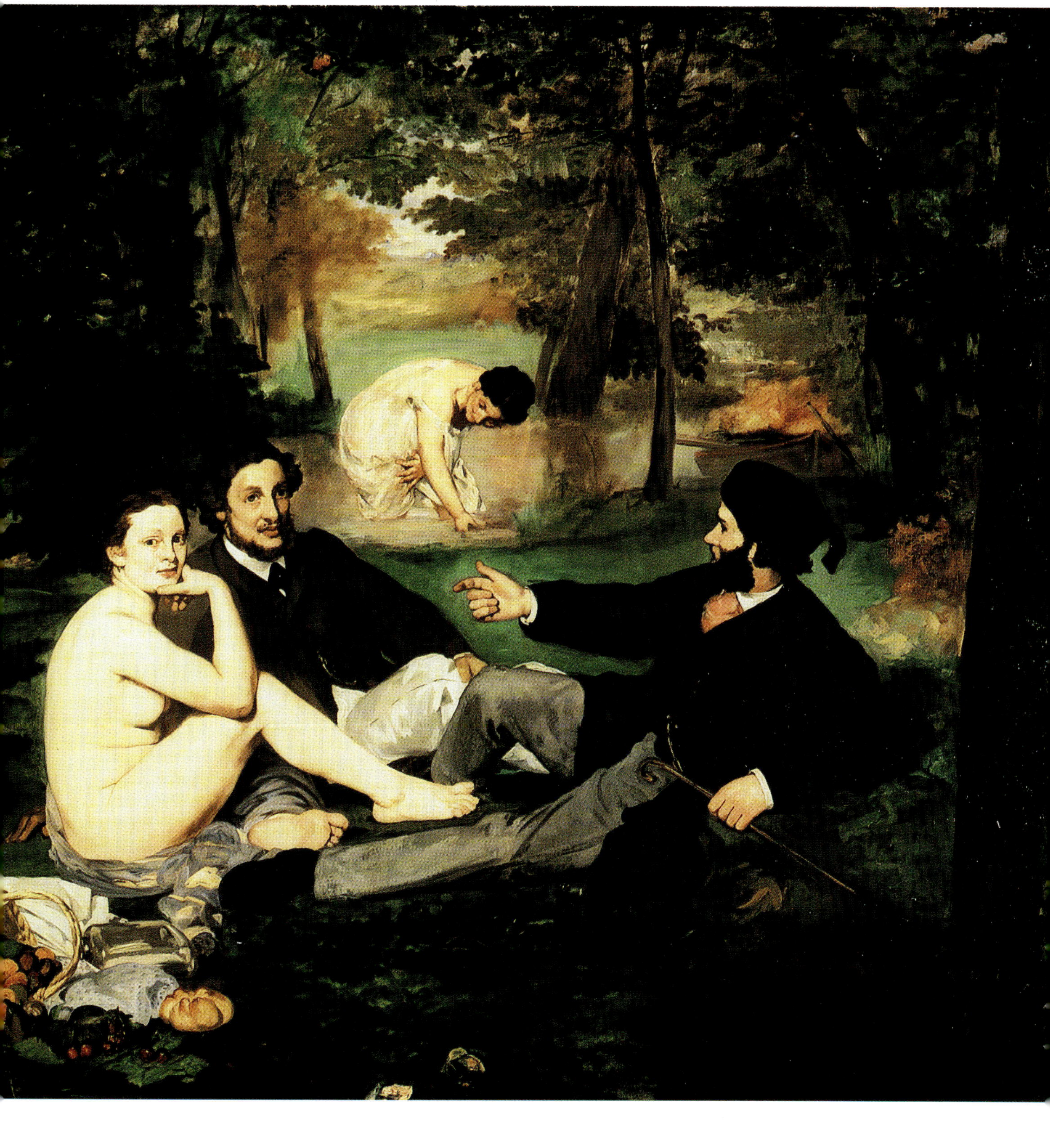

EDOUARD MANET
Olympia, 1863

Musée d'Orsay, Paris. Courtesy of AKG London/ Erich Lessing

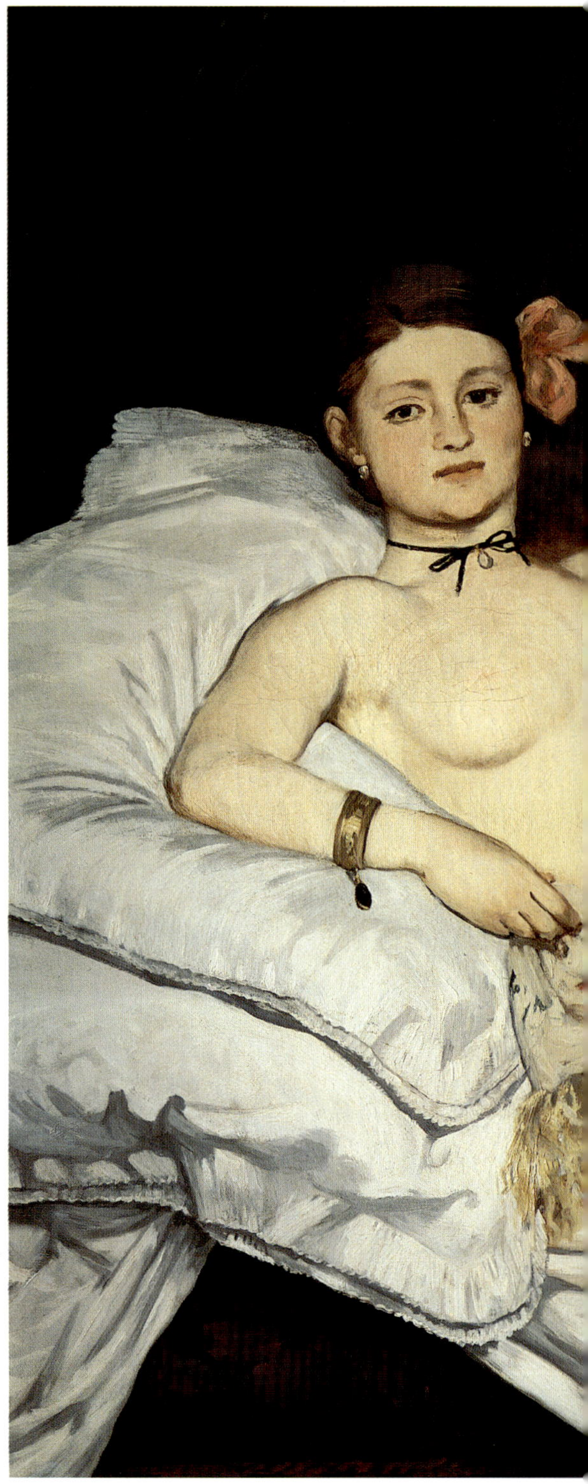

OLYMPIA, exhibited at the Salon of 1865, shows a nude in a pose reminiscent of works by Titian (*c.* 1485–1576), Velásquez (1599–1660), Goya (1746–1828) and Jean-Auguste Dominique Ingres (1780–1867). Like *The Lunch on the Grass* (1862–63), it was shocking in its modernity. First, Manet's nude stares out at the viewer, unsmiling, challenging. Second, she is wearing high-heeled slippers and a black ribbon around her neck, items that emphasise her nudity. She is no reclining Venus but a prostitute. Emerging from the shadows, a black maid brings flowers from a client, although they give the woman no pleasure, while crossing the bed is a black cat, a traditional symbol of sexual activity. Although the gesture is a conventional one, the reason why the woman covers herself with her hand is hardly chaste – you, the viewer, in the position of client, have not paid to see her.

The style, which is almost clinical, also has a fragile clarity. The subtlety and finesse of the modelling of the figure is typical of Manet's work and makes viewers even more acutely aware of the woman's body, increasing their discomfort. Her body contrasts with the dark, simplified background and flashes of colour (the bouquet and the flower in her hair). Yet it remains in harmony with the pale, silk shawl and the white linen of the bedclothes.

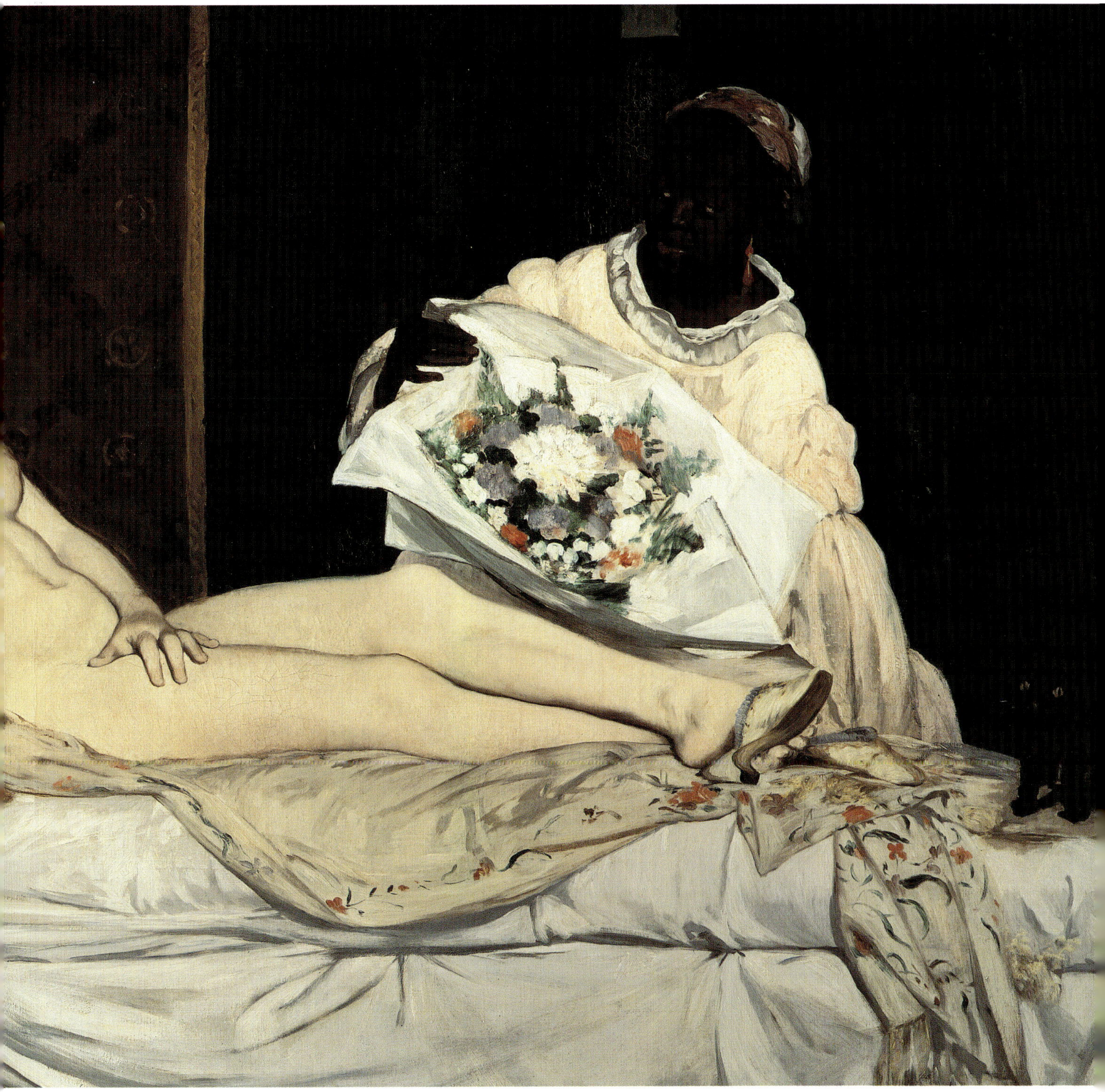

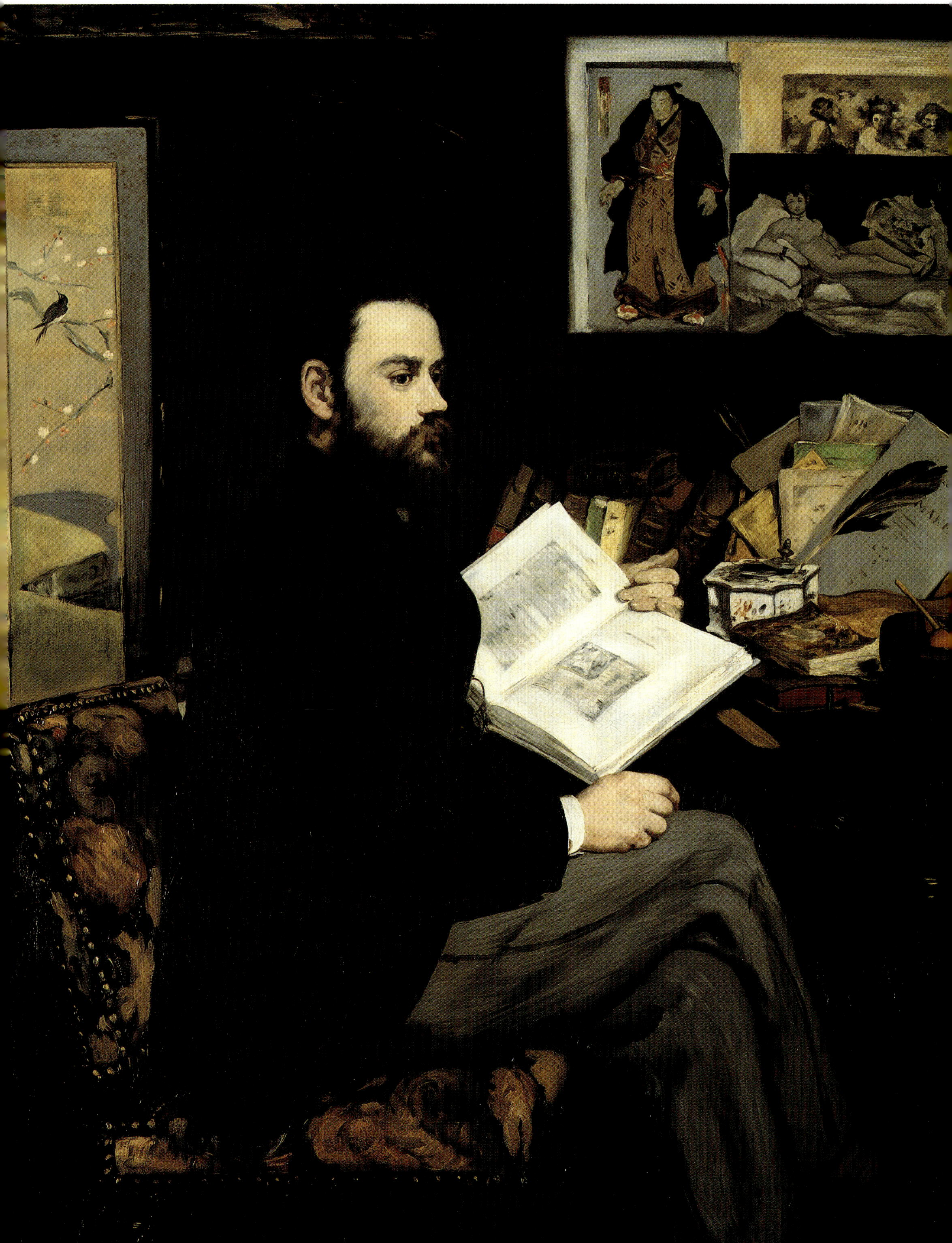

Edouard Manet
Portrait of Émile Zola, 1868

Musée du Louvre, Paris. Courtesy of AKG London

EMILE Zola (1840–1902), writer and childhood friend of Paul Cézanne (1839–1906), was a staunch supporter of Manet, whom he first championed in the journal *L'Événement* in 1866. The two men became lifelong friends.

As in traditional portraiture, Zola is surrounded by books and writing materials – *L'Événement* is in the 'fan' of journals behind the inkstand. His pale face glows in the darkness. The book in his hand, the Japanese prints, an engraving of Manet's *Olympia* (1863) and a glowing Japanese screen all indicate an interest in the avant-garde.

The emphasis on black and white tonal values is typical of early Manet. The book of Japanese prints, so newly arrived in Paris and a source of great interest to the artistic and literary worlds, glistens and is the focal point of the painting. The fine modelling of the face and hands contrasts with the looser brushwork of the trousers; the studio lighting picks up details such as Zola's ear, knuckles and the bridge of his nose.

Manet's limited palette may not yet reflect that of the Impressionists, but his refusal to 'make things up' corresponds with their desire to paint straight from nature. Zola describes how Manet refused to let him move during the long sittings: 'No,' he said, '... I can do nothing without Nature. I do not know how to make things up... . If my work has any real value today, it is because of the exact interpretation and truthful analysis.'

The painting was well received at the Salon of 1869.

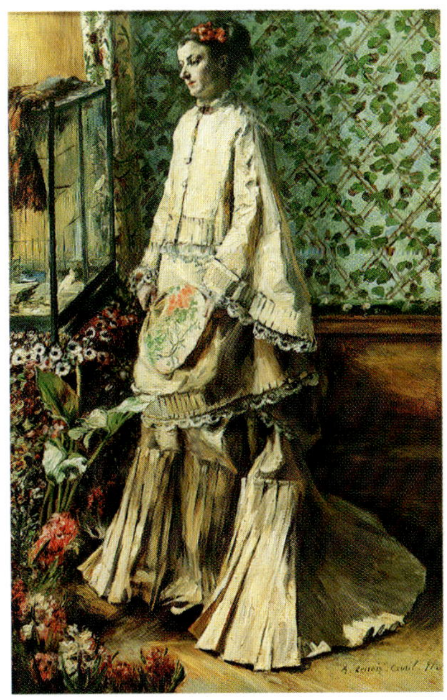

Pierre-Auguste Renoir
Portrait of Rapha, 1870–71
Private Collection. Courtesy of AKG London
(See p. 128)

EDOUARD MANET
Lunch in the Studio, 1868

Neue Pinakothek, Munich. Courtesy of AKG London

LUNCH *in the Studio* is one of Manet's most enigmatic paintings. A narrative is implied but not clear and the props on a chair are the only reference to the studio mentioned in the title.

The boy, who is clearly going out, is the main focus, and ignores the other figures. The lunch – the half-peeled lemon reminiscent of Jean-Baptiste-Siméon Chardin (1699–1779) and 17th-century Dutch still-life paintings, the half-filled wine glass and the glistening coffee cup – command the viewer's attention and are typical of many of Manet's compositions. A pot and an ivory-handled sword shine in the gloom on the left. A black cat washes itself – a humourous detail that creates a visual link with the boy's jacket, and brings to mind the dog in *The Balcony* (1868–69) – an animate element in an otherwise frozen scene.

Manet again uses predominantly greys, blacks and white with the odd splash of colour. As in *The Balcony*, an interplay of triangles binds the picture together. There are the triangles of the figures – the boy, woman and weaponry; of the bright patches of the man's hand, the boy's face, and the ivory handle; the flattened triangle of the handle, plant pot and the length of tablecloth; and the up-tilted triangle of the pot, the handle and the boy's face.

The influence of photography is evident in the cut-off figure on the right, although this 'snapshot' effect sits oddly with the otherwise static quality of the scene.

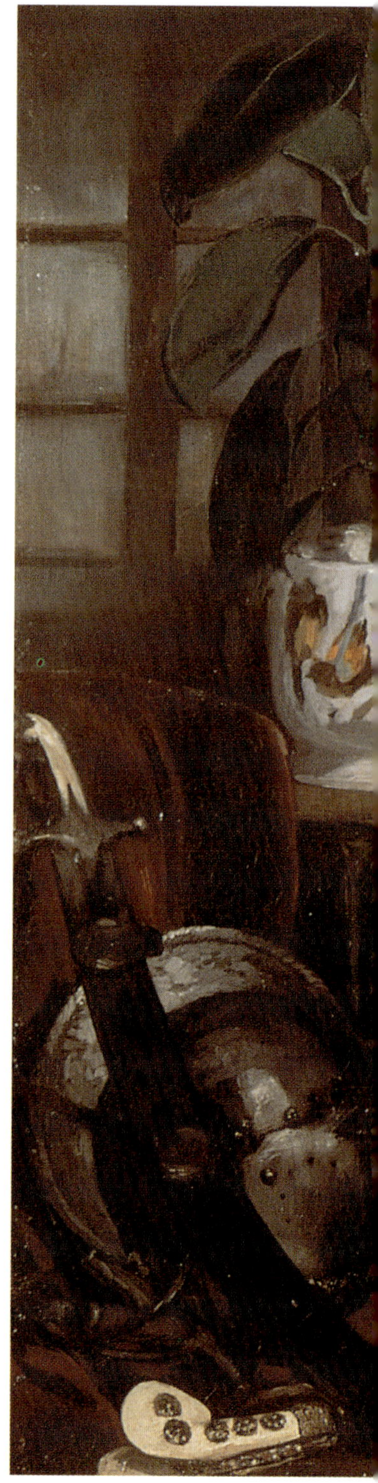

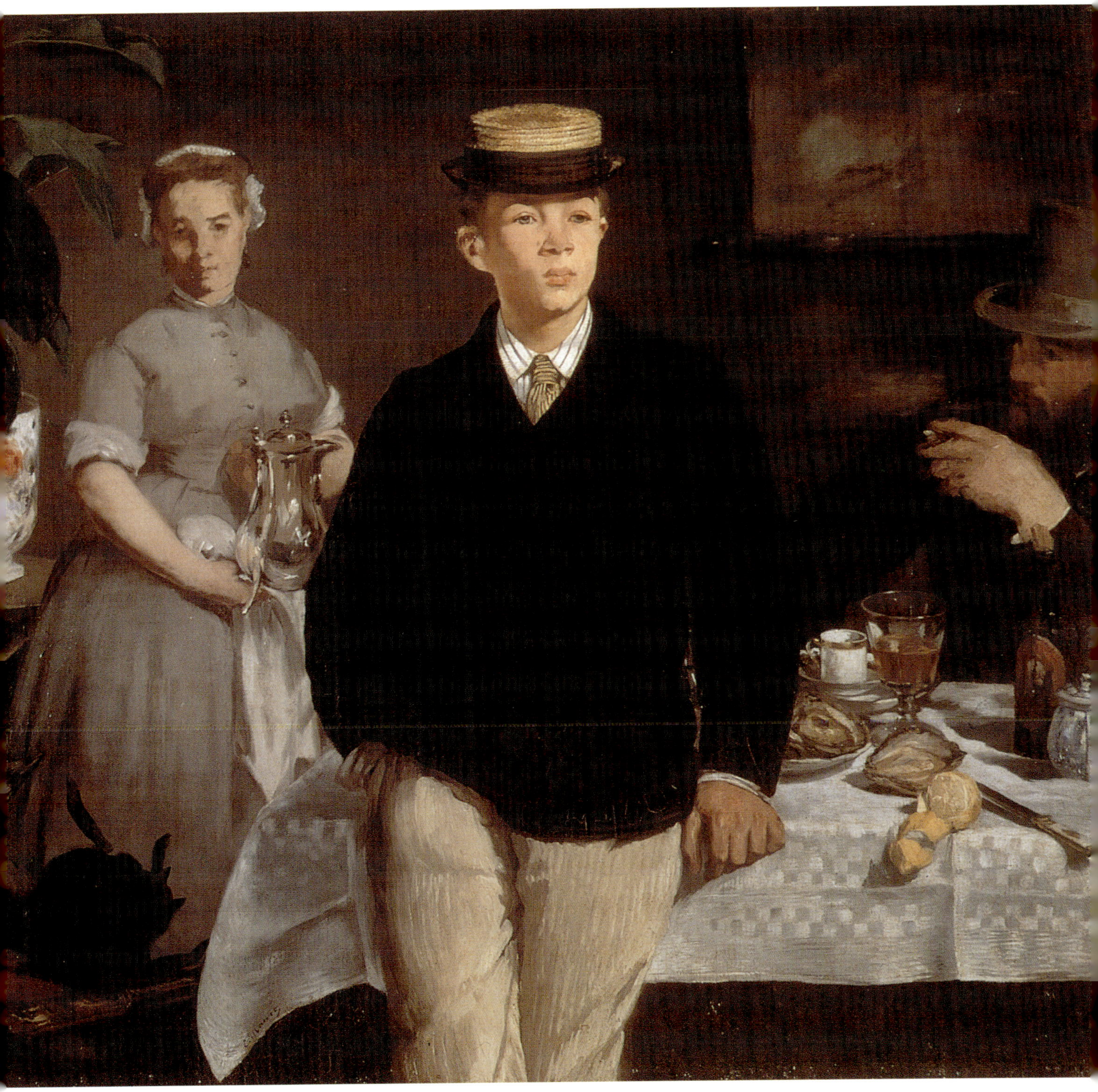

Edouard Manet
The Balcony, 1868-69

Musée d'Orsay, Paris. Courtesy of AKG London/Erich Lessing

EXHIBITED at the Salon of 1869, this picture met with public bewilderment. Despite their proximity, the three figures have no personal interaction. A fourth is barely visible. The Impressionist artist Berthe Morisot (1841–95) (seated) is painted the most heavily and stares, black-browed and intense, into the street. Fanny Claus (1846–77), the violinist, is painted with a light touch, in marked contrast with Morisot, and seems diaphanous and sketchy. She looks ahead, absent-mindedly putting on her gloves. Antoine Guillemet (1843–1918), the landscape artist, is also less firmly modelled than Morisot, and looks ahead. Yet all of them, posed as if for a formal photograph, avoid looking to camera. The scene is enigmatic, the players isolated in a frozen scene, which even the little dog fails to enliven.

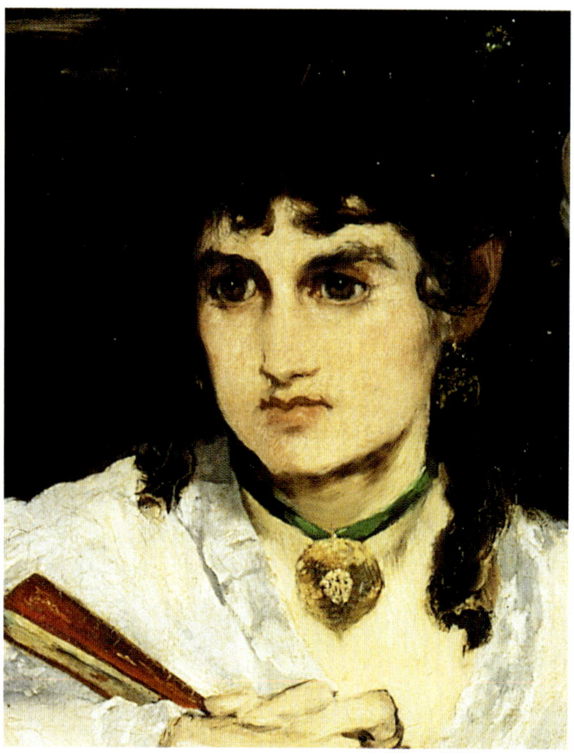

Painted in the studio, contrary to the Impressionist doctrine, *The Balcony* is fiercely geometric: the shutters confine the space; the house interior is black and flattened; the horizontal railing cuts the picture and the figures in two, while the diagonal and vertical bars point towards each figure. The figures form a triangular mass and the heads, bright against the dark background, also create a triangle, a shape reiterated in the balcony design. Again, Manet uses a limited palette, with an emphasis on blacks and whites. The contrast of bright colours – green shutters and balcony, the blue cravat, red fan, yellow gloves and green umbrella – also create their own directional forces within the canvas.

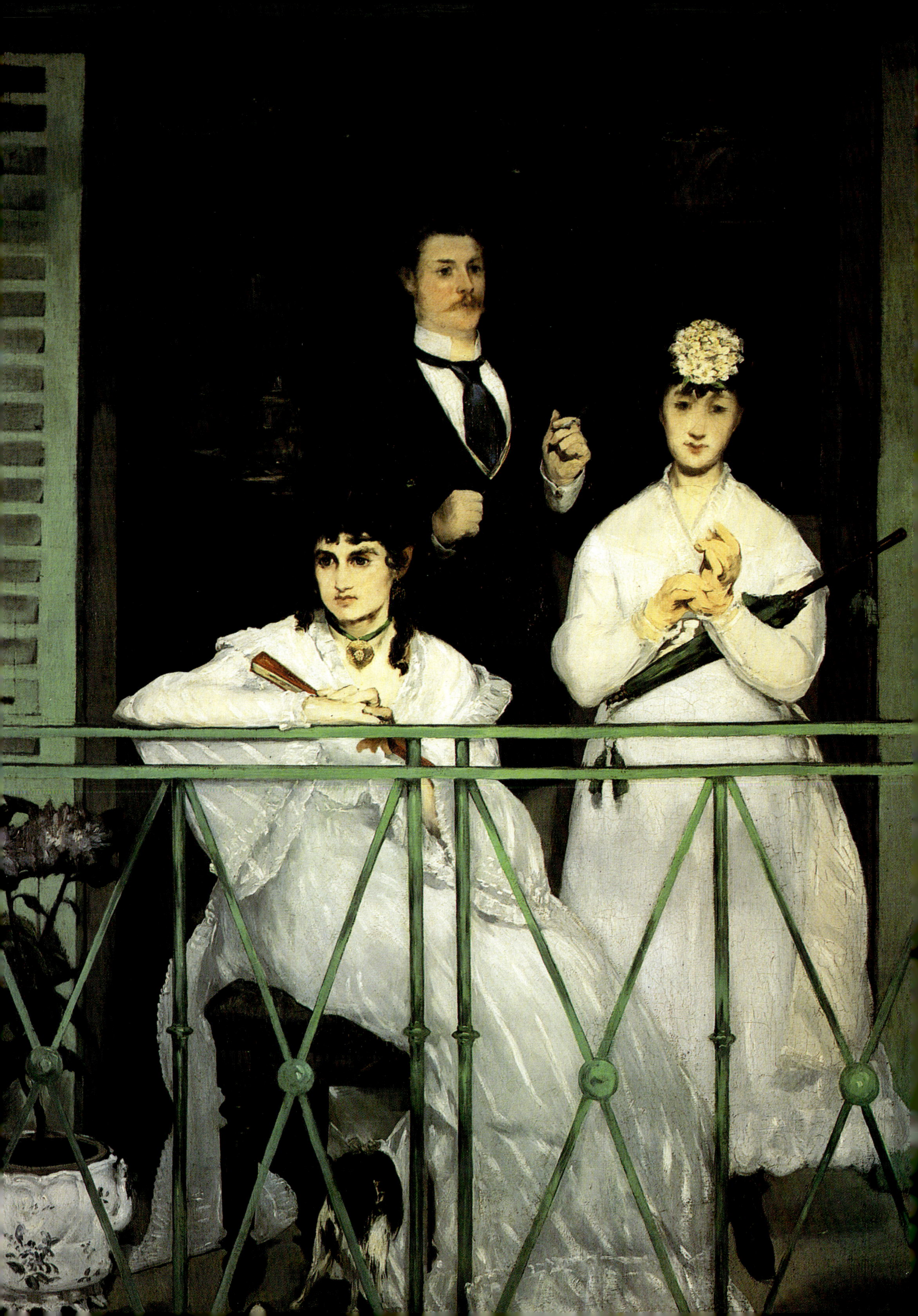

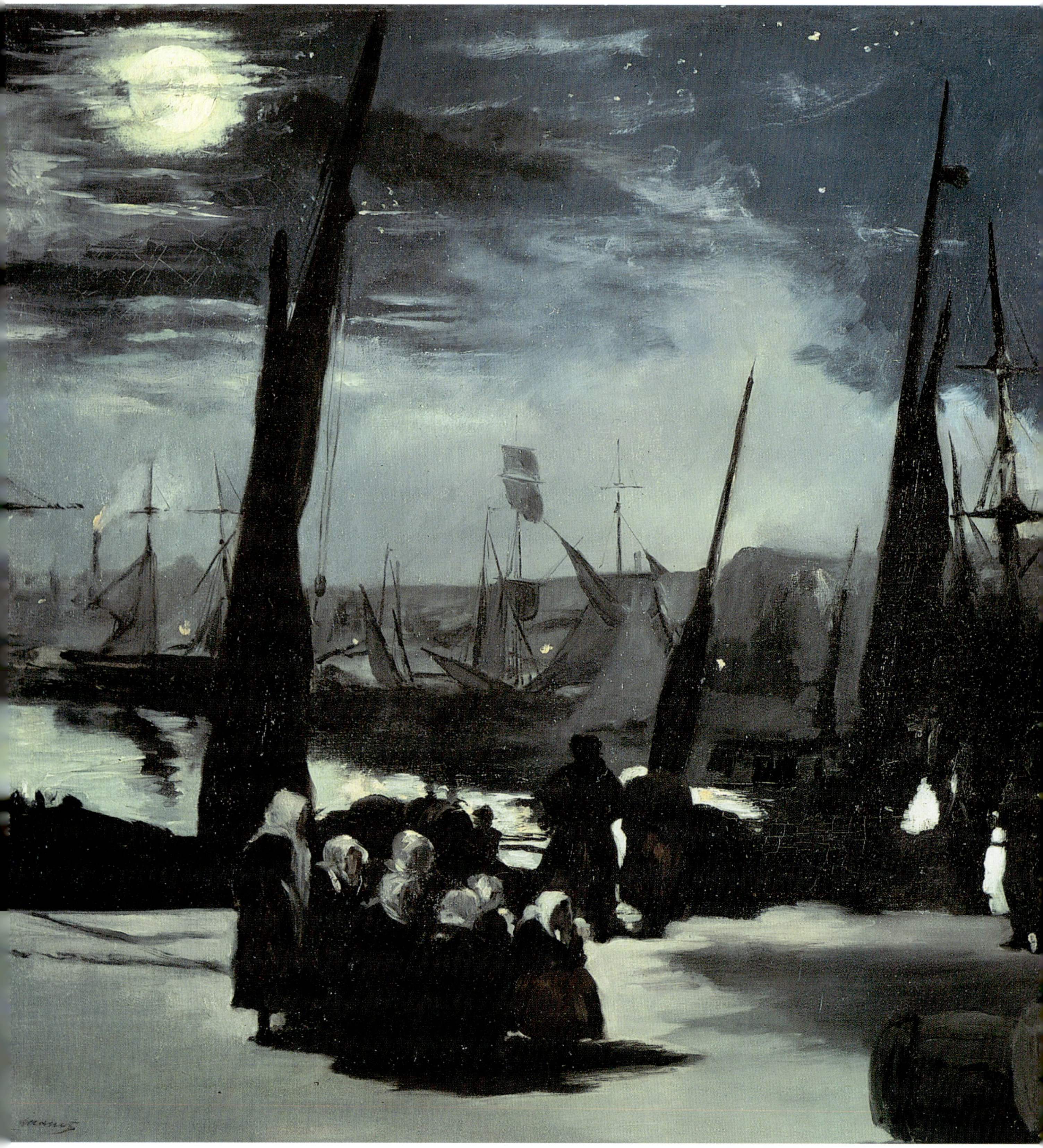

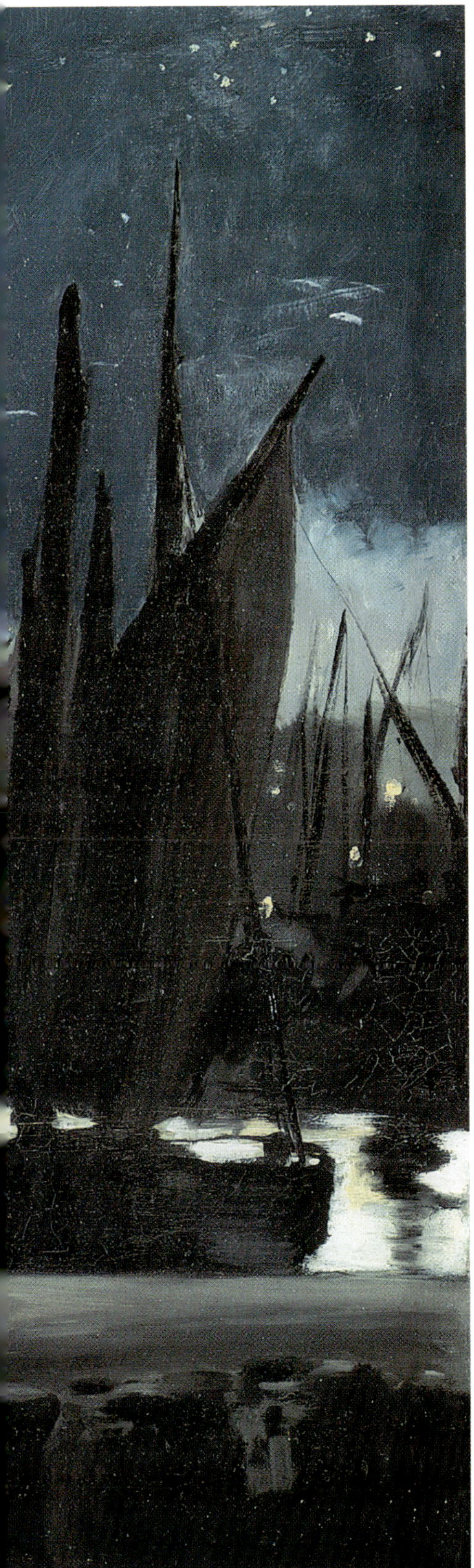

EDOUARD MANET
The Port of Boulogne in Moonlight, 1869
Musée d'Orsay, Paris. Courtesy of AKG London/Erich Lessing

MANET and his family spent the summer of 1869 at Boulogne, where he painted several harbour and sea scenes. This is a dramatic nocturnal scene with women huddled, apparently waiting, on the quay, their white headscarves, the water and the quay lit by moonlight. Although enigmatic, raising questions about a possible narrative, this is a less intimate painting than figure groups such as *The Balcony* (1868–69), or *Lunch in the Studio* (1868).

Manet painted a harmony of blues, greys, blacks and whites, with a thick impasto in several places, notably over the moon – X-rays reveal that it was originally lower down. Although the palette is dark, the style of the painting is beginning to show impressionist-type brushwork in places.

The ships in the harbour and the cloudy sky are reminiscent of Manet's first 'historical' painting, the *Battle of the Kearsage and the Alabama*, which he painted for the Salon in 1864, depicting a recent sea battle in the American Civil War off Cherbourg. This mingling of history, reportage and narrative is also evident in some of his other works, such as *The Execution of Maximilian* (1867), based on shocking news reports of the death of the Austrian Emperor of Mexico.

The strong verticals of the masts in the foreground are an interesting design device, possibly showing the early influence of Japanese prints, which were beginning to be imported and which became so important in the development of European art.

Edouard Manet
Argenteuil, 1874

Musée des Beaux-Arts, Tournai. Courtesy of AKG London/Erich Lessing

THIS is one of the first 'impressionist' paintings that Manet produced. The subject matter is contemporary, the palette is light and bright and Manet is concerned with showing a naturalistic background encompassing the luminosity and play of natural light. Even so, Manet's love of white and its different tonal values is still clear, and his 'punctuating' use of colour is still evident in the flash of red flowers.

As usual, the figures are the focus of Manet's composition – a young couple sit together, comfortably it seems, on a dock. But, even here, the interplay of emotions between the figures is unclear. The man seeks a connection with his companion; meanwhile she sits placidly, half-smiling, hands in lap, upright, looking ahead, formal, almost unaware of his presence. The man is Rodolphe Leenhof, Manet's brother-in-law; the girl is unidentified.

Boats in the foreground on either side of the couple face in opposite directions and are cut off on all sides – a 'snapshot' device suggested by photography and much used by Degas. Although there is no documentary evidence, it seems likely that this painting was executed, at least in part, out of doors – an unusual departure for Manet and one of the first times he would have tried it.

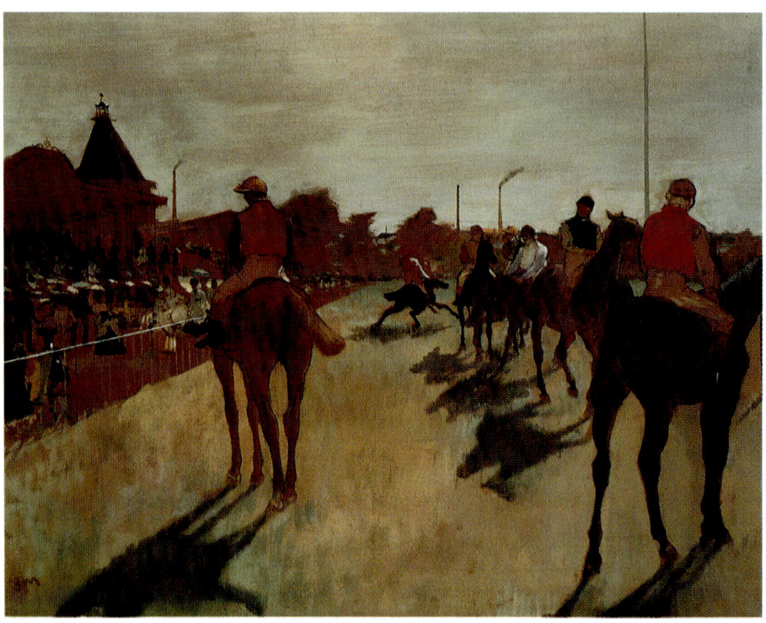

Edgar Degas
At the Races, in Front of the Stands, 1866–68
Musée d'Orsay, Paris. Courtesy of AKG London/Erich Lessing. *(See p. 162)*

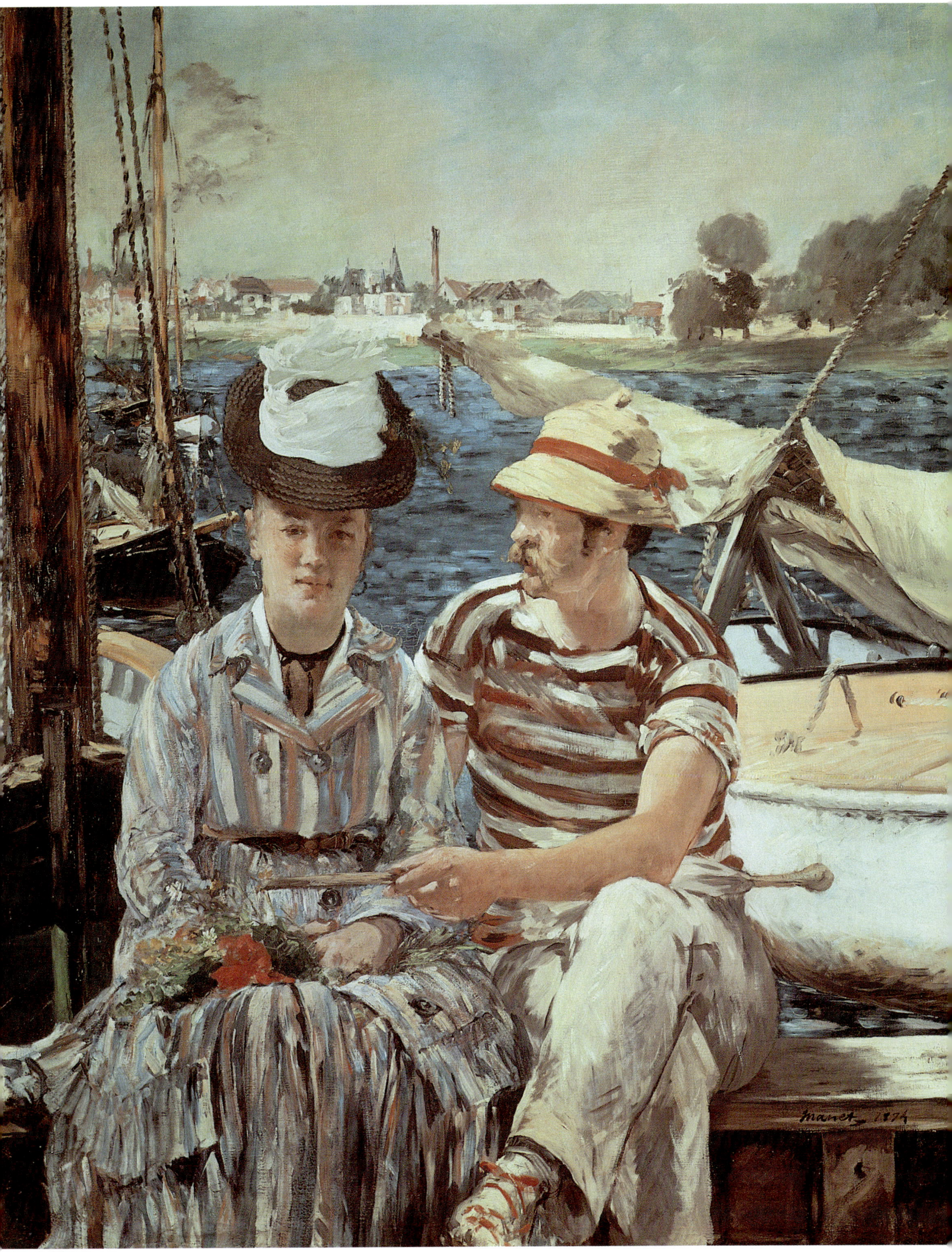
manet 1874

Edouard Manet
The Barge, 1874

Neue Pinakothek, Munich. Courtesy of AKG London

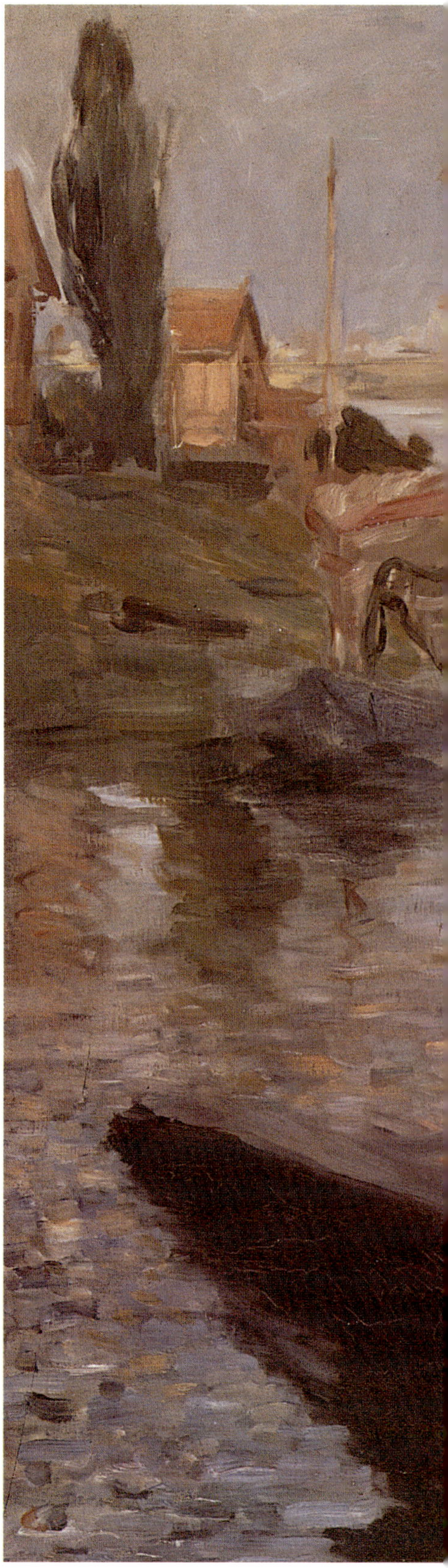

MANET first met the Impressionists in 1866, although they had admired his work since 1863. They used to meet him on Thursday evenings at the Café Guerbois but it was not until 1874, the year that they first exhibited independently of the Salon, that Manet experimented with their style of painting.

The Barge, which is unfinished because of the long sessions Manet needed to complete it, shows the painter Claude Monet on his floating studio on the river Seine at Argenteuil. In 1874, Manet spent the summer with his family on the opposite bank at Gennevilliers and painted alongside Monet and Pierre-Auguste Renoir (1841–1919). Under their influence, Manet discarded the dark tones and clear outlines of his earlier works and began to work in a more typical 'impressionist' style. But even here, Manet cannot quite give up his dark palette totally, as seen in the sombre treatment of the boat.

Moreover, true to form, the subject and focus of Manet's work are the people – in this case Monet and his wife Camille. Unlike Monet, Manet never painted a landscape just for itself. It was always part of a preconceived composition in the same way that the flat, dark backgrounds of some of his earlier works were conceived to work in harmony with his figures and were never just an absence of detail.

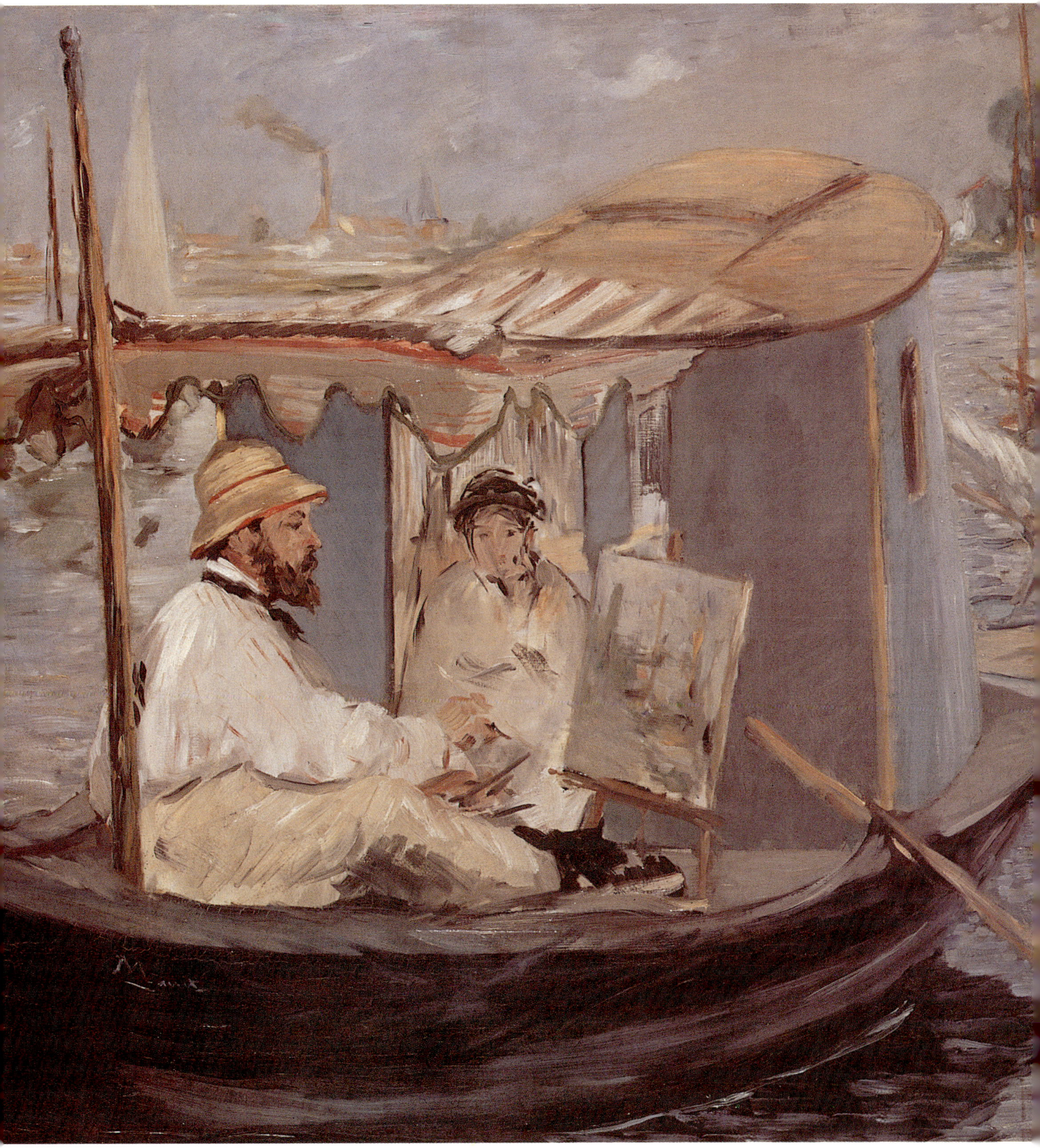

EDOUARD MANET
Inside the Café, 1878

Oskar Reinhart Collection, Winterthur. Courtesy of AKG London

SUNLIT, outdoor scenes were not the sole subject matter of the Impressionist group. Edgar Degas (1834–1917), Renoir and Manet also painted scenes of city life in the cafés, boulevards and theatres. Manet painted many café paintings in the late 1870s. Although the subject and the brushwork are in the Impressionist style, he has returned to his darker palette of grey, black and white tones. The only colour is in the beer and the matchstick holder on the left and a patch of red behind the auburn-haired waitress on the right.

For once, there is no tension in the relations between the figures – two people, heads together, enjoy a drink in a crowded café. The composition with the cut-off figures and table shows the influence of photography, possibly a result of Manet's friendship with Degas, whose similar subject matter sometimes caused tension between them. The diagonal of the table cutting across the composition also recalls compositions by Degas, particularly *The Tub* of 1886. Although Degas often experimented with different viewpoints, raising and lowering them, Manet rarely did. As usual, Manet shows an interest in the small, still-life objects that enliven the composition.

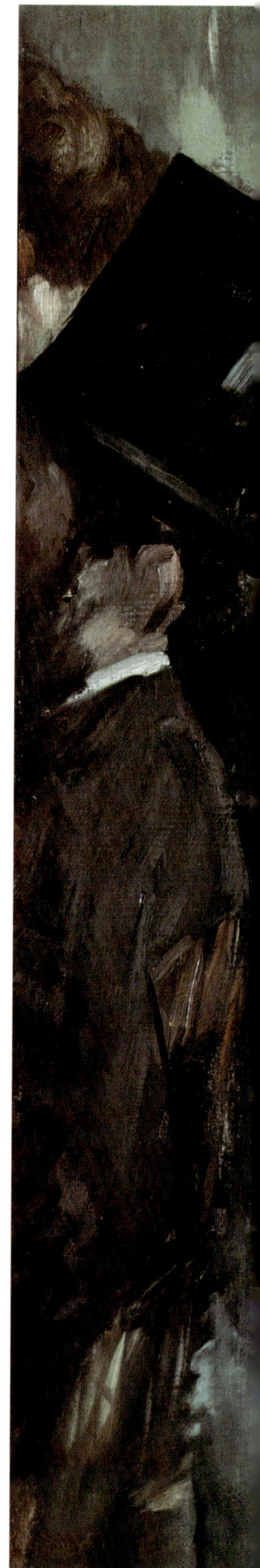

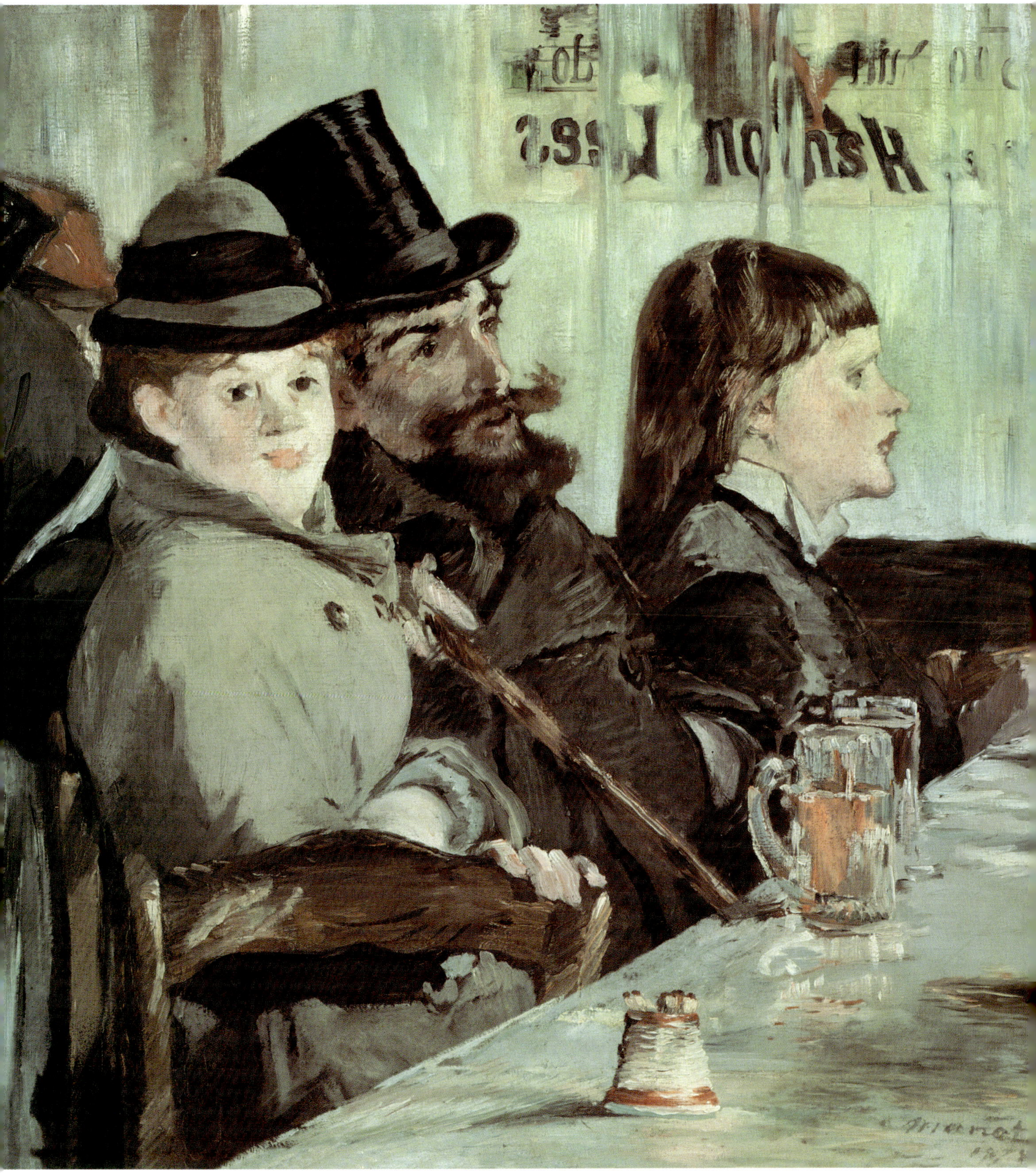

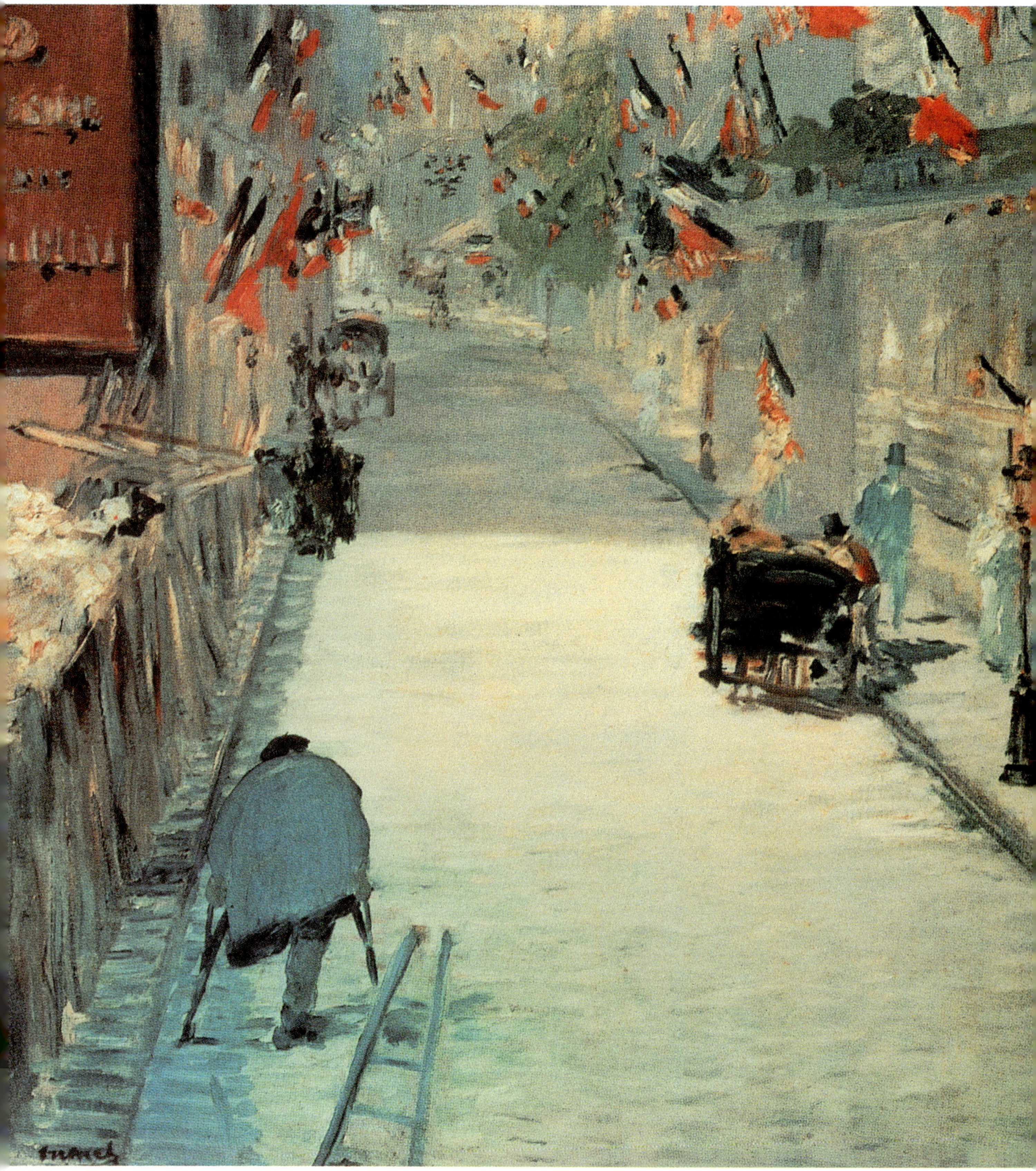

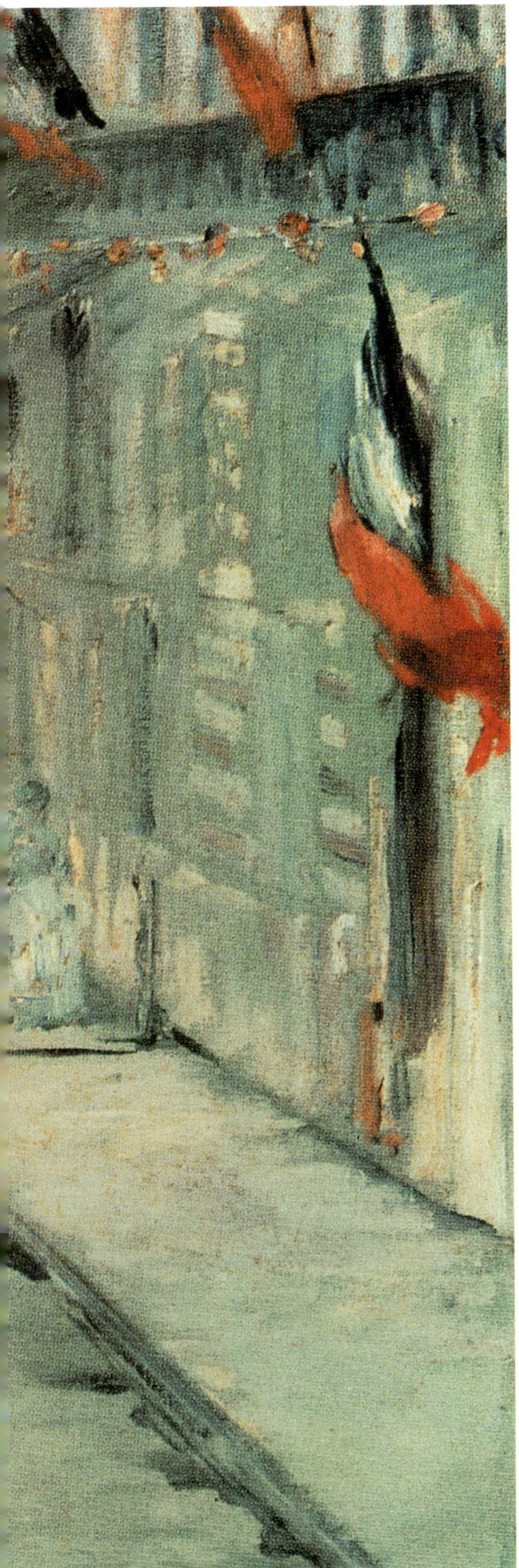

EDOUARD MANET
Rue Mosnier with Flags, 1878
Christie's. Courtesy of AKG London

MANET painted this street several times from his studio window on the rue Leningrad, which he rented between 1872 and 1878. It shows him using the Impressionist palette, stunning light effects, light-filled purple shadows and the effects of warm-cool colour.

The painting brings to mind other flag-filled street scenes of the same year (1878) painted by Monet and is very similar to Manet's own *Rue Mosnier with Pavers*. But, unlike Monet's work, which never had political overtones, Manet makes subtle, possibly political contrasts between the wealthy in their carriages and the street labourers in one painting and, in this one, between the festivity of the bright, flapping flags and the pathos of the one-legged man, half in and half out of the light, a local character who probably lost his leg in the Franco-Prussian war of 1870. A ladder, seen from above, partially separates him from the light-filled street and echoes the shape of his crutches.

In 1878 France had been a republic for a year and the flags celebrate the national holiday for the World Fair. This was one of the country's first efforts to re-establish full international status. That same year, Manet was rejected by the Salon and the group Impressionist exhibition was dropped, because the establishment wanted to remove all traces of radicalism, especially in the light of unrest in the worker's movement.

EDOUARD MANET
Blonde Woman with Bare Breasts, 1878

Musée d'Orsay, Paris. Courtesy of AKG London

THIS is an unusual painting for Manet and bears a strong resemblance to Renoir's *Nude in the Sunlight* (1876), although the light falling on this figure is uniform and she is not outside. The palette is typically impressionistic with none of the white, black and grey tones so typical of much of Manet's work. The woman is in a state of undress. The hint of a dress falls from her arms and she wears a hat on her head. Her pink skin and the green, flat background complement one another and are full of light, an effect partially created by the varying thickness of the green paint, which allows the colour of the canvas to help illuminate the painting. The top, left-hand, unpainted corner of the canvas contributes to this effect and reflects the golden straw of the hat. The red flowers contrast with the green.

Leaving areas of the canvas unpainted was not uncommon in Impressionist circles. Prepared canvases came in a range of pale to mid-tones and from the 1870s, with their bright palette and desire to represent natural light, it became logical to use the paler, primed canvases and to exploit the ground to play a role in the overall effect of colour and light.

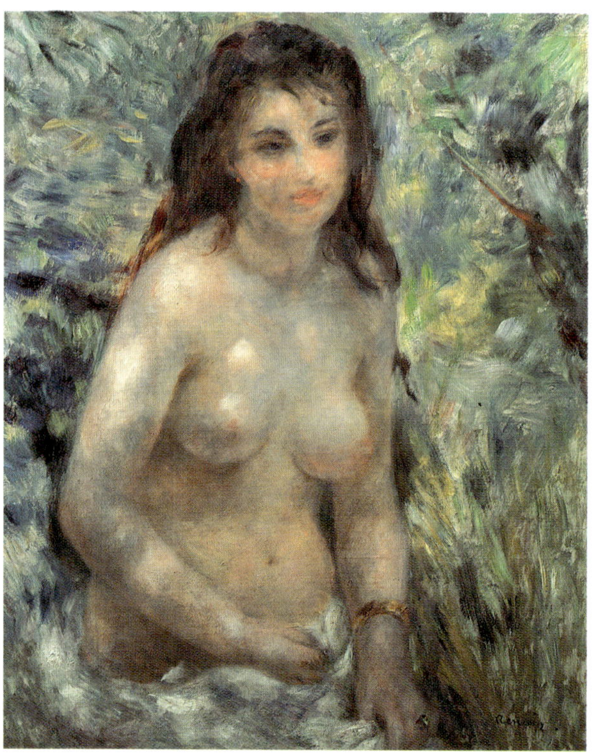

Pierre-Auguste Renoir
Nude in the Sunlight, 1876
Courtesy of AKG London/Erich Lessing.
(See p. 134)

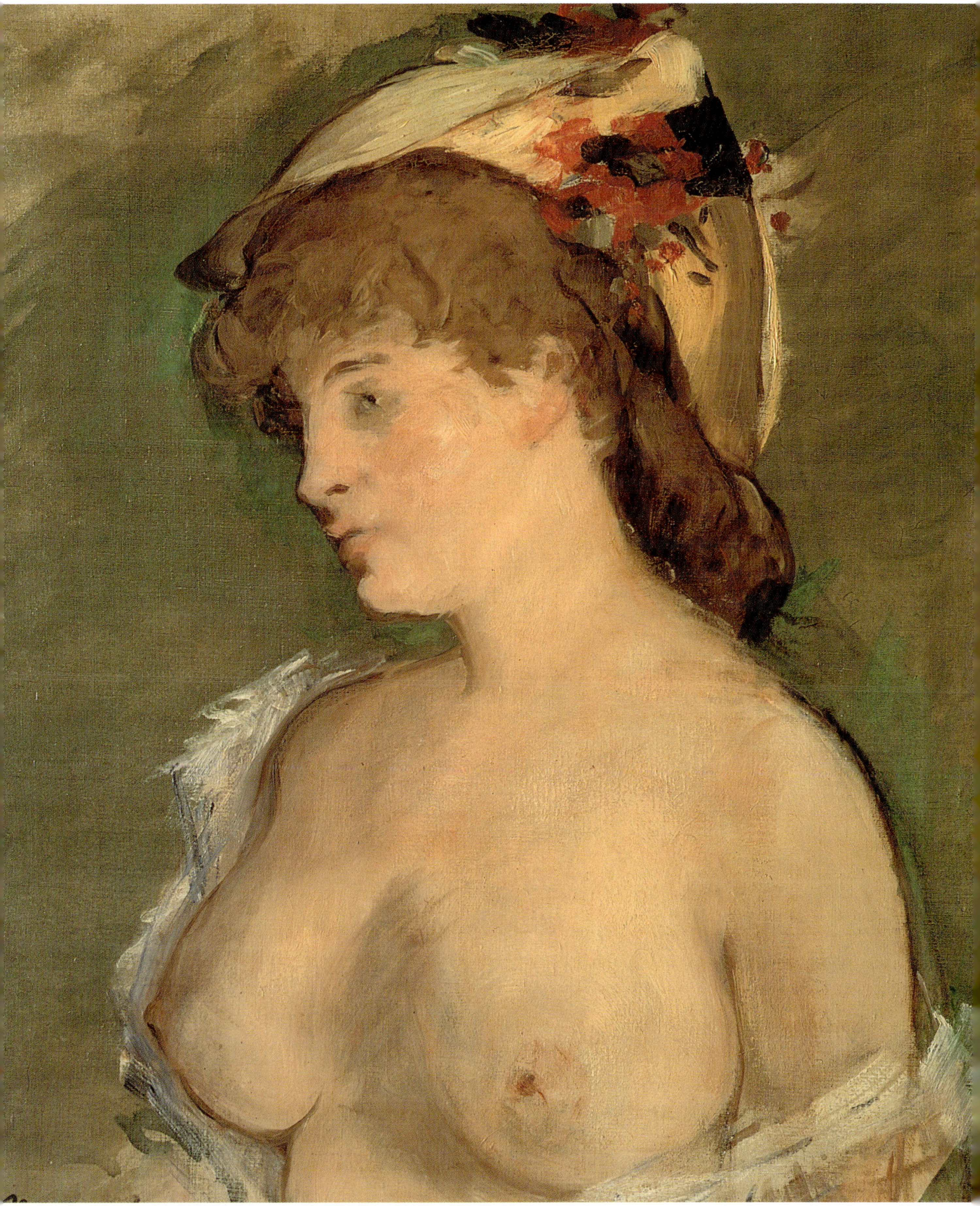

EDOUARD MANET
Bar at the Folies-Bergère, 1882

Courtauld Gallery, London. Courtesy of The Bridgeman Art Library

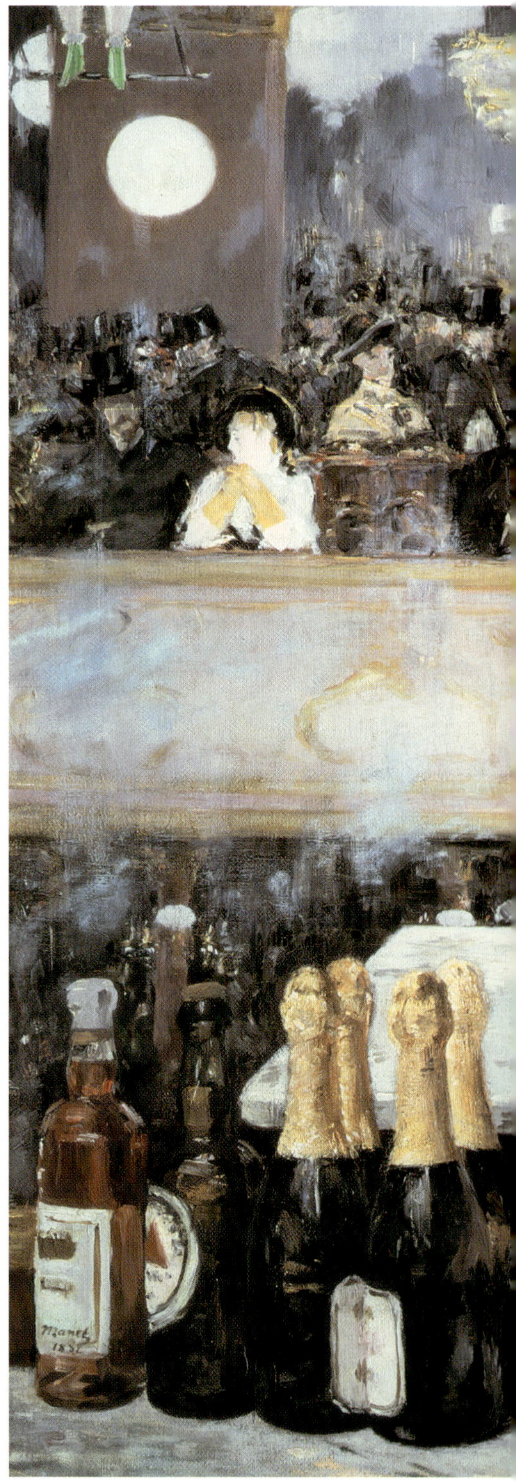

THIS is Manet's last large canvas and it was as reviled as *The Lunch on the Grass* (1862–63) almost 20 years earlier. Shown at the Salon of 1882, it was ridiculed for the 'mistake' of failing to show the customer, who is reflected in the mirror, in front of the bar.

This masterly canvas is full of visual and narrative riddles. The reflection of the girl is at an unexpected angle; the reflection of the customer is disconcerting and only makes sense if the viewer supposes it to be a reflection of themselves. The scene reflected in the expanse of mirror is of a balcony where people are enjoying an acrobatic display – note the feet, top left – which leads one to suppose that the bar is opposite the balcony, at the same level but virtually on the edge, and with no railings.

The reflection is full of lights, smoke and movement and contrasts keenly with the melancholic, lonely bar girl. She is so still that she has more in common with the lovingly painted objects on the bar (including English Bass beer) than with the noisy humanity behind (or before) her. Note the flowers – echoed in her corsage – an incongruous moment of innocent naturalism in the artificial world of the busy city.

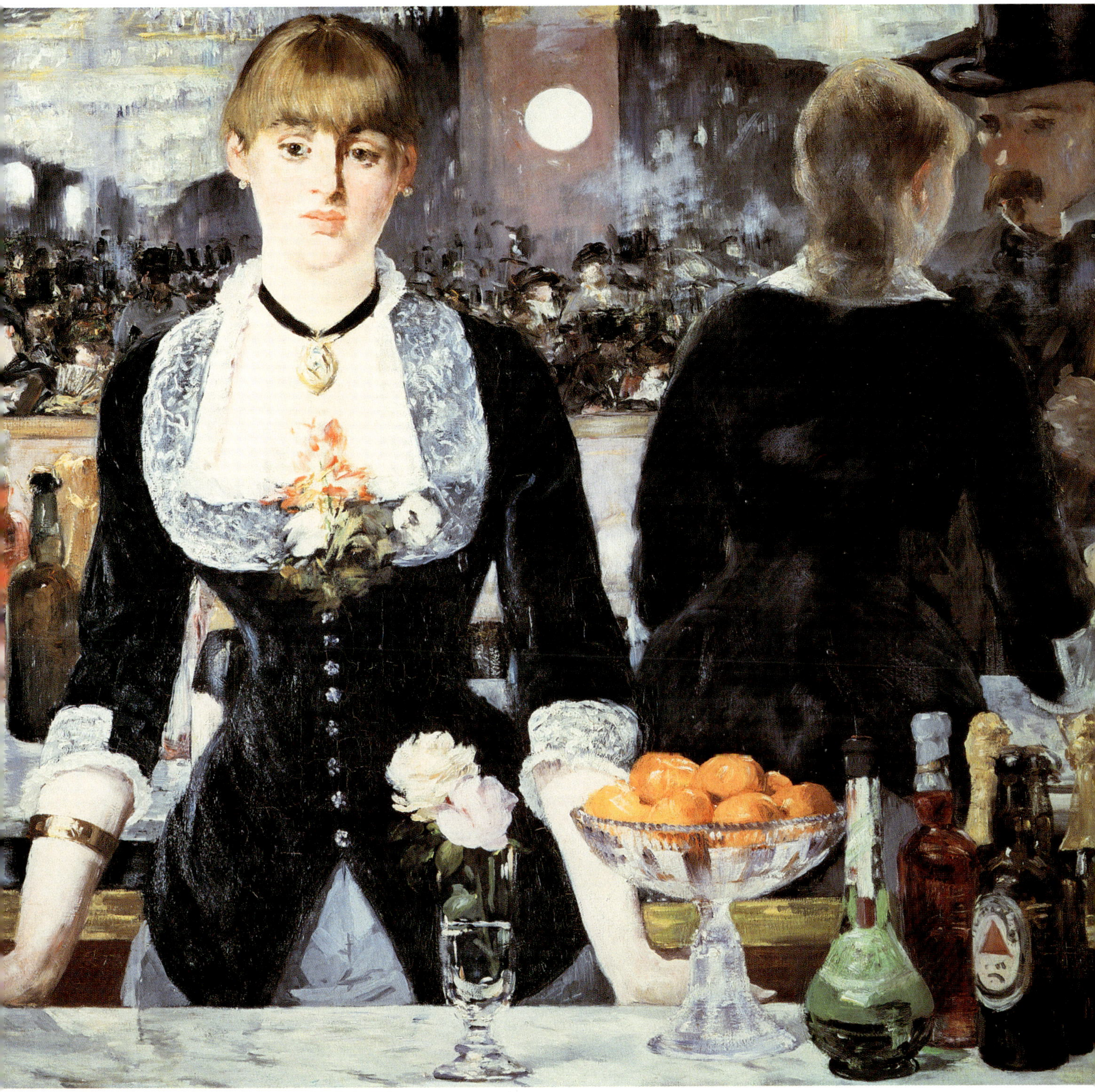

Edouard Manet
Woman in a Black Hat (Portrait of a Viennese, Irma Brunner), 1882

Musée du Louvre, Paris. Courtesy of AKG London

MANET painted many portraits throughout his life and did numerous half-length pastels of women during his last two years. The use of pastel in these works may show the influence of Degas.

One of his last pastels was of Irma Brunner, whom Manet met through his friend Mary Laurent, epitomizes the elegance and beauty of society Paris – a subject popular with Renoir. The soft treatment, so typical of pastel work, creates a misty quality; the pinks, greys, whites and shades of black harmonize gently; the only sharp definition is in the whiteness of the woman's profile against her black hat; the only sudden flash of colour in her scarlet lips.

The flat grey background is a perfect backdrop to the profile placed in the centre of the canvas to such effect. Any background detail would detract from the perfection of the colours and the form. This is a visual technique that Manet used throughout his career, but only if he thought it suitable for the work in hand. Théodore Duret (1838–1927), whose portrait he painted in 1868, describes how Manet added background details to his portrait when he was not happy with the effect of the plain background: ' ... missed the colours that might satisfy his eye, and not having put them in at first, he added them in the manner of still-life'.

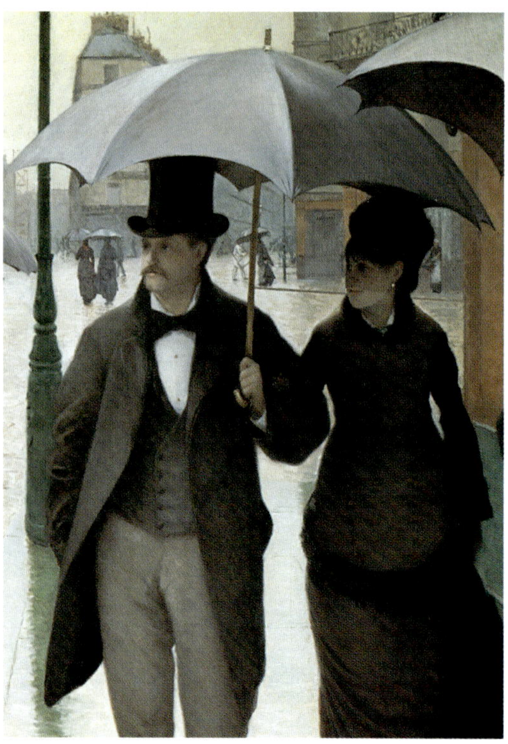

Gustave Caillebotte
Detail from *Street in Paris in the Rain*, 1877
Chicago Art Institute. Courtesy of AKG London/Erich Lessing. *(See p.194)*

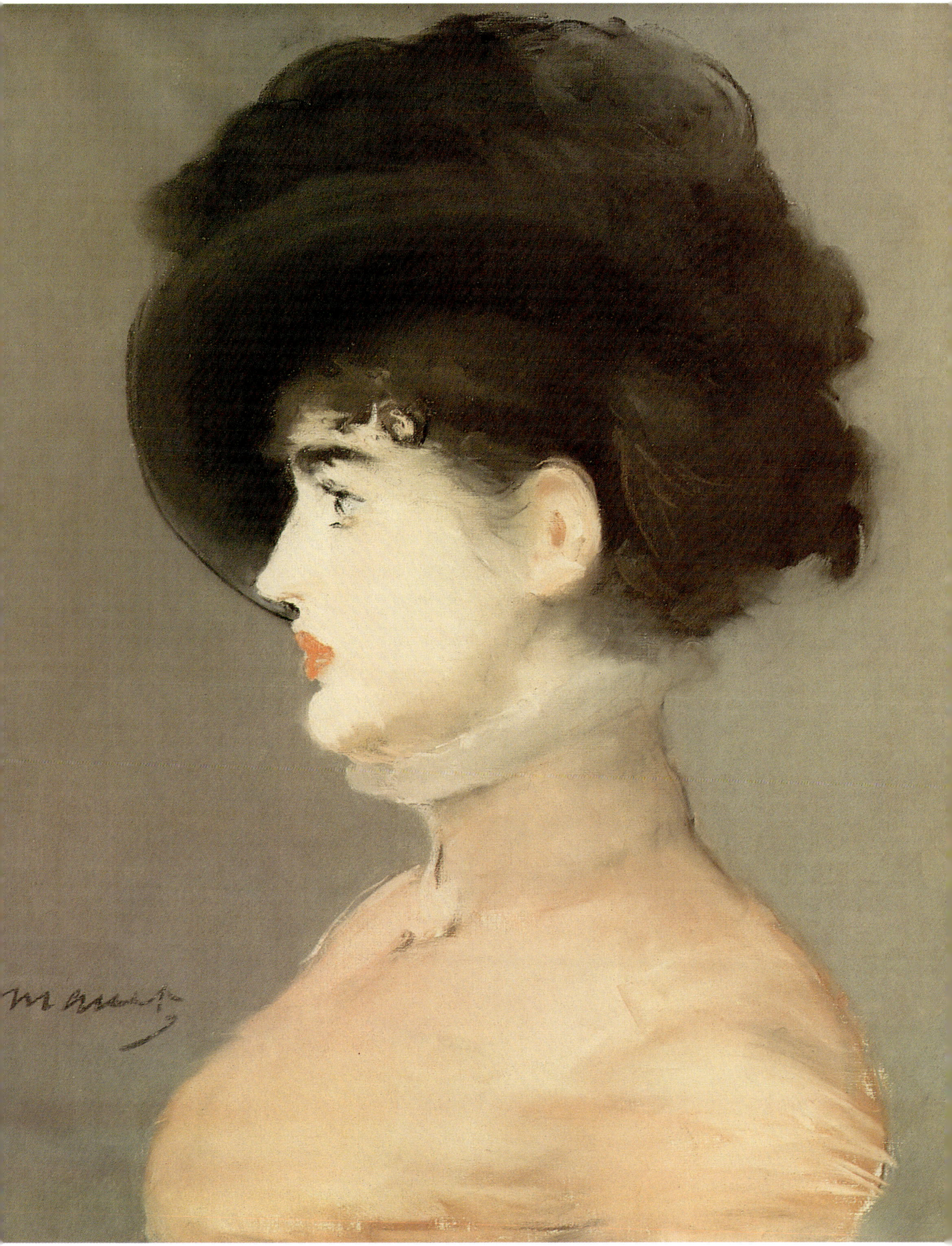

EDOUARD MANET
Rose and Tulip, 1882

Private Collection, Zurich. Courtesy of AKG London/Erich Lessing

THIS painting, probably executed in February 1883, is one of Manet's last. He died on 30 April 1883 from locomotor ataxia, a nervous disease resulting from undiagnosed syphilis, probably contracted as early as 1848.

Over the last two years of his life, Manet's movements were increasingly circumscribed and he often worked on small-scale still lifes such as this one, and garden views in the houses outside Paris where he spent the summer months on his doctor's advice.

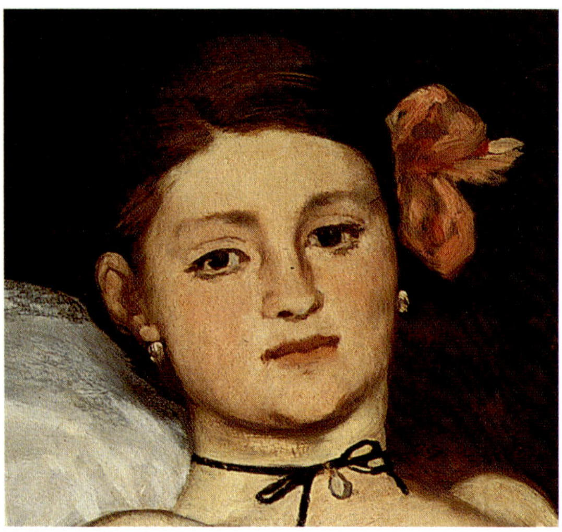

Edouard Manet
Detail from *Olympia, 1863*
Musée d'Orsay, Paris. Courtesy of AKG London/Erich Lessing. *(See p.22)*

This is one of 16 flower studies that he completed in the last year of his life – the last, *Roses in a Glass*, was executed on 1 March 1883. The flowers were probably brought to him by friends. 'There were always flowers in Manet's studio but never so many as there were in Rue d'Amsterdam in the early spring of 1883,' wrote Adolphe Tabarant, ' ... with what joy the patient welcomed these messengers of a springtime that he awaited with so much trust! He wanted to paint all of them; at least he painted some of them.' When he died, Degas said regretfully: 'He was greater than we thought.' Manet was buried in his beloved Paris; Monet was a pallbearer and a year later a retrospective of his work was held at the Académie des Beaux-Arts.

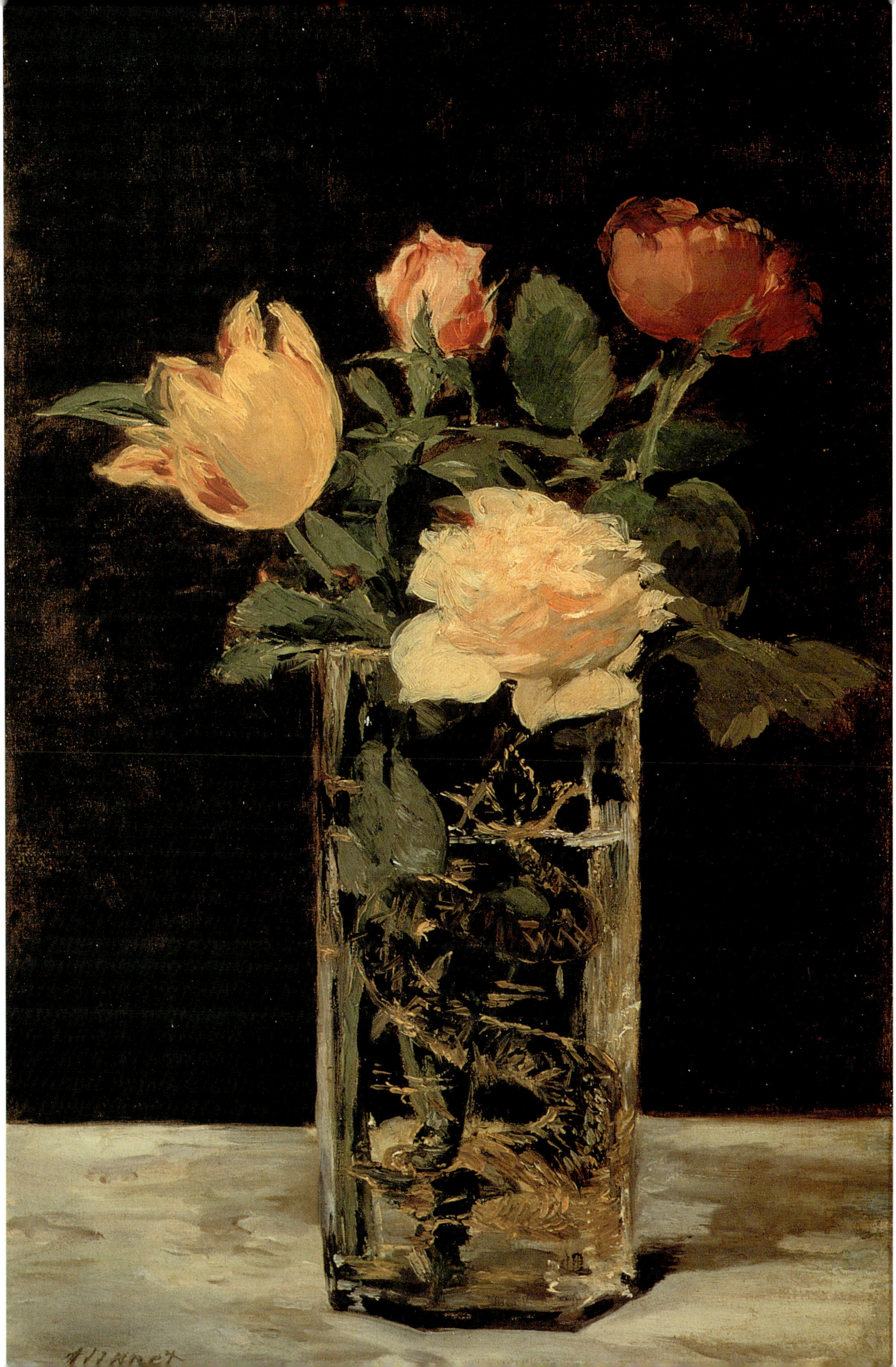

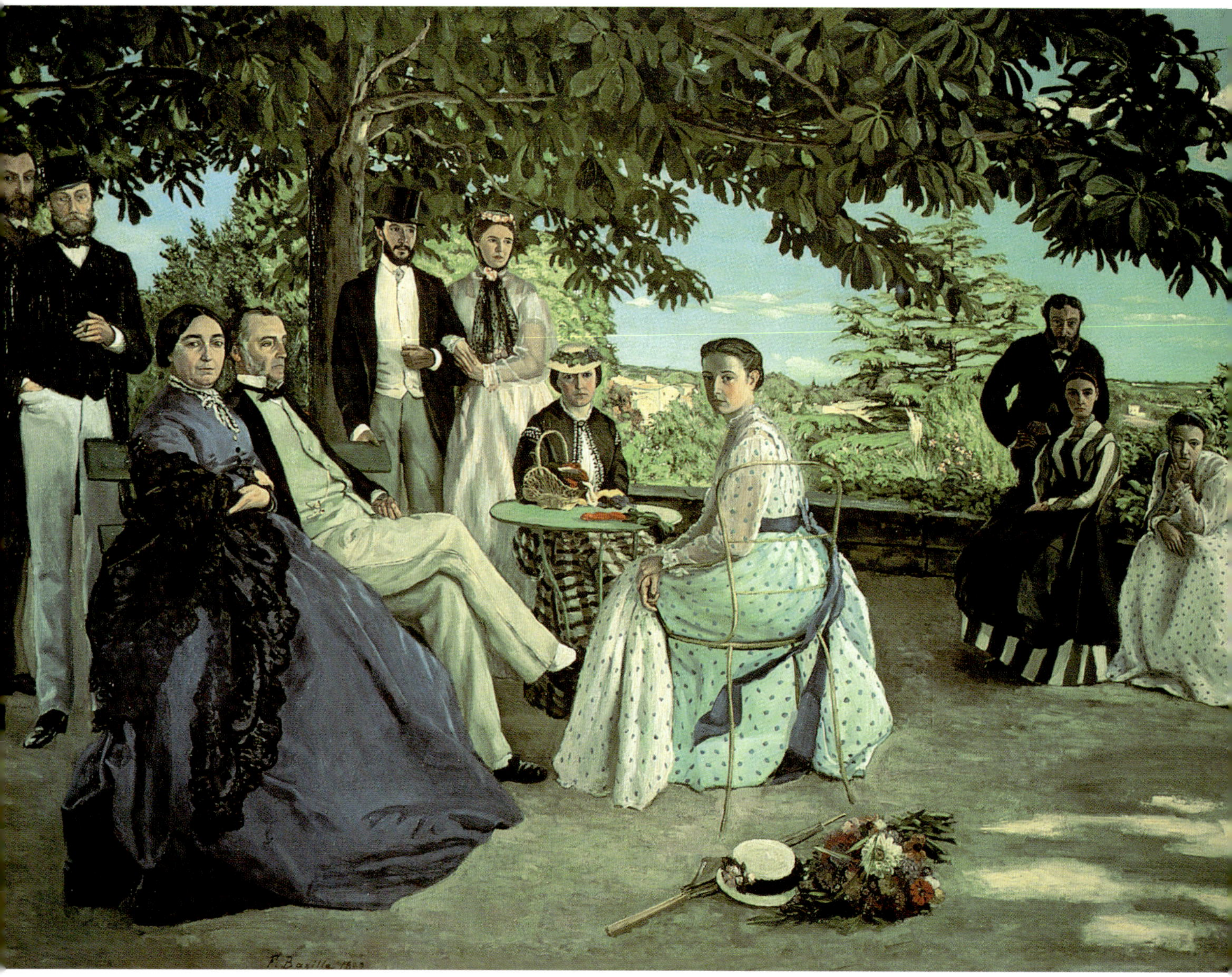

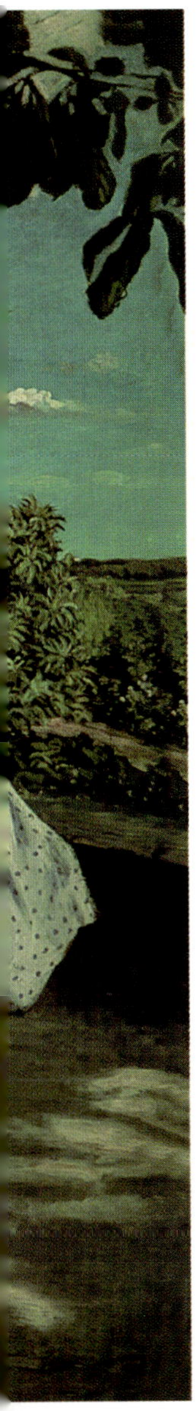

Frédéric Bazille (1841–70)
Family Reunion, 1867

Musée d'Orsay, Paris. Courtesy of AKG London

FRÉDÉRIC BAZILLE, a medical student, studied at the studio of the artist Gleyre (1808–74) in 1862 alongside Monet, Renoir and Sisley (1839–99). They became friends and used to go on trips outside Paris to paint in the open air. In 1863, Bazille wrote to his mother that he had spent 'eight days … near the Forest of Fontainebleau … with my friend Monet from Le Havre, who is rather good at landscapes. He gave me some tips that have helped me a lot.'

This painting shows members of Bazille's family. Bazille is standing on the far left. It bears comparison with Monet's *Women in the Garden*, which was painted later the same year. Both show bourgeois figures in a garden, and have been composed asymmetrically to create a snapshot effect. Both are concerned with the effects of sunlight and shadows on the ground and on the folds of the women's clothing. Bazille even goes so far as to paint the reflected light on the skirt of the girl in the centre in turquoise, which must have been just as astonishing at the time as the shadows in Monet's work. The emphasis of the two paintings, however, is different. Bazille's work is static, showing a ponderous, semi-formal grouping rather than a spontaneous moment and shows a shaded scene in which the light sneaks in through the leaves. Monet's, on the other hand, is a lively sunlit scene, interrupted by shade. However, Bazille's painting was accepted at the Salon of 1868, while Monet's was not.

FRÉDÉRIC BAZILLE
Bazille's Studio, 1870

Musée d'Orsay, Paris. Courtesy of AKG London/Erich Lessing

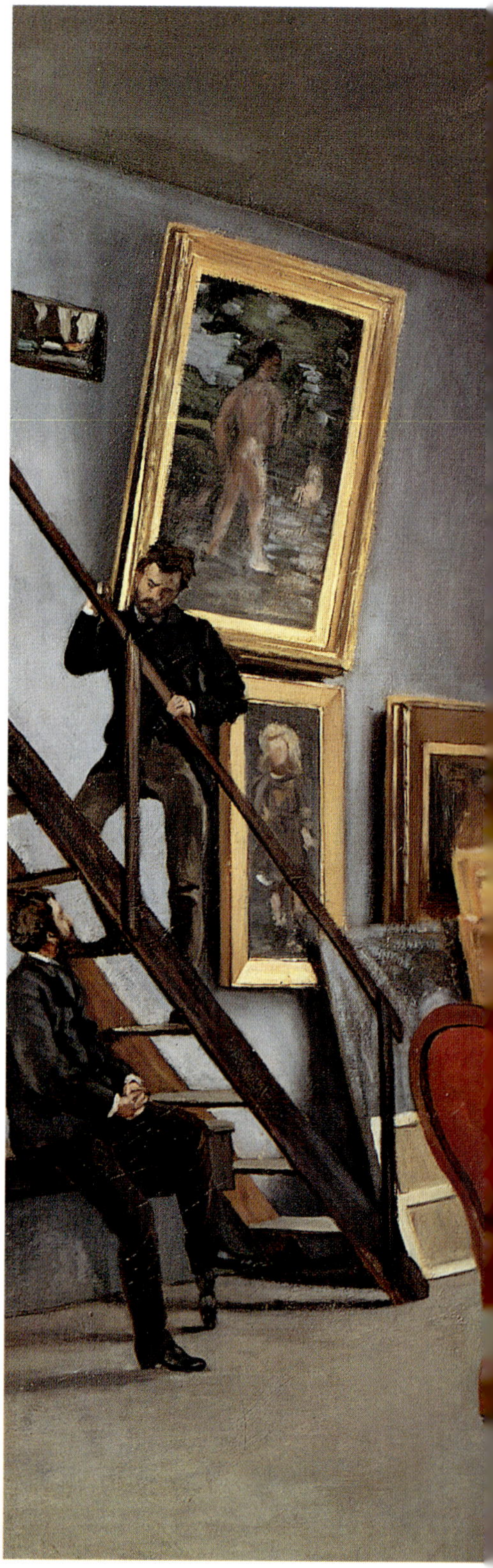

THIS painting shows Bazille's studio on the Rue de la Condamine, not far from the Café Guerbois where the group used to meet. Zola leans over the stairs, talking to Renoir; Manet inspects the canvas with Monet. The tall figure of Bazille, painted in afterwards (and out of proportion) stands by Manet holding the brush and palette. The pictures on the walls are by his friends, among them a still life above the piano that Bazille, much better off than most of the group, bought from the impecunious Monet.

It is an unusual composition, cut off on both sides and with a large, empty space on the right – a Japanese device much employed by Degas, in particular. The chair and the stove on either side channel the eye to the empty white sofa and the painting and wall behind it. On the right, Bazille's friend Maître (1840–98) plays the piano, separate from the crowd. The stove, the wall and the folded table also lead the eye towards this single figure. The left side of the painting is full and busy, showing an informal scene and the rapport between the friends.

Manet's influence is clear in the colours of the palette, although Bazille's is much lightened. The white sofa, the reds in the furniture and the golds of the picture frames provide bright accents of colour in an otherwise rather grey scene. Sadly, Bazille died the year that he painted this picture, killed fighting in the Franco-Prussian War.

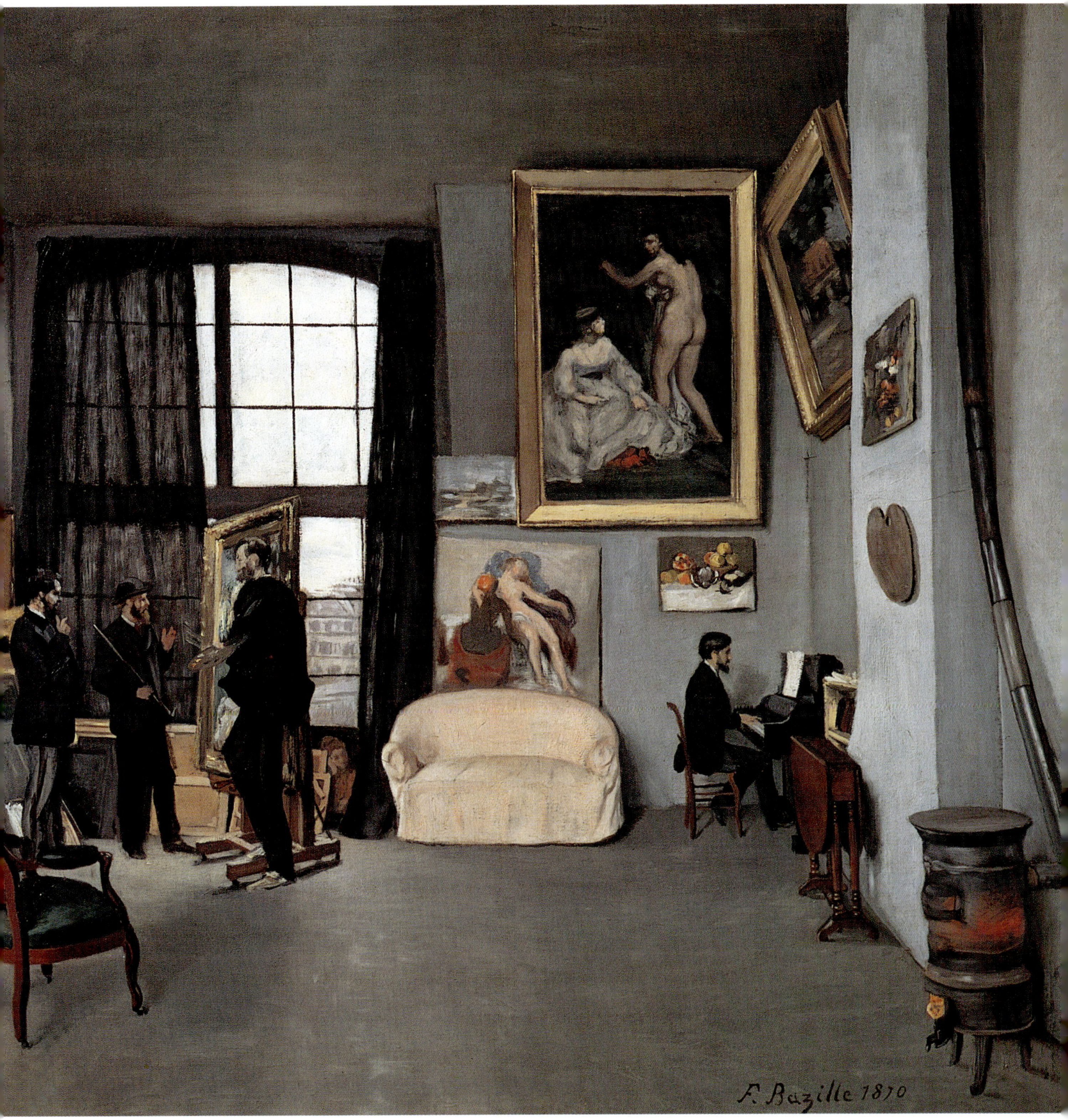
F. Bazille 1870

CLAUDE MONET (1840–1926)
Women in the Garden, 1867

Musée d'Orsay, Paris. Courtesy of AKG London/Erich Lessing

WHEN Monet painted this picture, he had already begun to paint outside, acting upon the advice of Boudin, whom he had met in 1858, and the Dutch painter Johan Jongkind (1819–91) to whom he said he owed 'the final development of my painter's eye'. *Women in the Garden* is a forerunner of the Impressionist style. It was painted *en plein air* and shows a fascination with the effects of natural light. The composition is cut off at the edges, trying to preserve in a big work the spontaneity of a sketch. However, the brushwork is still fairly traditional, the figures show an underlying draughtsmanship and Monet is concerned with details that in later years would disappear completely.

Monet had to have a trench dug in order to reach the top of this 3-m (9-ft 9-in) canvas. On one occasion the landscapist Gustave Courbet (1819–77) visited. Monet was not working and when he asked why not, Monet replied that he was 'waiting for the sun'. The older painter suggested that he paint in the background while he waited but Monet was adamant that everything had to be painted in the same light.

Refused by the Salon in 1867, Zola alone defended this *tour de force*, describing the then-extraordinary effects of light and shade cutting across the path and the women as 'Nothing stranger as an effect'

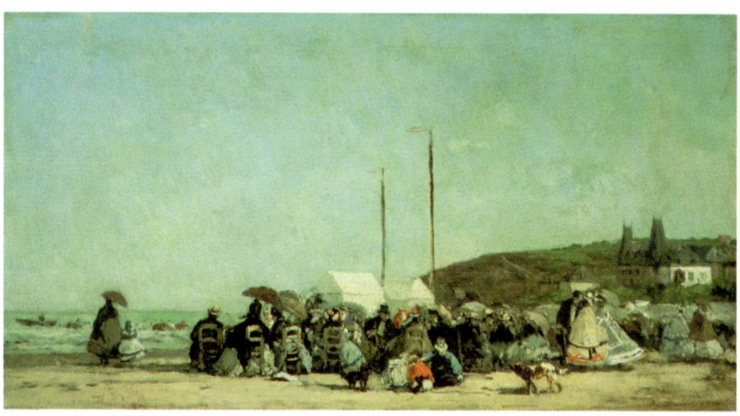

Eugène Boudin
The Beach at Trouville, 1864
Musée du Louvre, Paris. Courtesy of AKG London. *(See p. 16)*

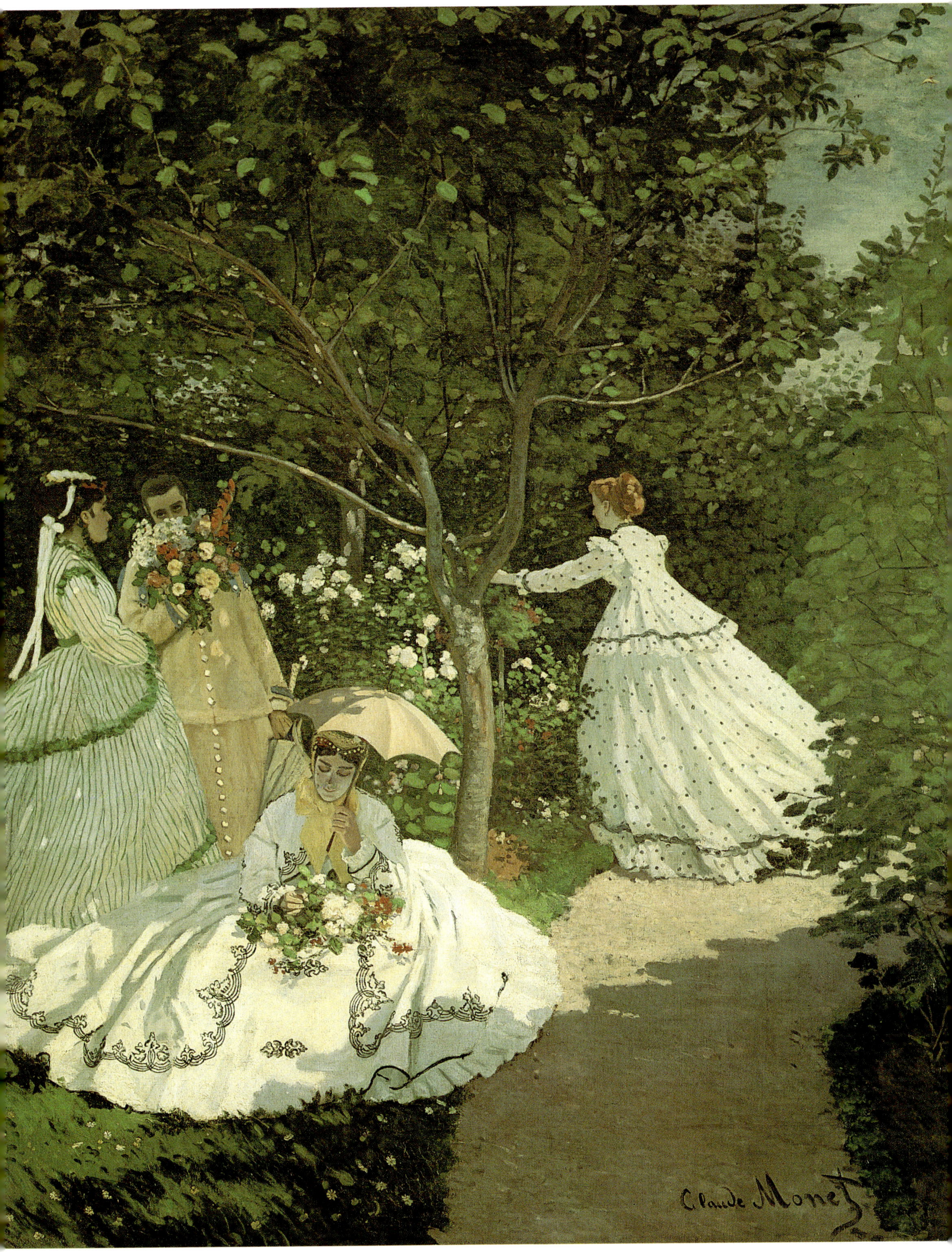
Claude Monet

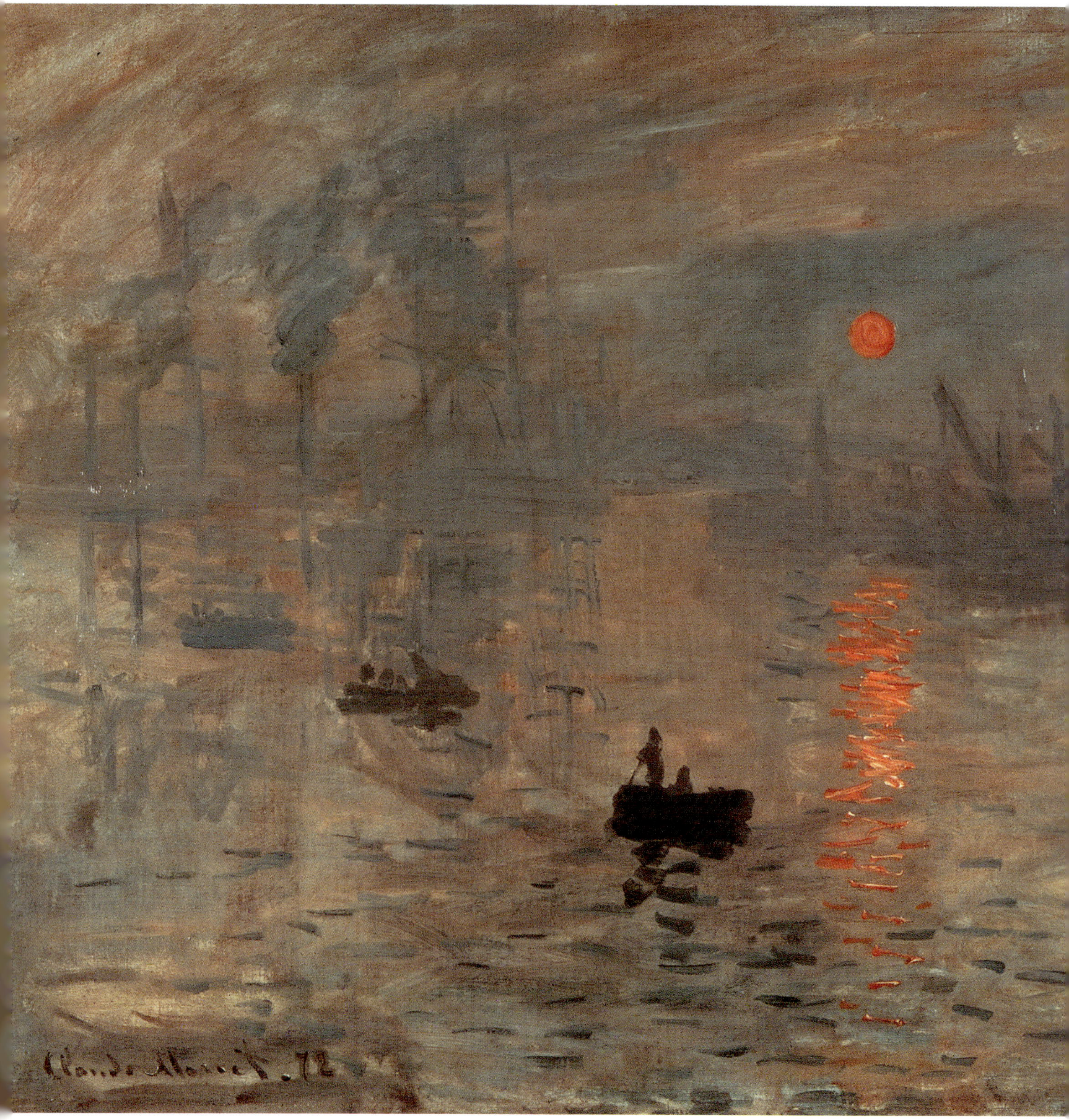
Claude Monet. 72

CLAUDE MONET
Impression: Sunrise, 1872

Musée Marmottan, Paris. Courtesy of AKG London

IN 1874 a group of artists led by Monet and his friends, dissatisfied with their dependence upon the selection of the official Salon for success, set up an exhibition to show their own work. The exhibition, at which 30 painters exhibited, including Boudin, Cézanne, Degas, Guillaumin (1841–1927), Morisot (1841–95), Pissarro (1830–1903), Renoir and Sisley, showed works that were considered typical of the new art's approach. But critics lashed out at the new aesthetic. They were horrified at the modern subject-matter, the unfinished quality of the pictures painted out in the open, the lack of draughtsmanship and the bright, pure colour that was used to depict the passing effects of light.

Impression: Sunrise, sketched early one morning at the docks in Le Havre, is the work that gave rise to 'Impressionism', a term first used in a satirical magazine in which the critic claimed to have seen the exhibition with a pupil of Ingres (renowned for his draughtsmanship). Confronted with these works, he cried out, 'Eheu, I am an impression on legs, the avenging palette knife'.

This was followed by another article that singled out Monet, Degas, Renoir, Sisley, Morisot and Pissarro, carefully differentiating their different styles and calling them Impressionists, 'in the sense that they do not produce a landscape but rather convey the sensation produced by the landscape'. But the name stuck and was used to describe all the artists of the new aesthetic regardless of their individual styles, subject-matter and techniques.

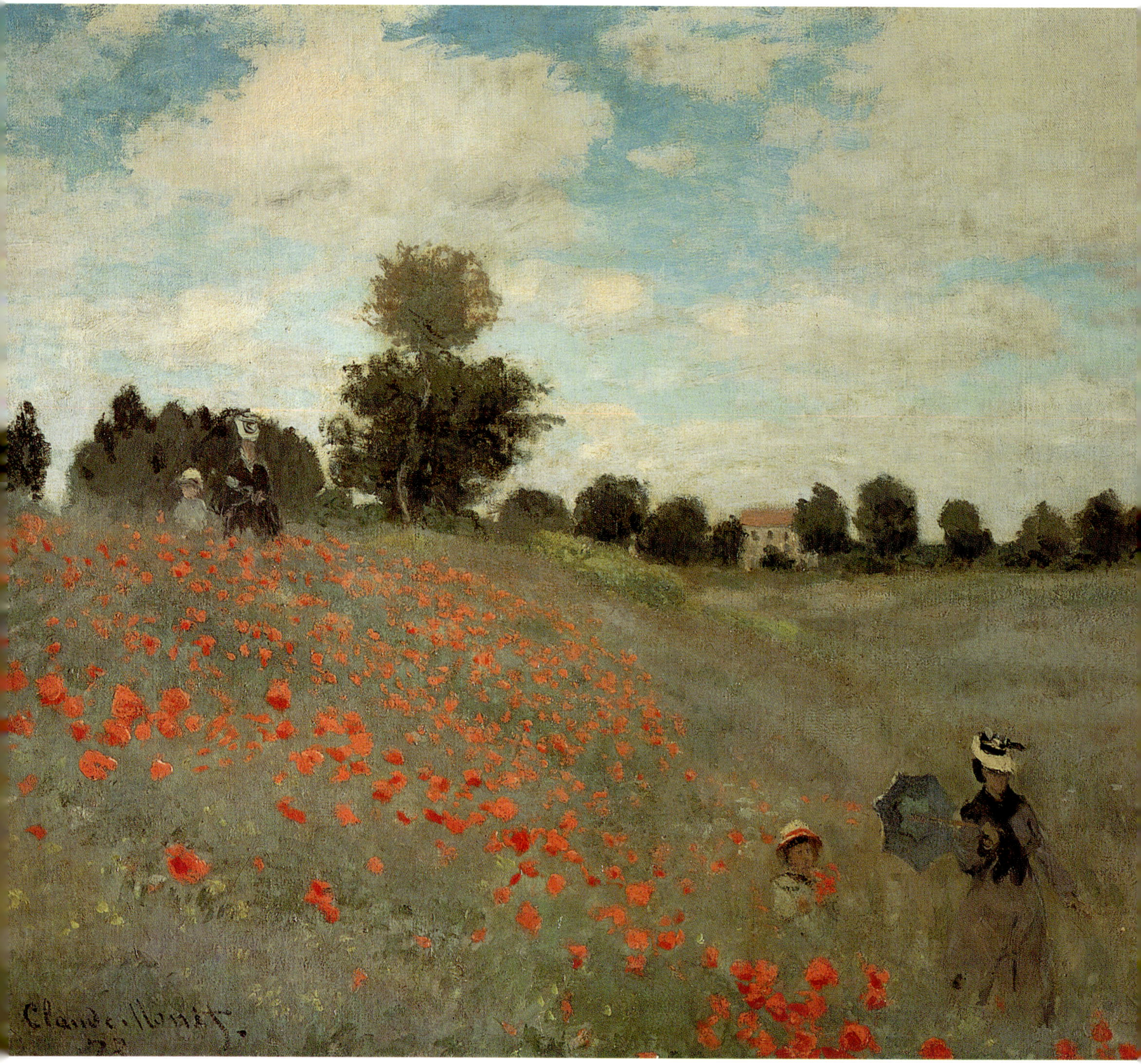

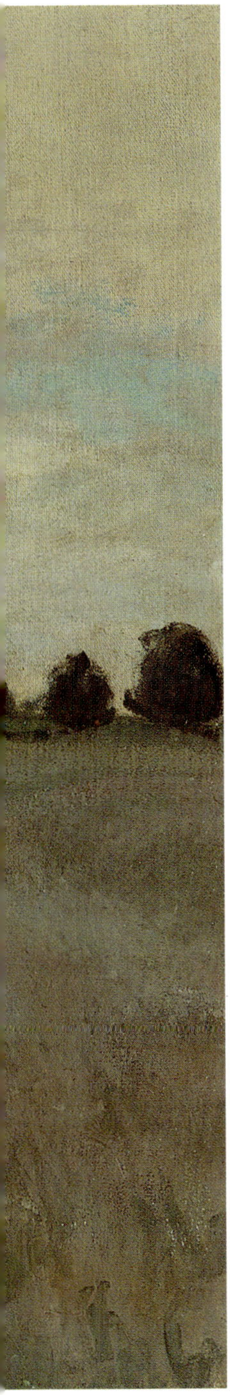

Claude Monet
Poppy Field at Argenteuil, 1873

Musée d'Orsay, Paris. Courtesy of AKG London/Erich Lessing

IN 1872 Monet settled with his wife Camille and son Jean at Argenteuil, having spent the years of the Franco-Prussian War of 1870–71 in London. Argenteuil provided him with plenty of idyllic subject matter. *Poppy Field at Argenteuil* is one of his most famous works and was shown at the first Impressionist exhibition in 1874. The small dabs of brilliant colour evoke the heat and vibrant atmosphere of a summer's day.

In this painting, in which the figures (Camille and Jean) seem so much part of the landscape, Monet creates an effect of time – not just of a fleeting moment, but of that moment within a broader time frame – in this case, a walk among the poppies. Beneath a broad sky, the poppy bank descends from the left in a swathe of vibrant colour. Two pairs of figures (almost like two frames of a moving film) come out into the sunlight – the tree on the far left echoing the upright female figure, implying the distance that they have come. The spontaneity of the scene is created not only by the sketch-like, faintly blurred effect of the paint, but by the figures in the foreground – the child with the flowers he has picked, his mother, with her arm swinging forward as she walks, and her parasol swung casually over her shoulder.

CLAUDE MONET
The Bridge at Argenteuil, 1874

Musée d'Orsay, Paris, Courtesy of AKG London/Erich Lessing

MONET presents us with an idyllic sunlit scene – although this painting would typically have been shown within the confines of suburban Paris. He uses pure colour to create the effects of light and the reflections in and of water – note the walls reflected back on themselves inside the arches of the bridge. The warm colours – blues, golds, pinks and whites – repeat, echoing each other from one side of the painting to the other and, above all, in the reflections in the water. But the water is not just a large mirror (interestingly, mirror effects play a part in the works of other artists such as Degas), it ripples and sparkles, an effect created by applying the paint in short and long strokes or in flat patches of colour.

The composition, which is so natural, does not lack structure and shows an informed balancing of the strong verticals of the trees, the mast and the piers of the bridge (and their reflections), with the strong horizontals of the boat, bank, sky and river.

Modern eyes hardly question the Impressionist style but even this painting was not easily acceptable at the time. Taken out of context, the broken dabs of colour would not clearly represent anything at all – their power is in their relation to everything else and the effect that is seen at a distance.

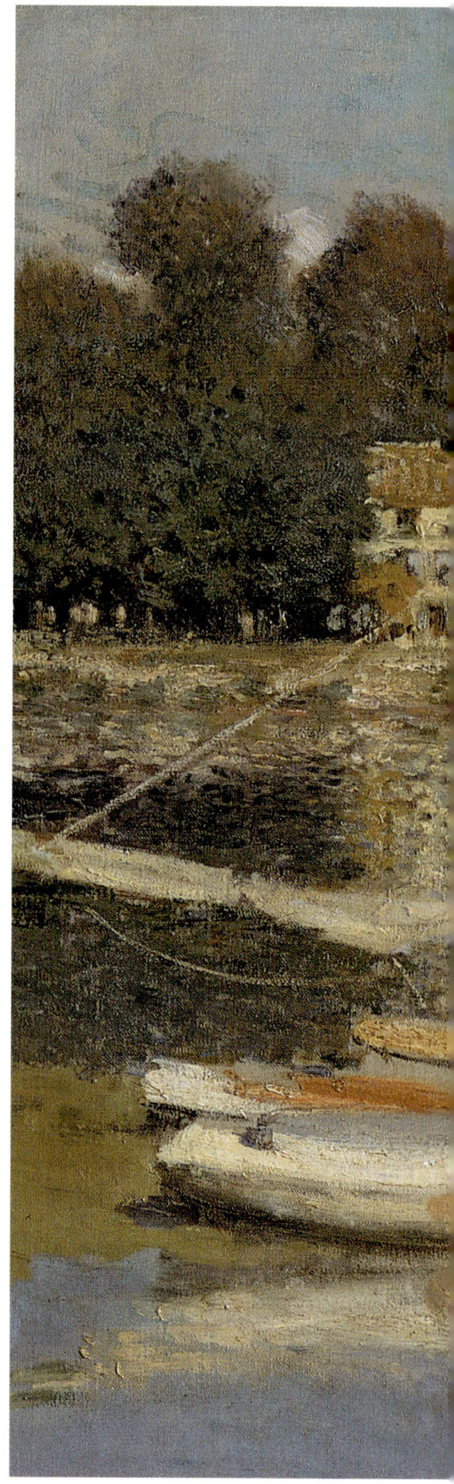

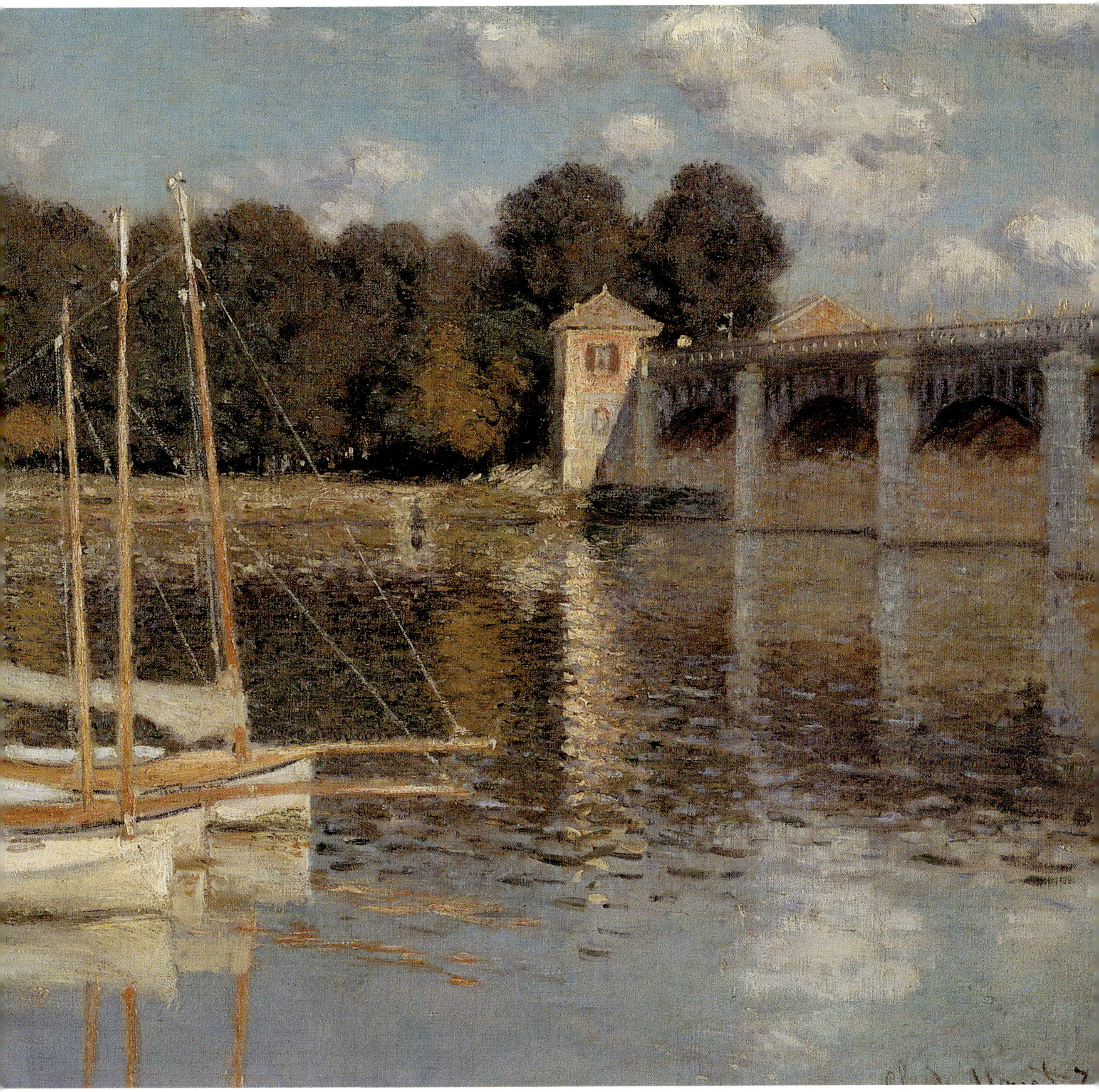

CLAUDE MONET
Turkeys, 1876

Musée d'Orsay, Paris. Courtesy of AKG London/Erich Lessing

TURKEYS was part of one of four decorative panels that Monet painted for the Chateau de Rottembourg at Montgeron for his patron Ernest Hoschedé (1838–90), who owned a textile business. Here, he returned to a large format and created a daring, innovative design influenced by the unusual viewpoints found in Japanese prints. Viewed from below, the turkeys loom tall, with the trees and the chateau in the distance. They are separated by size, colour and the evening sunlight highlighting their feathers and contours in bright yellow. The turkey cut off from the chest downwards at the bottom of the canvas increases the immediacy of the scene and positions the viewer who is lying silently in the grass, so close to the birds, looking up a slope. As usual, Monet's palette in confined to blues, yellows, whites and reds, which are used, particularly in the 'white' turkeys, to great effect.

Monet returned from this commission to Argenteuil. He had many money worries and feared he would have to leave 'this nice little house … where I have worked so well'. The family did eventually leave in January 1878 and returned to Paris where Monet had also worked over the last few years on scenes of Paris parks and stations.

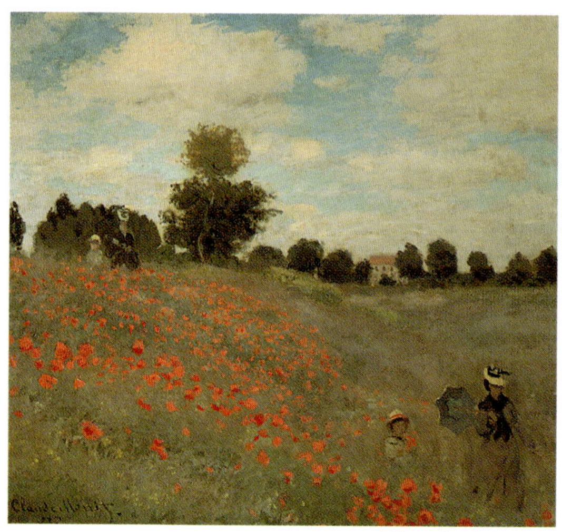

Claude Monet
Poppy Field at Argenteuil, 1873
Musée d'Orsay, Paris. Courtesy of AKG London/Erich Lessing. *(See p. 57)*

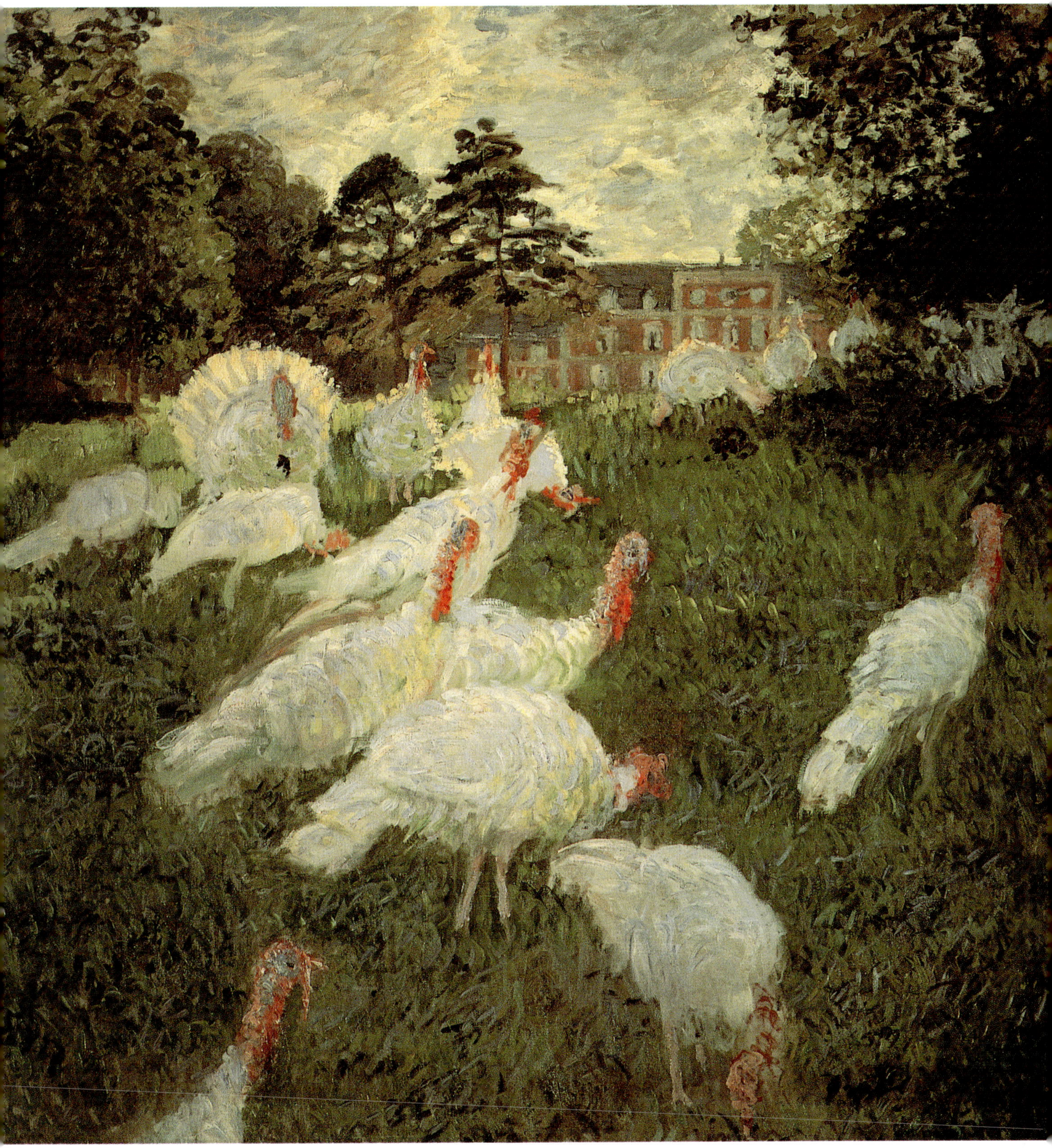

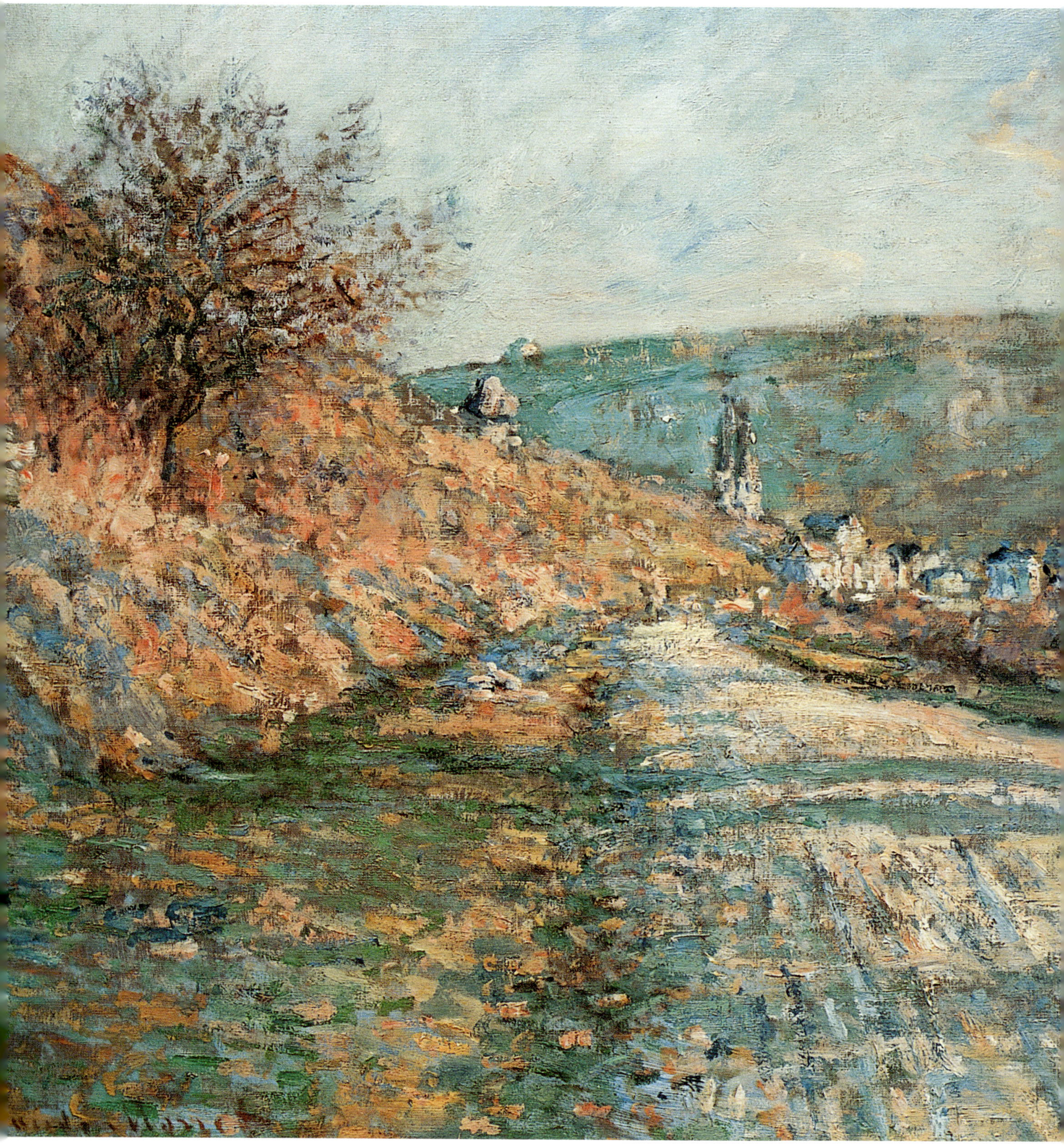

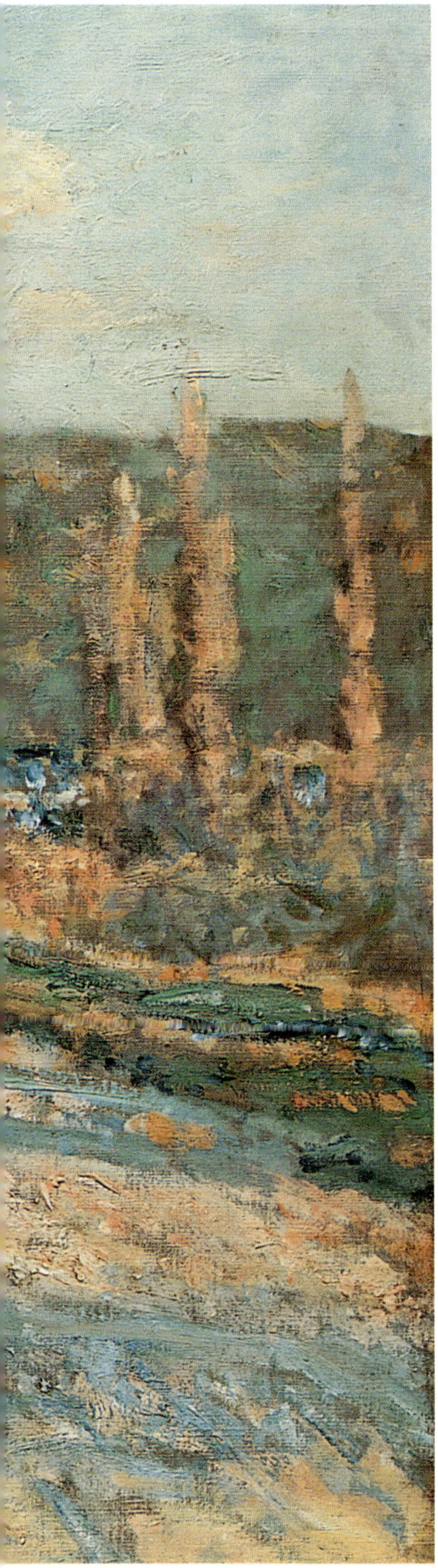

CLAUDE MONET
The Road to Vétheuil, 1880

Phillips Collection, Washington D. C.. Courtesy of AKG London

IN 1878, Monet and his family had moved to Vétheuil and rented a house with Ernest Hoschedé – who had gone bankrupt that year – and his family. The period in Vétheuil was not a happy one. Monet's finances were bad and in September 1879, his wife died shortly after the birth of their son Michel. The following winter, still living with the Hoschedés, Monet spent his time painting beautiful but desolate pictures of ice floes on the Seine – perhaps reflecting his inner melancholy.

This picture was painted early in 1880 and is a study in the effects of light on the road going towards Vétheuil, pictured in the distance. With his typically limited palette, Monet creates the effect of a cold, fresh morning – the light white and clear, bleaching the landscape of its colour, the trees on the right (not included in the picture) throwing long blue shadows. The same colour is repeated in the mist above the town.

The composition is clever, although it seems so simple. From left to right, four rough triangles take up the foreground, sweeping down the bank to the road below. They roughly converge on Vétheuil, leading the eye into the picture from the silence and clarity of the road to the busy human habitation beyond. The patchy blue horizontals of the shadows across the road are forceful and balance the band of sky, which loses its severity thanks to the soft curves of the hillsides and a tree breaking in on the right.

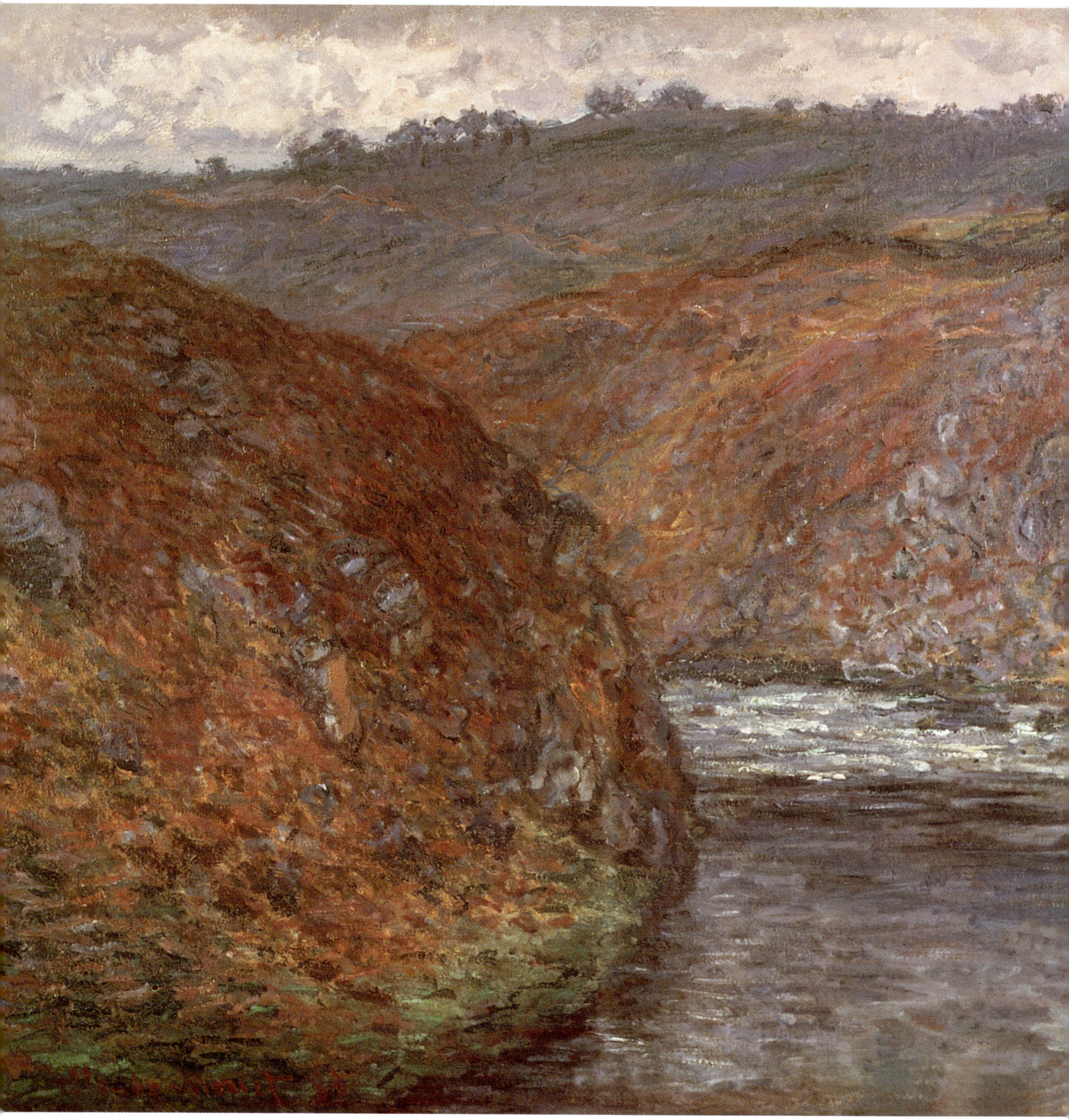

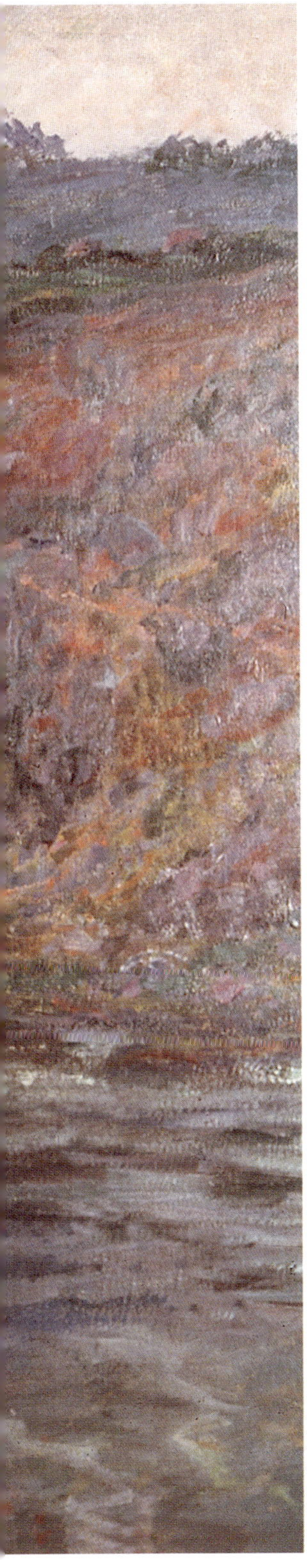

Claude Monet

View of the River Creuse on a Cloudy Day, 1889

Heydt Museum, Wuppertal. Courtesy of The Bridgeman Art Library

IN 1889 (now living at Giverny with Alice Hoschedé and both sets of children) Monet joined his friend, the critic Geffroy, and two others on a trip to Fresselines, a village in the Massif Central in the centre of France. There, overwhelmed by its wild beauty, he began a series of paintings of the river Creuse.

The Creuse is two rivers, the Grande and the Petite Creuse, which meet below Fresselines in a wide expanse of water. The area is well known for its rugged terrain and rock quarries and Monet wrote to Alice of its 'awesome wildness'.

In total, Monet completed 24 canvases of this dramatic valley, most of which he painted from the same vantage point. They constitute the first works that Monet painted as a series. Of all his work, they are the most brooding and lugubrious, many of them executed as the last rays of light disappeared.

These paintings formed a large part of the exhibition that Monet staged with the sculptor Auguste Rodin (1840–1917) in 1889, the year of the Universal Exhibition. After public disappointment at his previous exhibition of paintings done in Antibes, about which Pissarro had written to his son, 'they are beautiful but Fénéon is correct; while good, they do not represent a highly developed art,' this exhibition, and the Creuse paintings in particular, met with enthusiastic reviews.

Claude Monet
The Three Poplars, Autumn, 1891

Museum of Art, Philadelphia. Courtesy of AKG London

THIS light-filled canvas is one of a series of 24 pictures showing poplars on the banks of the river Epte, which Monet painted in the spring to autumn of 1891. Here, three poplars, placed slightly off-centre, stand out, golden and white against a bright blue sky. Another row recedes in to the background, the trees visible but dissolving in the light, as they cut diagonally across the canvas to make up the point of a triangle with the river bank in the foreground. The blue and green bank, which is slightly angled, runs across the canvas, barely interrupting the elegant thrust of the trees that continues in its reflection in the river, which also reflects the sky and the treetops directly above that we never see.

This series follows on from Monet's haystacks of the previous year, recording one scene at different times of day as well as in different weathers. The idea of using the same motif to explore the effects of light moment by moment had gradually come to Monet over the 1880s when he was away much of the time, often painting seascapes in all kinds of weather. Monet said that each poplar painting represented only seven minutes of the day: when the light left a certain leaf, he would take out the next canvas and work on that.

The poplars, like the haystacks, met with major approbation.

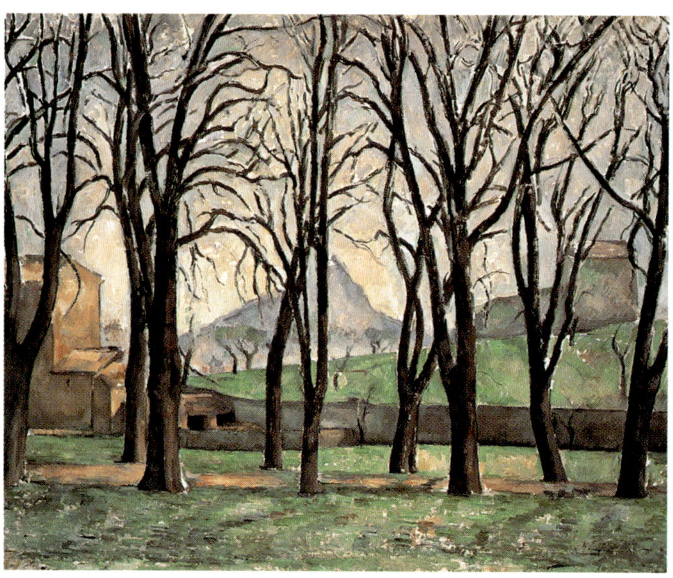

Paul Cézanne
Chestnut Trees in the Jas de Bouffan in Winter, 1885–86
Institute of Arts, Minneapolis. Courtesy of AKG London. *(See p. 229)*

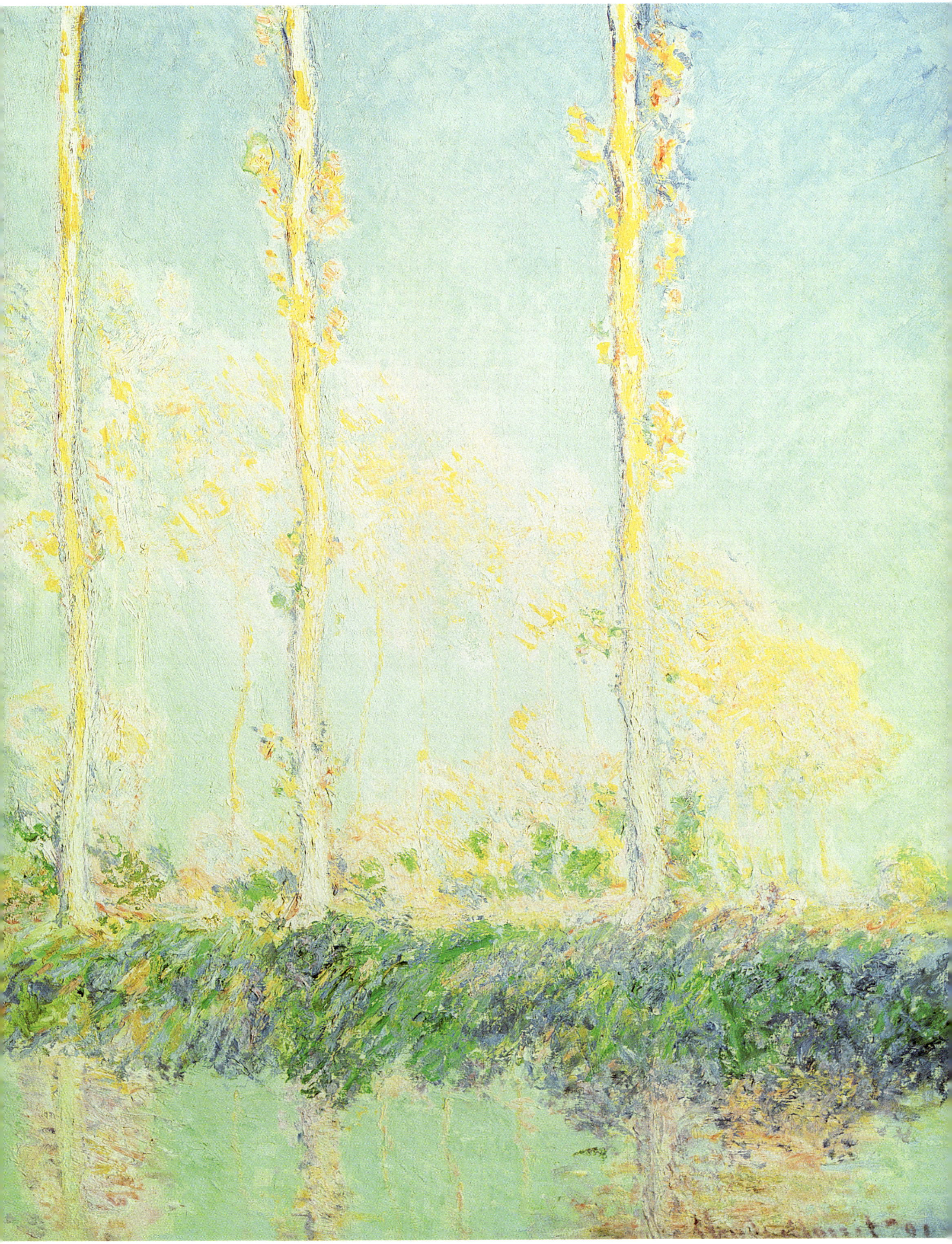

Claude Monet
Rouen Cathedral, The Portal, Morning Sun, Blue Harmony, 1893

Musée d'Orsay, Paris. Courtesy of AKG London/Erich Lessing

MONET travelled less and less during the 1890s but in 1892 and 1893 he went to Rouen to work on a systematic series of paintings of the west façade of Rouen Cathedral at different times of day. These he finished in his studio at Giverny. The effect was startling – over 30 paintings from three slightly different angles, ranging through shades of blue, purple, pink and yellow. Monet wrote to Alice, whom he had married in 1892, 'I am broken … I had a night filled with bad dreams … the Cathedral was collapsing on me, it seemed to be blue or pink or yellow.'

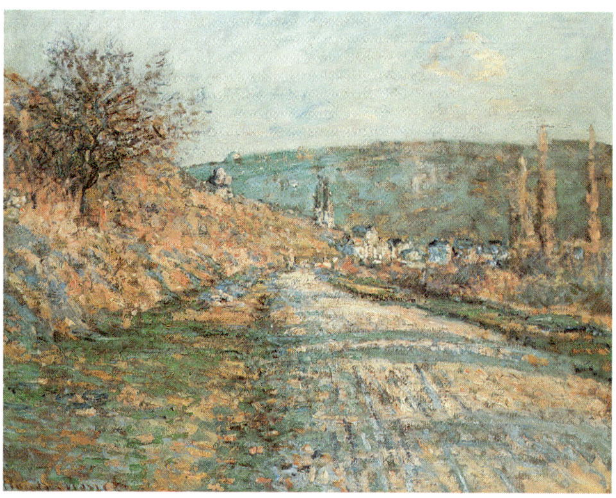

Claude Monet
The Road to Vétheuil, 1880
Phillips Collection, Washington, D. C.. Courtesy of AKG London. *(See p. 63)*

This image, *Morning Sun, Blue Harmony*, recalls the colours in Monet's *The Road to Vétheuil* (1880), but here, he is not really interested in the object upon which the light is falling. The stonework is only interesting in providing a vehicle for his research into the effects of light and atmosphere. The details dissolve under the light blue, pink and dark gold by turns, depending on how much they are in the light or shade.

Monet's series paintings were recognised as ground-breaking. In 1913, the German abstract painter Wassily Kandinsky (1866–1944) wrote that seeing Monet's haystacks in 1897 'set the seal on my entire life … suddenly, for the first time, I *saw* a painting … one thing was quite clear: the undreamt of power of the palette … But also, unconsciously, the idea that an object is an indispensable element of any painting had been discredited.'

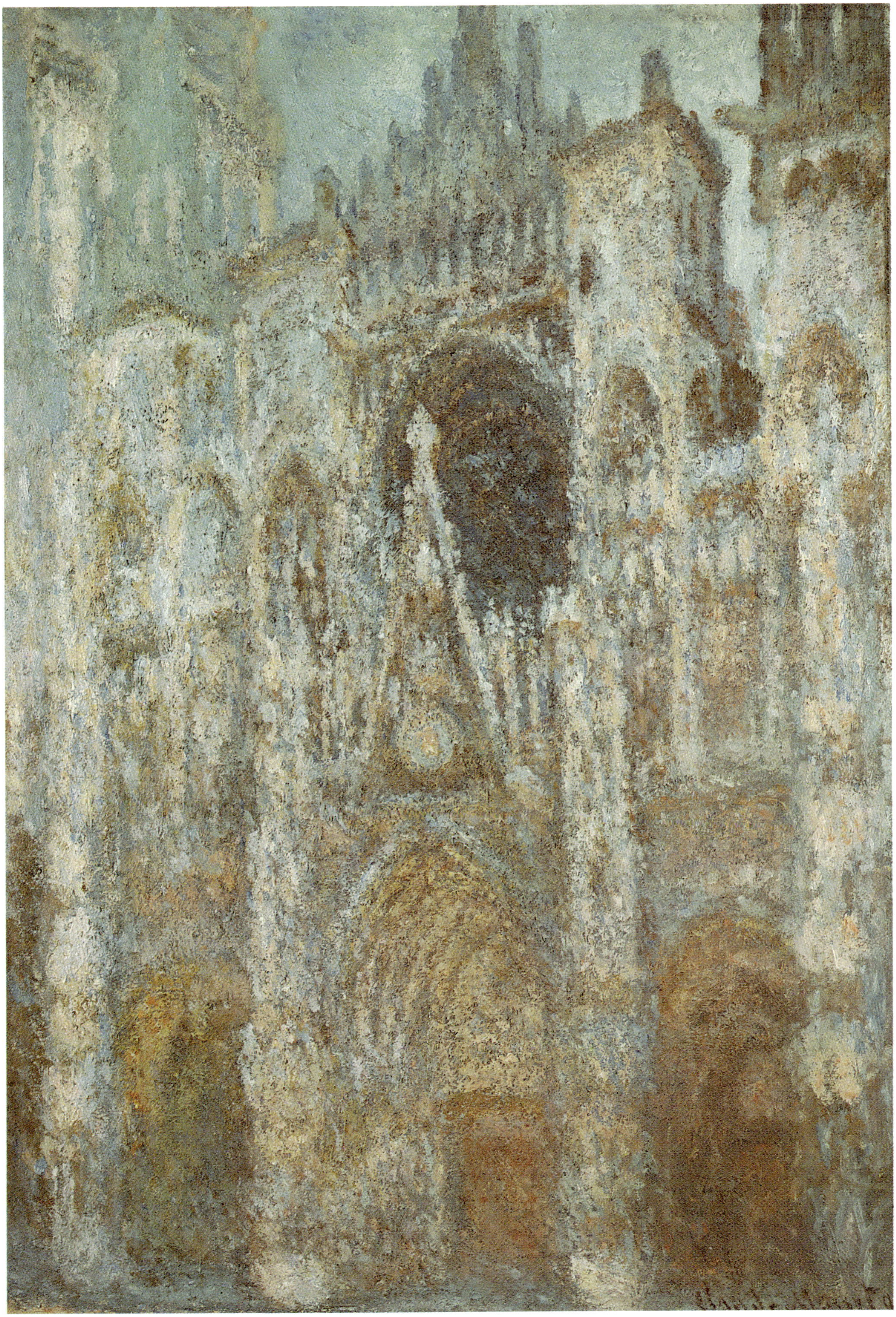

Claude Monet
White Water Lilies, 1899

Pushkin Museum, Moscow. Courtesy of AKG London

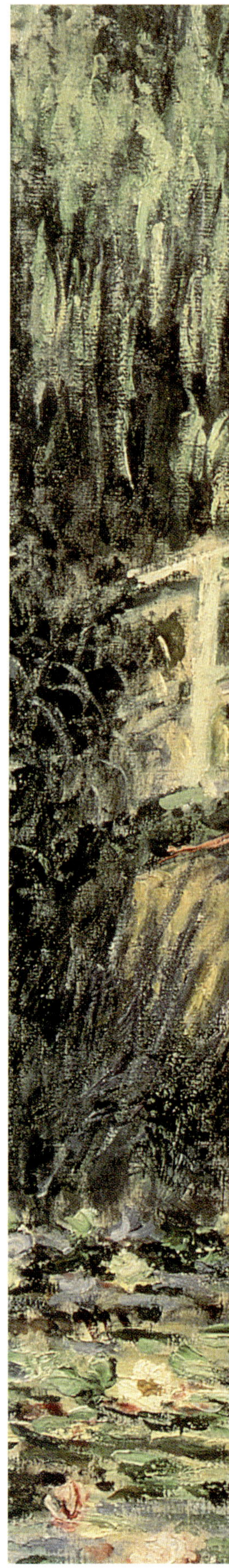

MONET had moved to Giverny with Alice Hoschedé and all their children in 1883. Here, he painted the garden that was the culmination of his lifelong passion for horticulture. 'My most beautiful work of art,' he said, 'is my garden.'

Monet and many of the other Impressionists had painted gardens throughout their careers but these paintings of the 1890s are no longer full of people. They become beautiful landscapes of colour and reflection rather than spaces that people inhabit.

This is one of 18 views of the lily pond that Monet painted in 1899 – the motif that, apart from a trip to London and one to Venice, was to dominate the last 20 years of his work. He called them his 'water landscapes'.

Painted in an almost square format, the sunlit bridge arches across the canvas, cutting it in two slightly above the midpoint. Below, the water, covered with lilies, recedes into the distance. Above, the sunlit trees on each side guide us into the leafy darkness beyond. Trees and rushes rise up, only to be reflected down in the water below, creating verticals that run straight through the mirror surface of the water, suggesting the depths below.

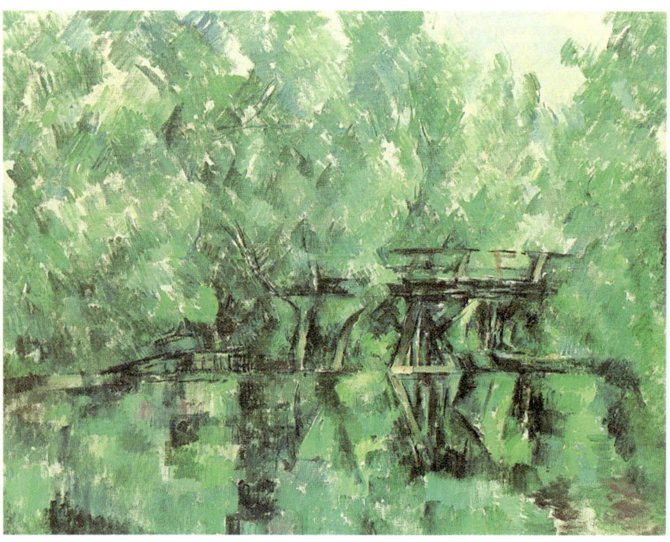

Paul Cézanne
Bridge Over the Pond, c. 1898
Morosoz Collection, Pushkin Museum, Moscow. Courtesy of AKG London.
(See p. 238)

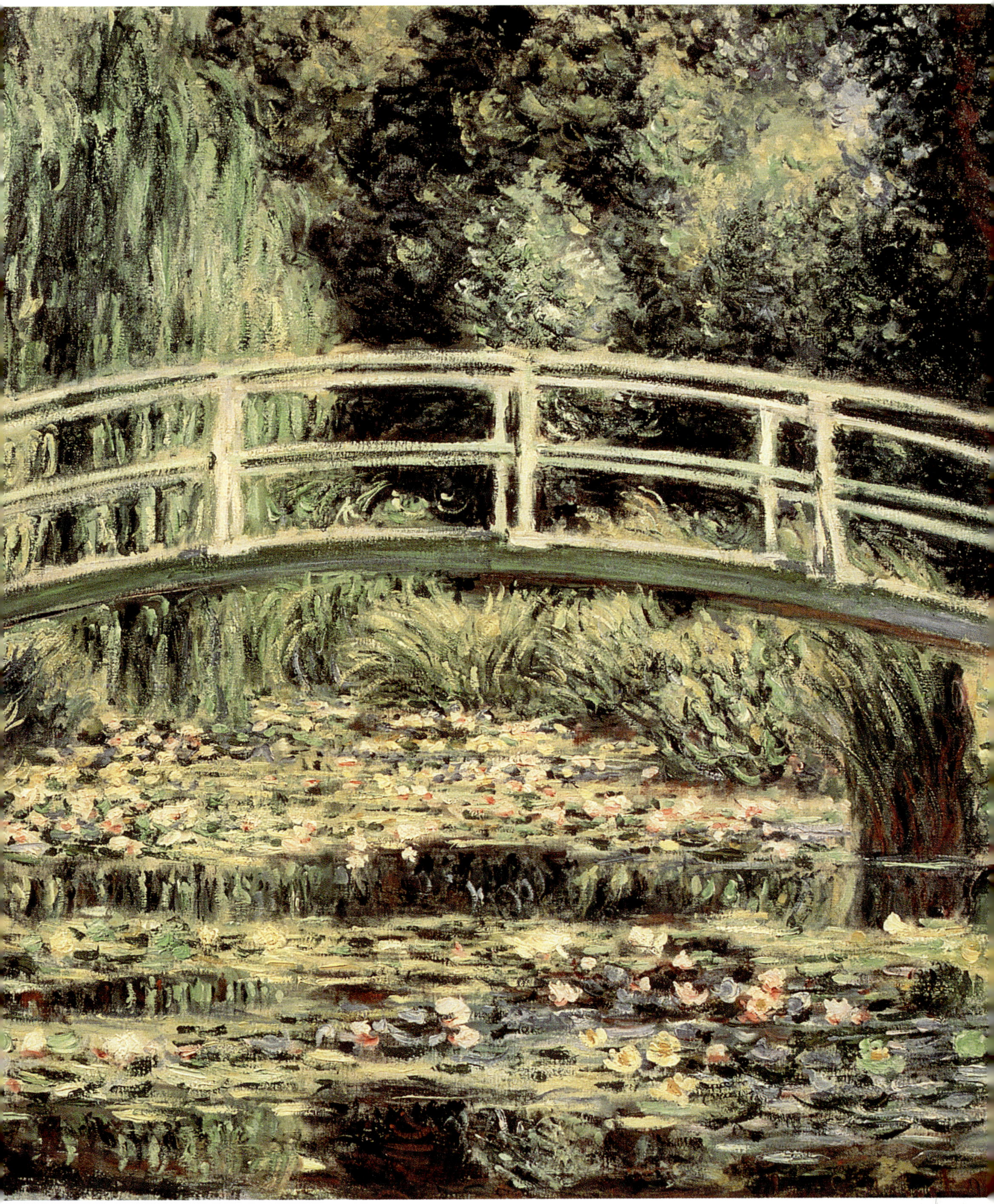

CLAUDE MONET
Water Lilies, 1907

Musée Marmottan, Paris. Courtesy of AKG London

MONET'S water garden was to become his most important motif in later life, and he explored this theme until his death in 1926. The colours in his palette were changing as his eye-sight deteriorated; in later works in the series, as we see here, he moved again to hues of purple and lilac. As in the Poplar series of the 1890s, there are some things that we see only from their reflection in the water.

Based on the complementary shades of green and orange, this vivid work is, nonethless, peaceful. The composition is verging on the abstract and works in several directions. Looking straight down, as if from the bridge, we see the two lily pads in the left-hand foreground. At water level, we look across the pond and see the lilies receding in the middle- and background. But we also perceive the reflections of the willows to be plunging into the pond, which gives an indication of depth and, by association, height. This is reinforced by the realisation that the glorious golden water is a reflection of the ephemeral effects of the sky above.

This interplay of horizontal and vertical planes is further complicated by the flat surface of the canvas, which is emphasised by the vigorous textural brushwork over most of the painting.

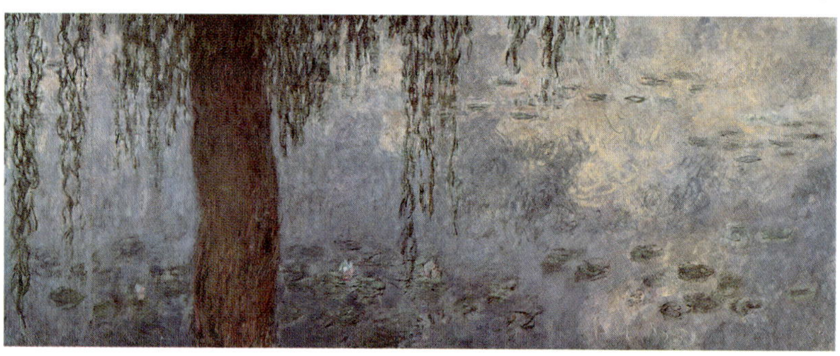

Claude Monet
Water Lilies, 1915–26
Musée de l'Orangerie, Paris. Courtesy of AKG London/Erich Lessing. *(See p. 82)*

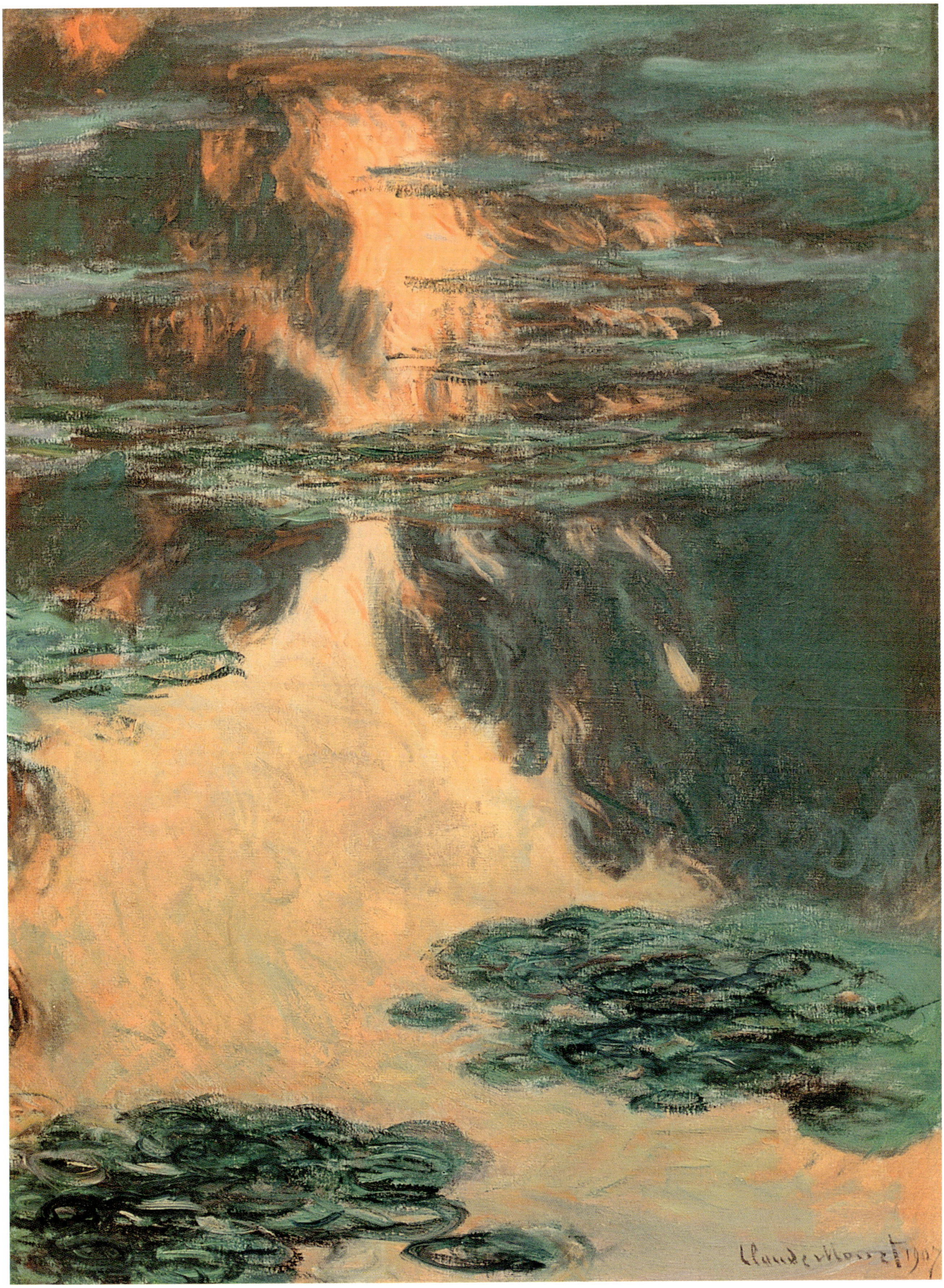
Claude Monet 1907

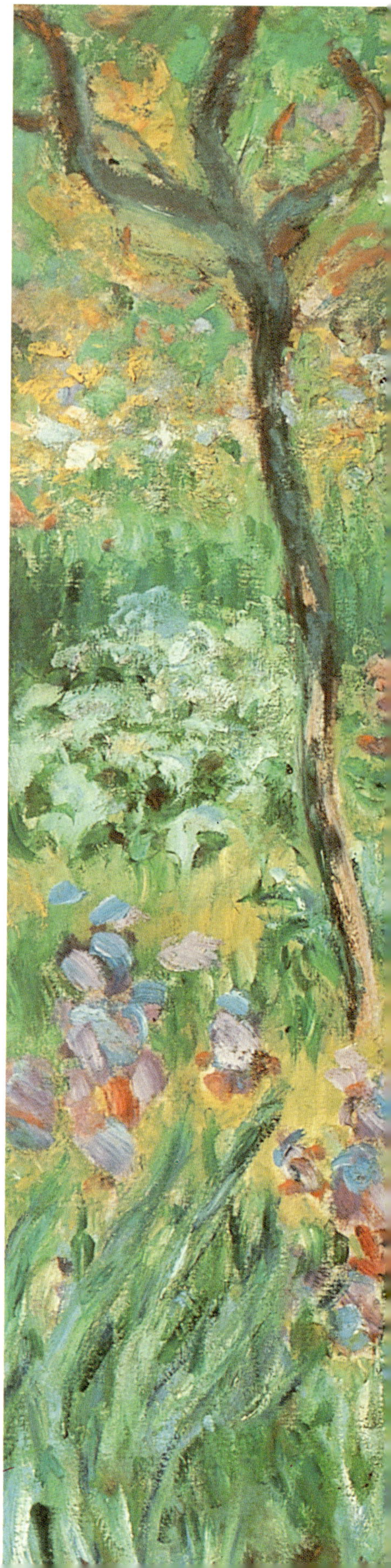

Claude Monet
Giverny: Spring, 1900

Yale University Art Gallery. Courtesy of AKG London

ON the other side of his garden from the water lily pond was Monet's more western, formal flower garden, which he painted eight times between 1900 and 1902.

Like the bridge paintings of 1900, the colours are strong in this joyful depiction of nature, in which yellow and green dominate. The composition is arranged asymmetrically with the long, straight, sun-dappled path coming in diagonally from bottom right, so that we do not see the first tree in the avenue. This emphasis to the left is enhanced by the direction of the brushwork and the tree on the left, which seems to lean outward, giving an open feeling to this enclosed space where we do not see the sky. The vantage point is slightly raised to enhance the perspective. The formal underlying structure of this riot of colour is ensured by the verticals of the trees, the receding path and the two horizontals created by shadow on the plants and suggestive of an obscured path. To the right and in the foreground, blue and purple irises create new rhythms and directions, harmonising with the greens and making the yellows more vivid. Dabs of red poppies in the middle ground complement the green.

Monet knew the effects of all his plants, arranging them, said his stepson Jean Hoschedé-Monet, 'with foreknowledge of what role they would play … rather as he painted a picture….'

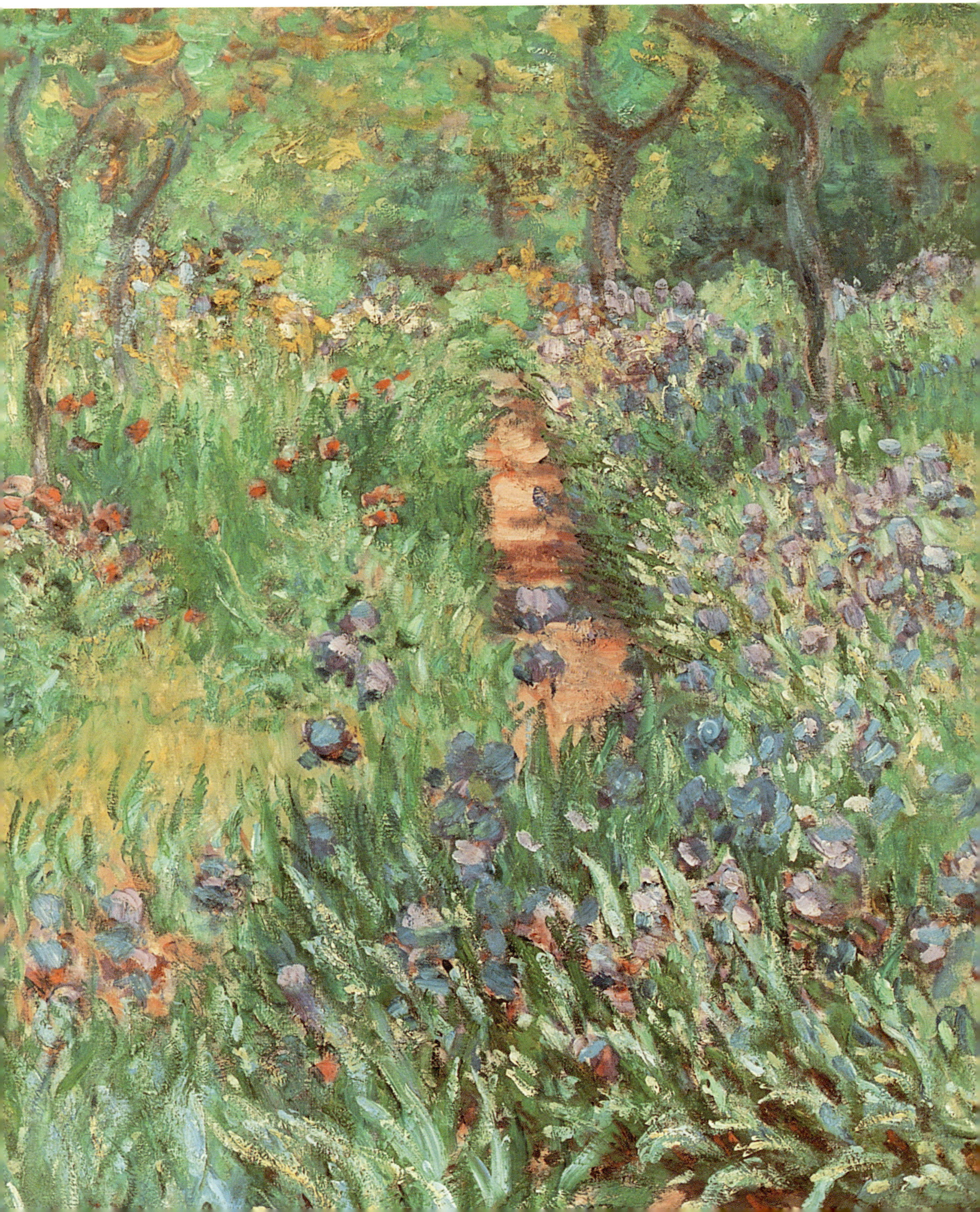

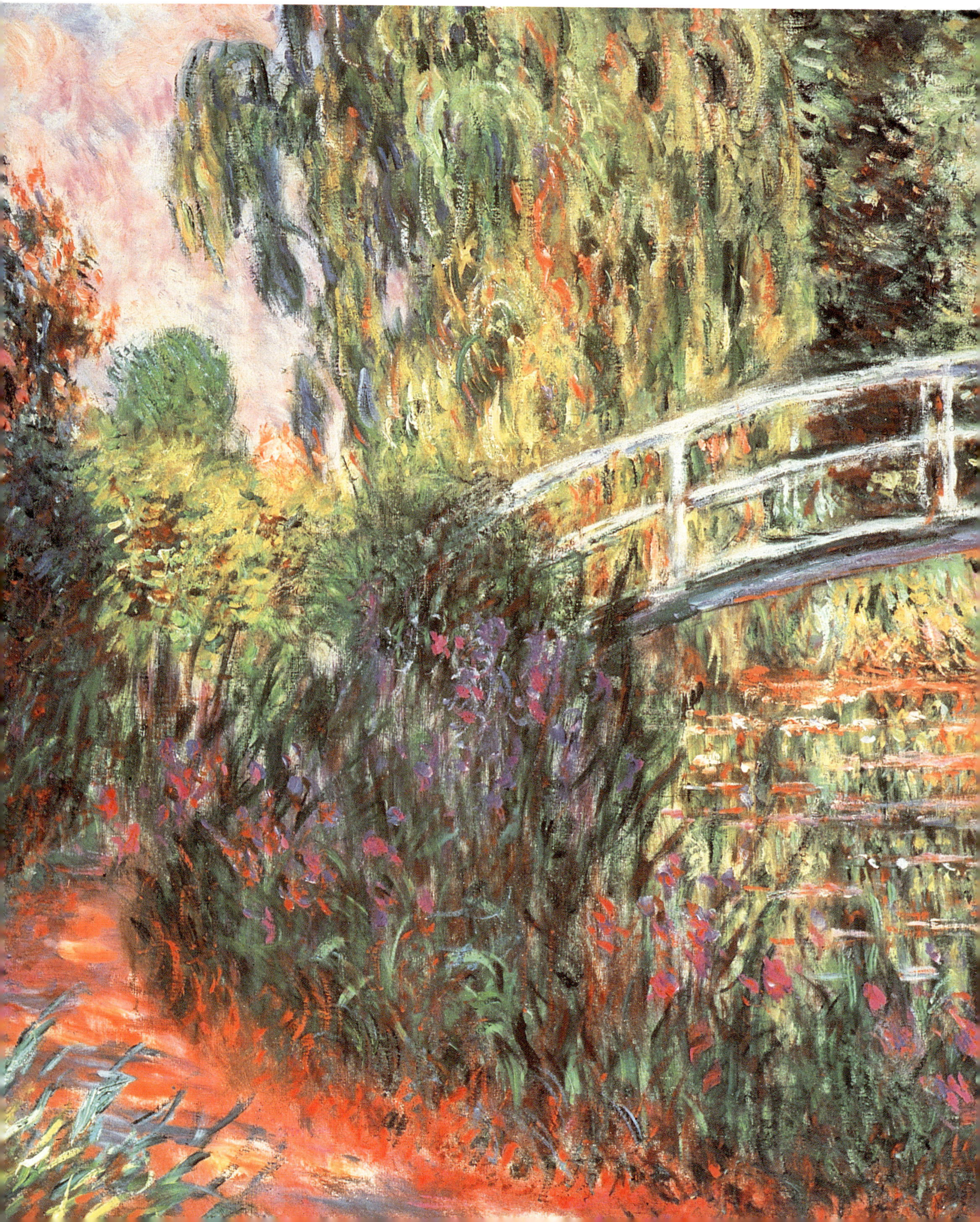

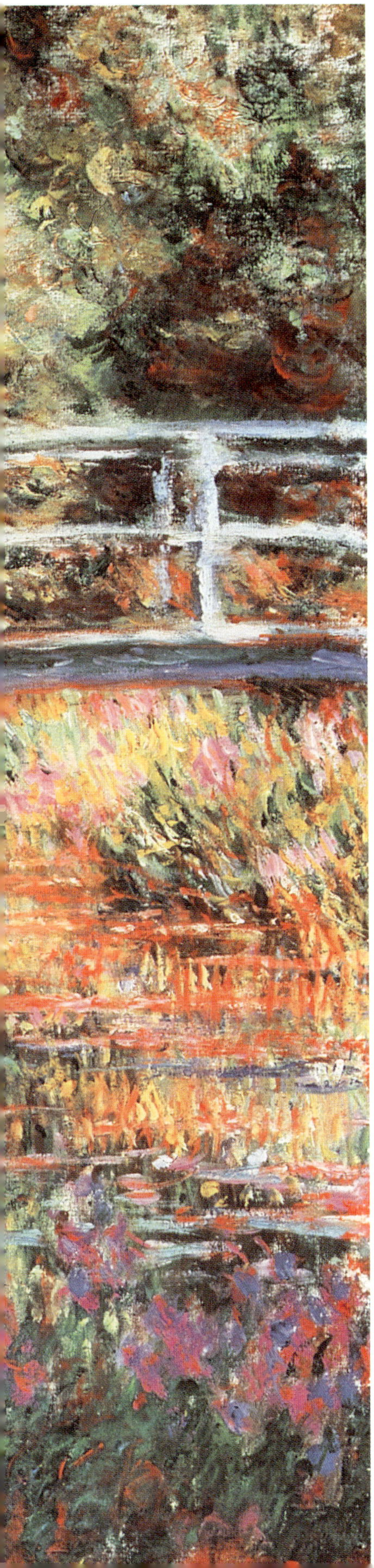

Claude Monet
The Japanese Bridge, 1900
Courtesy of Christie's Images

MONET painted another six paintings of his Japanese bridge in 1900. In these, he shifts his viewpoint, no longer painting the bridge head-on, and his palette becomes more intense.

Here, he had moved his easel to the left so that the bridge was cut in two and we see the curve of the path, the flowers and the sky. He emphasises hot pinks and reds and complements them with intense greens – an exotic, sharp contrast with the limpid, meditative, mysterious greens and pinks of the bridge pictures of 1899. As if to give us a breath of fresh air from the sultry heat of this view, we see a pale patch of pink-and-blue sky at top left.

The composition, as ever, is well planned with an interesting juxtaposition of planes, horizontals and verticals. But note, too, its roundness and softness – the circular patch of water and the enclosing rushes on the far side and the mirroring of the bridge in the sweep of the path in the foreground.

Monet exhibited his bridge paintings in 1900 at Paul Durand-Ruel's (1831–1922) gallery. In general, they met with favourable comment for Monet, after decades of struggle, was now an established figure and his work considered to be the essence of France and the French spirit. 'To discredit it [this series]', wrote the critic Julien Leclerq passionately, 'is to discredit France.'

Claude Monet
London, Parliament, 1904

Musée d'Orsay, Paris. Courtesy of AKG London/Erich Lessing

IN 1904, Monet revisited London, where he had spent the years of the Franco-Prussian war. From a suite of rooms at the Savoy – he was now very comfortably off – he painted many views of the Thames, with the Parliament building as here, or Charing Cross and Waterloo bridge.

The style of his work has moved away from the dab-like brushmarks of his typical Impressionist manner, as it did for a while in the 1990s when he painted views of the Seine,. Here, the brushworks seem to fuse, shining through or obscuring one another – as the sun sets through the pall of the London fog.

These Parliament pictures, along with the Rouen Cathedral series, are Monet's only paintings of architectural monuments. As with the Rouen series, the building is an excuse for effects of light and colour, and in this case, shape, which Monet has simplified dramatically – a green and purple spiky shadow between two flaming orange and gold patches of light and reflection. The light struggling through the mist creates a stunning, focussed effect.

Of his paintings at this time, Monet said, 'I want to paint the air in which the bridge, the house and the boat lie, the beauty in which they are, and that's nothing other than impossible.' The air in which the Parliament 'lies' here, pervades the entire scene.

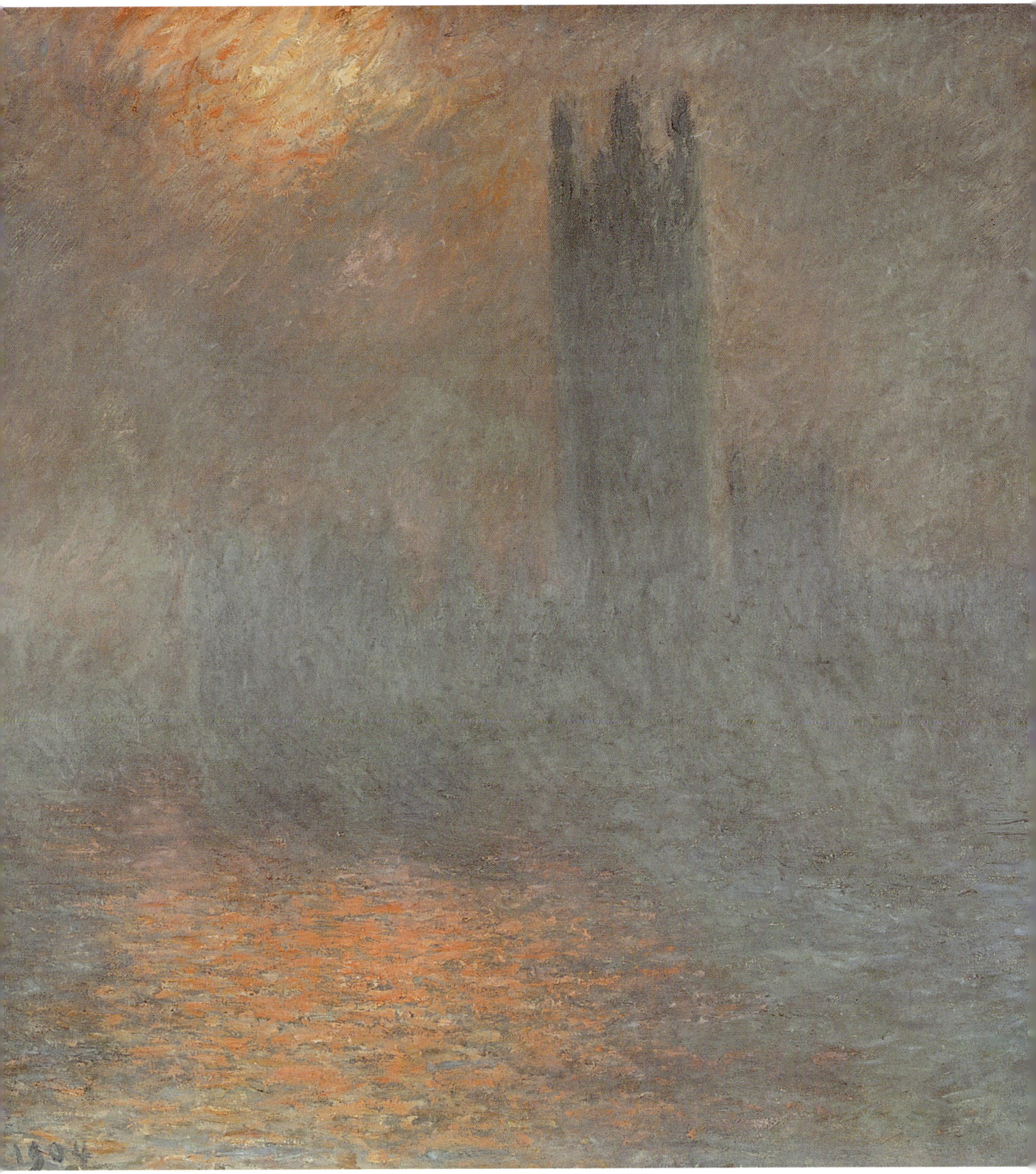

CLAUDE MONET
Santa Maria della Salute and the Grand Canal, Venice, 1908

Sotheby's. Courtesy of AKG London

IN 1908 Monet and Alice visited Venice, where Monet was stunned by the light in this historic city. Although his intention was to take a two-month holiday, Monet produced 37 paintings, 35 of which he finished in his studio at Giverny.

Enveloping the scene with the blue air around it, Monet's painting reveals the same interests and concerns as in his water lily paintings, although here he includes the real world in a dream-like haze, as well as its rippling reflection in the Grand Canal. Recalling the arches of the bridge in *The Bridge at Argenteuil* of 1874, Monet marks the reflection of the buildings on to the water and reflects it back on to the stonework.

Apart from the poles and the boat cut off on the left, which remind us of the influence exerted by Japanese prints and photography from the early days of Impressionism, this is a conservative composition, particularly in comparison with some of the water lily paintings. Although the pole in the foreground creates a dynamic vertical that brings the viewer up short, Monet has not created an ambiguity of planes. Reflections are surface-deep only and spread across the water rather than down into it. The water ripples and recedes to Santa Maria in the background.

Twenty-nine canvases depicting Venice were exhibited in 1912 at the Bernheim-Jeune gallery. On seeing them, the painter Paul Signac (1863–1935) wrote in a letter to Monet, 'I admire these paintings as the highest expression of your art.'

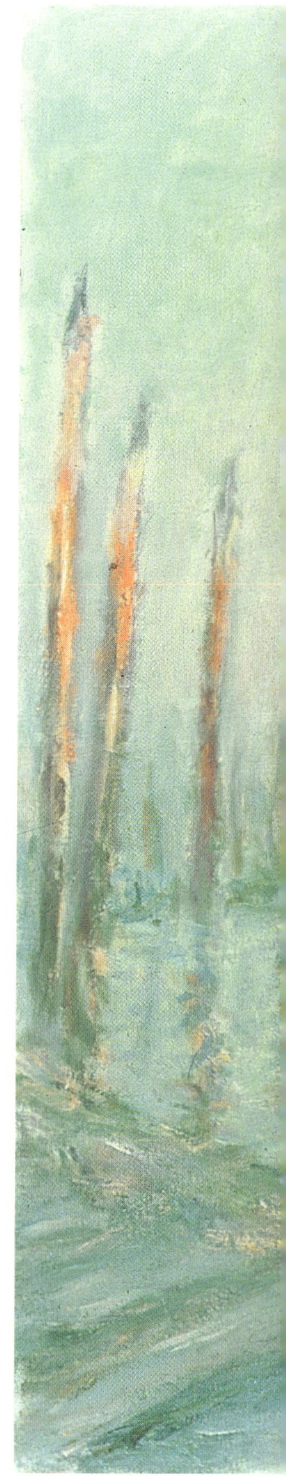

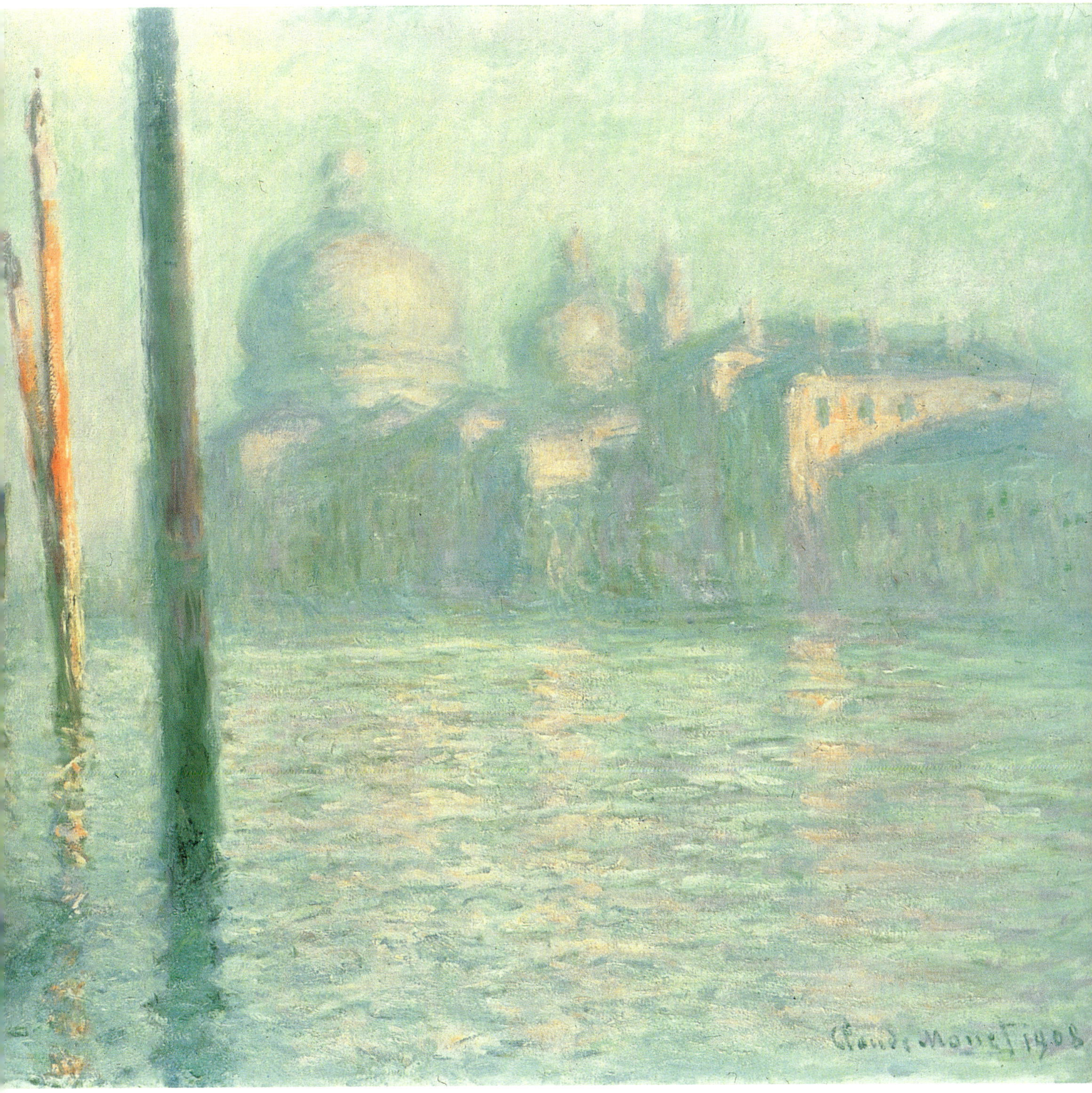
Claude Monet 1908

CLAUDE MONET
Water Lilies, 1915–26
Musée de l'Orangerie, Paris. Courtesy of AKG London/Erich Lessing

BETWEEN 1911, when his wife Alice died, and 1914 Monet hardly painted at all. In 1912 Monet was diagnosed with cataracts and his son Jean had a stroke – he subsequently died in February 1914.

In April 1914, Monet began to work again – predominantly on large-scale decorative panels, 2 m (6 ft 6 in) square. In 1915 he built a larger studio to accommodate them and larger ones, measuring 3 x 6 m (9 ft 9 in x 19 ft 6 in), followed. In 1918 he offered two of these *Grandes Décorations* to the State in celebration of France's victory in

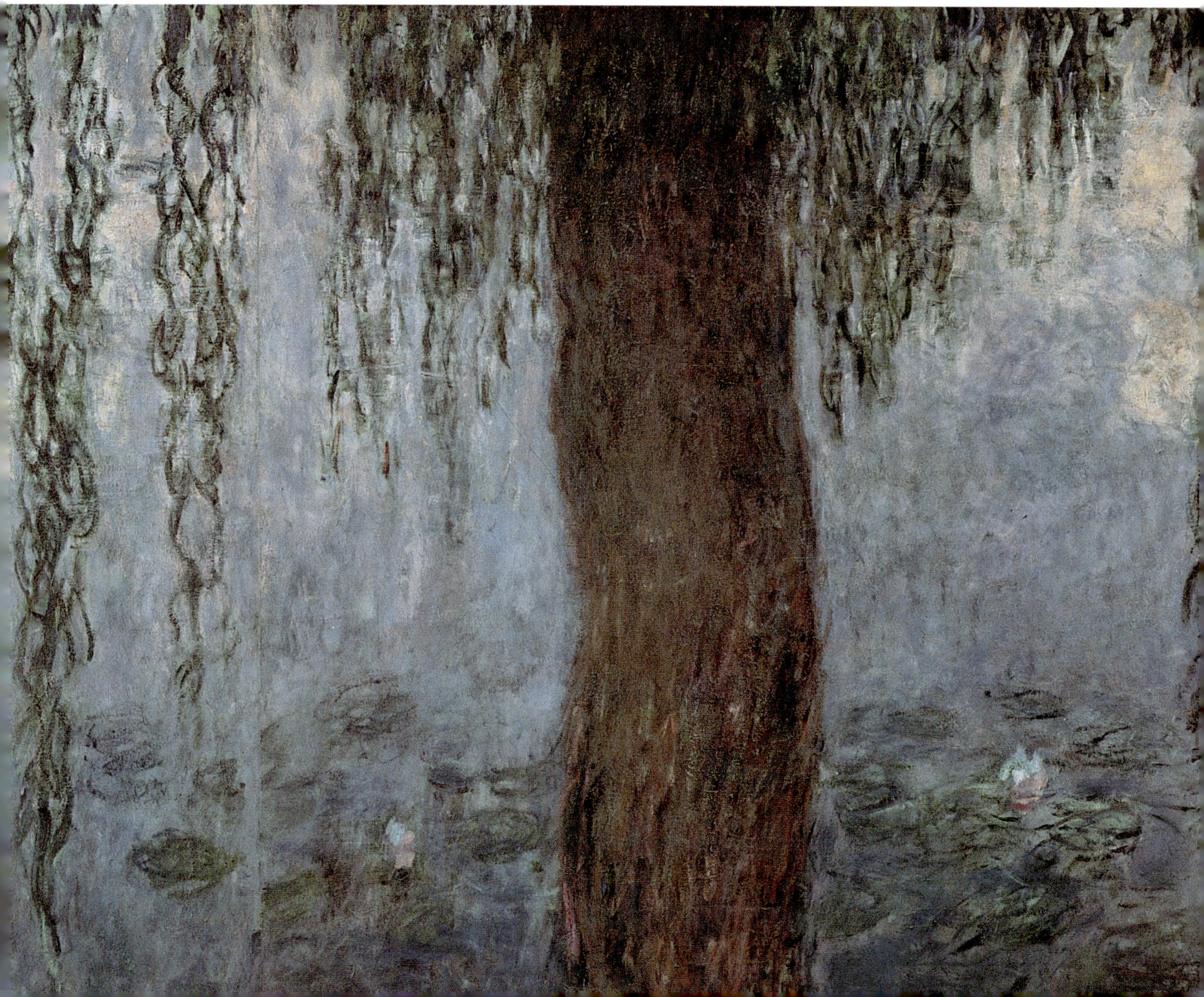

the First World War. In 1922, it was agreed that eight panels would be hung, after Monet's death, in the Orangerie at the Tuileries Gardens. By this time he was 82 and, with the exception of the critic Geffroy and Armand Guillaumin, was the last survivor of the original Impressionist group. Monet found much of this work frustrating and he destroyed many panels. In 1923, he had his cataracts operated upon and his vision improved and cleared of the red and yellow cast that is particularly evident in some of his canvases from about 1918.

He died in December 1926, aged 86, still an artistic rebel and an inspiration for the abstract movement and the work and ideas of artists of the new *avant-garde*.

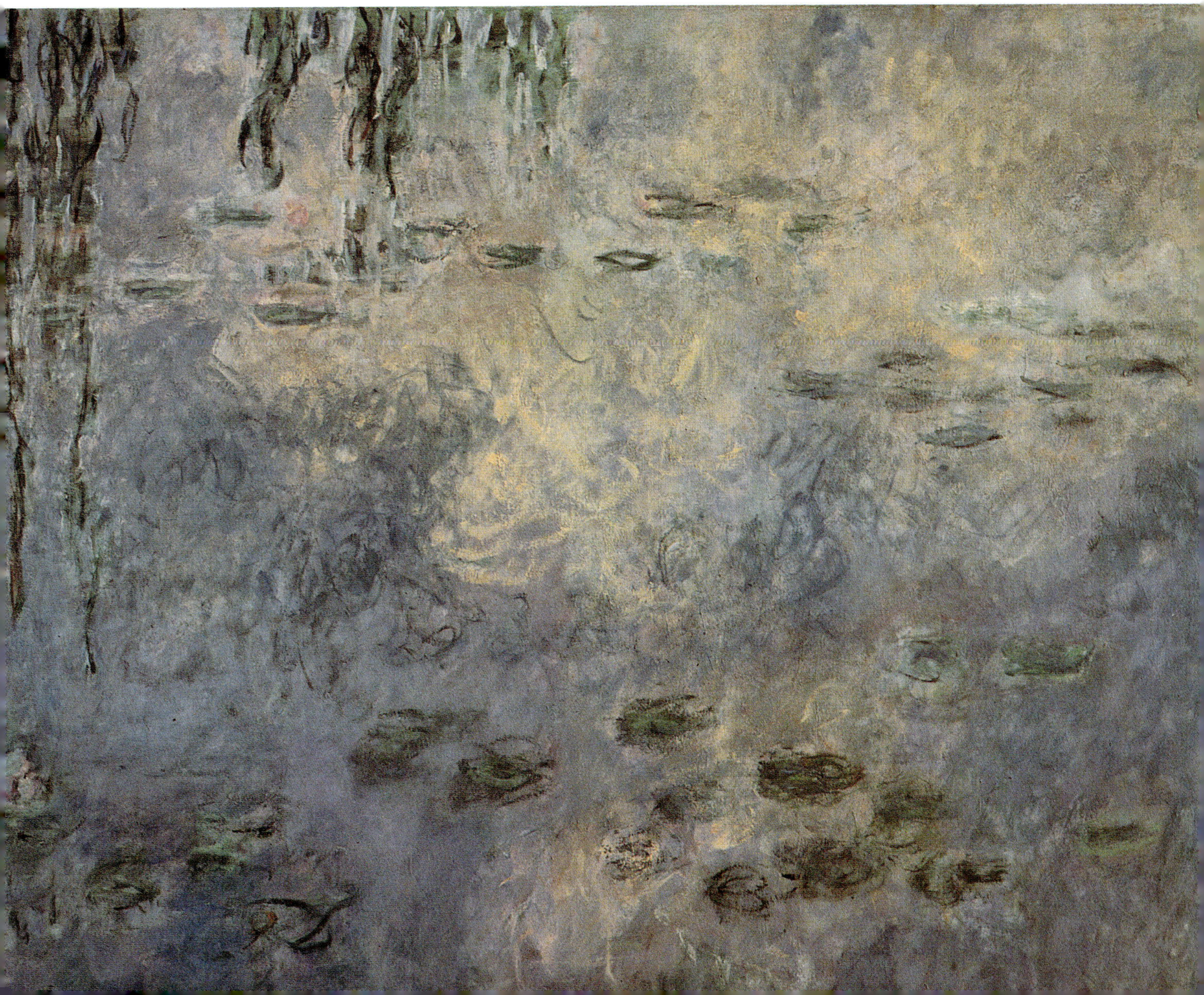

ALFRED SISLEY (1839–99)
View of the St Martin Canal, Paris, 1870

Musée d'Orsay, Paris. Courtesy of AKG London/Erich Lessing

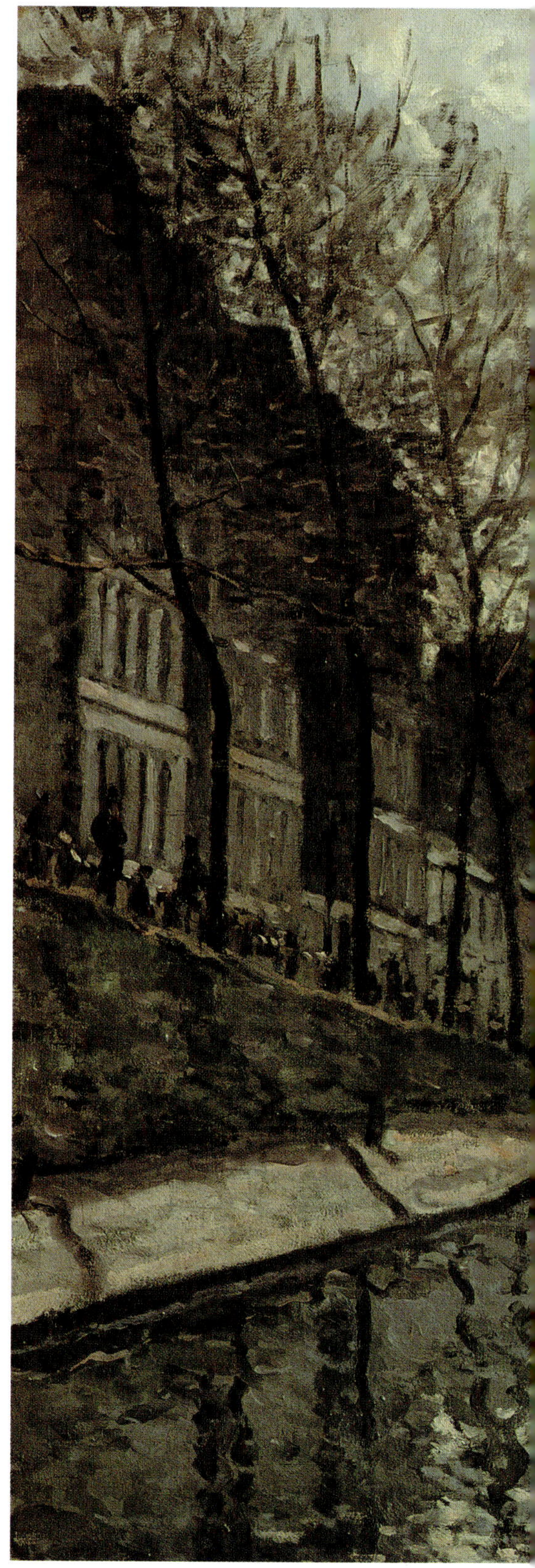

ALFRED SISLEY, born in Paris but the son of wealthy English parents, is the English Impressionist. He intended to make a career in business but in 1857 began to draw. In 1862 he entered the studio of the artist Gleyre where he met Monet, Bazille and Renoir – the latter painted his picture in 1868. With them, he painted in the woods near Barbizon, an area popular with landscape artists.

Sisley was a committed landscape artist and his art generally focused on the riverside villages to the west of Paris where he lived. He had little interest in the human figure or the modern urban scenes that fascinated his colleagues.

This picture shows a view of the Saint Martin Canal, almost the only site that Sisley ever painted in Paris itself. It shows a traditional composition receding to a central vanishing point on the horizon – something he tended to maintain throughout his work.

As in many of his paintings, Sisley favours a big sky. 'Not only does it give the picture depth through its successive planes, it also gives movement,' he once said. Much like Monet, he shows a love of water and sky and their relationship with each other – a mutual source of light and reflection, here enhanced by the darkness of the buildings and trees on either side.

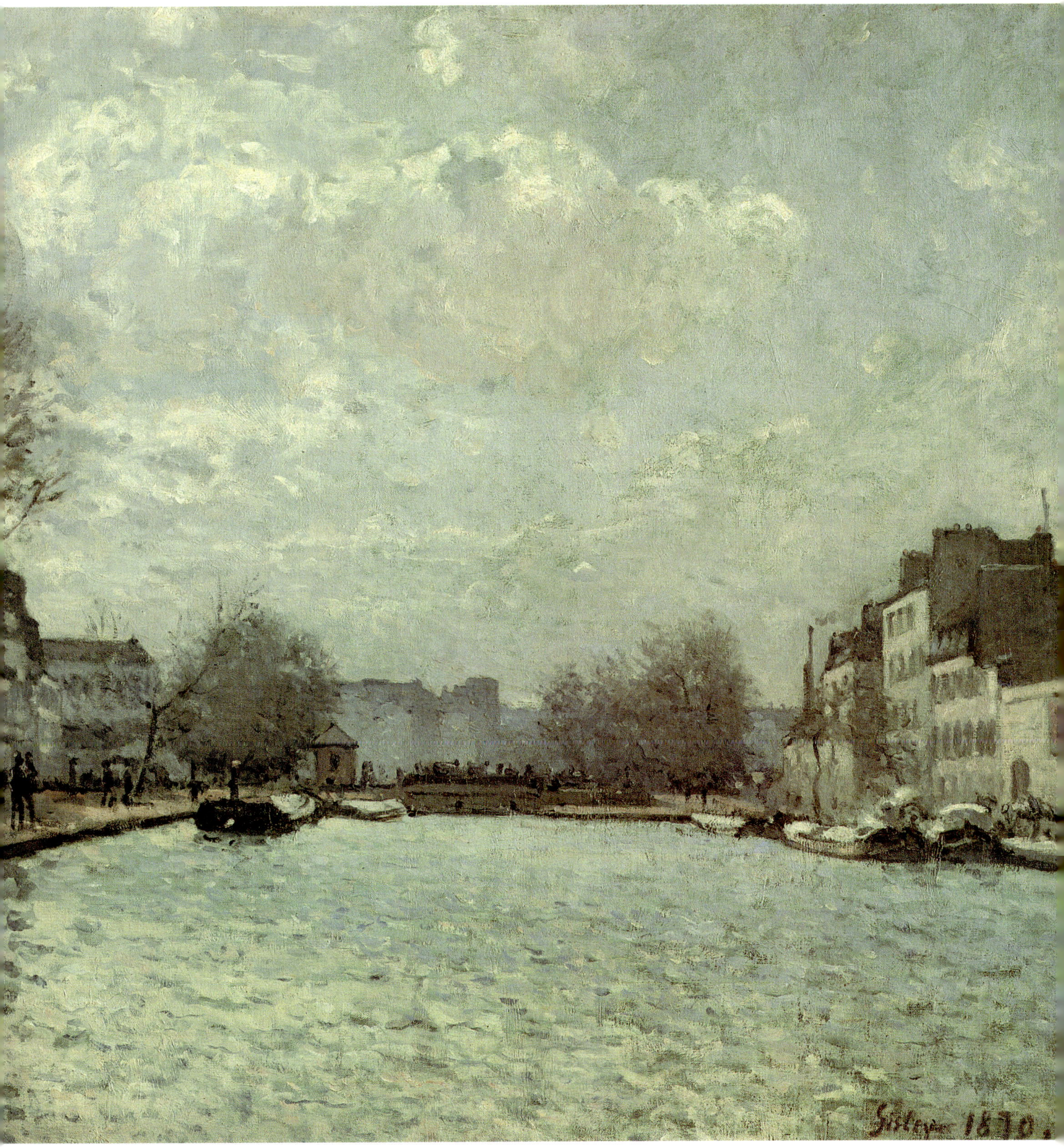
Sisley 1870.

ALFRED SISLEY
Misty Morning, 1874

Musée d'Orsay, Paris. Courtesy of AKG London/Erich Lessing

THIS was painted the year of the first Impressionist exhibition in 1874. By this time Sisley had lost his family fortune as his father's business went bankrupt during the Franco-Prussian War. But he was managing to sell some pictures to the dealer Durand-Ruel, although his prices were never as high as Monet's, whose work his own reflects. Of all the Impressionists, Sisley experimented the least, painting in the Impressionist style throughout his entire career.

Even so, this is an unusual picture, showing as it does, the muffling of light and vision by the mist. Sisley presents delicate harmony of colours – pinks, blues and greens. The trees are a soft blue, as is the fence that defines the limit of what we can see before the soft mantle of fog takes over. The softness of the treatment contrasts with some of the more vigorous brushwork in other paintings such as *View of the St Martin Canal* (1870).

The flowers in the foreground and the woman bending over in the middle ground are more clearly defined, but are still softened and enveloped in the mist. The informal brushwork varies, according to Sisley's belief that there should be a variety of treatment, even in a single painting, corresponding to the needs of the subject matter and the effect being sought. This is one of the reasons that Impressionist paintings in general create such a feeling of vitality.

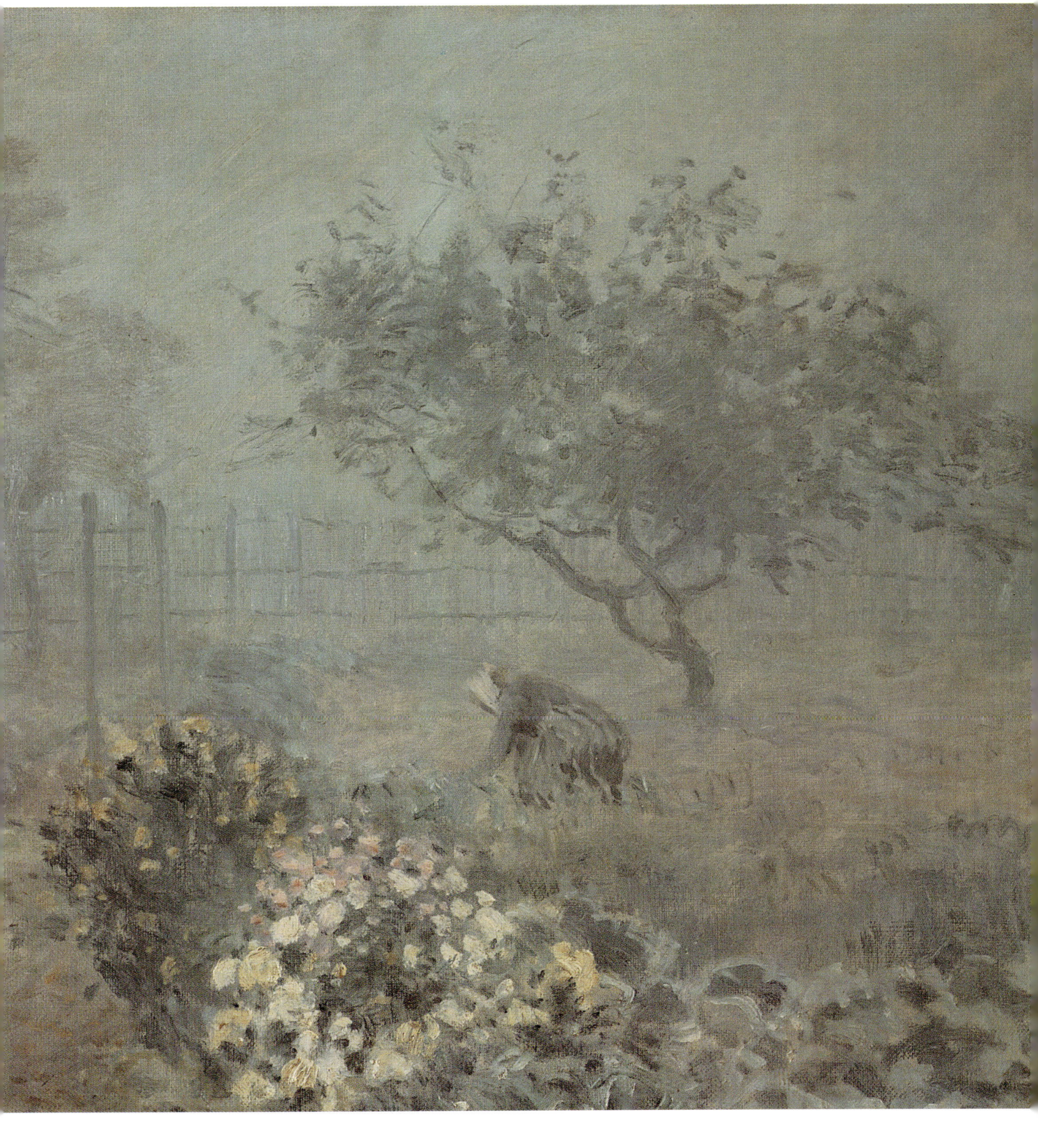

ALFRED SISLEY
Snow at Louveciennes, 1878

Musée d'Orsay, Paris. Courtesy of AKG London/Erich Lessing

IN 1876 and 1877, Sisley exhibited at the second and third Impressionist exhibitions and moved to Sèvres. But his finances were not good and he was being supported by the collector Eugène Murer (1845–1906), who was a hotelier and friend of Armand Guillaumin, and also by Georges Charpentier (1846–1905), another collector who was a patron, in particular of Renoir. The years 1878 and 1879 were very lean for Sisley, with few purchases of his paintings.

This snow scene of Louveciennes, where both Pissarro and Cézanne lived, shows a muteness of colour and a solitary figure that perhaps reflect Sisley's anxiety in those difficult years. The effect is bleak. A leaden yellowish-grey sky lowers over a country lane. Thick, white snow covers the ground, the fences, the trees, the tops of the wall and the church roof in the distance. But there is no sunshine to make the snow glisten and sparkle, or create pink or blue shadows and reflections. There is no warmth. A subtle use of black predominates.

The vertical format has an elongating effect and increases the sense of emptiness, as there are no trees to connect the upper and lower edges of the painting. The large triangle of sky holds our attention as much as the triangle of snow that comes to meet it in the figure of the lone, dark woman heading towards a dead end.

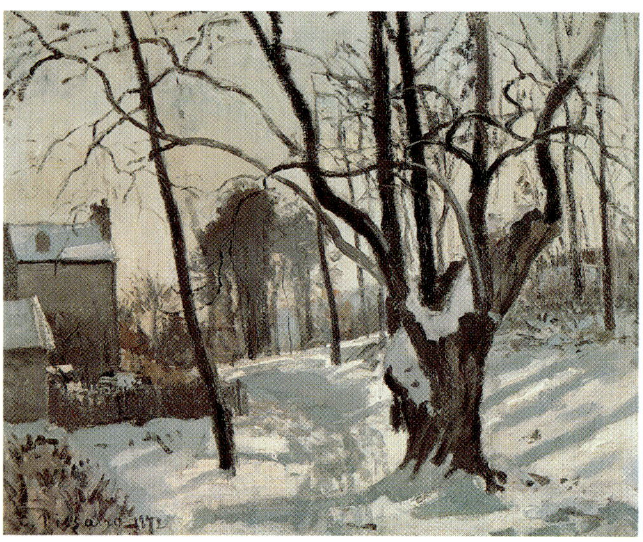

Camille Pissarro
Louveciennes, 1872
Museum Folkwang, Essen. Courtesy of AKG London.
(See p. 99)

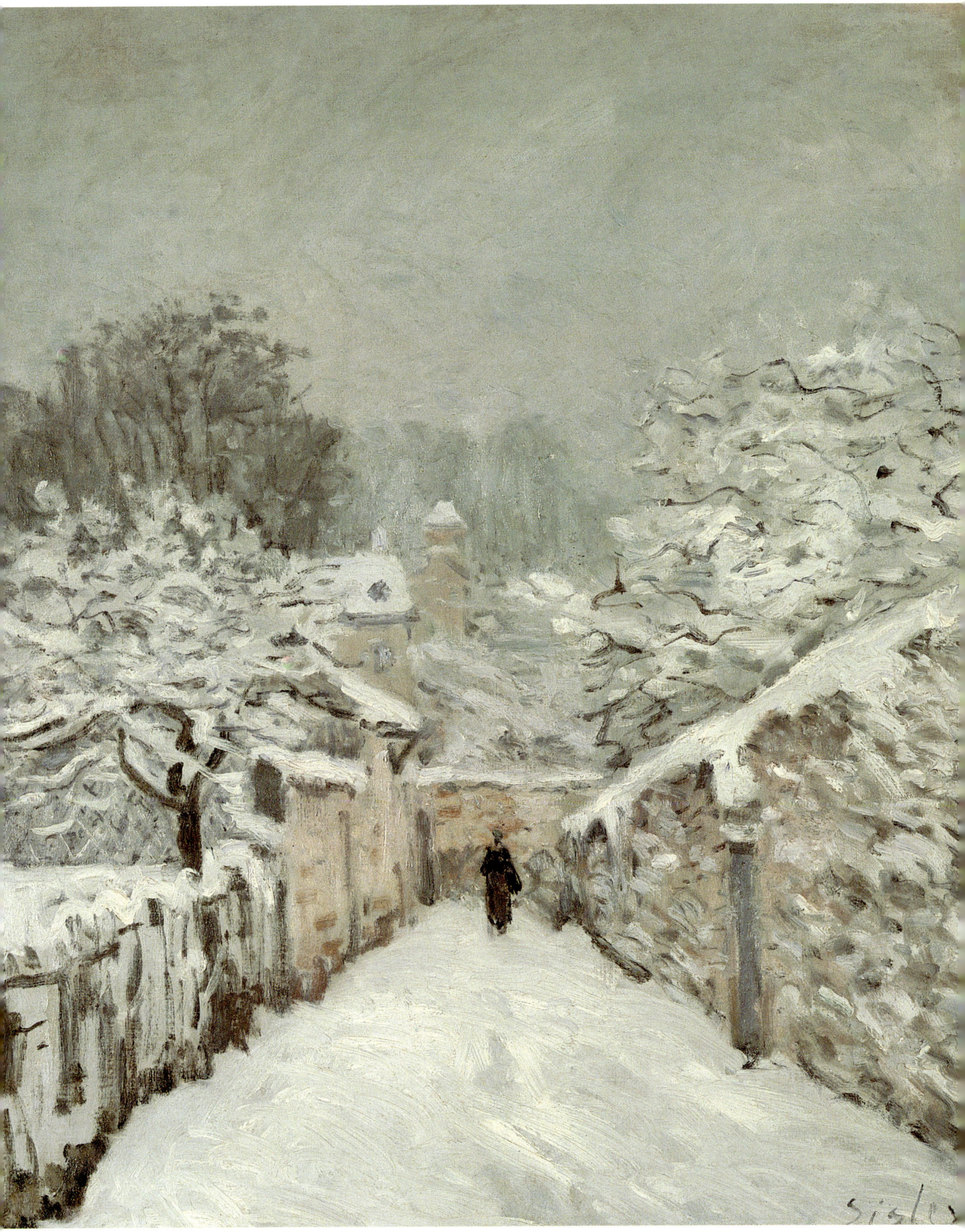

ALFRED SISLEY
Winter Morning, 1878

Private Collection. Courtesy of AKG London

THIS river scene has a similar composition to *Spring in Moret-sur-Loing* (*c.* 1888), with a view out across a lake. However, on close inspection, although the diagonal of the bank from right to left leads us into the picture, the bank swings round and we follow the river towards the horizon. As we do so, we pass through the trees, their spindly trunks and branches reminding us of works by Pissarro and, as a dramatic element in the foreground, owing something to the influence of Japanese prints. We follow the road into the shade and there, discover a tiny figure, like those in the *View of the St Martin Canal*, walking away from us, towards the patch of dazzling sunshine that illumines the trees on the bank further along. These throw a golden reflection into the water below. The golden haze is continued along the horizon and effects a warm, rosy glow throughout the painting, belying the thin, meagre leafless trees in the foreground.

The treatment of the trees in the distance is reminiscent of paintings by the English artist Joseph Mallord William Turner (1775–1851), which Sisley would have seen on a trip to London in 1874. This trip was paid for by opera singer Jean-Baptiste Faure (1830–1914), who was an admirer and collector of Impressionist paintings.

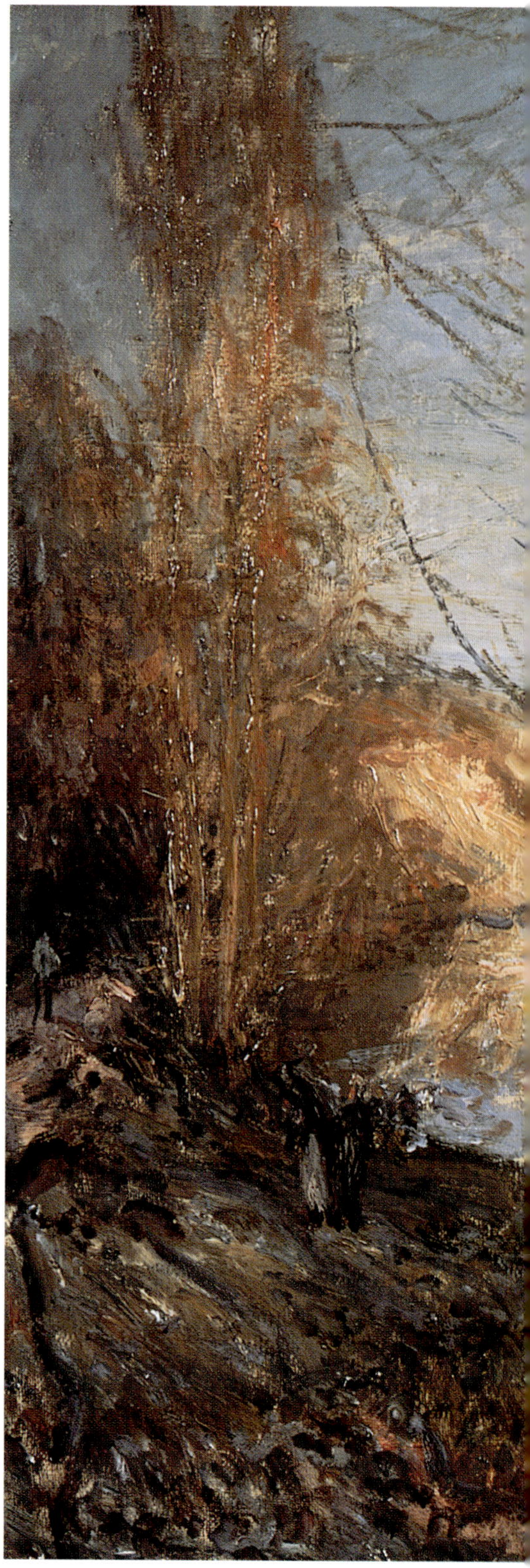

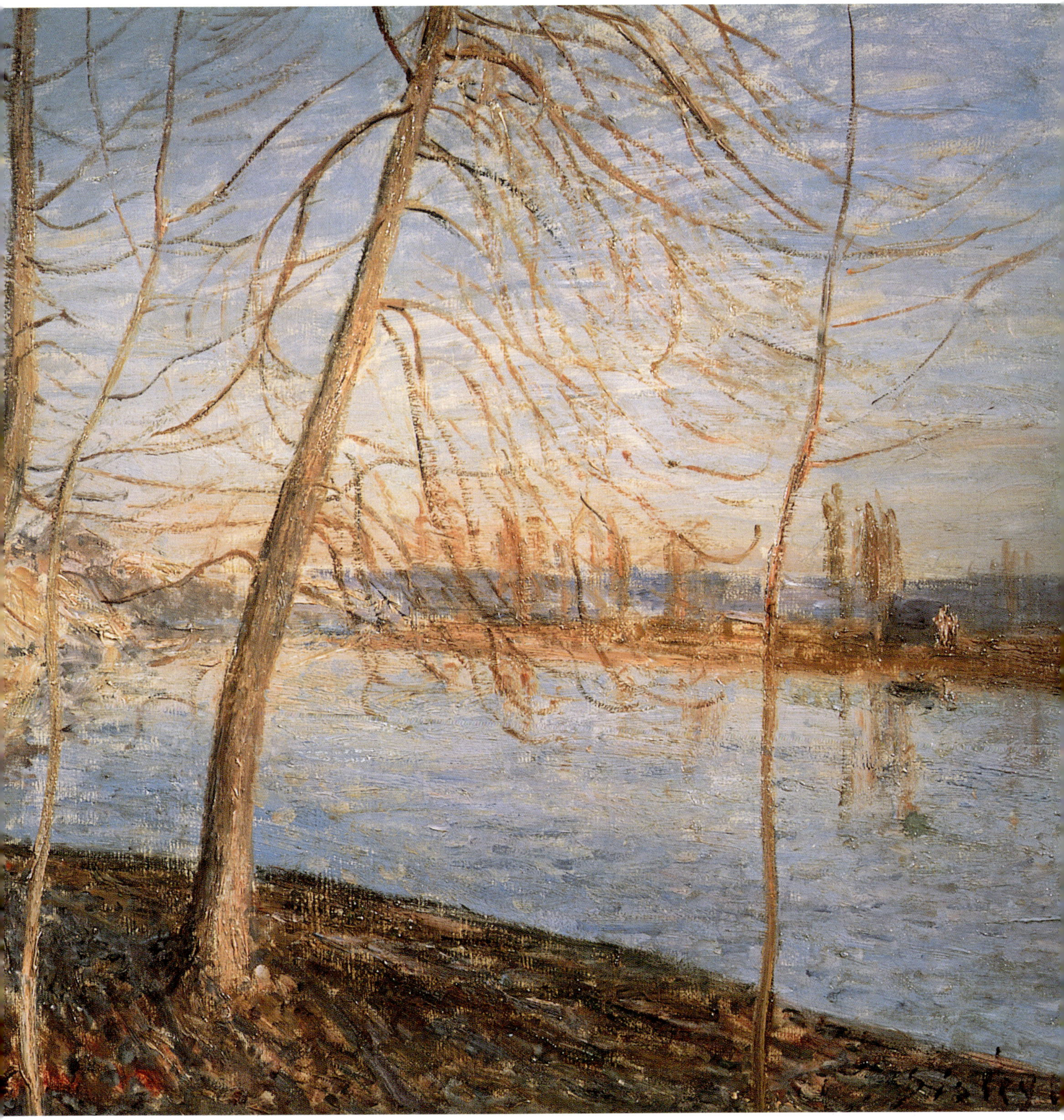

ALFRED SISLEY
The Bridge at Moret-sur-Loing, 1888

Private Collection. Courtesy of AKG London

THIS was painted two years after the last Impressionist exhibition, at which Sisley did not exhibit. It shows a view which is typical of most of Sisley's work, revealing how little his style changed over the years. It also brings to mind Monet's *The Three Poplars* painted three years later, but the contrast shows how Monet moved on in his art while still maintaining Impressionist values, whereas Sisley did not.

Sisley, who always suffered from being a follower of Monet, also remained true to these values but, unlike Monet, he did not paint the effects of light for their own sake. His perception remained one in which the landscape around him, usually viewed from a distance and disappearing to a vanishing point on the horizon, remained the object of his endeavour.

As with his earlier works, this painting offers us many avenues to look down as if we are turning our heads. Composed asymmetrically and cut off on both sides, the world continues ahead of us and to our left and right. When he died, Sisley's finances were so poor that his fellow artists made a collection for his children. Ironically, at the posthumous auction of his works, the previously low prices rose dramatically.

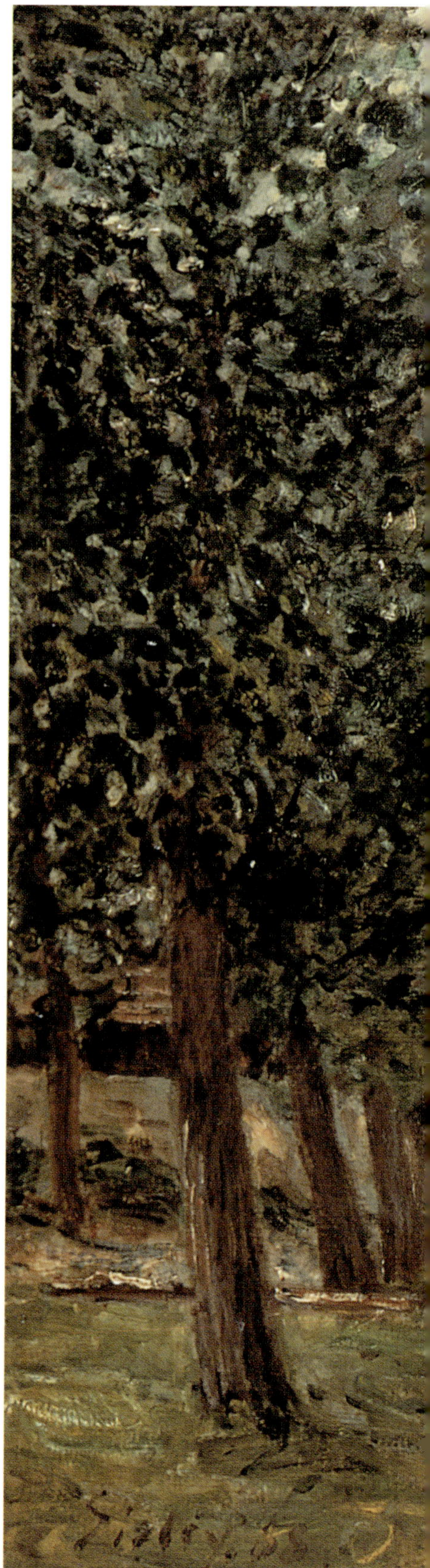

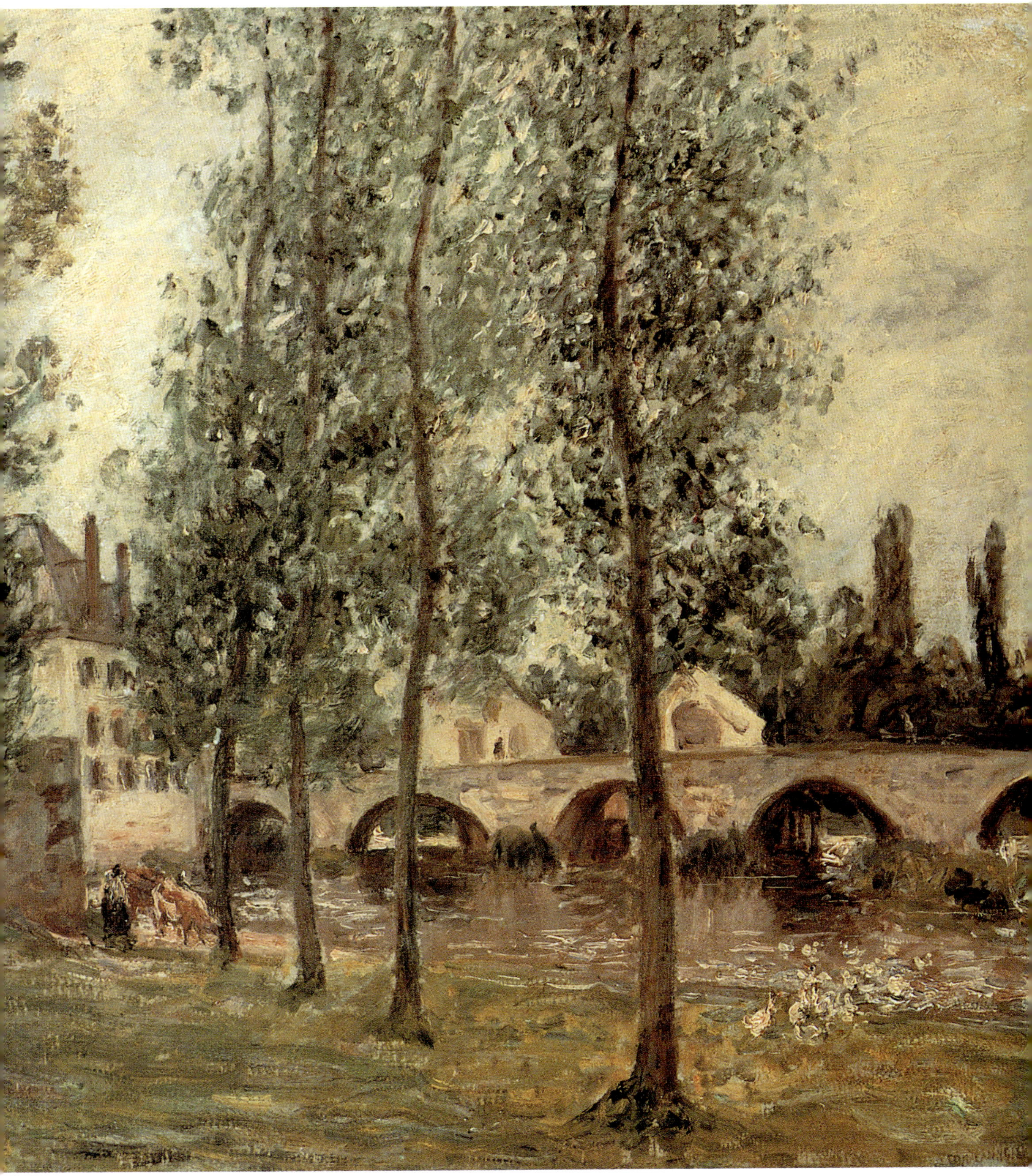

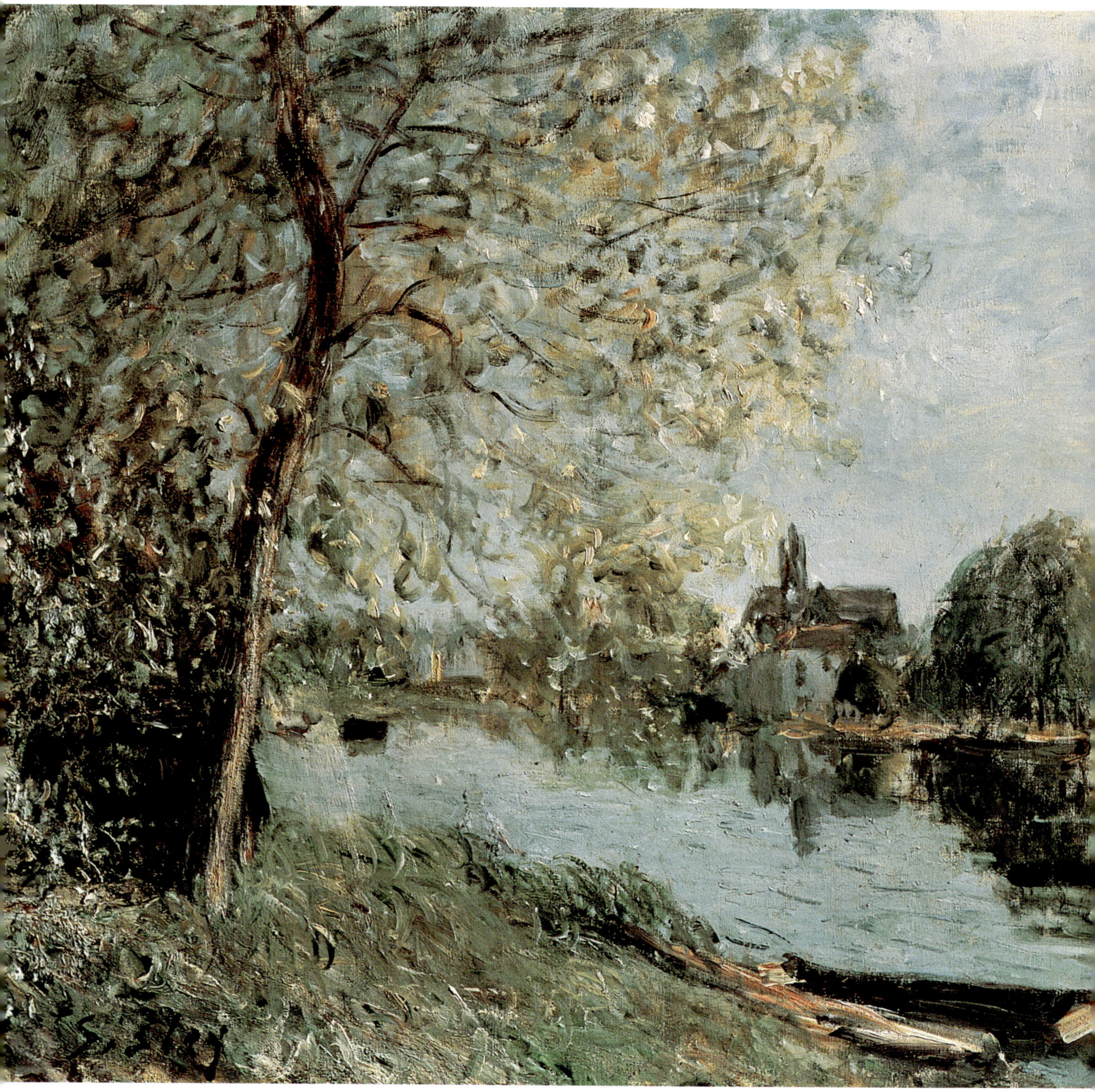

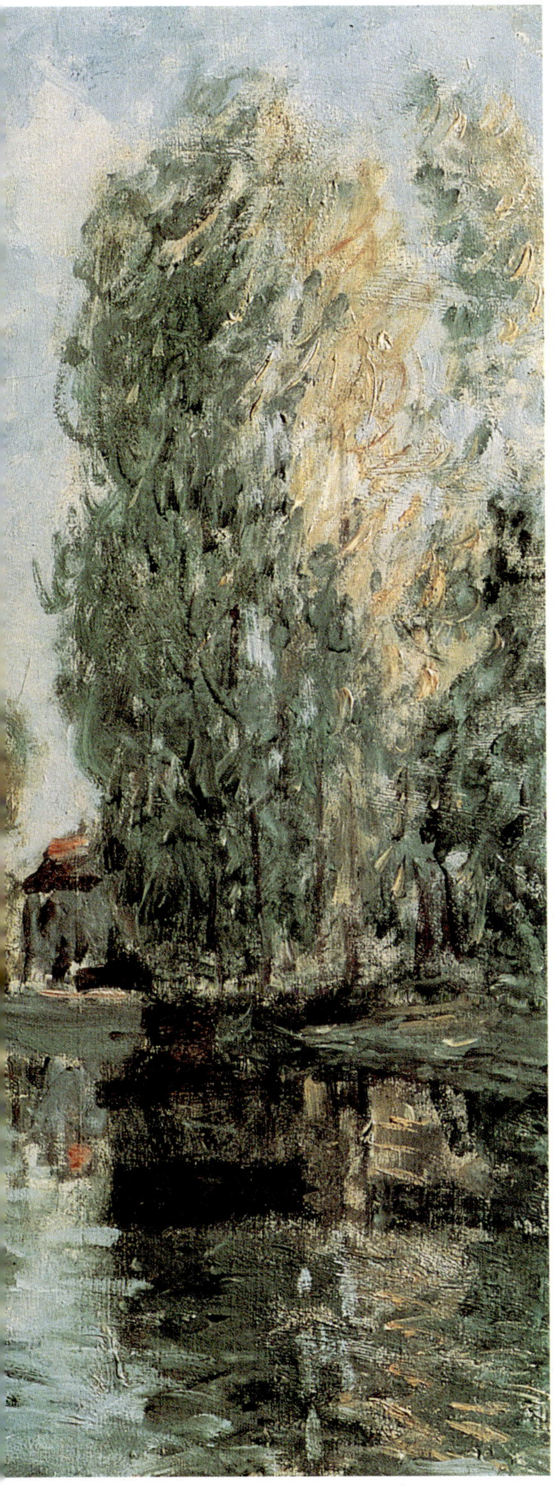

ALFRED SISLEY
***Spring in Moret-sur-Loing,* c. 1888**
Courtesy of AKG London

THIS is painted in a typically free Impressionist style, the colours and brushstrokes imbuing the work with a vivacity and joyfulness that suggest a landscape of constant light with a slight breeze rippling through the leaves. Note how Sisley applies the paint to create different effects – the thin broad strokes on the tree dissolve in the light, and yet the thick dabs of white suggest strong direct light on the leaves and branches.

The view is a particularly interesting one across the river where Sisley lived. He has split the composition into three planes, which are viewed diagonally from left to right – the bank, the river and the far bank. The tree leaning in on the left directs our gaze out over the water; the boats disappearing from view under the bank indicate the lower level of the river further down and echo the dark patches on the other side. The tree on the right bank stands directly opposite the tree on the left bank.

The house, halfway down the far bank, is also in the centre of the painting and when we look straight ahead it leads us to the high blue and white sky beyond. The river then leads us off to the right. We have the impression that we can look around this painting, gazing off in several directions.

CAMILLE PISSARRO (1830–1903)
Landscape with Ploughman, 1868

Kunsthalle, Bremen. Courtesy of AKG London

PISSARRO was the oldest member of the Impressionist group, older by two years than Manet. He had started to draw in 1855 and first painted like landscapist Gustave Courbet (1819–77), whose work he had first admired at the World Fair in Paris in 1855.

He met Cézanne and Guillaumin, who considered him their mentor, in 1862 at the Académie Suisse. Like the rest of the group, he exhibited at the Salon des Refusés in 1863. Between 1864 and 1868 he was in financial difficulties and spent part of 1868 painting shop signs with Guillaumin to earn some more money.

He concentrated on landscapes and painted views of villages outside Paris, on the banks of the Seine, the Marne and the Oise. He began to use a brighter palette, without black, from 1865. From 1866, he lived at Pontoise.

Painted in the open air, this painting shows a ploughman and his white horse in the middle ground, with green fields in front and behind. It is typical of Pissarro's work at this time. The stately composition reveals his concern for presenting readable space and forms, using only colour to define edges and contours. Typically, he creates a sense of movement and depth by indicating a 'path', in this case the furrows in the middle ground, to take the viewer into the space. The picture has a calm, gentle quality that is particular to Pissarro's work.

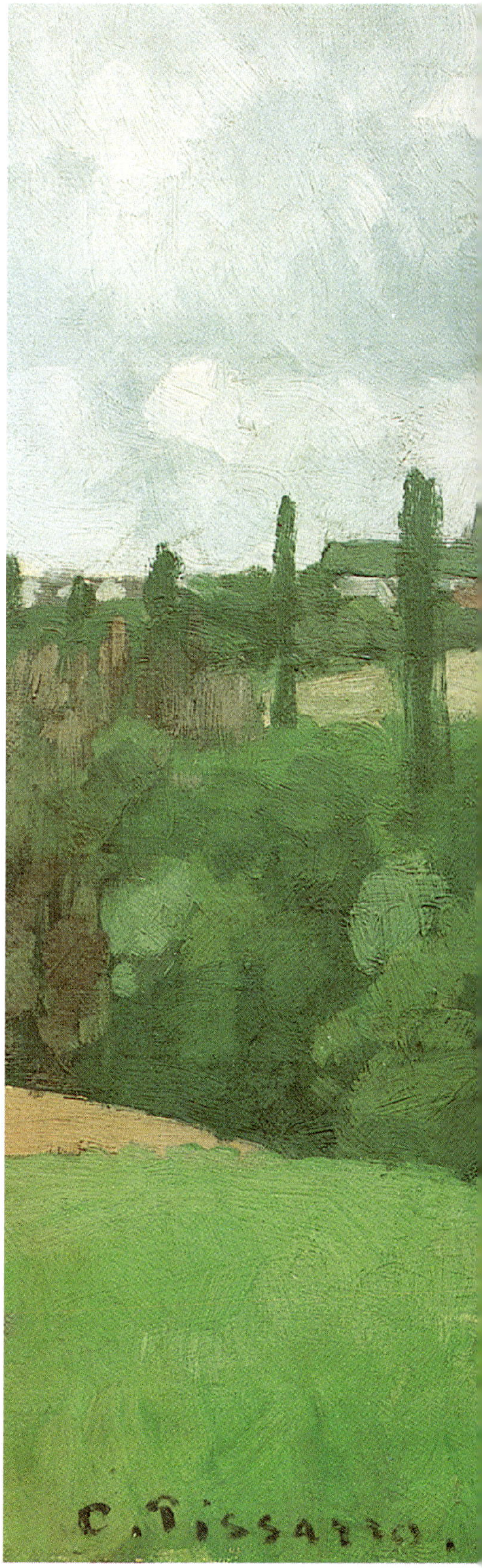

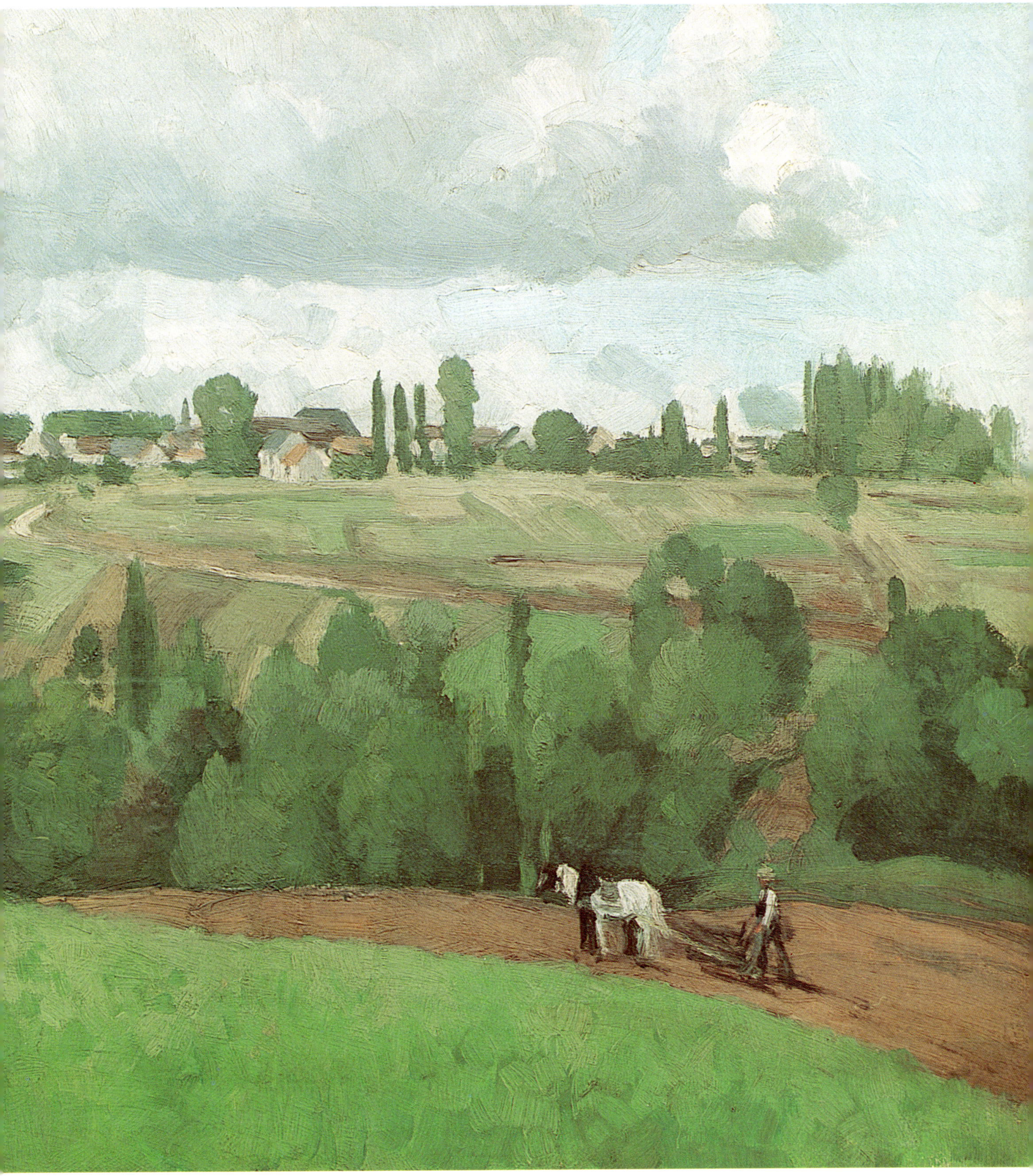

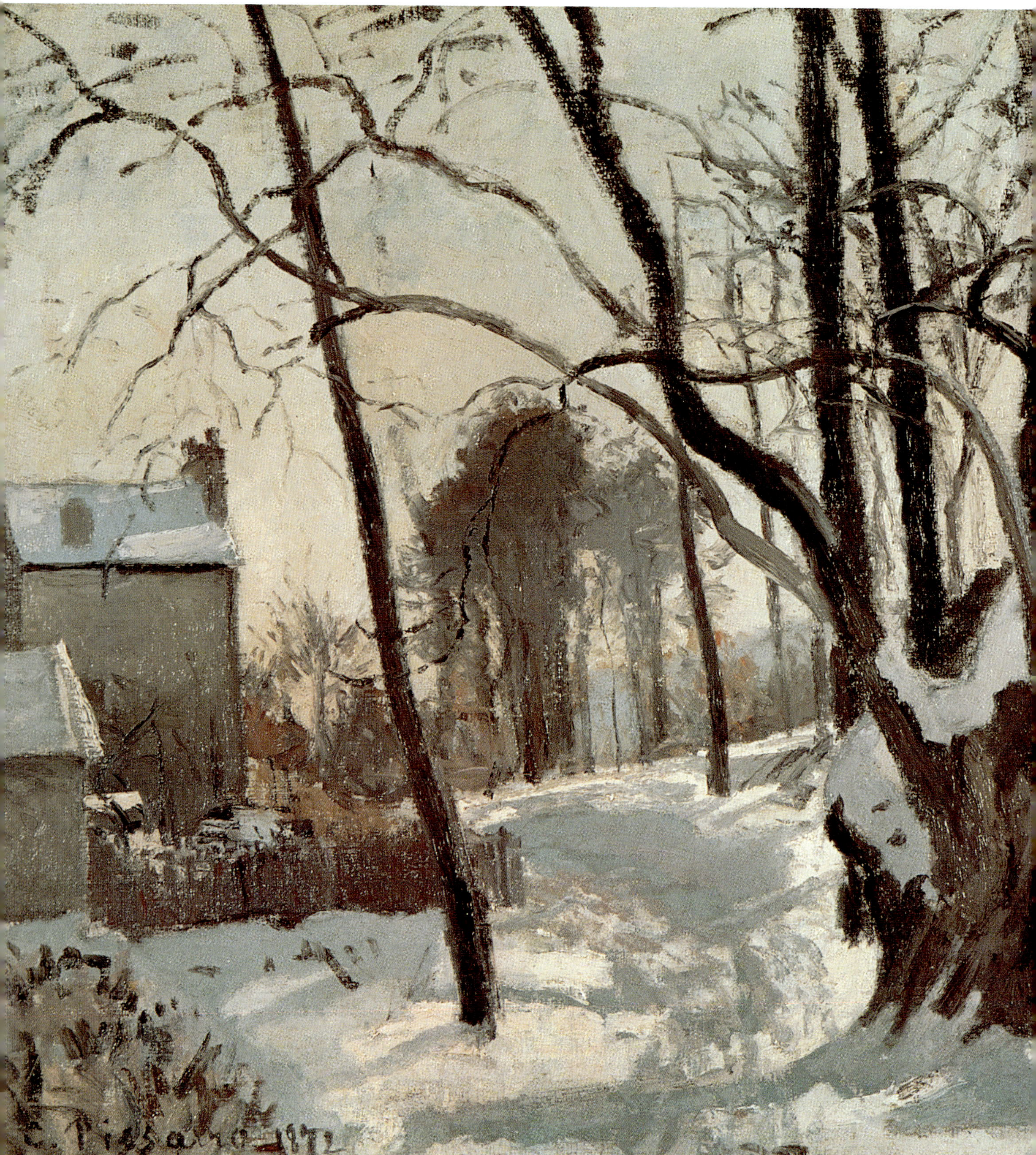
C. Pissarro 1872

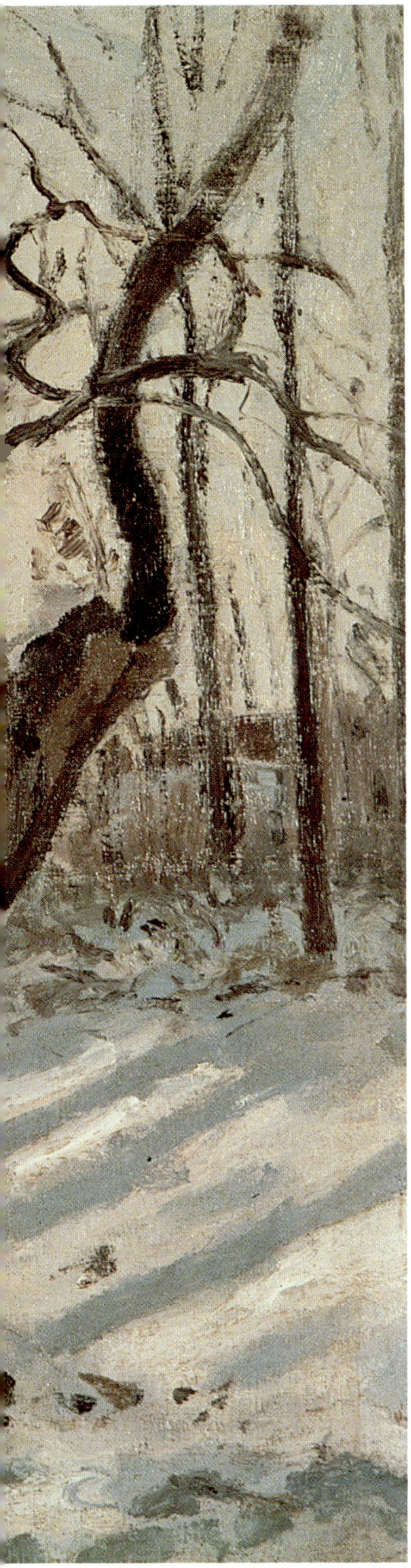

CAMILLE PISSARRO
Louveciennes, 1872

Museum Folkwang, Essen. Courtesy of AKG London

PISSARRO, who was born in the West Indies and had Danish nationality, fled France during the Franco-Prussian War and spent the years 1870–71 in London where he painted country lanes in the suburbs. Many of the works that he left behind in France were looted and destroyed.

After the war, he returned to Louveciennes. Cézanne moved close by and the two worked together in the region for the next ten years. Here Pissarro fully developed his own distinctive style of Impressionism.

In this snow scene, Pissarro is concerned with the way in which the light is reflected off the snow, creating pink, blue and lilac shadows in the shade and dazzling brightness in direct light.

Typically, he depicts a fairly nondescript corner of the world – a few trees at the bottom of a slope with houses to the right. The charm lies in his delicate rendering of light effects and his ability to create an atmosphere of bright, chill calm on a winter morning. He channels our gaze to the left out of the picture via the diagonal of the trees and the blue shadows running down the slope from the left. The picture is cut off on each side, creating a sense of immediacy, and viewed from a slight height, as if we are newly come down a slope to this place, looking to left and right.

The composition also shows the influence of early photography and the strong, dark verticals in the foreground are suggestive of Japanese compositions and contrast with the soft colours around them.

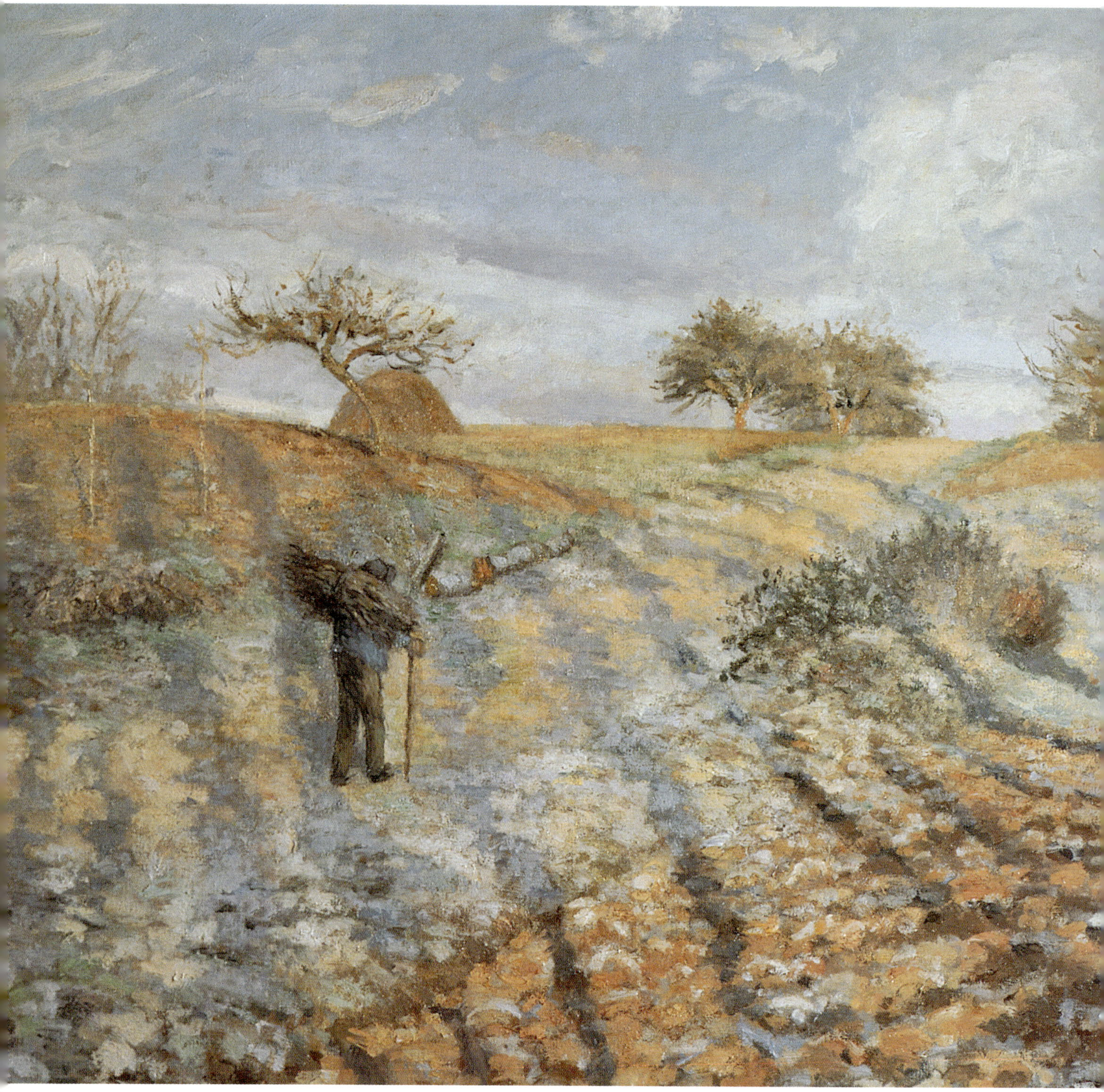

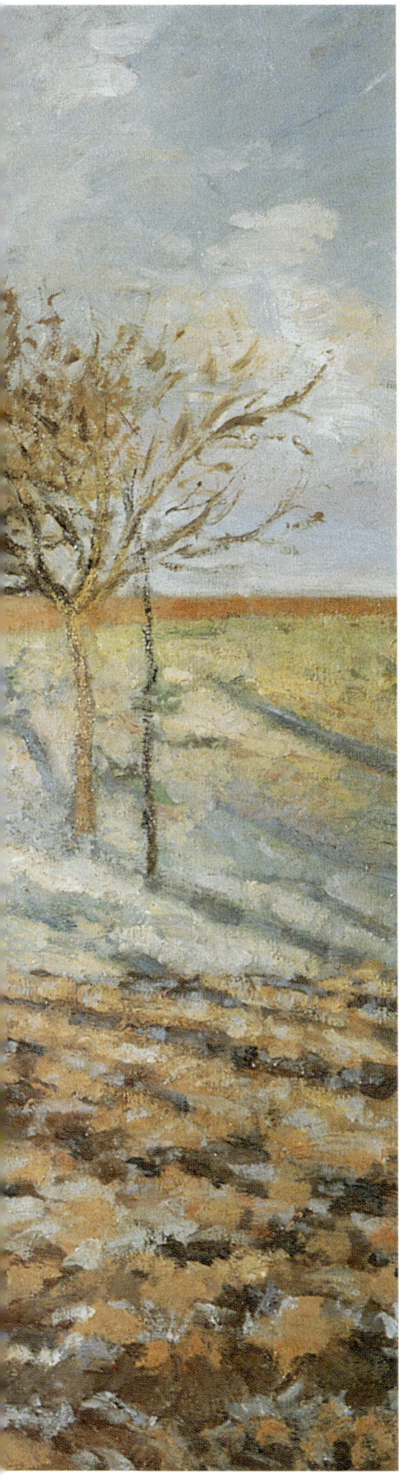

CAMILLE PISSARRO
Hoar Frost, 1873

Musée du Louvre, Paris. Courtesy of AKG London/Erich Lessing

THIS painting of a field at Louveciennes aroused much vitriolic comment at the first independent Impressionist exhibition of 1874. 'What?' spluttered the critics. 'Are those furrows? Is that meant to be frost ... they are just scratchings of paint placed in strips on a dirty canvas. It's got neither a head nor a tail, a high nor a low, a front nor a back... .'

Not only were the critics distressed at the technique but also at the lack of subject matter. They did not understand or appreciate Pissarro's desire to convey reflections of morning light on a tilled field with the frost still on the ground in a complementary harmony of golden and blue tones.

Pissarro has put together a composition in which horizontal and diagonal lines dominate, emphasising the breadth and depth of the scene. The geometry is immediately obvious in the strips of light and shade that run as far as the horizon from right to left and the broader edges of the fields that run the other way, drawing the viewer's gaze in opposite directions. The central point is marked by the sunlit bushes in the middle ground, where four triangles roughly intersect below the trees placed centrally on the horizon.

The brushwork is typical and lends itself to the texture of the rough clods of tilled earth. Although a lot of white is used, which creates a fresh tonality, there is an overall contrast of cool 'blue' colours and warmer reds and yellows. In this shimmering atmosphere, the wood gatherer stands out, finely contoured and suggestive of the hard work involved in country living as he toils along the road.

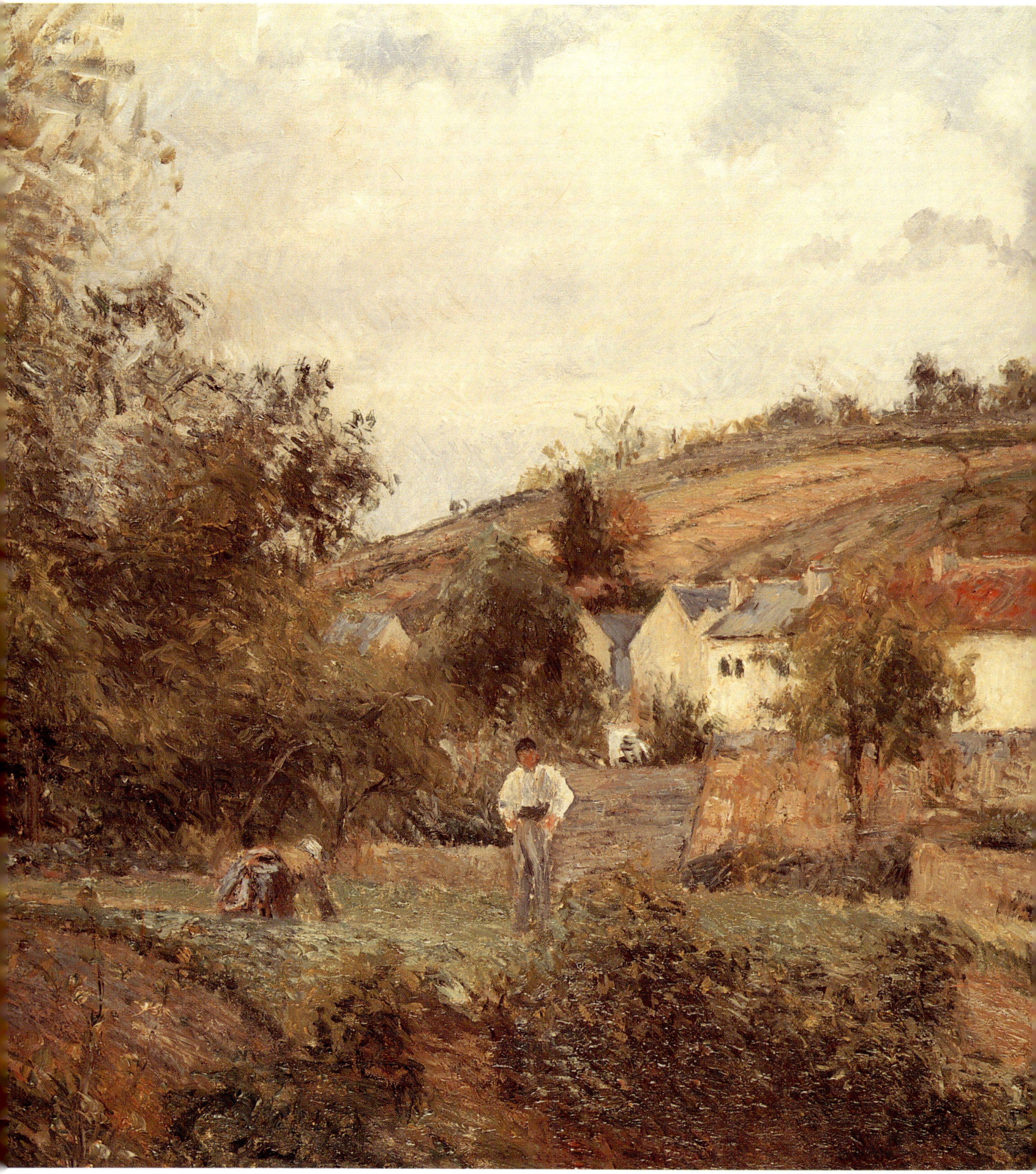

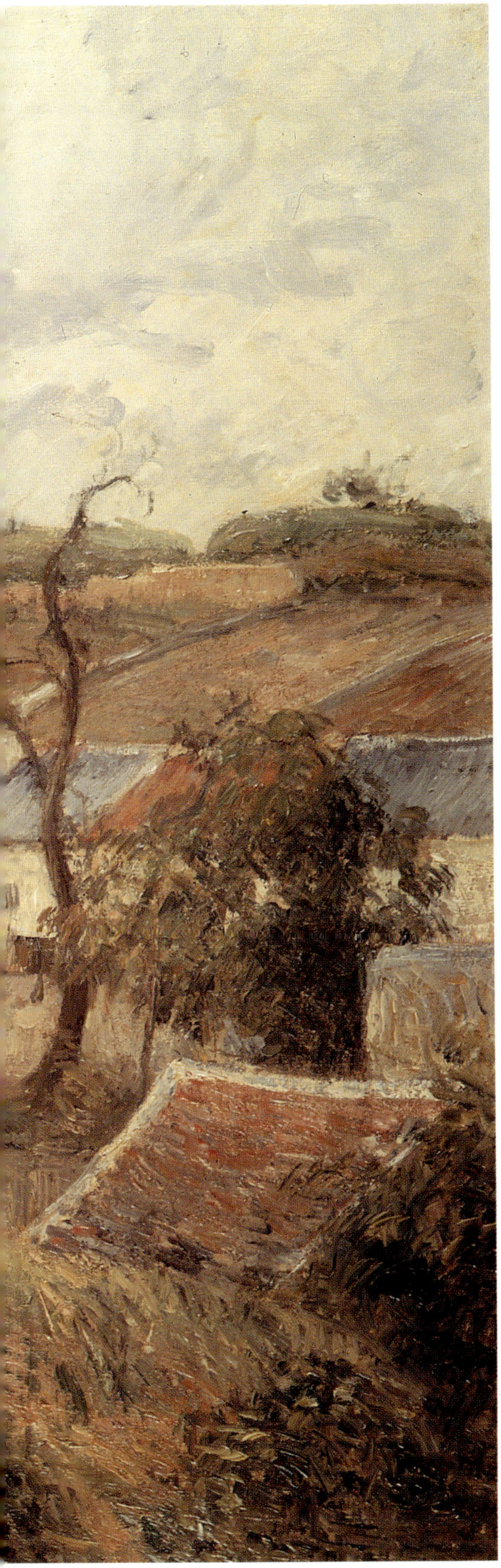

Camille Pissarro

Village Near Pontoise, 1873

Offentliche Kunstsammlung, Basel. Courtesy of AKG London

HERE, Pissarro is beginning to use the small, fleeting directional brushstrokes for which he became known. He has completely banished black from his palette and is only using the primaries and their derivatives. However, although he describes the effect of light, the colours are muted and recall the more earth-toned landscapes of Corot (1796–1875).

Pissarro was always interested in the structure of his paintings and here, despite the light touch, we are still aware of every succeeding plane. Each contour is clear and yet true to Impressionist principle, the lines are created by colour and tone alone.

Pissarro creates great breadth and height with the horizontal of the land juxtaposed with the tall tree on the left that is disappearing at the top. The effect recalls Cézanne's advice to the young Emile Bernard (1868–1941) in 1904: 'Lines horizontal to the horizon give breadth … Lines perpendicular to this horizon give depth;' a lesson probably learned with Pissarro.

Here, nature and man's constructions blend and, typically, Pissarro includes two little figures, at one and yet distinct from the land around them and the soft, cloudy sky above. Again, we feel as if we have chanced upon a scene – an effect increased by the man in the white shirt having stopped to look at us.

CAMILLE PISSARRO
Woman Doing her Washing, 1875

Courtesy of Christie's Images

UNTIL the 1880s, Pissarro was essentially a landscape painter, whose views, seen from a distance, often included small figures working on the land. This painting shows him moving towards the depiction of figures that were to take a prominent place in his work in later years.

It is the country equivalent of Degas' female city workers, ironing in the sweat shops of Paris. But whereas Degas was mainly interested in these women from an artistic viewpoint rather than one of social concern, Pissarro seems to be offering us a commentary on the wholesome qualities of honest work in the country.

The sun shines and the woman washes the last piece of clothing, rubbing it along a board in a wooden tub outside. She is immersed in her domestic world. This impression is enhanced by the brick wall that encloses her, the lack of horizon and her central position, her head at the apex of a balanced triangular configuration. The palette is warm and inviting, based on complementary pink and green tones. The sun warms,her back and her white shirt shines. Pissarro, even when portraying figures as the focal point of a painting, makes them at one with their surroundings, through a harmony of colours and a rhythm of lines and shapes across the canvas. The brushwork, which creates the pattern, and the surface of the brick wall also suggest the influence of Cézanne, who began to build up shapes with mosaic-like brushstrokes.

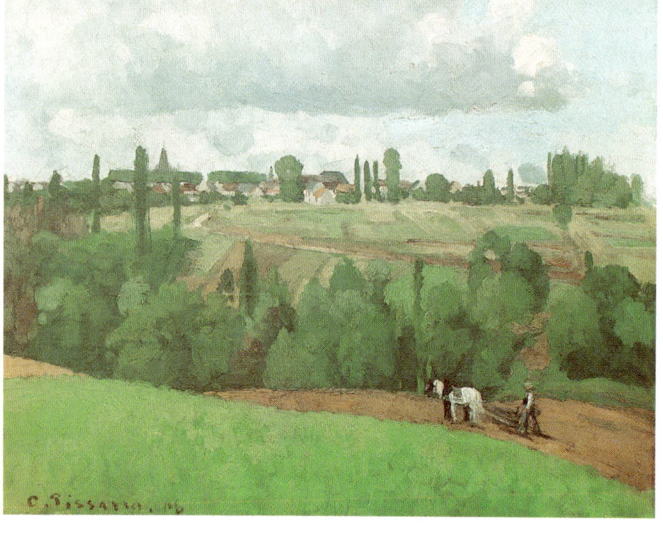

Camille Pisarro
Landscape with Ploughman, 1868
Kunsthalle, Bremen. Courtesy of AKG London. *(See p. 96)*

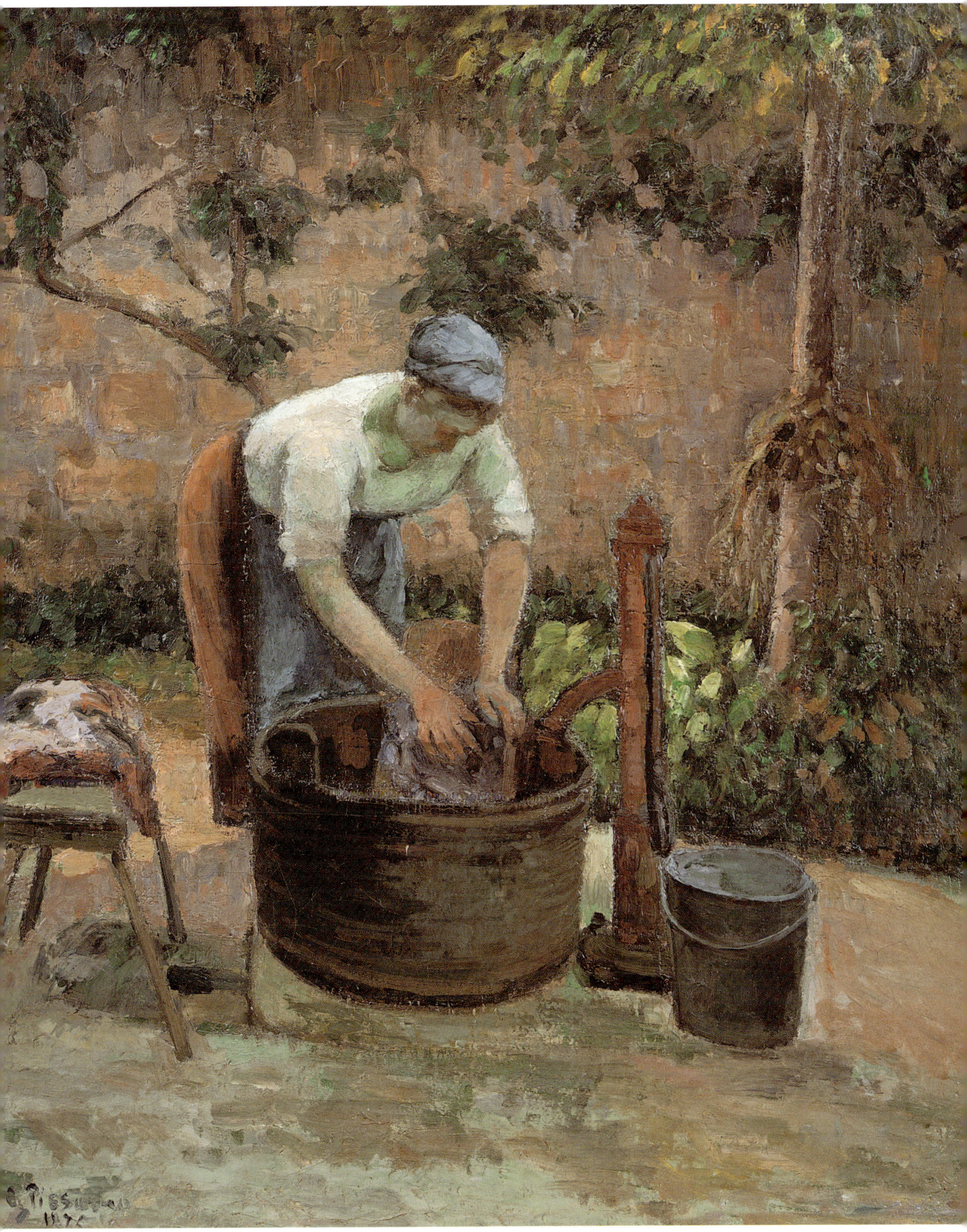

Camille Pissarro
Landscape: the Village of Melleraye, 1876

Niedersaechsisches Landesmueu, Hanover. Courtesy of AKG London

PISSARRO portrays this pastoral scene in the intense heat of the day using only yellow, blue and green – two primary colours and their secondary colour. Light is painted in vivid yellow, eliminating the colour of the grass and the leaves upon which it falls.

The composition is made up of a long rectangle in the foreground, another on the right and a square on the left, two-thirds of which makes up the sky. The low trees and cottages, painted with a restrained vigour reminiscent of Corot, nestle between the hot yellow earth and the luminous blue sky. The technique used by many of the Impressionists, of allowing the white priming of the canvas to glow through in the lower reaches of the painting, creates a shimmering light rising up from the horizon.

The rhythm of the design is created by the repetition of colour and by the echoing of forms, such as the cottage roofs and the gentle curve of the bridge. A relatively shady respite is created in the upright rectangular space on the right, which is dominated by blues and greens, and it is here that we suddenly spy the little figure that we expect in Pissarro's work. In a few tiny, quick dabs Pissarro has painted a man lying on his elbow, chin in hands and he seems to be looking at us. A second figure, virtually obliterated in the play of light, seems to be working, unaware of us, by the far tree.

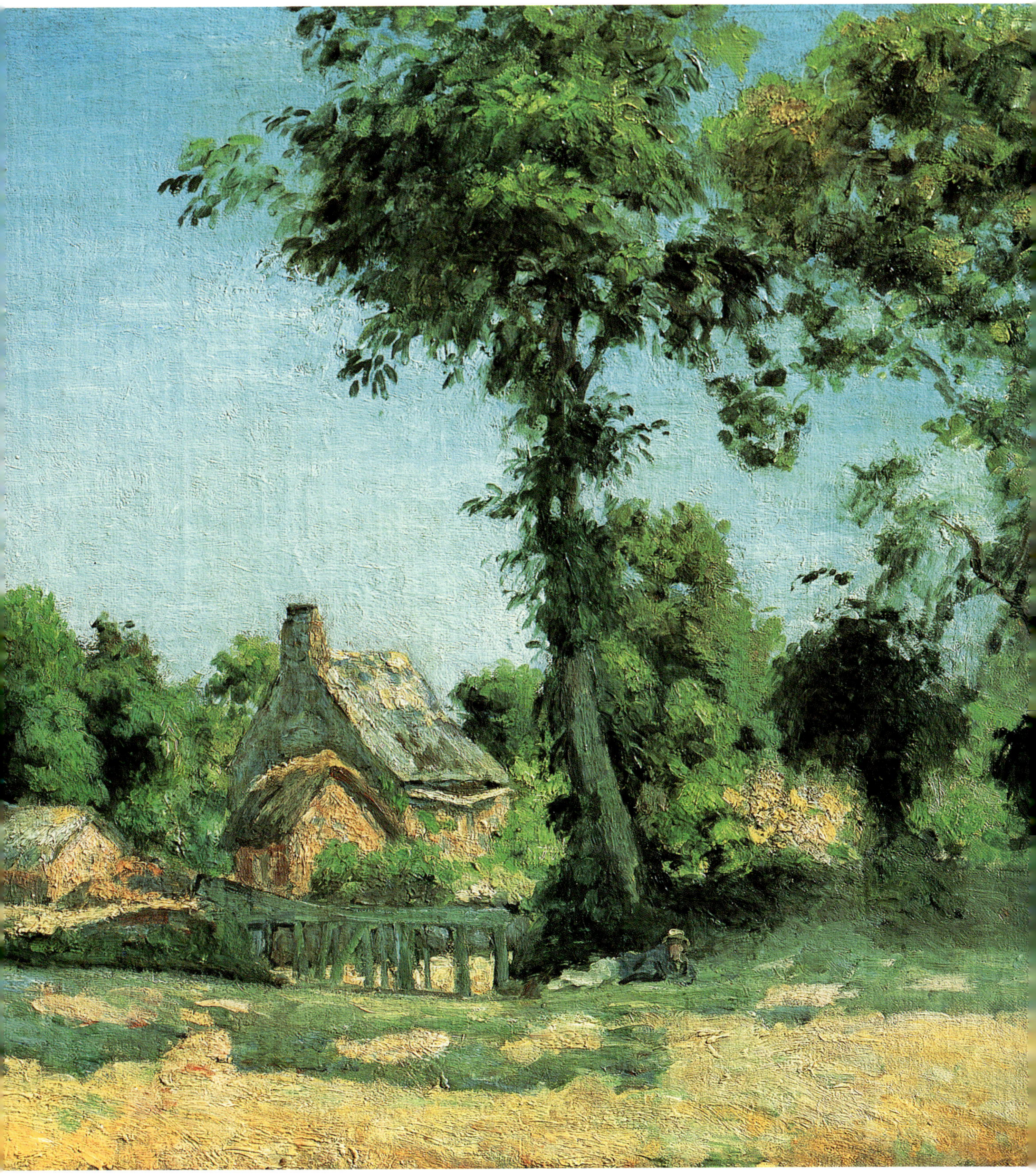

Camille Pissarro
Red Roofs, Corner of a Village, 1877

Musée d'Orsay, Paris. Courtesy of AKG London/Erich Lessing

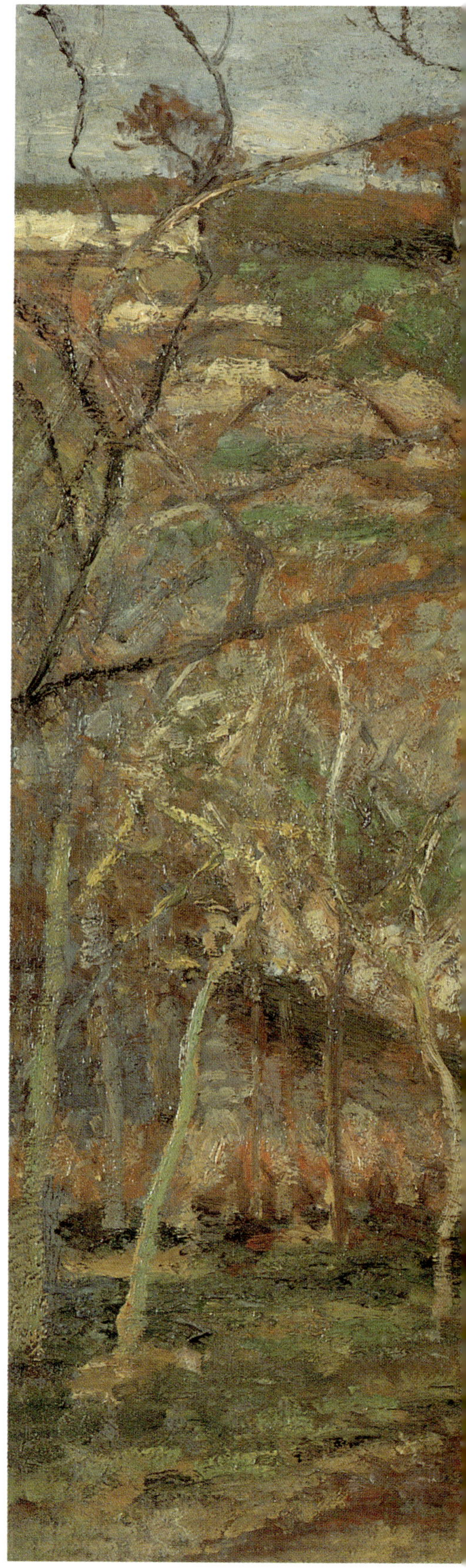

THIS is another scene from around Pissarro's home village of Pontoise and reminiscent of the pretty, but unstartling view depicted in Louveciennes (1872). In style, it bears comparison with Cézanne's *House of Dr Gachet* (1872), but by 1877, the latter was beginning to develop an idiom of his own that solidified nature into a timeless, geometric weight. Pissarro's work is firmly in the Impressionist style and shows the light effects on a particular afternoon.

In 1867, the critic Zola described a work of art as 'a corner of creation seen through a temperament'. Much of Pissarro's work, including this one, reflects this statement quite literally. As here, he often chooses enclosed views, surrounded by trees that do not stun by their majesty and grandeur. The scene is rendered extraordinary by Pissarro's treatment of it.

The green and brown earth, littered with sinuous young saplings, recedes to the white buildings with blue doors and red roofs, which are lit by the golden light that suffuses the whole canvas. The red, yellow and green slope, farmed in strips, rises to a high diagonal blue horizon, which is fragmented by the delicate tracery of the trees in the foreground. The complicated relationships are devised solely through the use of colour, which are not localised but repeated in different areas of the painting to create an overall harmony of colour and design.

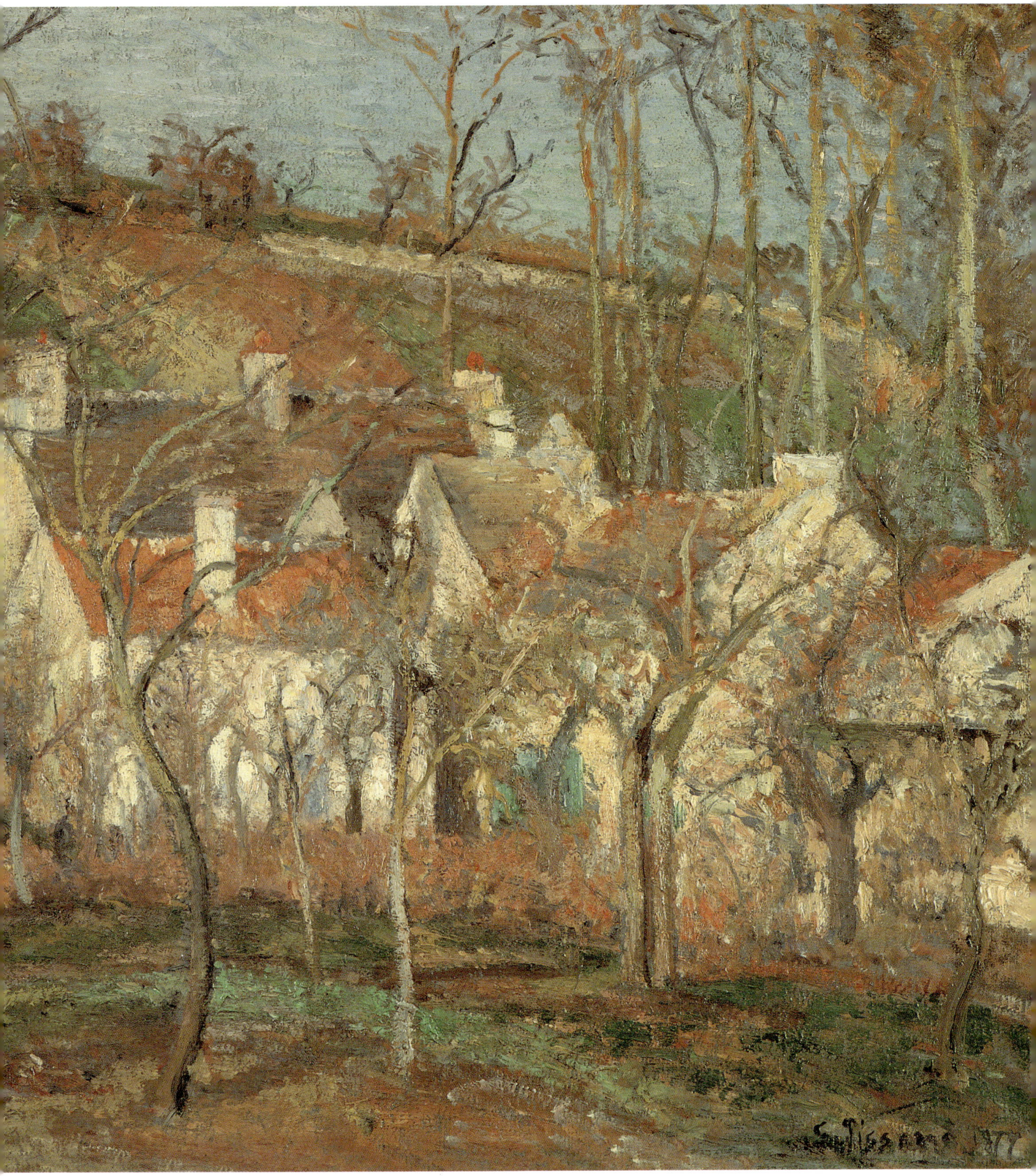

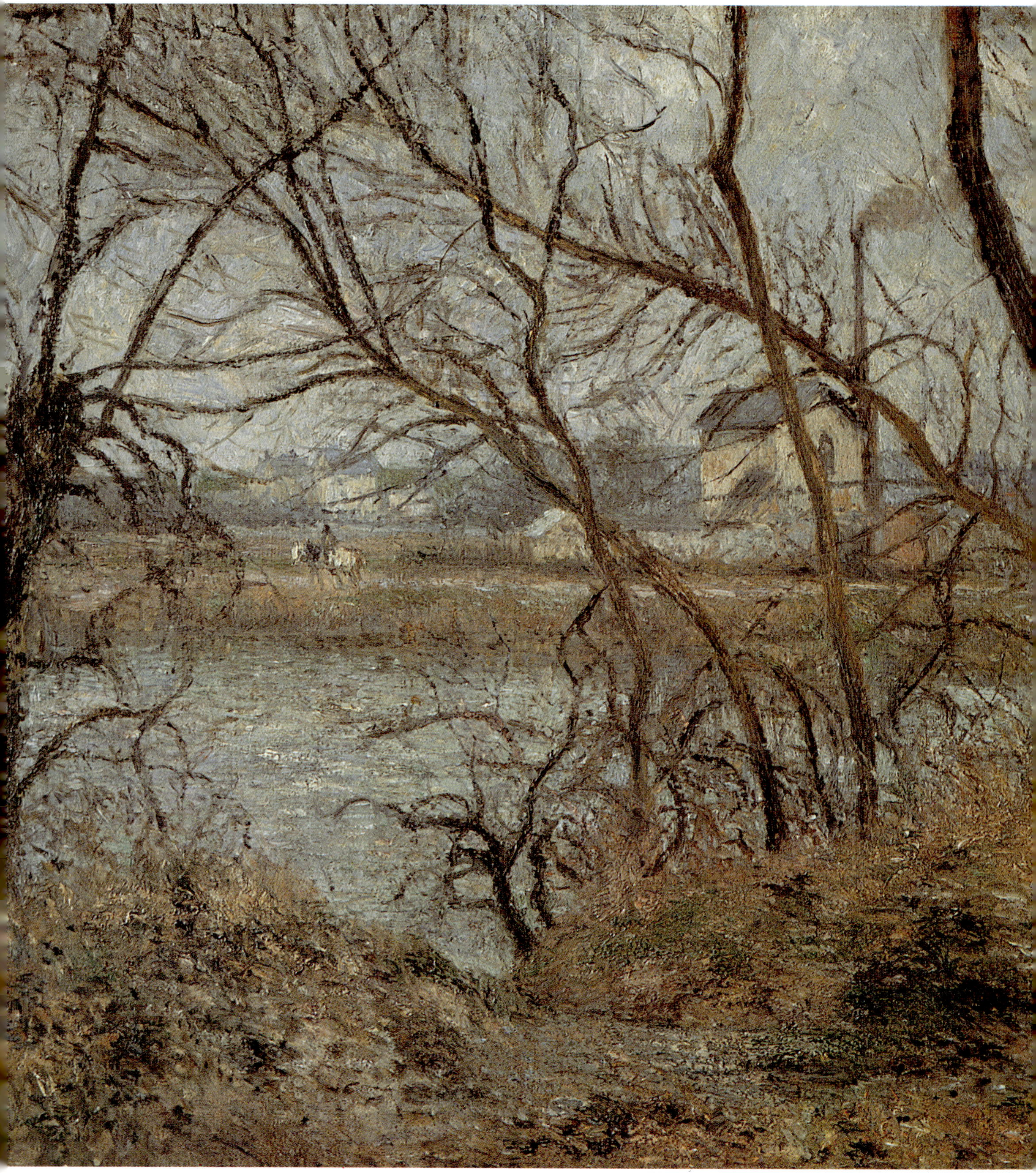

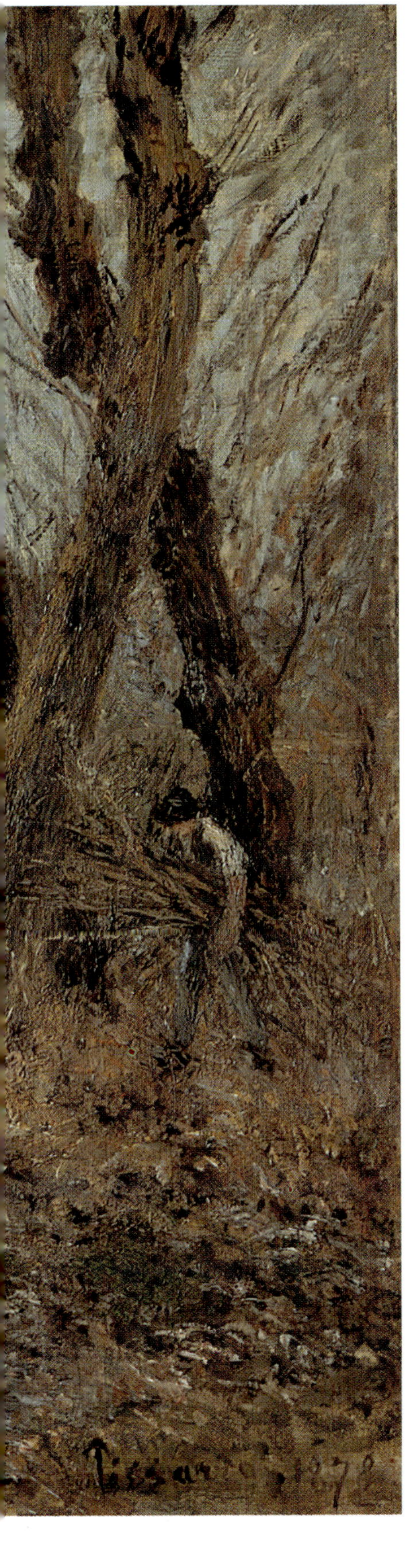

CAMILLE PISSARRO

Bank of the River Oise, 1878

Musée du Louvre, Paris. Courtesy of AKG London

ON a grey day by the river Oise, Pissarro takes a view across the water to the opposite bank where a man rides a white horse. The viewer is led straight into this scene on the left by the structural composition of the foreground in which the bending, leafless trees create a kind of viewfinder focused on the scene beyond. The effect is tiny and delicate, with the trees providing a fragile framework.

Pissarro's artistic skill causes the viewer to look to the right, where in the foreground we see the sturdy, trunks of larger trees through which we see a house, or possibly a factory, with a tall smoking chimney. Only at the last moment do we see the figure gathering wood, part of the diagonal created by the bending tree behind him and barely highlighted by a dab of light on his shoulder. Although Pissarro works in the Impressionist manner, in this painting he is rather more concerned with the absence of bright light, without which the colours subside and do not vibrate and dazzle. The painting recalls the muted colours of some of his earlier works, and Pissarro's longstanding admiration for Corot's grey-toned landscapes is clear. In 1866 Cézanne had written to Pissarro, 'you are quite right what you say about grey, it alone prevails in nature, but it frightfully difficult to capture'.

Camille Pissarro
The Toilette, c. 1883

Private Collection. Courtesy of AKG London

IN 1882 Pissarro and his large family moved to Osny. The move ended the 10-year period in which he and Cézanne worked closely, although they still kept in touch. The year 1883 was an eventful one for Pissarro. He had the first of several solo exhibitions at the gallery of the dealer Paul Durand-Ruel; his son Lucien, also an artist, moved to London, which initiated a long correspondence, and he became interested in Socialism. He also renewed his interest, after painting landscapes for so long, in depicting women at their work, in the fields or at home. He exhibited a series of peasant women at the seventh Impressionist exhibition of 1882. The critic J-K Huysman called them 'truly little masterpieces' and Degas approved them as 'angels who go to market'.

This quick watercolour sketch is utterly charming and shows the vigour and liveliness of Pissarro's style – the child's mother is really rubbing away at those ears – which is not always evident in his oils.

The watercolour technique is different to the technique he uses to build up colour and shape in his oils. The comparison shows how the usual Impressionist style differed so greatly from traditional painting. Here, as a traditional artist would do in oil, Pissarro describes his shapes with black contours, which he then fills in with colour.

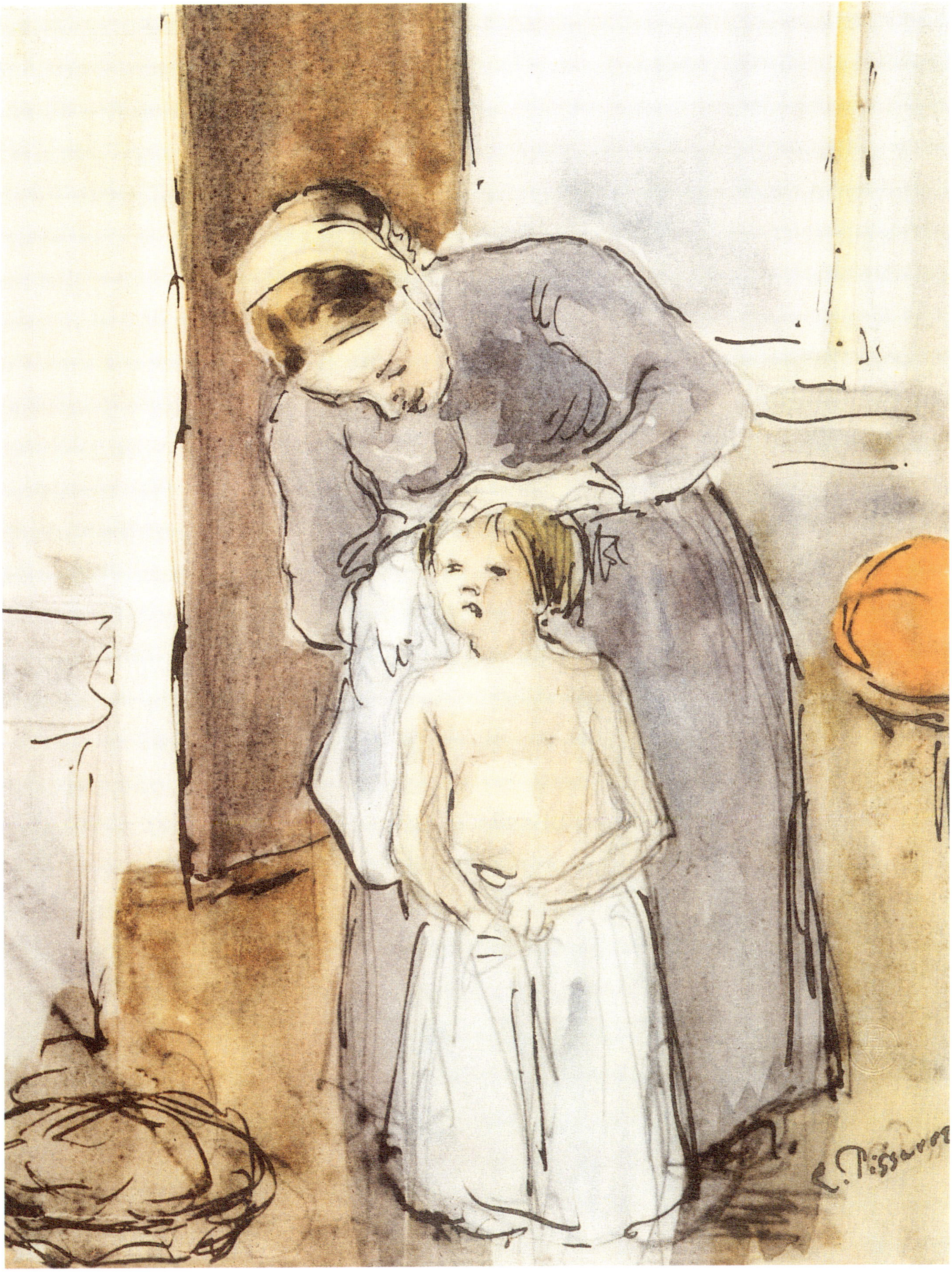
C. Pissarro

Camille Pissarro
Woman Hanging Out the Washing, 1887

Musée d'Orsay, Paris. Courtesy of AKG London/Erich Lessing

THIS is one of Pissarro's later works in which he focuses on a full-length figure. Although the composition suggests quite a large painting, as with many of the others, the dimensions are not big (41 x 32.5 cm/16 x 13 in). The portrait formula lends itself to showing a full-length figure because it emphasises the vertical. For landscapes, particularly with a fairly uninterrupted horizon, such as *Hoar Frost* (1873), which measures 65 x 93 cm (25.5 x 37 in), he turned the canvases round.

This is another charming picture in which Pissarro uses small dabs of paint in a semi-divisionist manner. The only area where he seems to combine pure colour for an optical effect is in the apron, in which blue predominates with a greeny tinge appearing around the folds, where bright yellow has been added.

In spite of the increased formality of the technique, Pissarro creates a feeling of movement as the young woman hangs up the washing and talks to the child. This is created by elements such as the linen on the left blowing in the breeze, the flickering quality of the brushstrokes and the lines leading from right to left across the canvas out of the picture. Pissarro also expresses a very real tenderness for the child, whom he depicts with a charm akin to the child portraits painted by Renoir.

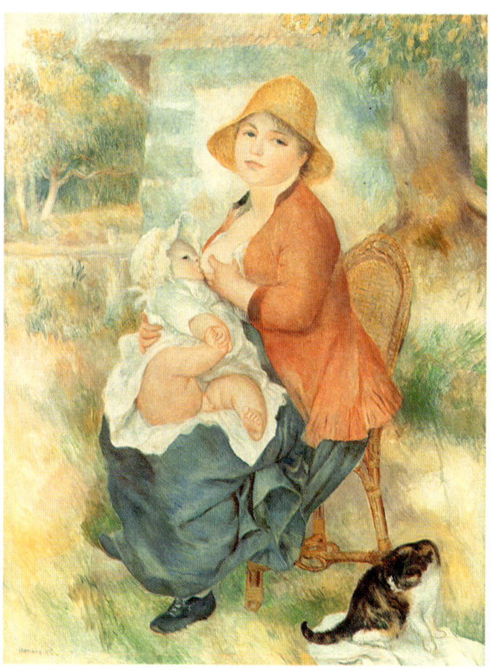

Pierre-Auguste Renoir
Maternity; Woman Feeding her Baby, 1886
Courtesy of AKG London. *(See p. 145)*

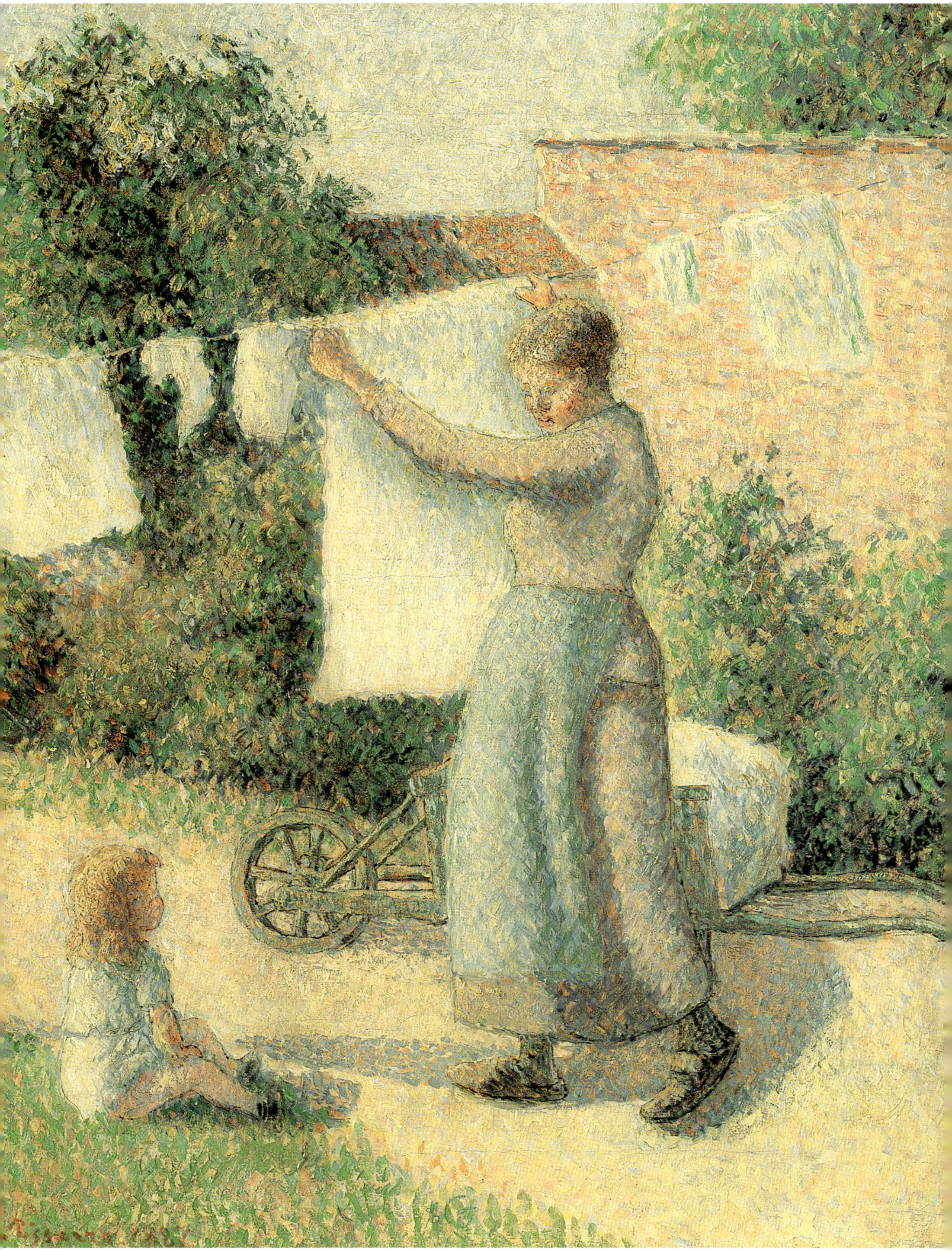

Camille Pissarro
Woman in an Orchard (Spring Sunshine on the Field at Eragny), 1887

Musée d'Orsay, Paris. Courtesy of AKG London/Erich Lessing

PISSARRO moved to Eragny-sur-Epte, where he painted this picture, in 1884 and stayed there until his death in 1903. It was painted a year after the eighth Impressionist exhibition, which proved to be the last owing to differences in opinion among the group regarding new exhibitors such as Paul Signac (1836–1935), Seurat (1859–91), Gauguin (1848–1903) (who began to exhibit in 1879) and Odilon Redon (1840–1916). Of the original core group, only Pissarro, Morisot, Guillaumin and Degas took part. Pissarro was the only founder member to have exhibited at all eight shows.

From 1886, Pissarro, who was more open to new ideas than other members of the group, was influenced by the 'Divisionist' technique of Georges Seurat in which bright dots of pure colour were placed side by side with the intention that the colour should be mixed optically by the eye.

Pissarro is partially adopting the technique in this painting, which otherwise shows a fairly typical landscape with a little figure that would almost be overlooked in the dazzling sunlight were it not for her red headscarf. Even though he has apparently taken on this new 'scientific' approach, Pissarro is not applying the rules consistently. The green we see, for example, is not a combination of blue and yellow dots on the canvas as, theoretically, it should be. Pissarro was taking no chances and painted his greens green. Deep down, he remained a loyal supporter of the Impressionist ideal.

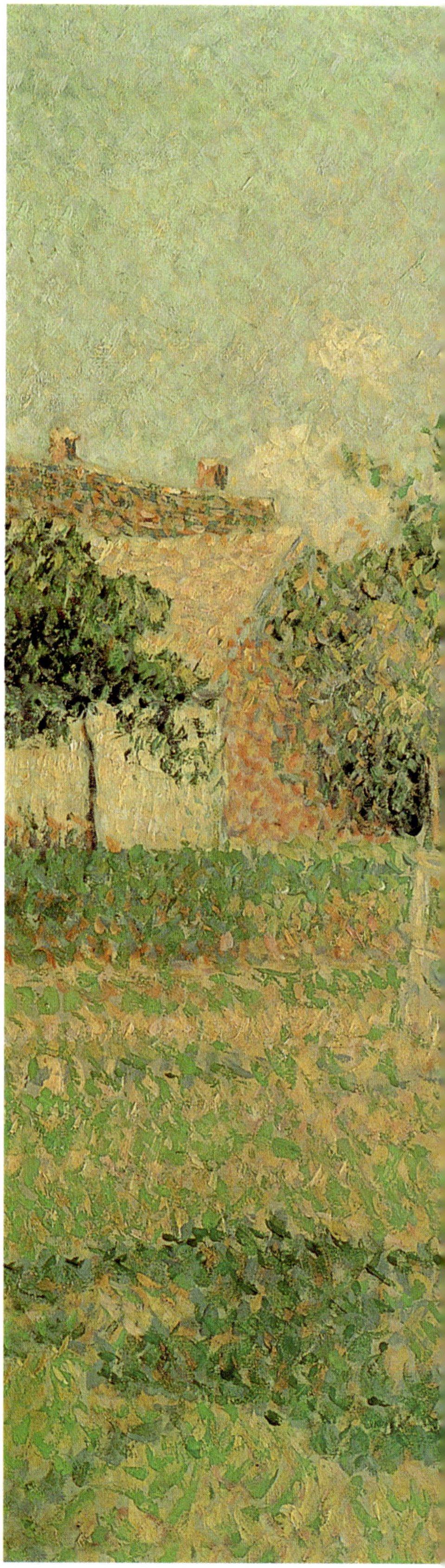

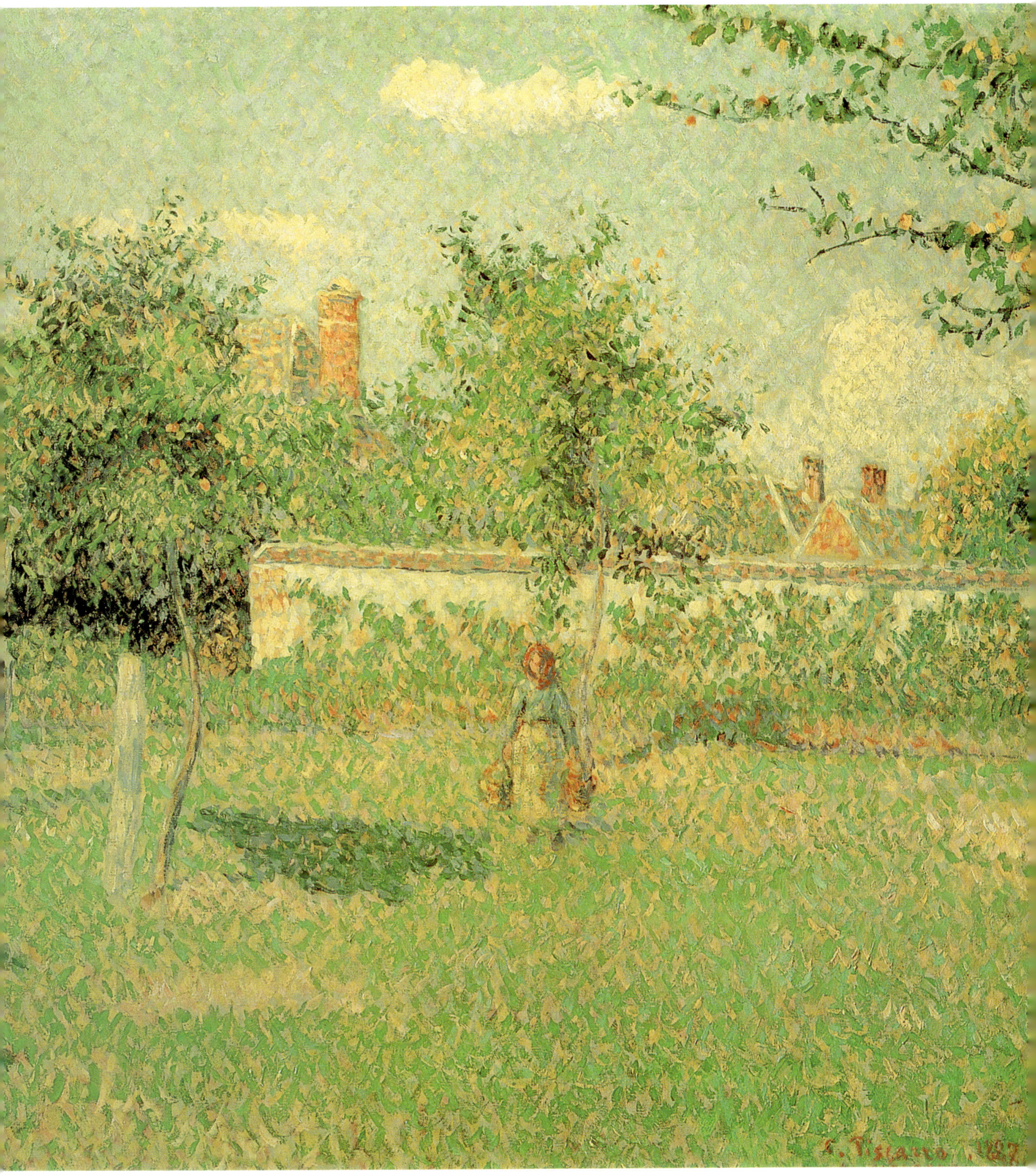

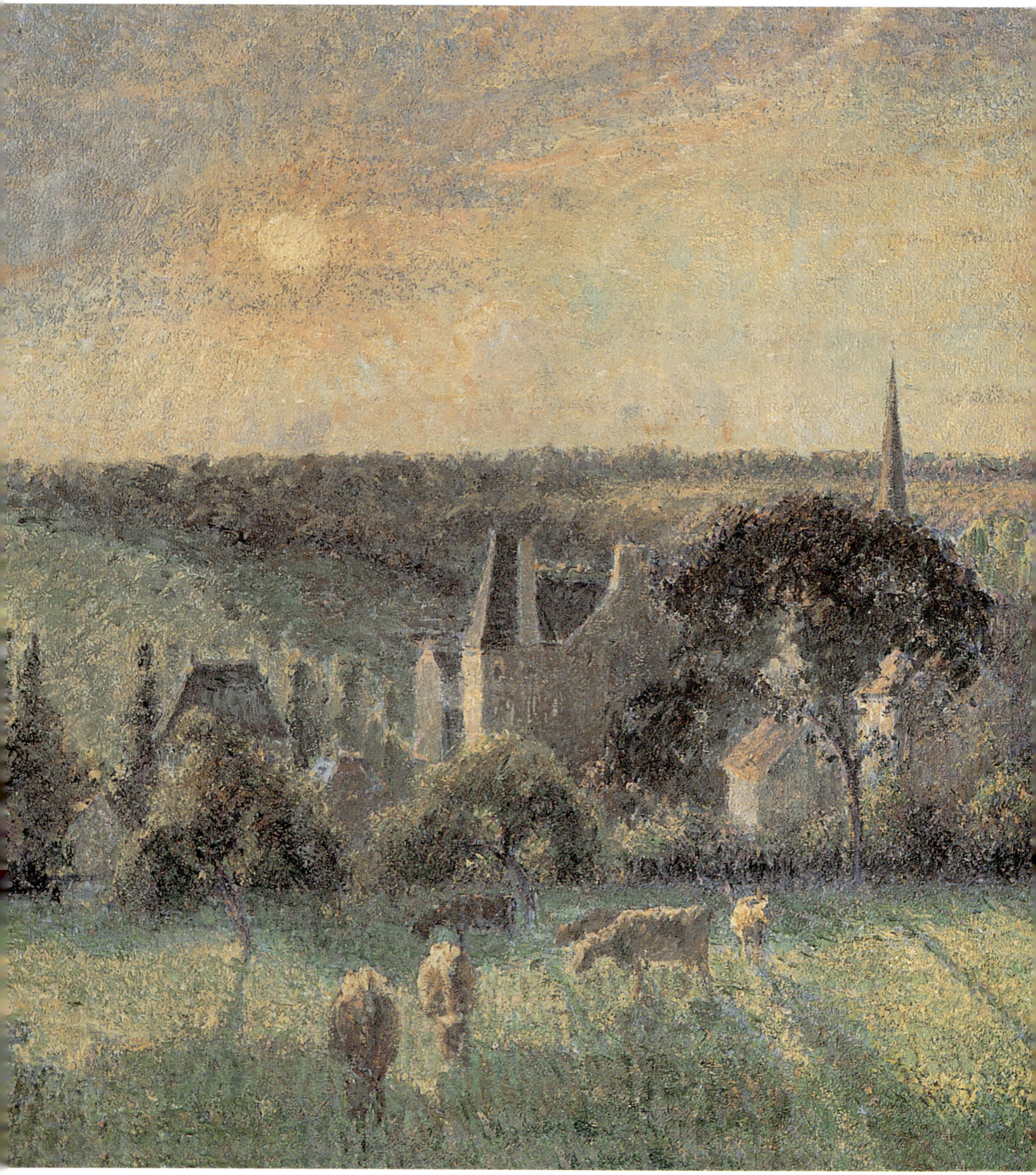

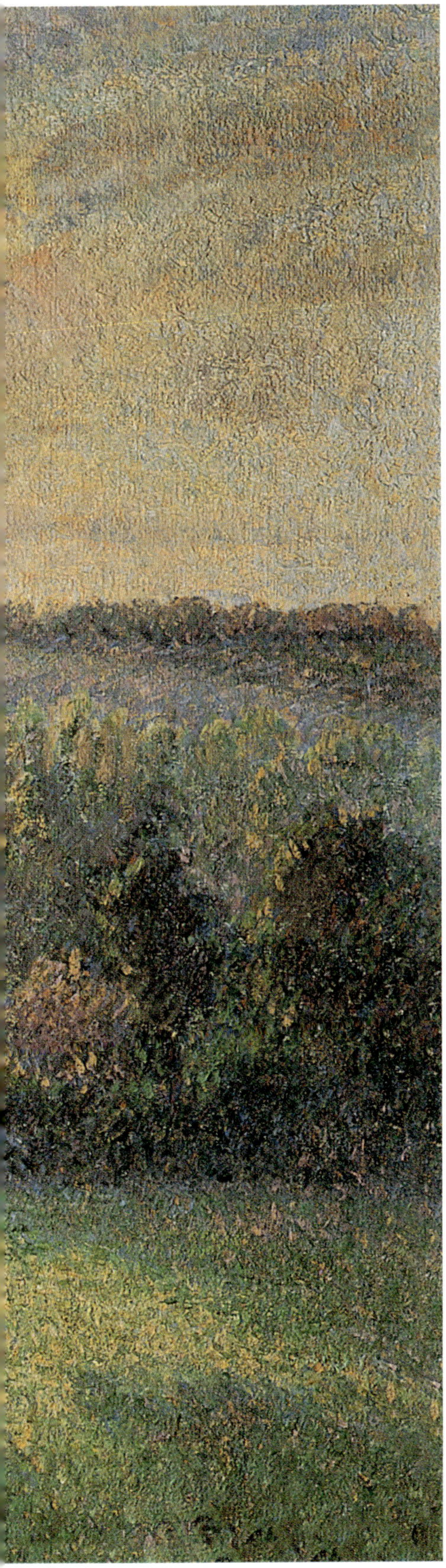

Camille Pissarro
Landscape at Eragny: Church and Farm at Eragny, 1895

Musée d'Orsay, Paris. Courtesy of AKG London/Erich Lessing

THE decade of the 1890s was a fairly active one for Pissarro. He was becoming well-known, thanks to the dealer Durand-Ruel, and with the other Impressionists had had work exhibited at the Century Exhibit at the Paris World Fair in 1889. From 1890 he also made several visits to his son in London and in 1894 he fled to Belgium to escape political persecution as an anarchist.

After 1890, Pissarro stopped painting in the Divisionist style and later regretted that he had spent so long working in that way, which he felt denied his emotions and restricted movement. Here, the calm and tranquillity that we have come to expect is to the fore. The pastoral scene is peaceful, the composition is balanced in three bands and the colours harmonise.

Pissarro's work, particularly that which depicted peasants, was often compared to the work of Jean-François Millet (1814–75), which had religious or biblical overtones. Pissarro, who was Jewish but had no religious beliefs, had become an anarchist in 1885 and felt that religion hindered social reform and objected to these comparisons. However, this landscape, with the luminous sky and the lengthening shadows, not to mention the church steeple in the town, creates an atmosphere that could almost be deemed to be religious. It seems to suggest a peacefulness after the drama of his flight in 1894.

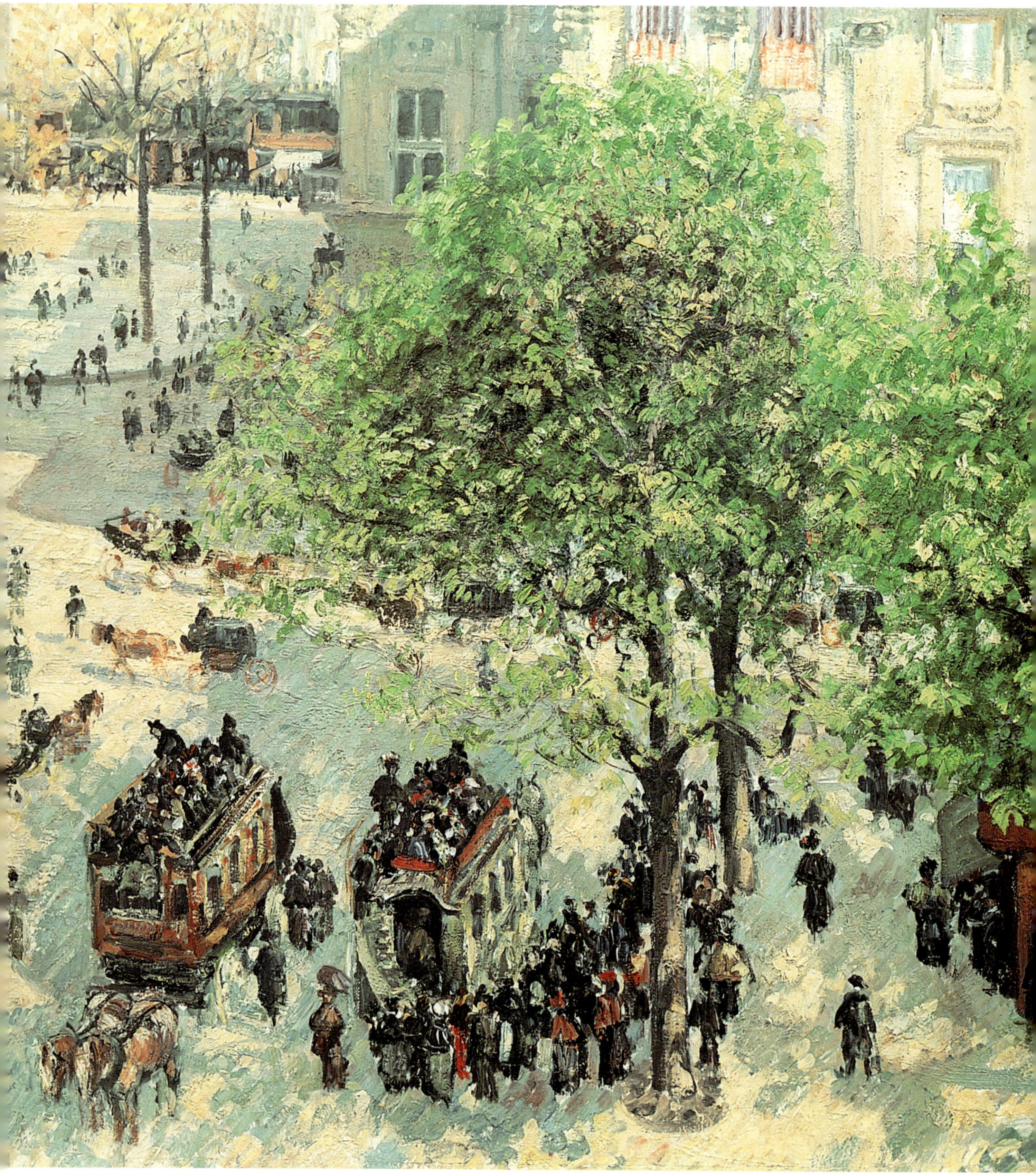

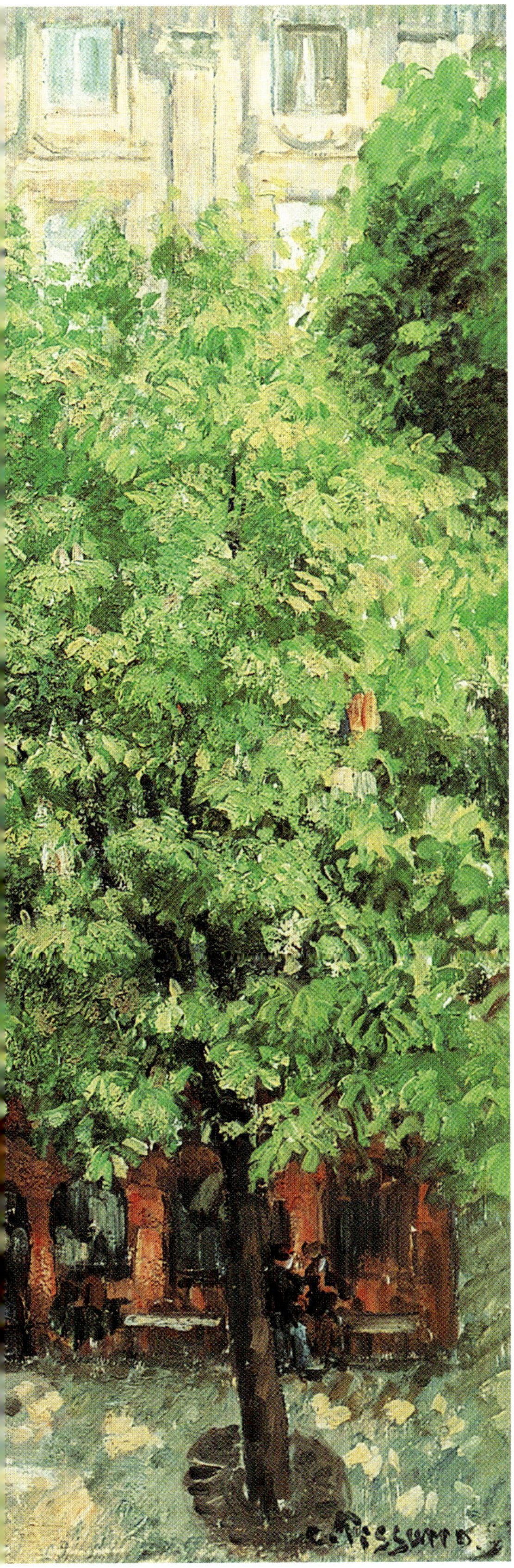

CAMILLE PISSARRO

Place du Théâtre Français, 1898

St Petersburg State Hermitage. Courtesy of AKG London

IN 1888 Pissarro had begun to suffer from eye problems. This meant that, increasingly, he avoided painting in the open air, where he was disturbed by the wind. Instead he painted through open windows and from 1896 he began to concentrate on views of city life. In the same way that he had often taken a raised view point on the landscapes of Pontoise and Eragny, he now painted bridges, boulevards and squares in Rouen, Paris and Le Havre, in scenes that recall paintings by Monet and Manet.

Pissarro painted a number of views of the Place du Théâtre Français from the Hotel du Louvre in the winter and spring of 1898. Here he creates a sunlit, spring scene of people getting on and off the bus in the square below. He now returned to a truly Impressionist way of painting in terms of his aims and the application of paint. He increases the brilliancy of the busy scene with marked use of the complementary opposites, red, green, yellow and blue.

His figures are lively and individual, in spite of being treated so briefly. Each one has a life of its own. Note, for example, the woman leaning over the top of the bus on the left and the people chatting in the open carriage a little further up as it rolls along.

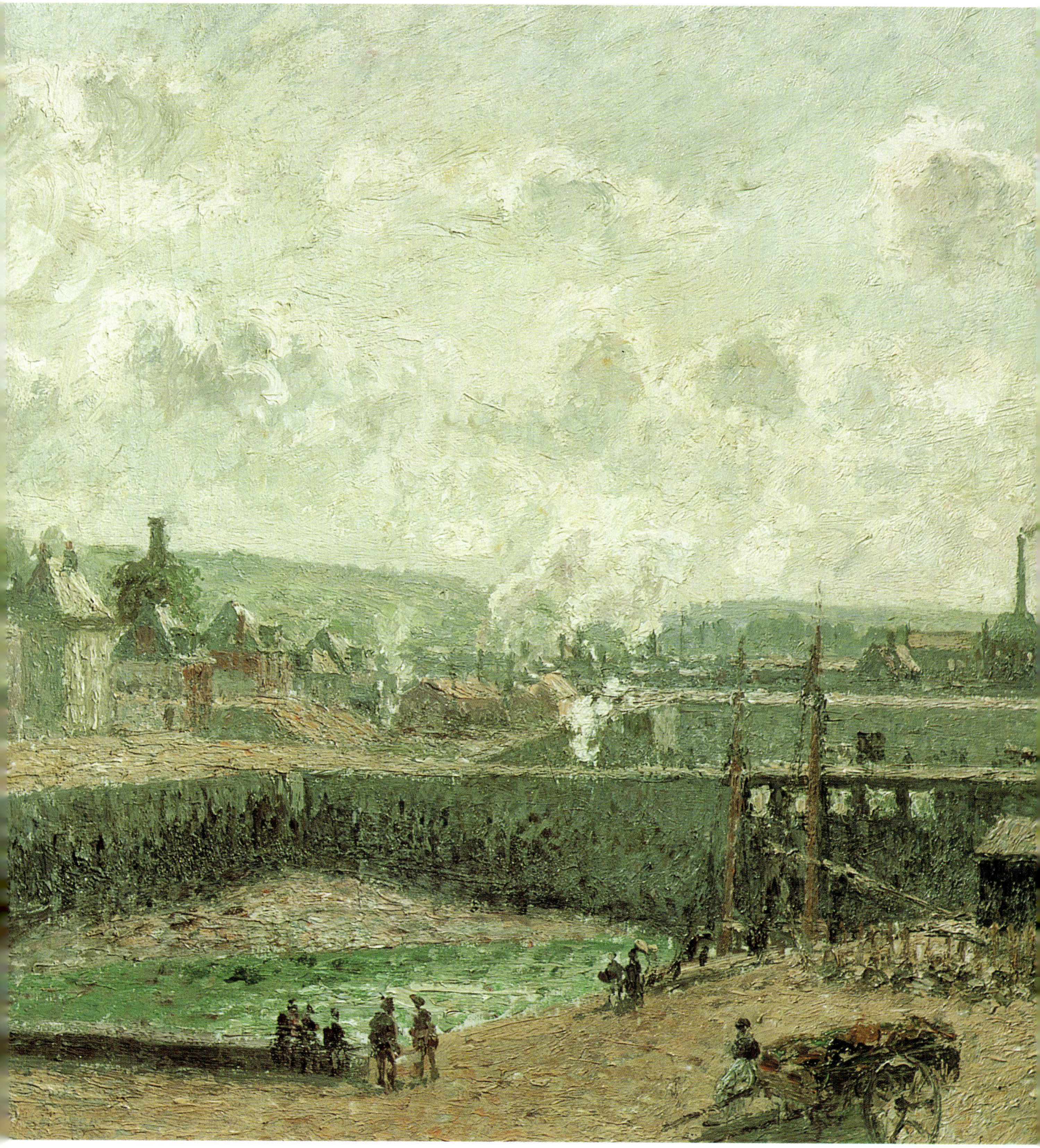

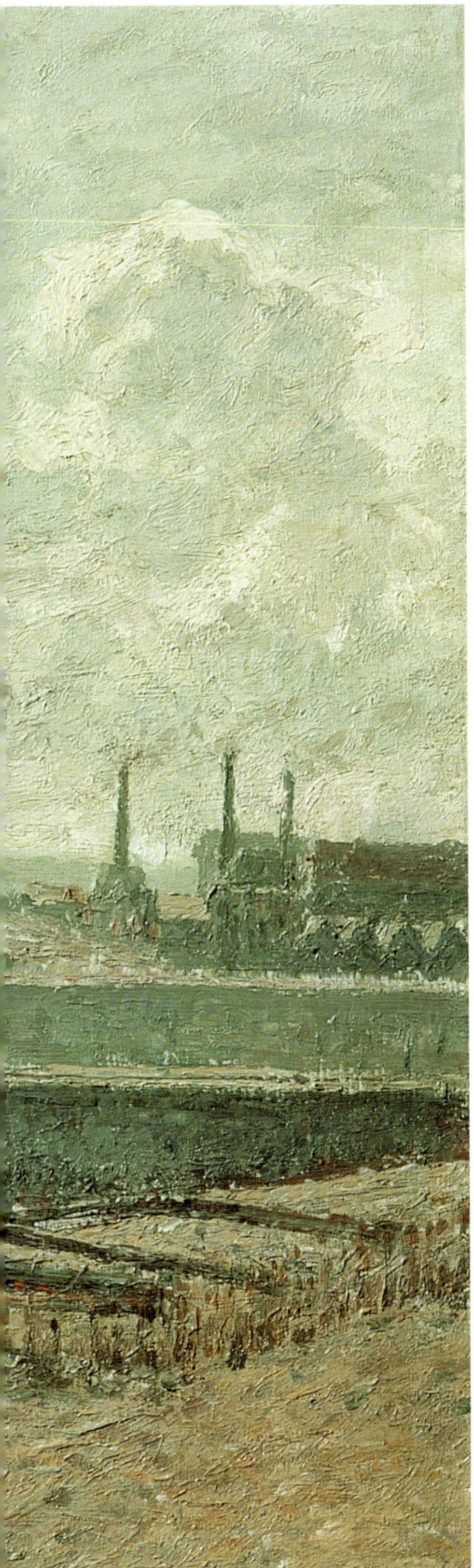

Camille Pissarro
Duquesne Basin, Dieppe, 1902

Musée d'Orsay, Paris. Courtesy of AKG London/Erich Lessing

THIS is one of several paintings of Dieppe harbour and town that Pissarro painted the year before his death. In it, he has returned to his early roots and the muted tones reminiscent of Corot as well as the slightly raised viewpoint from which he paints his subject at a distance. It is a tranquil painting, an effect achieved by the predominantly horizontal composition, the muted colours and the soft, rounded quality of the clouds, which merge so seamlessly with the smoke from the factory chimneys.

In 1903, Pissarro explained to his son how he painted: 'All I see is dabs of colour. When I begin a painting, the first thing that I fix is the accord ... The great problem that has to be solved is to bring everything in line with the overall harmony, with that accord I have spoken of.'

Pissarro died in Paris on 12 November 1903, while planning a series of paintings at Le Havre.

PIERRE-AUGUSTE RENOIR (1841–1919)
Engaged Couple (The Sisley Family), 1868

Wallraf-Richartz-Museum, Cologne. Courtesy of AKG London

RENOIR came from quite a poor family and worked as an apprentice in a ceramics factory and then a decorator of blinds before he entered the Académie des Beaux-Arts in 1862. He met Sisley the same year, along with Monet and Bazille, in the studio of the painter Gleyre. In 1864, he painted William Sisley, his friend's father, and the portrait was accepted at the Salon in 1865.

Ostensibly, this painting is a double portrait of Renoir's friend Alfred Sisley and his companion Eugène Lescouezec, although the woman may be Lise Tréhot, Renoir's mistress and favourite model at this time. Like the other artists of the group, Renoir has not yet come to the *plein-air*, 'impressionist' style that was to hold his attention during the 1870s. The background is flat - like a backdrop in a photographer's studio - and he shows very little interest in the natural effects of light. His handling of the figures is firm and the drawing precise (note the drawn contours of Sisley's leg). The palette is strong, using bold colours and black, and the style is suggestive of Manet. In 1919, a young Picasso (1881–1973) paid the painting homage in a series of line drawings.

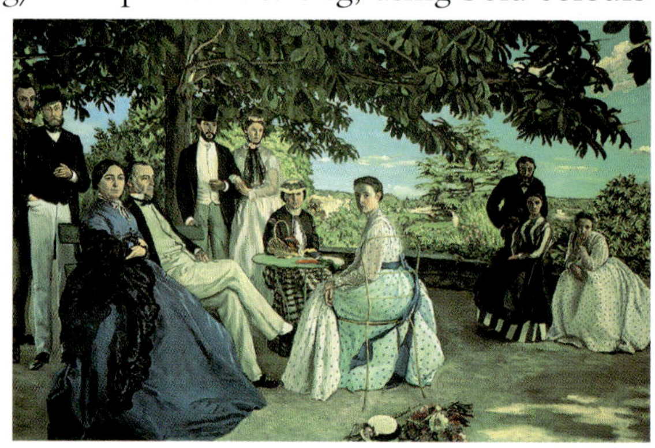

Frédéric Bazille
Family Reunion, 1867
Musée d'Orsay, Paris. Courtesy of AKG London. *(See p. 49)*

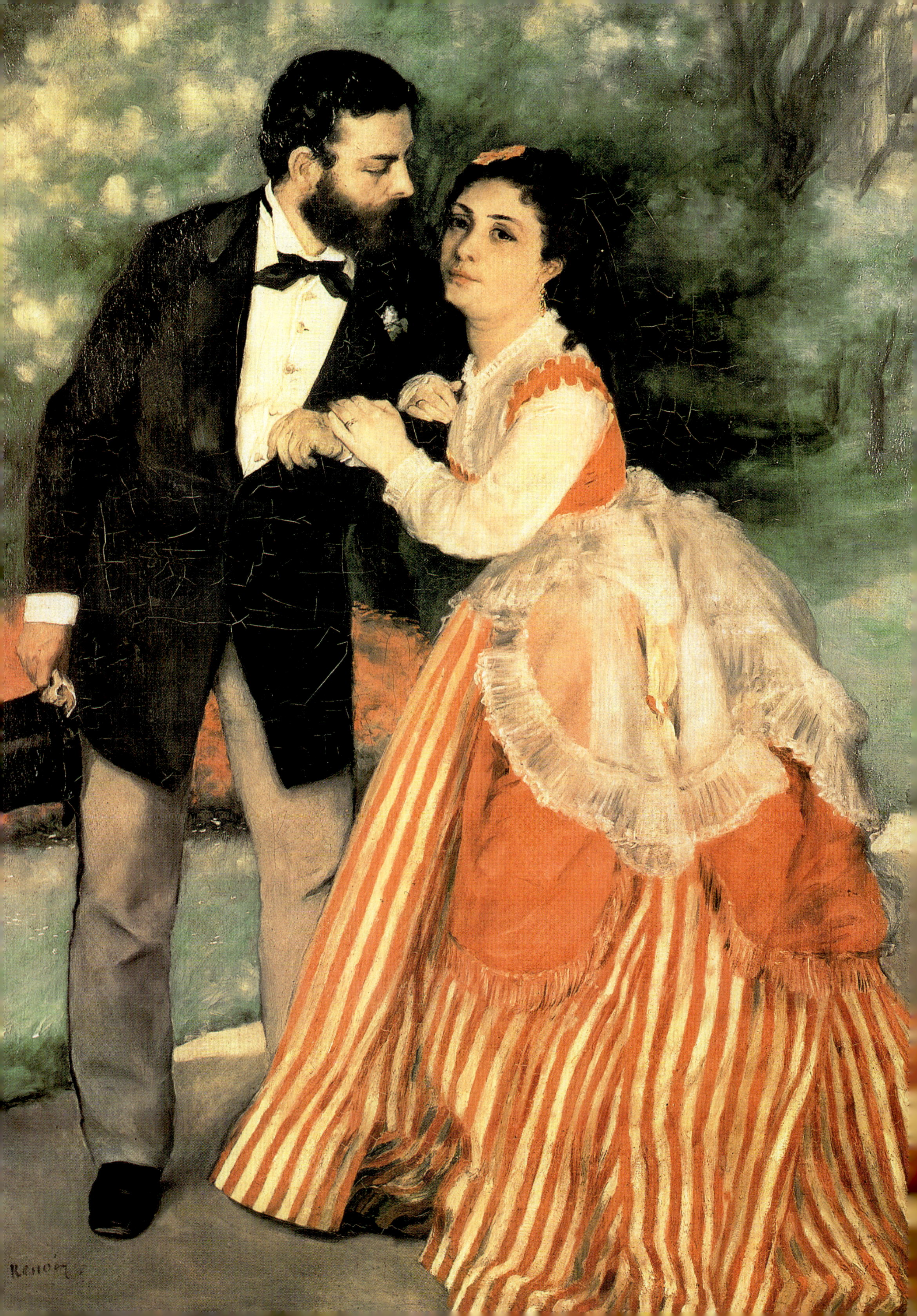
Renoir

Pierre-Auguste Renoir
La Grenouillère, 1870–71

Private Collection. Courtesy of AKG London

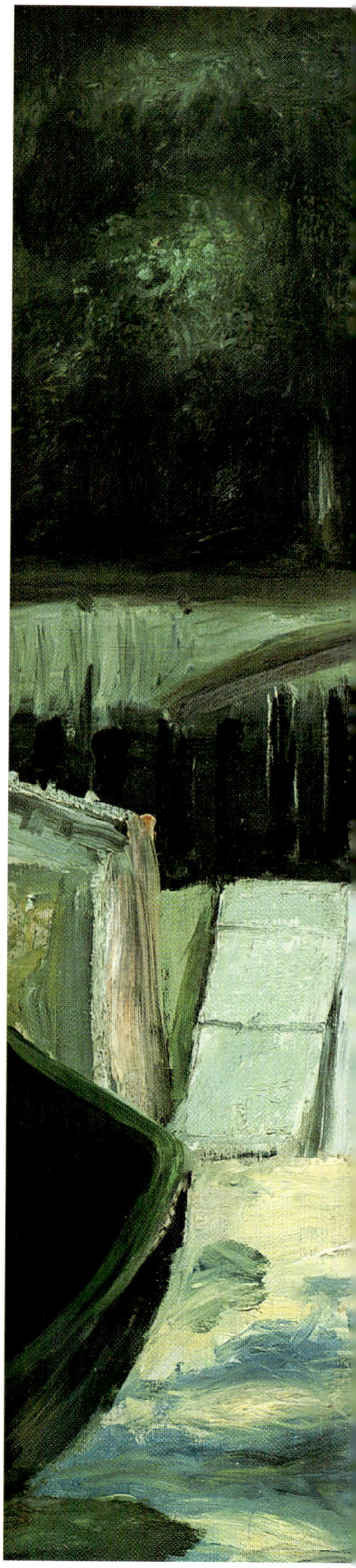

FROM 1869 Renoir painted several canvases of La Grenouillère, an open-air bathing establishment and café. He worked there in company with Monet. In September 1869, Monet wrote to Bazille of his intentions for the Salon of the following year: 'I have a dream, a painting of the bathing place at La Grenouillère. I have made a few poor sketches, but it is only a dream. Renoir, who has just spent two months here, also wants to paint the same picture.' Some of the paintings of the two friends are virtually identical and must have been painted side by side.

This painting, and the others, show Monet's growing influence on Renoir's palette and style. Painted outdoors to catch the effect of natural light on the world around him with brisk, fleeting brushmarks, his palette has lightened and the world dissolves in a light- and shadow-filled haze.

However, the young, flirting couple indicate where Renoir's interests also lie. He is as captivated by their fun as he is by the effects of light on nature – a light-heartedness increased by the 'snapshot' effect created by the hull of the boat on the left and the rather large dog in the middle. His interest in people is made clear by the choice of contemporary, human subjects in many of his other works.

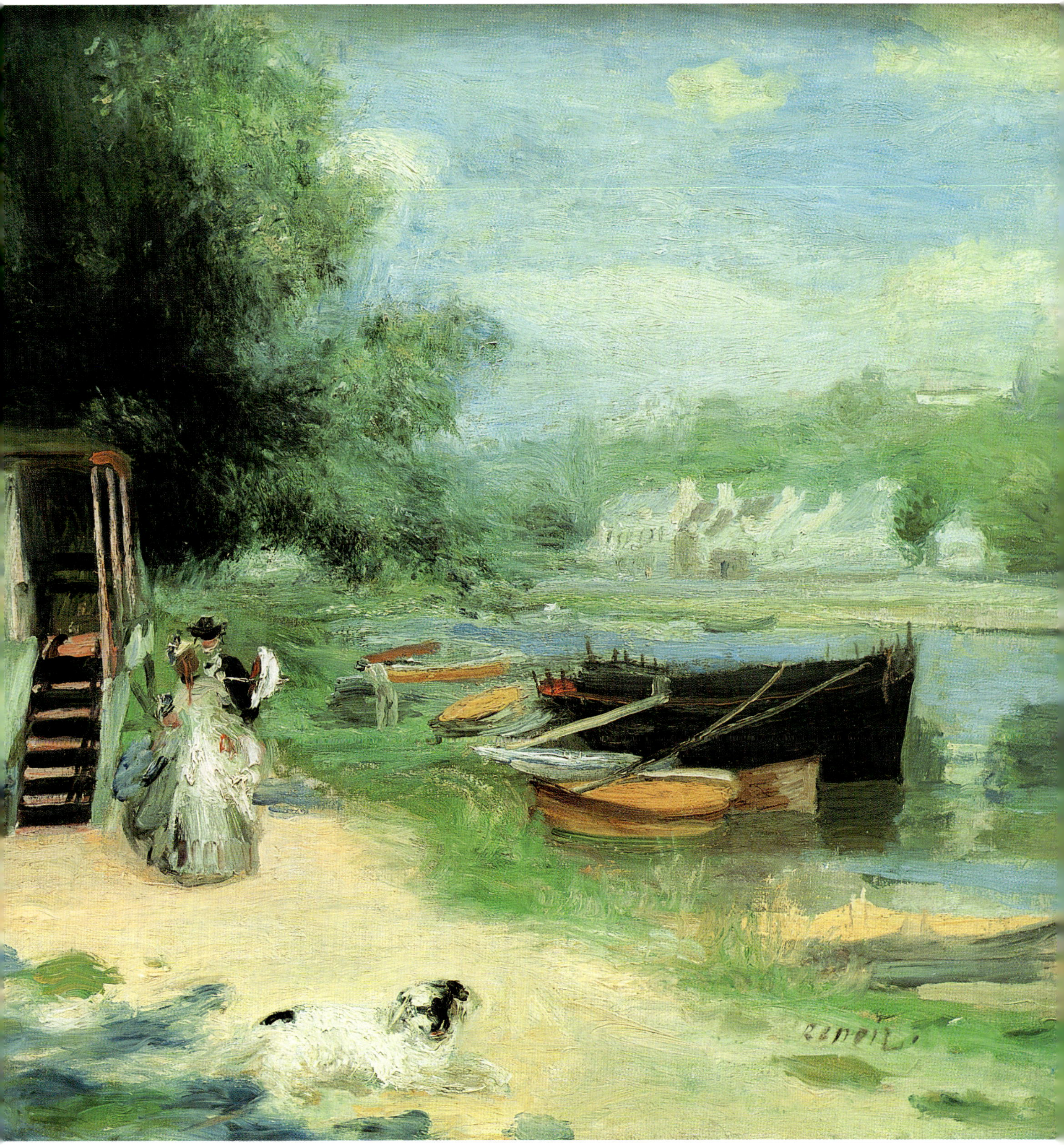

Pierre-Auguste Renoir
Portrait of Rapha, 1870–71

Private Collection. Courtesy of AKG London

BY the time this portrait was painted the craze for all things Japanese was upon the art world of Paris. This is believed to be a portrait of the mistress of Edmond Maître, a close friend of Bazille, who is seen playing the piano in *Bazille's Studio* (1870).

This painting shows a tall, elegant girl against a formal patterned wallpaper holding a japanese fan and staring out of a window. The light floods in, falling on her dress and the flowers that half surround her. The wall behind her is in shadow, indicated by a darker tone rather than an 'impressionist' change in colour. A birdcage stands in front of the window, suggesting a genre scene of the type popular in eighteenth-century French painting, evident in the work of painters such a François Boucher (1703–70) and Jean-Honoré Fragonard (1732– 1806), which Renoir always admired. In his later work, the influence of their light touch and joyfulness are plain to see. It is an informal portrait in the way that it depicts Rapha, but the composition, with the flowers, the fan and the trellised wallpaper, and the tight brushwork, give the painting formal air. Unusually for Renoir, whose work is characterised by a *joie de vivre*, Rapha seems pensive.

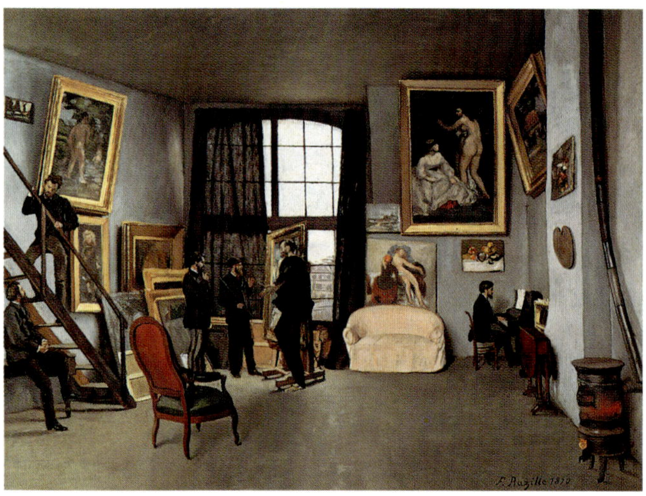

Frédéric Bazille
Bazille's Studio, 1870
Musée d'Orsay, Paris. Courtesy of AKG London/Erich Lessing. *(See p.50)*

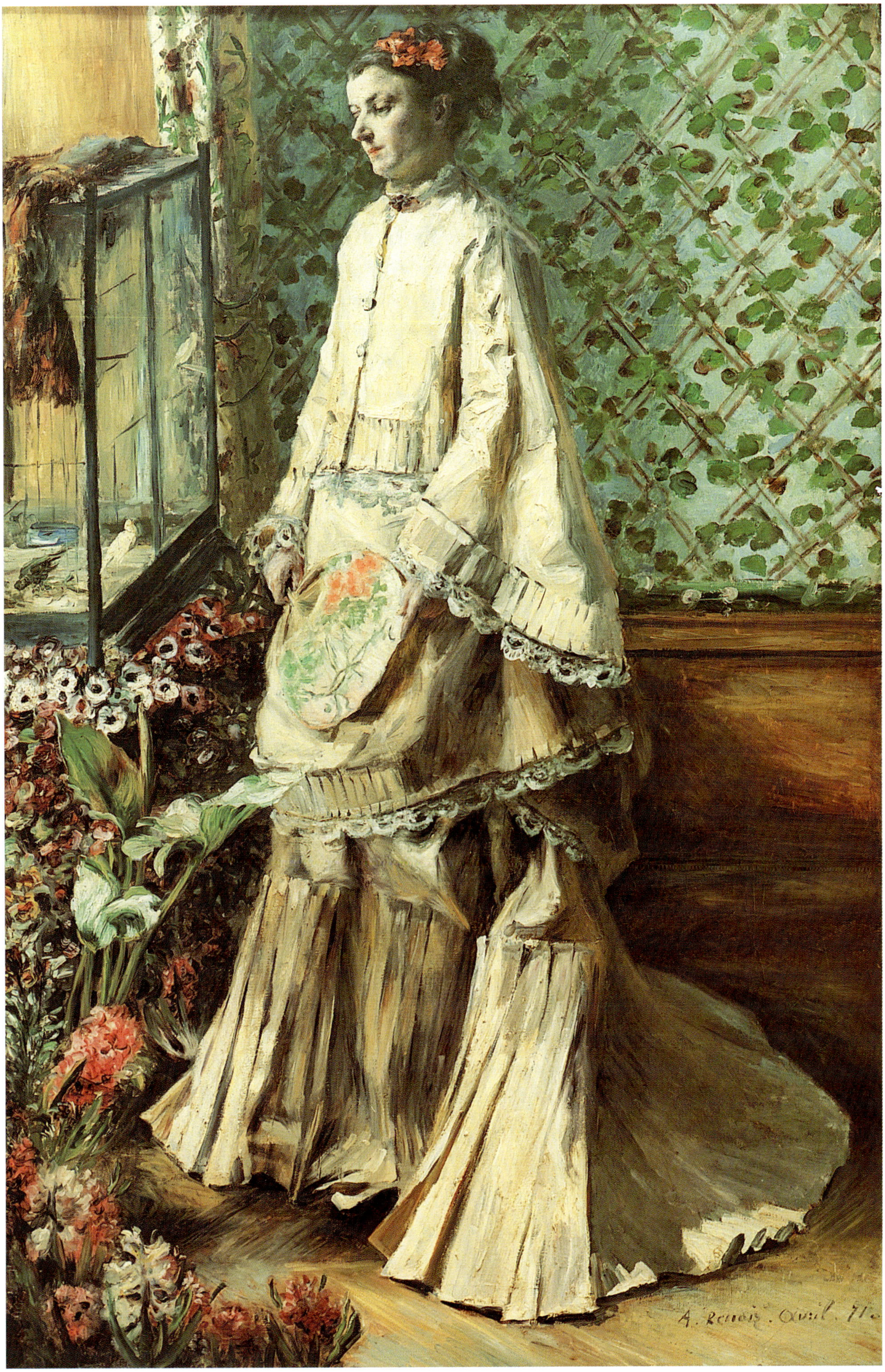
A. Renoir. Avril. 71.

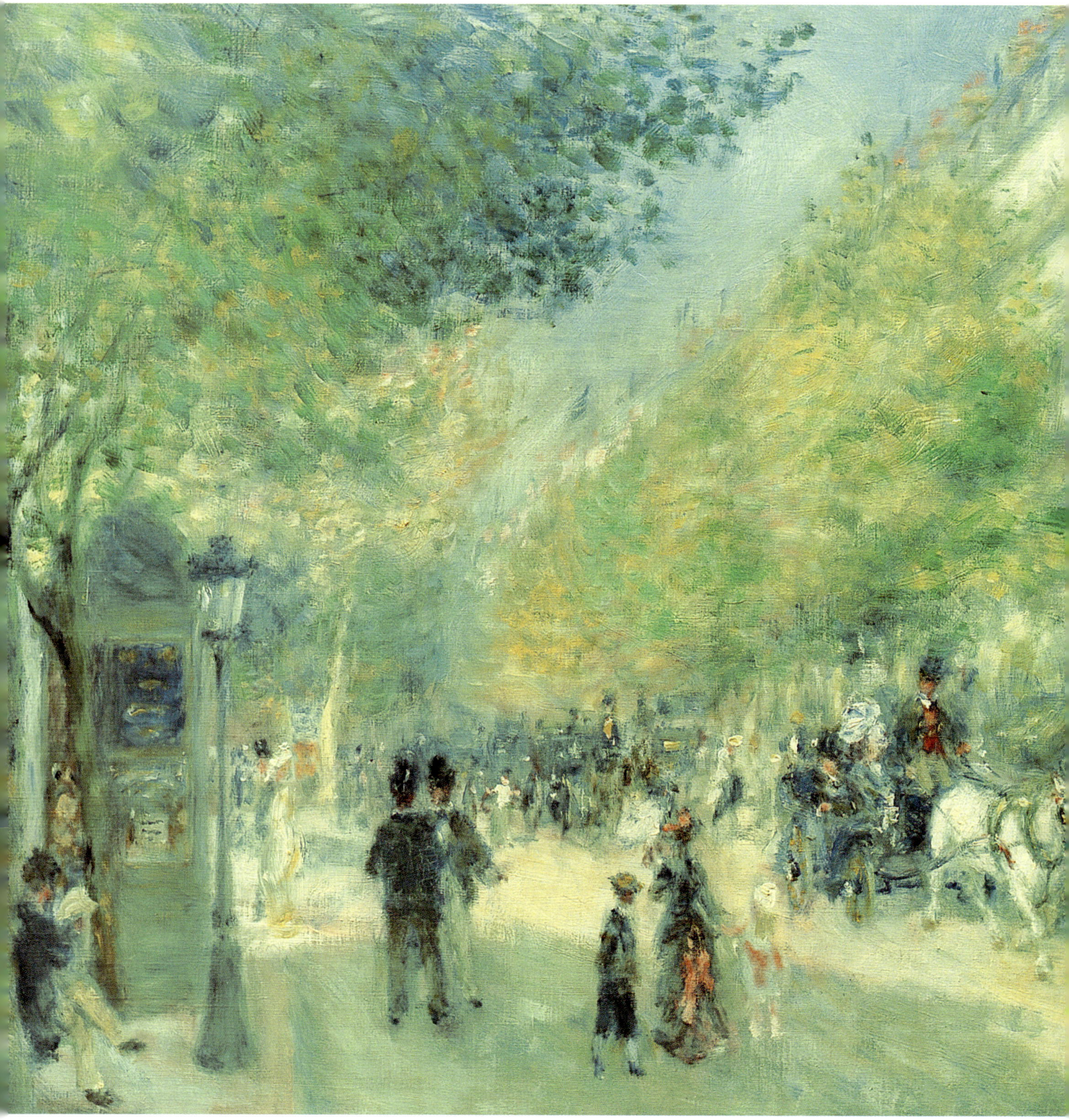

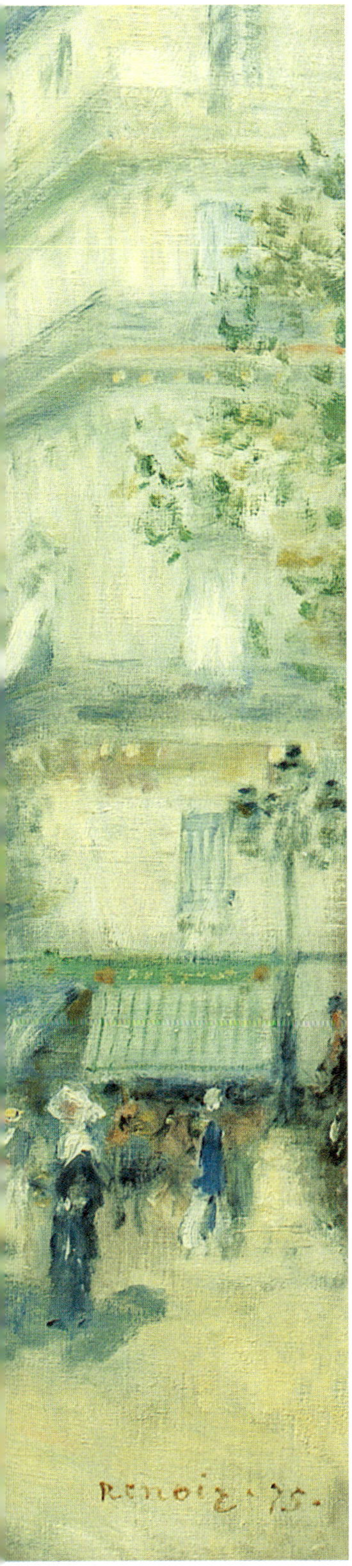

Pierre-Auguste Renoir
The Boulevards, 1875

Museum of Art, Philadelphia. Courtesy of AKG London

PAINTED during the great decade of Impressionism and a year after the first Impressionist exhibition in 1874, Renoir's street scene was reflected in the work of other artists such as Manet, Monet and Caillebotte. It shows a busy Parisian street painted in the shades you might expect to find in a painting of a summer afternoon in the country, and uses the limited, light, bright palette typical of the group.

The composition is full of busy detail, swift movement, people and horses moving in all directions. The figures, some of them brought to our attention by little dabs of red paint, are sketchy but surprisingly individual – note the nun on the right, the little girl holding her mother's hand as she seems to ask directions from the two men talking, the boy running between the wheels of the carriages in the background, the man reading a newspaper in the foreground on the left.

This painting revolves around white, blue and yellow. The sun is falling on to the street between the trees and the buildings; the shadows are blue – a feature shocking to the public of the time, who were used light changes being indicated by a change in the tonal value of the colour affected. The Impressionists were the first to use pure colour to indicate a change in light effects.

Pierre-Auguste Renoir
Moulin de la Galette, 1876

Musée d'Orsay, Paris. Courtesy of AKG London/Erich Lessing

RENOIR painted several scenes of Parisians enjoying themselves, and this is the first. It was exhibited at the third Impressionist exhibition (1877) and was well-received. According to Renoir's friend and biographer Georges Rivière, it was painted on the spot.

It is painted in a typically Impressionist manner, although the soft, caressing quality of the brushstrokes is a hallmark of Renoir's very specific style. He delights in the effect of the sunshine filtering through the trees, dappling the revellers with light. Pink and blue predominate – true to the Impressionist ideals even black is not shown as black but as a colour (or lack of colour) that changes when light falls on it. The light dissolves the shapes and contours and, in the left corner, even flattens the distance between the little girl and her mother and the area where people are dancing.

As ever, Renoir is fascinated by the people in his paintings and has created a lively scene with plenty of stories being played out. Cut off on all sides like a photograph, the painting shows a Japanese influence in an innovative composition, which divides the canvas almost diagonally from top right to bottom left with the foreground animation in the bottom half and the background details in the top half. The two sides are linked by the head of the standing girl but there is no loss of depth – the figures in the background rapidly diminish in size, drawing the eye in to the canvas.

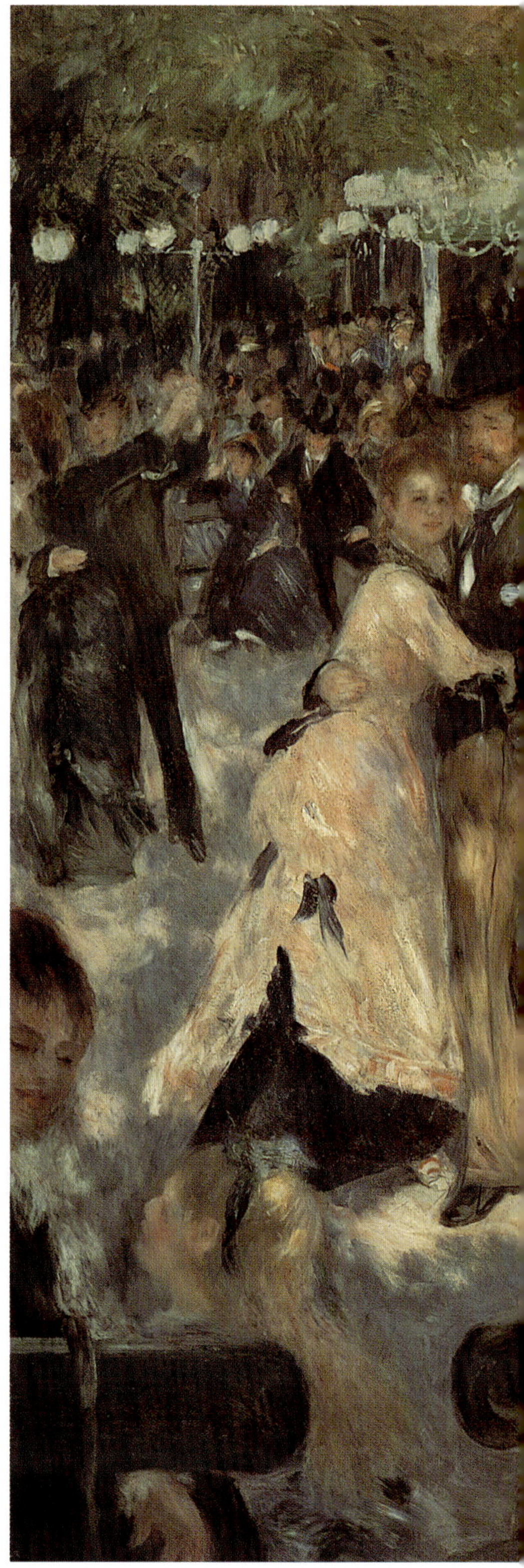

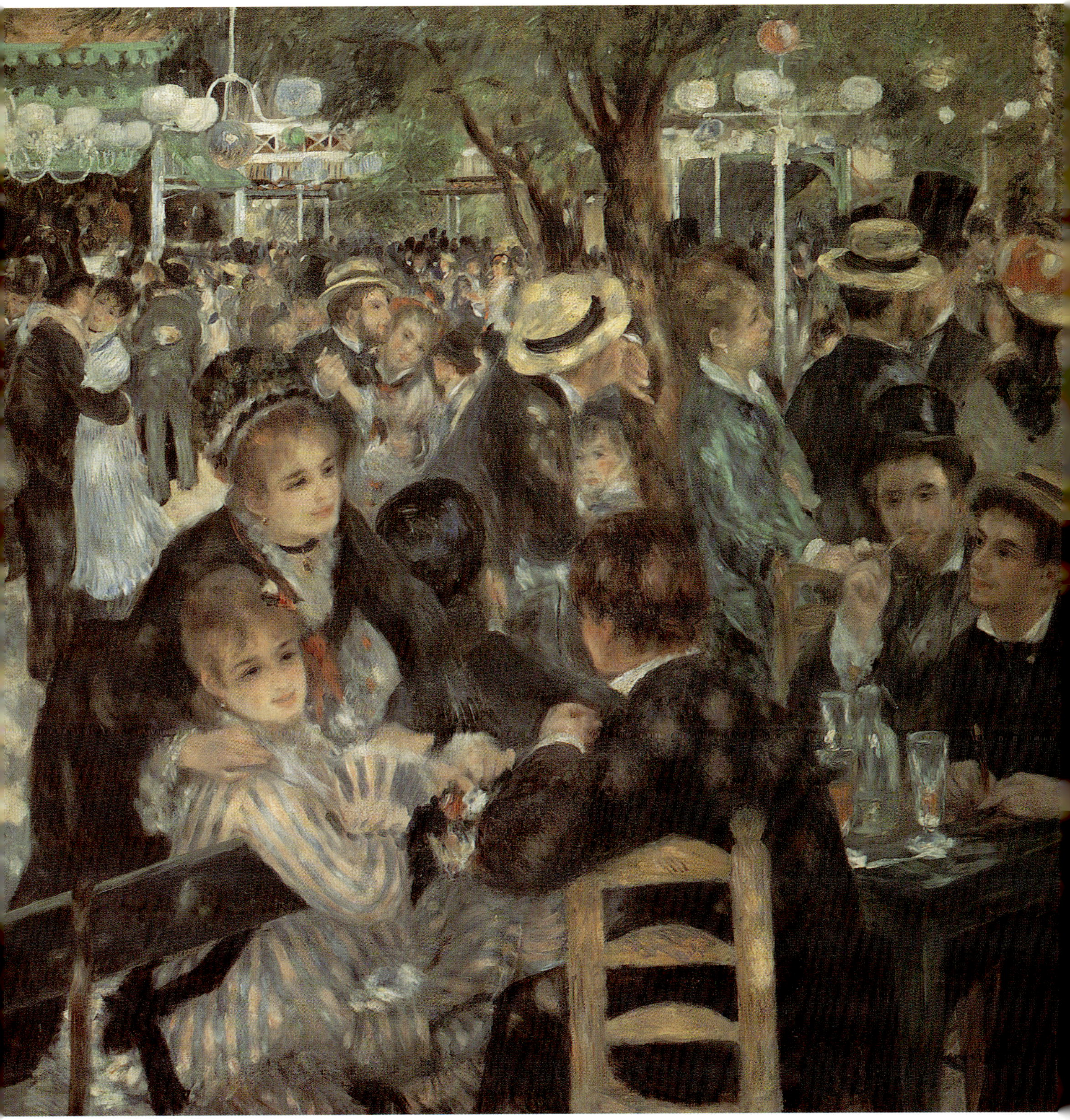

Pierre-Auguste Renoir
Nude in the Sunlight, 1876

Musée d'Orsay, Paris. Courtesy of AKG London/Erich Lessing

THIS delightful study of a nude was shown at the second Impressionist exhibition of 1876. A few critics liked it, calling it a 'superbly coloured study', 'well posed and well-lit' and the critic Armand Sylvestre wrote of '[the] delightful pink flesh tone … the work of a great colourist'. But Albert Wolff, critic for the French daily newspaper, *Le Figaro,* savaged it: 'Try to explain to M. Renoir that a woman's torso is not a mass of flesh in the process of decomposition with the green and purplish blotches which denote the state of complete putrefaction of a corpse …!'

In exhibiting a study, Renoir was challenging the critics. The composition is daring: the nude is slightly off-centre, the brushwork loose (something for which Renoir had already been criticised) and the background abstract, with parts of the canvas bare. The light, filtered through leaves above that we cannot see, falls on the girl's body, dappling it with light and blue shadows. Her face blurs under the diffusing qualities of the light. Except for the bracelet and the ring that indicate her modern status, she is a timeless nymph. The change in style since *Portrait of Rafa* (1870–71), for example, is clear.

The model may be a girl called Anna who died, aged 23, in February 1879. Renoir wrote to his friend Dr Gachet (1828–1909) asking him to go and see her.

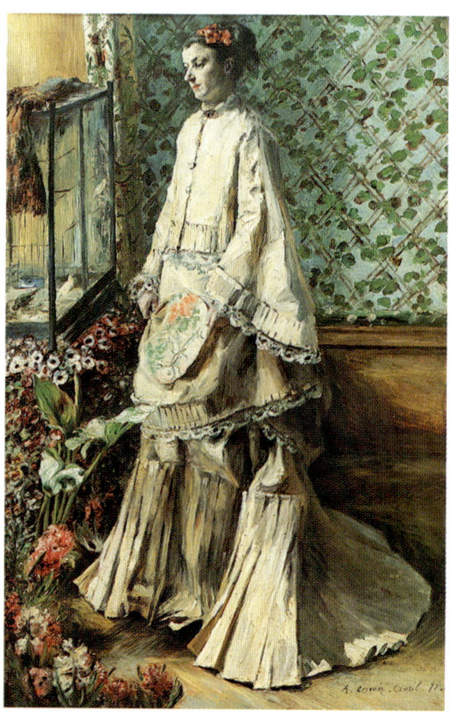

Pierre-Auguste Renoir
Portrait of Rapha, 1870–71
Private Collection. Courtesy of AKG London.
(See p. 128)

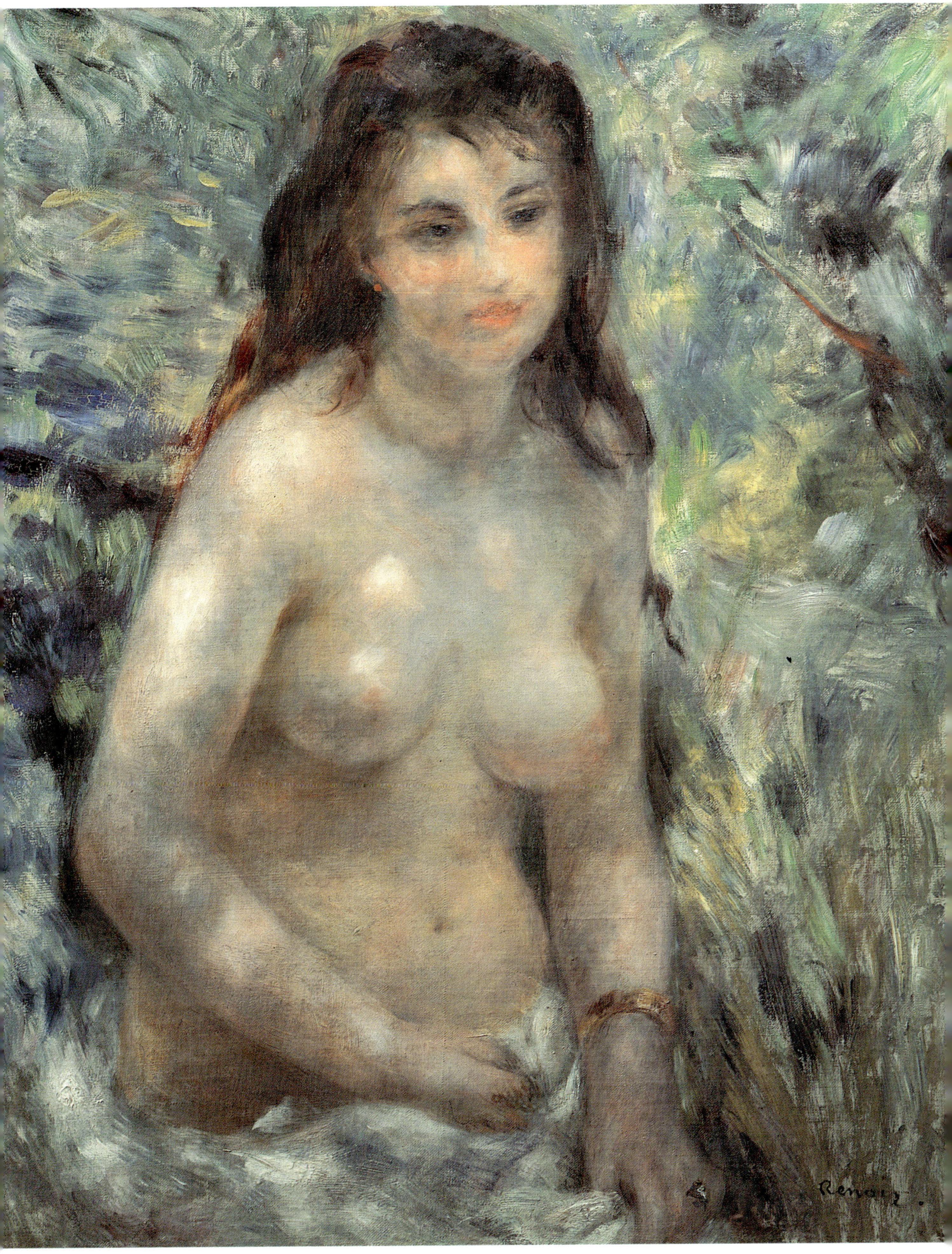
Renoir.

Pierre-Auguste Renoir
Path Climbing Up Through the Tall Grass, c. 1876–77

Musée d'Orsay, Paris. Courtesy of AKG London/Erich Lessing

THIS lovely painting shows Impressionism in true Monet style and bears a resemblance to his paintings of poppy fields of 1873. Four patchy figures descend a path towards the viewer, a little girl in front, a woman with a red parasol behind her followed, at a distance, by two figures side by side and deep in conversation – a theme Renoir treated in closer proximity on several occasions in paintings such as *The Moulin de la Galette* (1876), for example.

Only the trees betray a darker effect than one might expect – bearing little relation, for example, to the bright trees of *The Boulevards* (1875) painted the same year. These, in their dark delicacy, recall the influence of the landscapist Corot, whom Renoir admired. The contrast between the trees and the hillside is enhanced by the wet-on-wet technique that Renoir uses to paint the soft, light-filled blurry background of the hillside. In the foreground and middleground, where the light falls, he has used a thick impasto. As is often the case in these green, blue, white, and yellow canvases, Renoir uses tiny dabs of red to create a stronger contrast and make the colours resonate. In this case, it also leads the eye towards the apex of a triangle – the woman's red parasol.

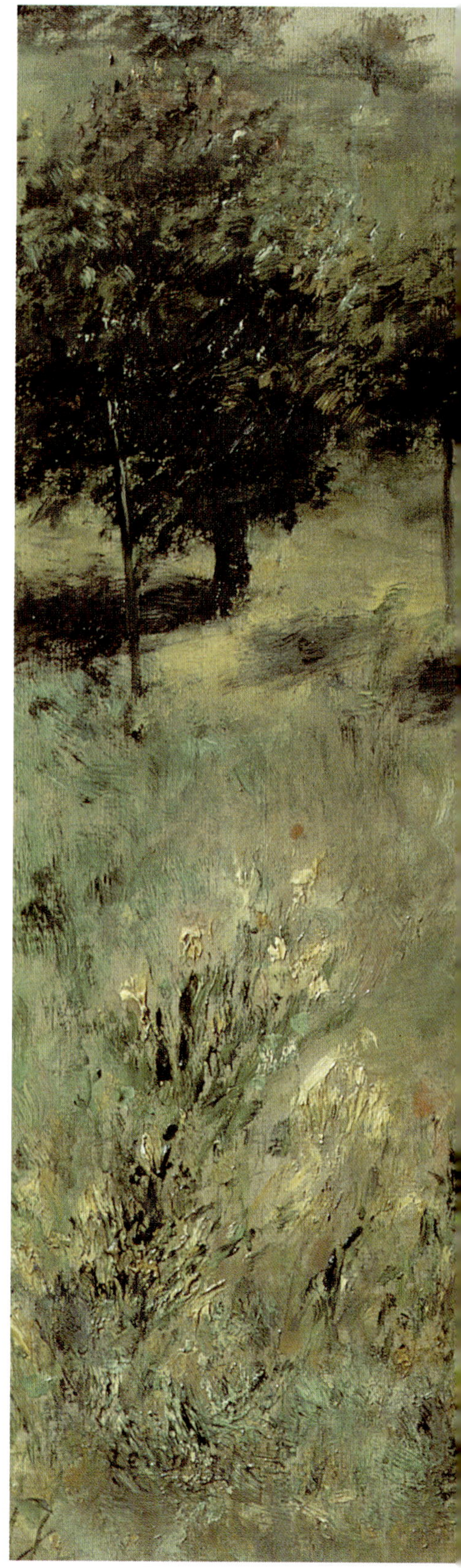

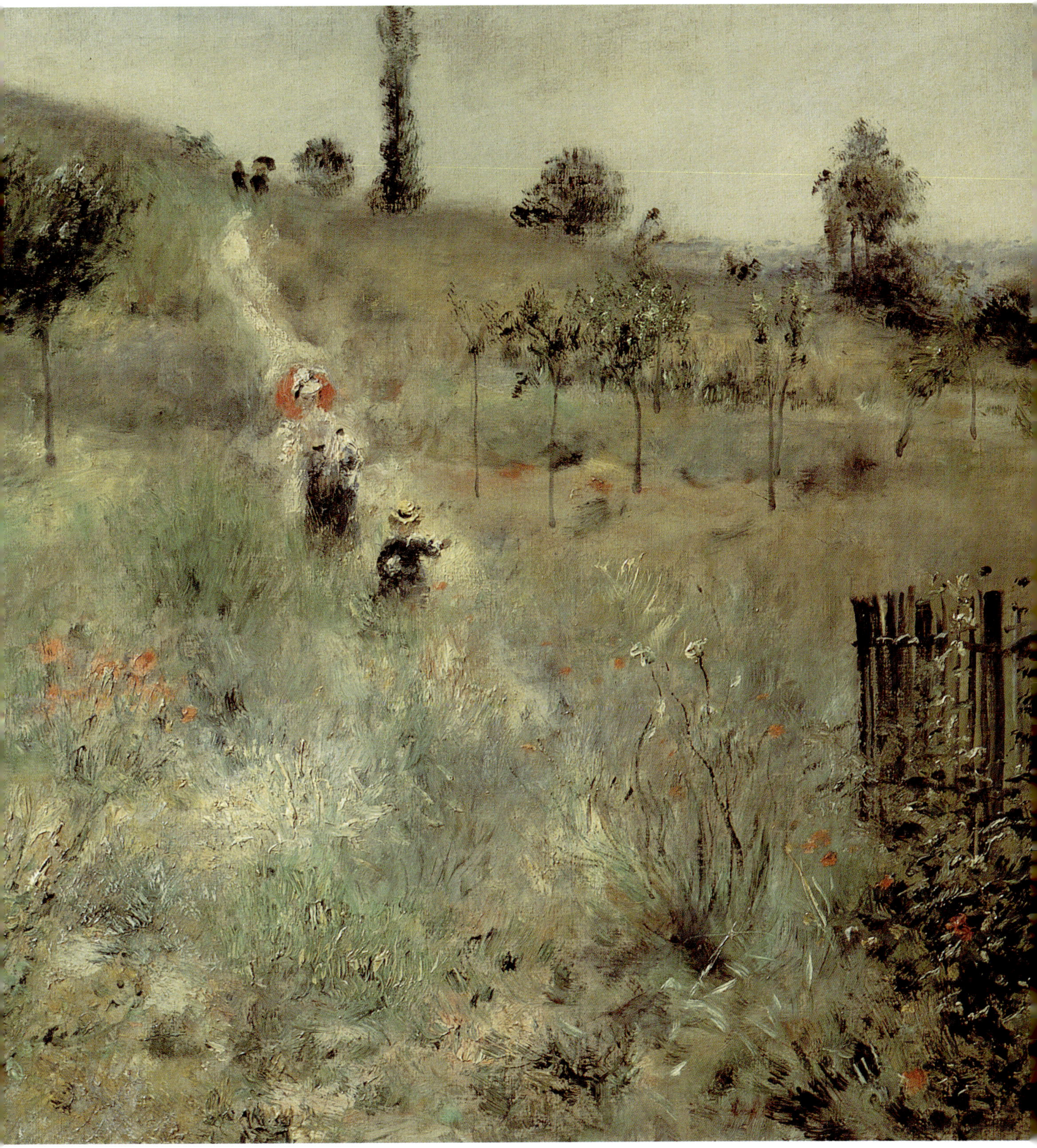

Pierre-Auguste Renoir
Madame Georges Charpentier, 1876–78
Musée d'Orsay, Paris. Courtesy of AKG London/Erich Lessing

MADAME Georges Charpentier (1848–1905) was the wife of the publisher Georges Charpentier, one of Renoir's early patrons. Married in 1872, Madame Charpentier's salon soon became a famous literary and left-wing meeting place. Her guests included Renoir and Manet.

Charpentier first bought three of Renoir's paintings in 1875. Through him, Renoir received several commissions that kept him solvent. In 1879, he had a great success at the Salon with a landscape portrait of *Madame Charpentier and her Two Children* (1878). In 1880, the art dealer Durand-Ruel began to buy Renoir's work regularly, after which Renoir was never financially insecure again.

This portrait is fairly conventional in style – as was necessary in order to attract commissions – but the Impressionistic patchy, loose brushwork, seen in Renoir's works as soft, feathery brushstrokes, is clear and especially flattering to female sitters. Renoir continued in this style until the early to mid 1980s. But until then he was painting contemporary Parisian scenes and portraits – especially of children, whom he portrayed in all their childlike softness and gentle innocence. Renoir did not exhibit at the fourth, fifth and sixth Impressionist exhibitions in 1879, 1880 and 1881. By 1880, the dynamics of the group were changing, with severe internal disagreements.

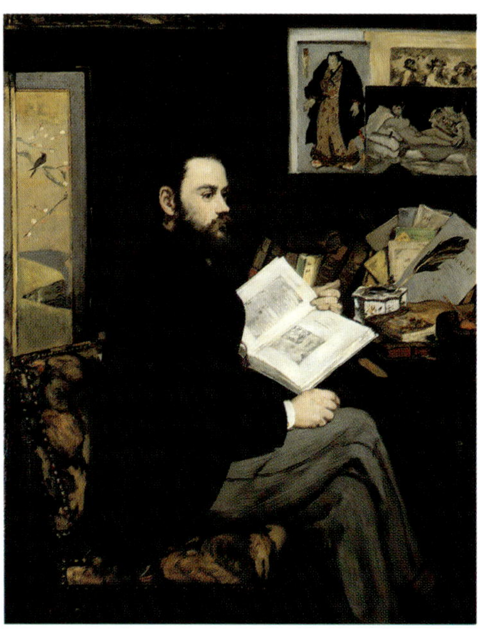

Edouard Manet
Portrait of Émile Zola, 1868
Musée du Louvre, Paris. Courtesy of AKG London. *(See p. 25)*

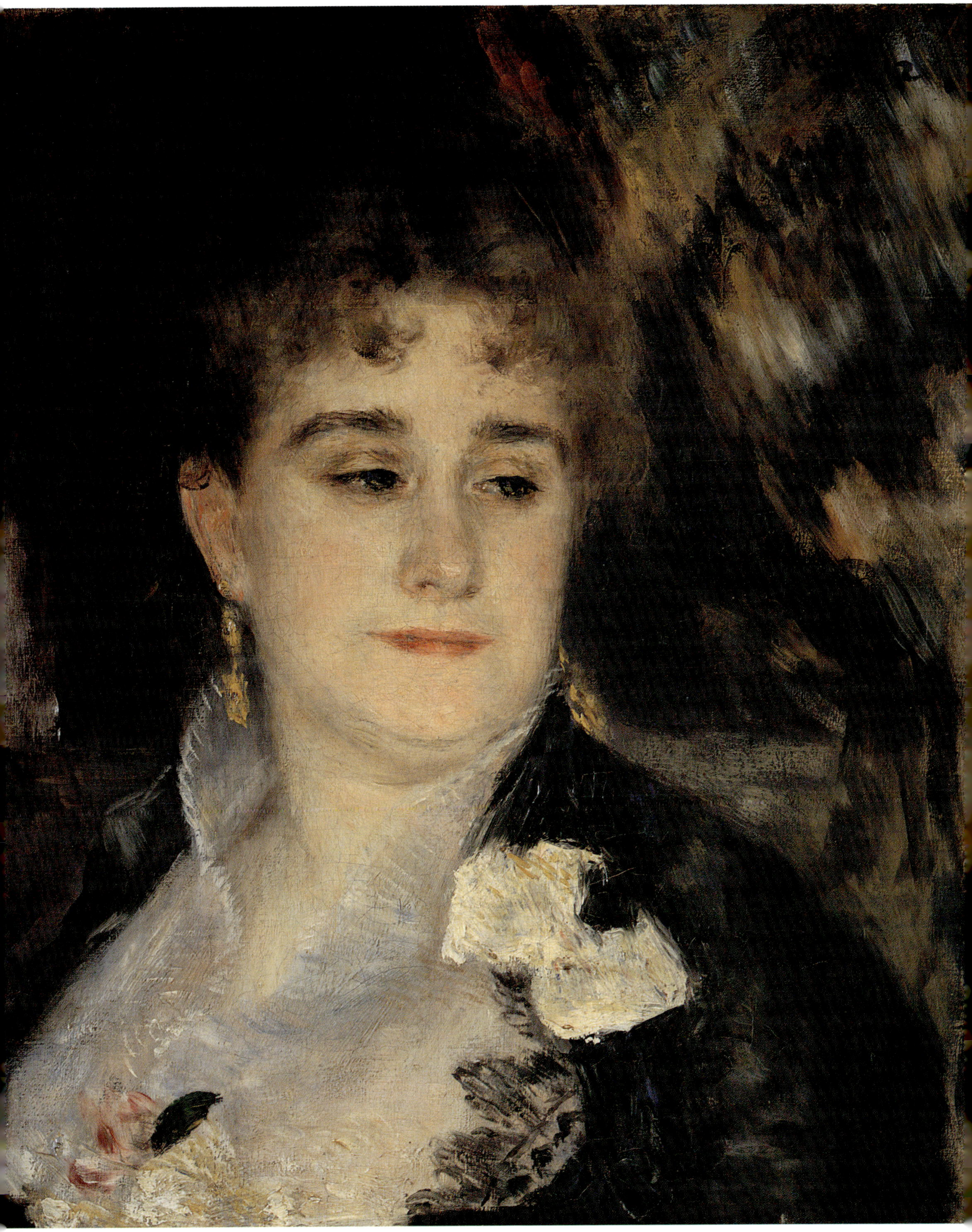

Pierre-Auguste Renoir
Dance in the Country, 1883

Musée d'Orsay, Paris. Courtesy of AKG London

THIS is one of Renoir's many scenes of contemporary life in which people are shown enjoying themselves. A young couple dance energetically, the man's hat having already fallen off, enjoying the closeness that social dancing allows. The scene is firmly placed at a specific moment, with the remnants of a meal to the right and, to the left, people continuing their meals.

It was designed as a pendant to *Dance in the City*, one of three almost life-size canvases of dancing couples that Renoir began in spring 1883. They were among the last of his paintings to show contemporary life.

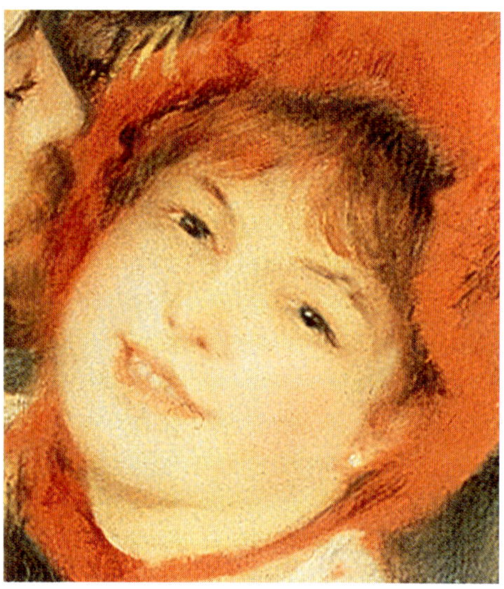

Dance in the Country shows Renoir's incessant *joie de vivre*, his belief that all paintings should be a pleasurable experience arousing the senses. Here, the young woman, Renoir's mistress Aline Charigot whom he met in about 1880, smiles at the viewer – a picture of sturdy, rude health so typical of Renoir's models.

The Impressionist palette remains, as does the blurry background and the use of complementary colours to enhance brightness, but the figures have taken on a new clarity. This, coupled with the clean contours of the dancers, reflects the lessons Renoir learnt on a trip to Italy in 1881 where he had discovered Raphael (1483–1520) and concluded that he had never really learnt how to draw or paint. By the mid-1880s he had turned to the severest form of Classicism.

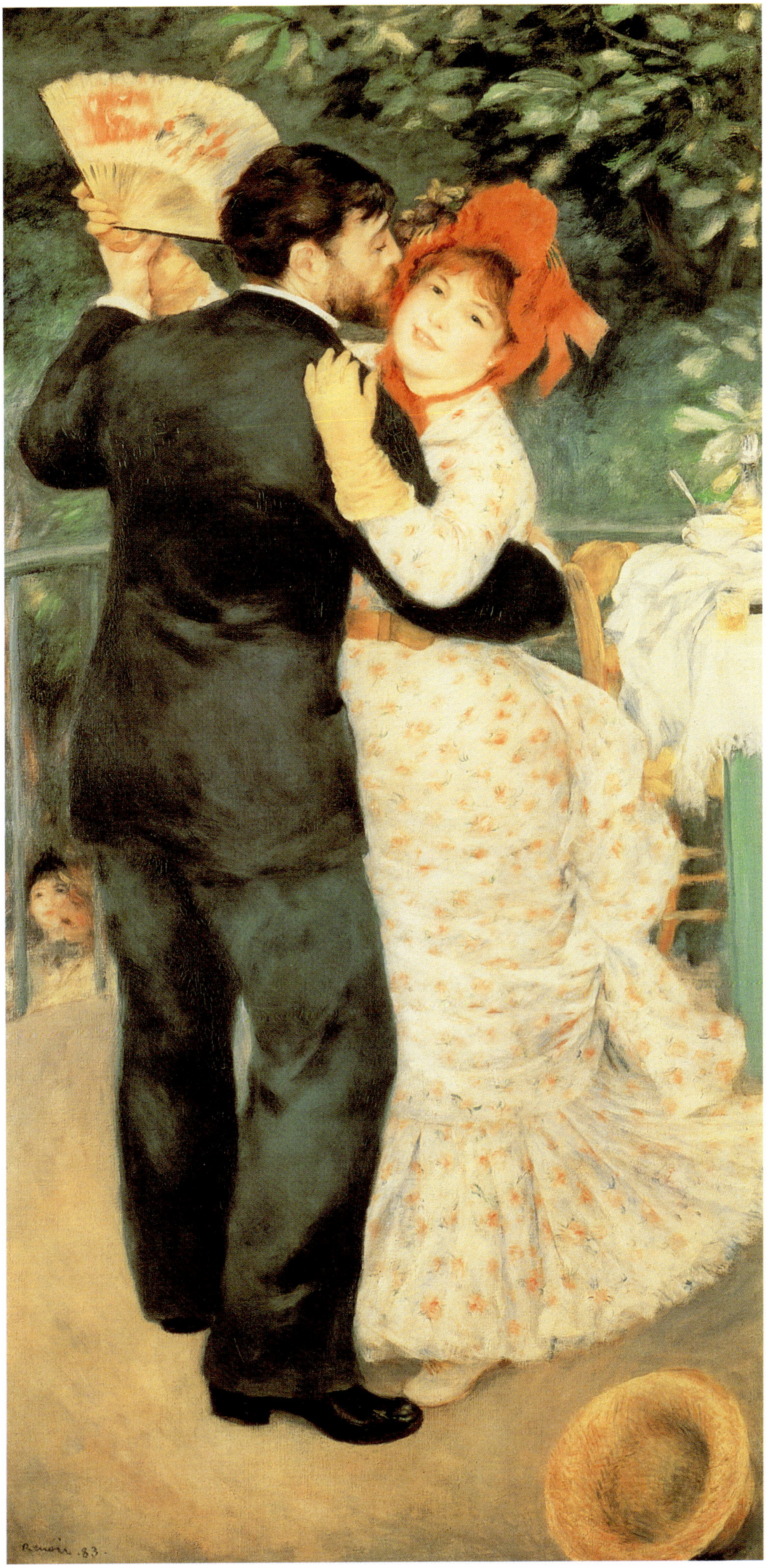
Renoir .83.

Pierre-Auguste Renoir
The Plait, 1884

Stiftong, Baden. Courtesy of AKG London

THE *Plait* is a clear example of the 'dry', severely classical style that Renoir followed in the 1880s. It concentrates on well-moulded, clear-cut forms that are based on draughtsmanship. Gone are the sensuous, velvety forms of the 1870s and early 1880s, although the feathery brushstrokes, now much controlled, can still be seen in the treatment of the background. But everything has a firm contour, every edge is defined. Moreover, the subject-matter has a timeless quality – neither the girl's clothes, nor the background, betray the present day. In her state of semi-undress, we presume that she has just been or is about to go bathing outdoors, suggesting a pastoral theme. In contrast with Degas' nudes, for example, Renoir's girl and the bathers that were to follow over the next few years were depicted outside with no (or few) references to contemporary life. In later years Renoir was to refer to them as his 'nymphs'.

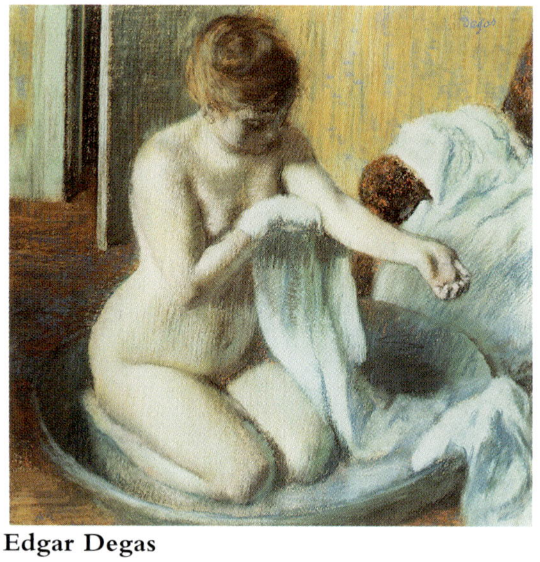

Edgar Degas
Woman in a Tub, 1885
Courtesy of AKG London. *(See p.182)*

The change in Renoir's work was the result of trips abroad that he had taken in 1881. Becoming dissatisfied with the Impressionist style and the path that he seemed to be taking as a portrait painter, he went to Algiers and to Italy. It was the Italian trip that brought about the style that he later distastefully referred to as 'sharp'. From his early days as a ceramic painter he had believed that the art of the past taught lessons and that, furthermore 'it is in the museums that one learns to paint'.

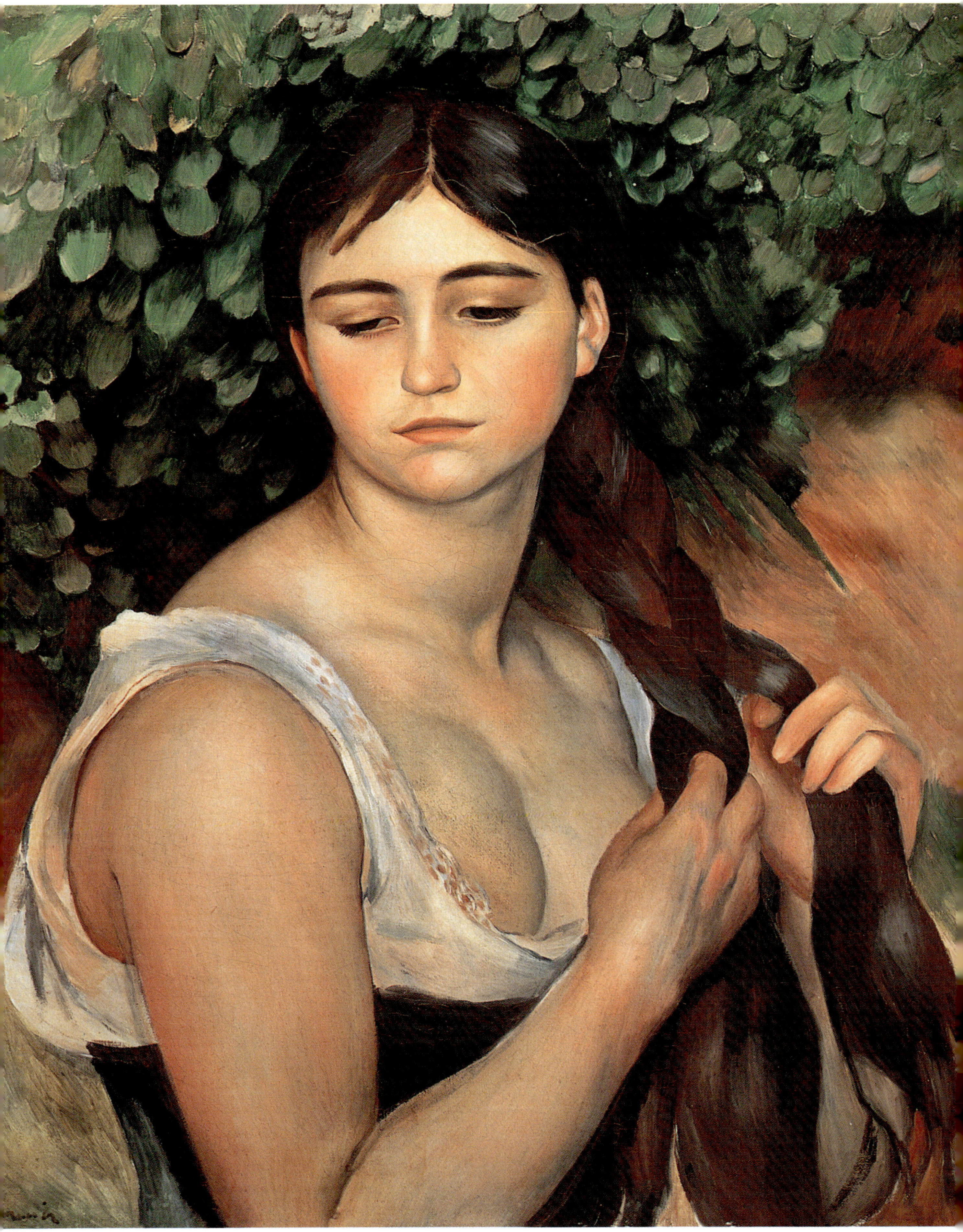

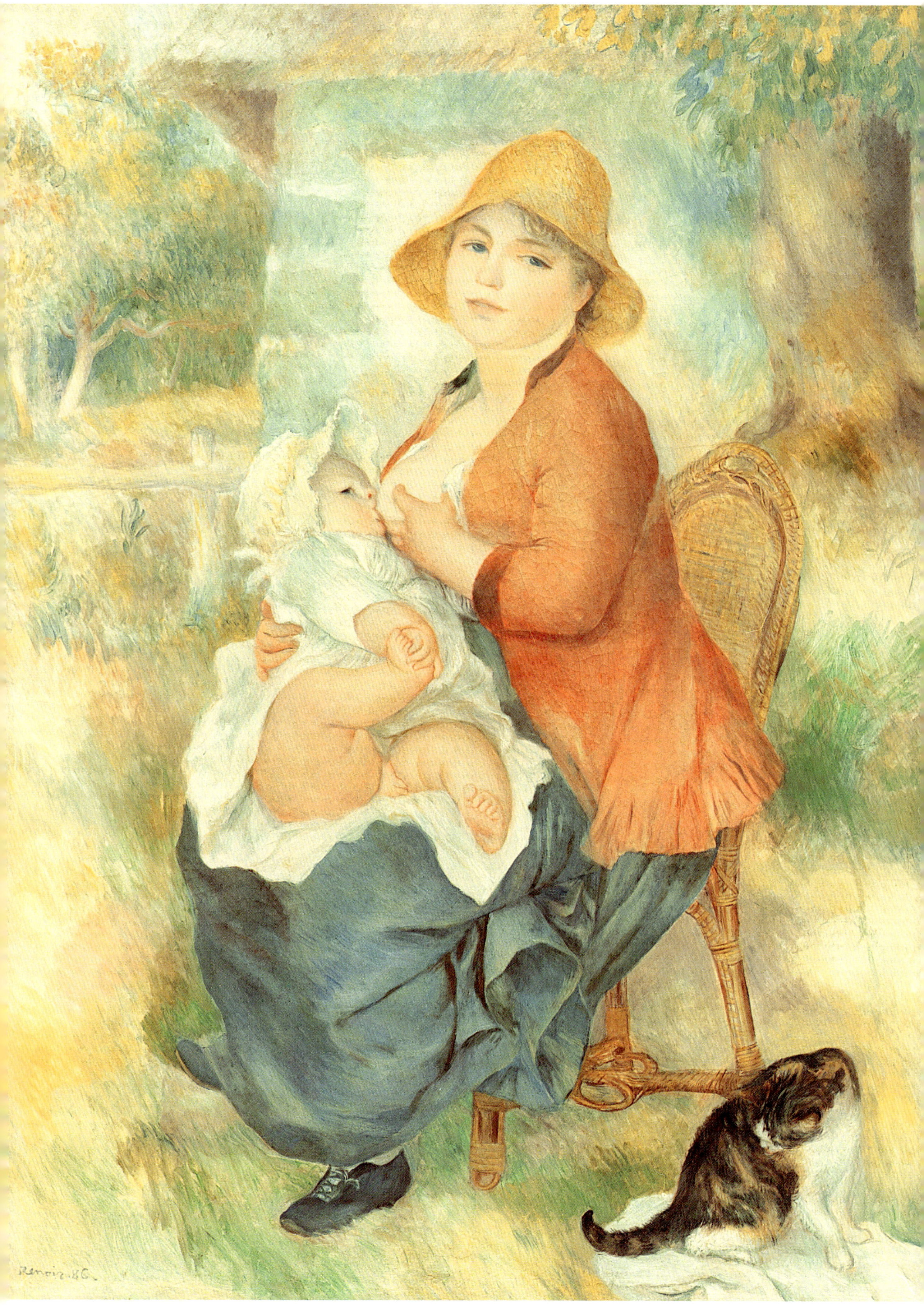
Renoir.86.

PIERRE-AUGUSTE RENOIR
Maternity; Woman Feeding Her Baby, 1886

Courtesy of AKG London

PAINTED in 1886, the year of the last Impressionist exhibition, Renoir did not submit this, or any other entry. Of the old guard, only Degas, Pissarro and Morisot exhibited. Nonetheless, the group still saw each other and between 1880 and 1894 had monthly dinners at the Café Riche in Paris.

This painting is in the Classical style that Renoir had favoured from the mid-1880s, although the palette and the brushstrokes are in the Impressionist style. Painted in oils, but so thinly and with such a light touch that you might think it pencil and wash, it shows Renoir's partner Aline with their baby, Pierre, who was born in 1884.

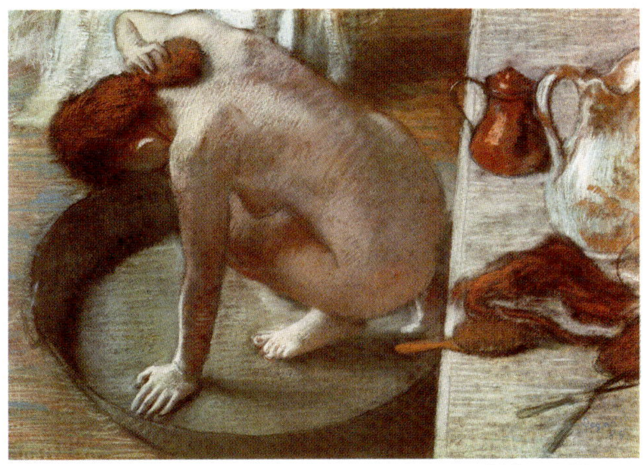

Edgar Degas
The Tub, 1886
Musée d'Orsay, Paris. Courtesy of AKG London. *(See p. 185)*

Berthe Morisot, who became a good friend of Renoir's, mentions her first visit to his studio in 1886 where she saw ' ... a red pencil and chalk drawing of a young woman nursing her child, charming and gracious in its subtlety' – a sketch relating to this painting. Morisot clearly did not recognise the models. Few people in his cultivated, society group of patrons and friends knew of Renoir's ménage. Renoir kept his two worlds separate. Morisot only learnt of Aline and Pierre's existence in 1891, 15 months after the couple married, when Renoir, who used to stay with Morisot's family in the country, sometimes for weeks at a time, brought his wife and child on a visit one day, although he failed to introduce them to Morisot.

Pierre-Auguste Renoir
Young Girls at the Piano, 1892

Musée d'Orsay, Paris. Courtesy of AKG London/Erich Lessing

SIX versions of this painting exist. The earliest was painted in 1889 and the rest when the French government asked Renoir to paint a new picture for the Musée de Luxembourg, which exhibited the work of France's leading, living artists. The commission caused Renoir much worry – hence the many versions, which showed slight variations in the backgrounds and in the poses of the two girls, particularly the arm of the brunette. This is the version that the Luxembourg chose.

The theme is very much in keeping with the overall tenor of Renoir's work in the 1890s – genre scenes depicting natural, harmonious youth, usually young girls walking, talking, gathering flowers or sitting in meadows. The piano theme has clear links with the images painted by the French eighteenth-century artists that Renoir so much admired. The models in all these paintings appear to be the same, and the brunette in pink and the blonde in white with a blue sash (although the dress patterns vary) run throughout.

This picture is not a double portrait; there is no psychological intent. Harmony rules in a timeless world; this is no 'passing moment'. The soft, supple brushwork so typical of Renoir is still in evidence and the pure, bright palette remains, but there is no doubt that he is no longer working in the Impressionist idiom of the 1870s.

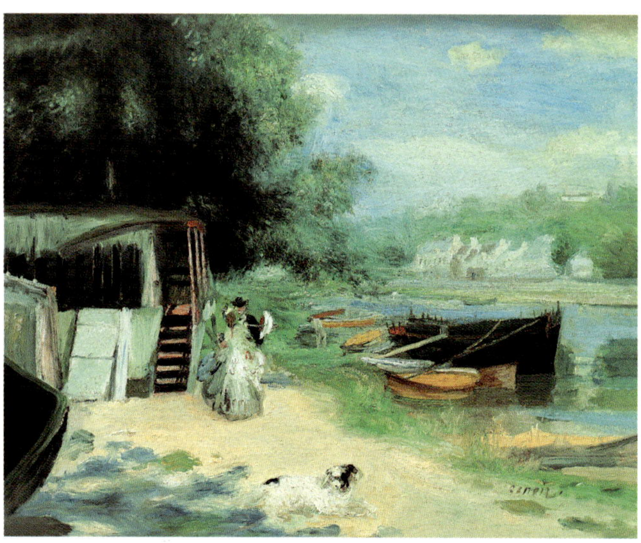

Pierre-Auguste Renoir
La Grenouillère, 1870–71
Private Collection. Courtesy of AKG London. *(See p. 126)*

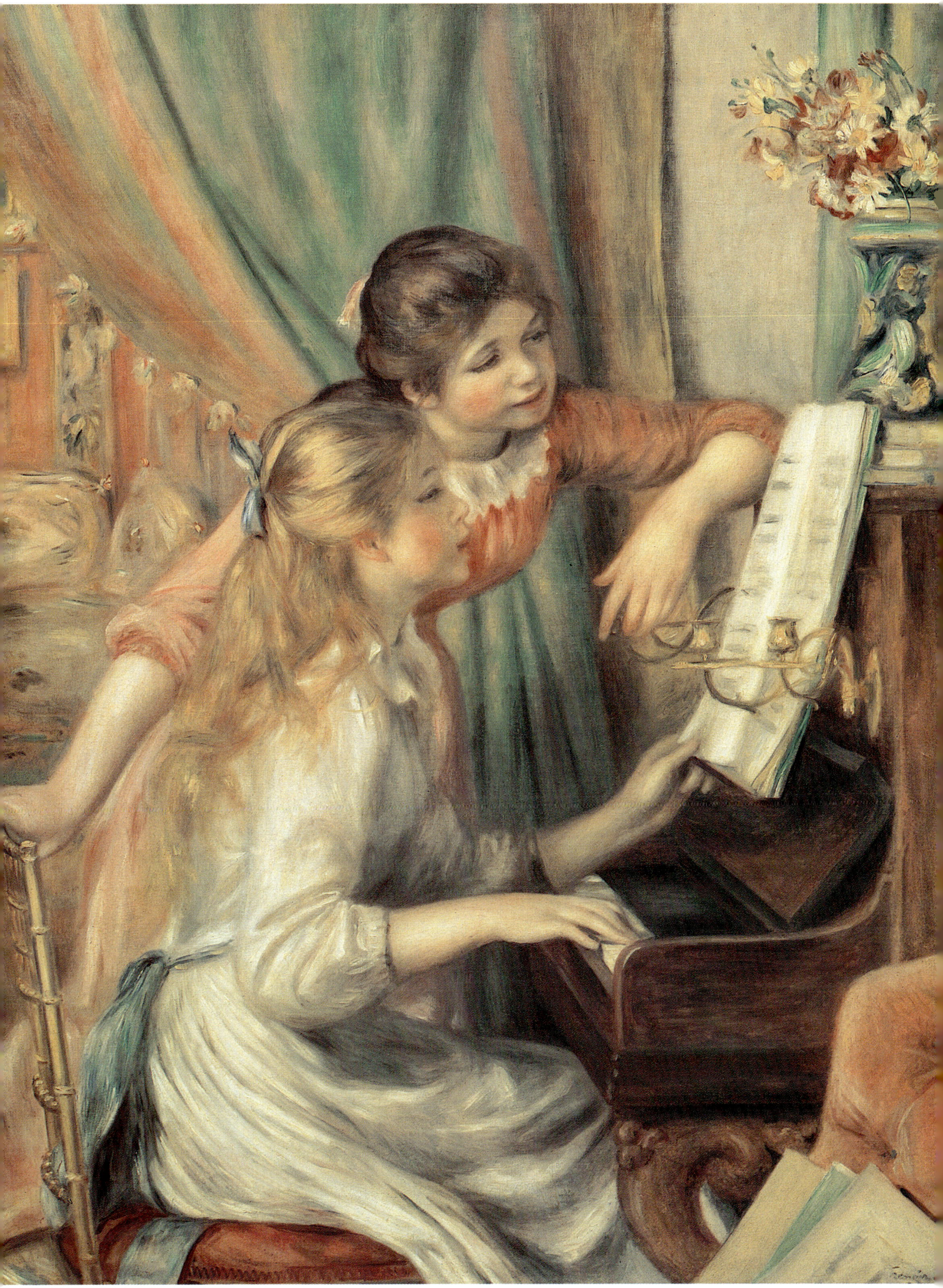

PIERRE-AUGUSTE RENOIR
Cagnes, c. 1909–10

Kunsthalle, Bremen. Courtesy of AKG London

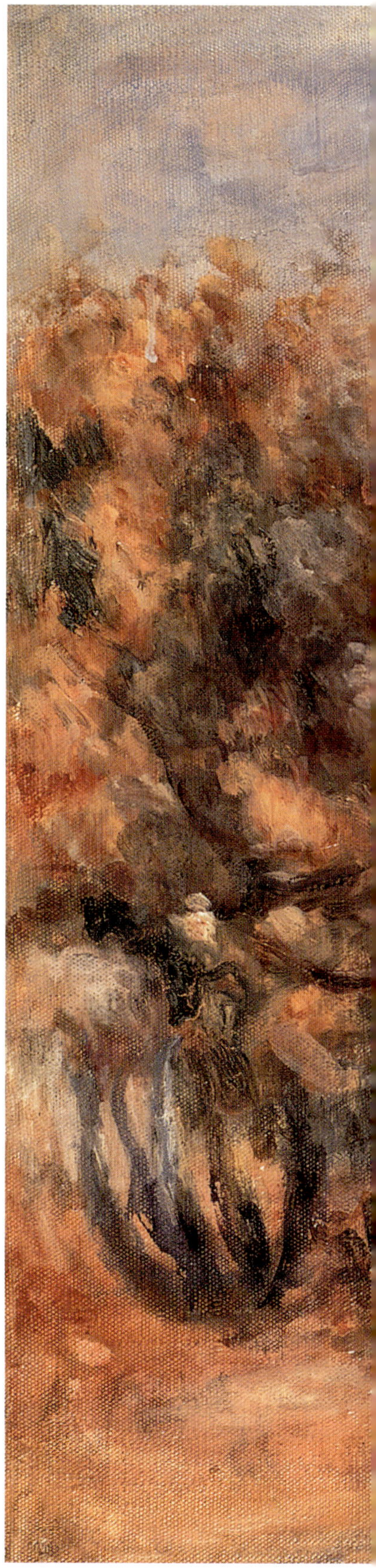

ACCORDING to his son Jean, from about 1900 onwards Renoir seemed to have resolved his insecurities as a painter and, while insisting that it was essential to study and learn from the masters of line, such as Raphael and Ingres, from 1905 his palette became increasingly warm and he seems to have thrown in his lot with the colourists such as Eugène Delacroix (1789–1863), Rubens (1577–1640) and Titian.

In 1907 Renoir and Aline bought a property in Cagnes in the south of France. The move south was partly because of Renoir's health, which was deteriorating. By the end of summer 1910, he could not walk and became so arthritic that it was difficult for him even to hold a brush.

Owing to his increasing difficulty in dealing with large subjects, Renoir painted many small still lifes and landscapes such as this – sun drenched and fantastically coloured. The silky lushness and 'touchiness' is typically Renoir and seems to go beyond Impressionism. With virtually all Renoir's work, except his more classical pieces of the 1890s, this supple touch is tangible. He is quoted earlier in his life as saying: 'What is inside my head doesn't interest me. I want to touch, or at least to see … .' Here he seems to combine both touch and sight.

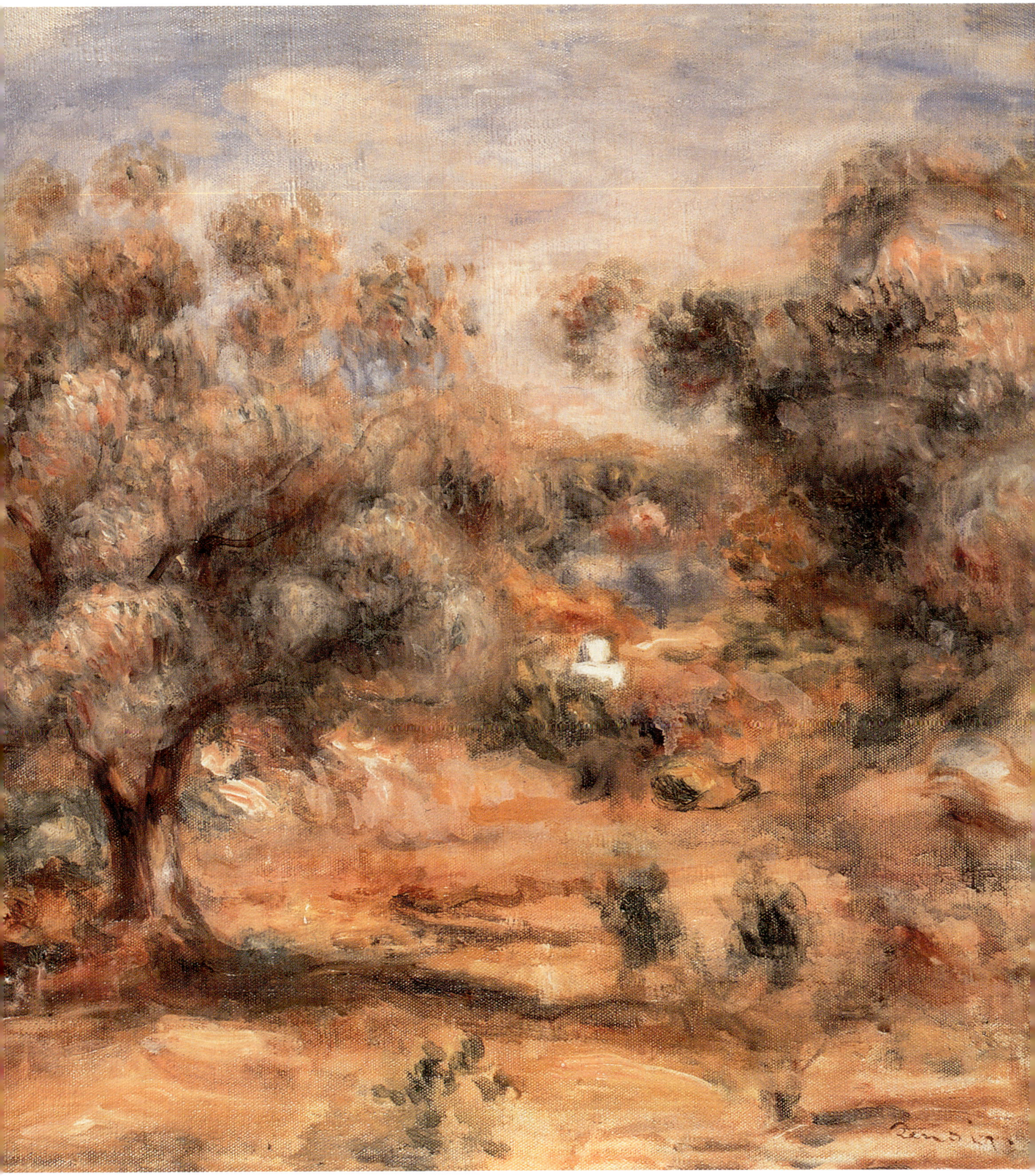

Richard Guino
Head of a Woman, 1916

Musée d'Orsay, Paris. Courtesy of AKG London

THIS is a bust of Aline Renoir, Renoir's partner and wife of over 35 years, who died in 1915. Renoir was devastated and in 1916 asked the Catalan sculptor Richard Guino (1890–1973) to model a bust of her from a seated study. This is a return to the material of Renoir's early years as a painter of ceramics and a direct connection with the marble busts of the 18th century that he admired so much.

Aline is shown in her youth in a charming hat with roses, a bright smile on her face recalling her image in *Luncheon of the Boating Party* (1880-81) in which, in virtually the same hat, she sits on the left playing with a small dog. Other paintings for which she posed also spring to mind, such as *Maternity* (1886), in which she suckles her baby, and *Dance in the Country* (1883), in which she dances so very cheerfully and gaily.

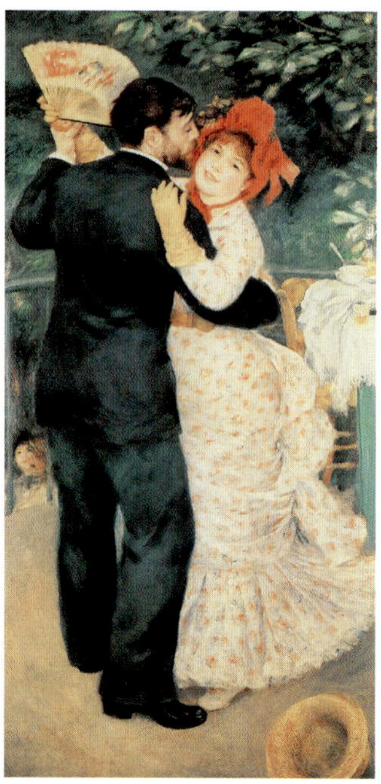

Pierre-Auguste Renoir
Dance in the Country, 1883
Musée d'Orsay, Paris. Courtesy of AKG London. (See p. 140)

Renoir, who could not handle clay properly owing to his severe rheumatism, was clearly showing a renewed interest in the medium when he began to teach his son Claude how to make pottery in the autumn of 1916. Unfortunately, when Guino left Cagnes in December, Renoir became disenchanted with his collaboration with him and lost interest in pottery.

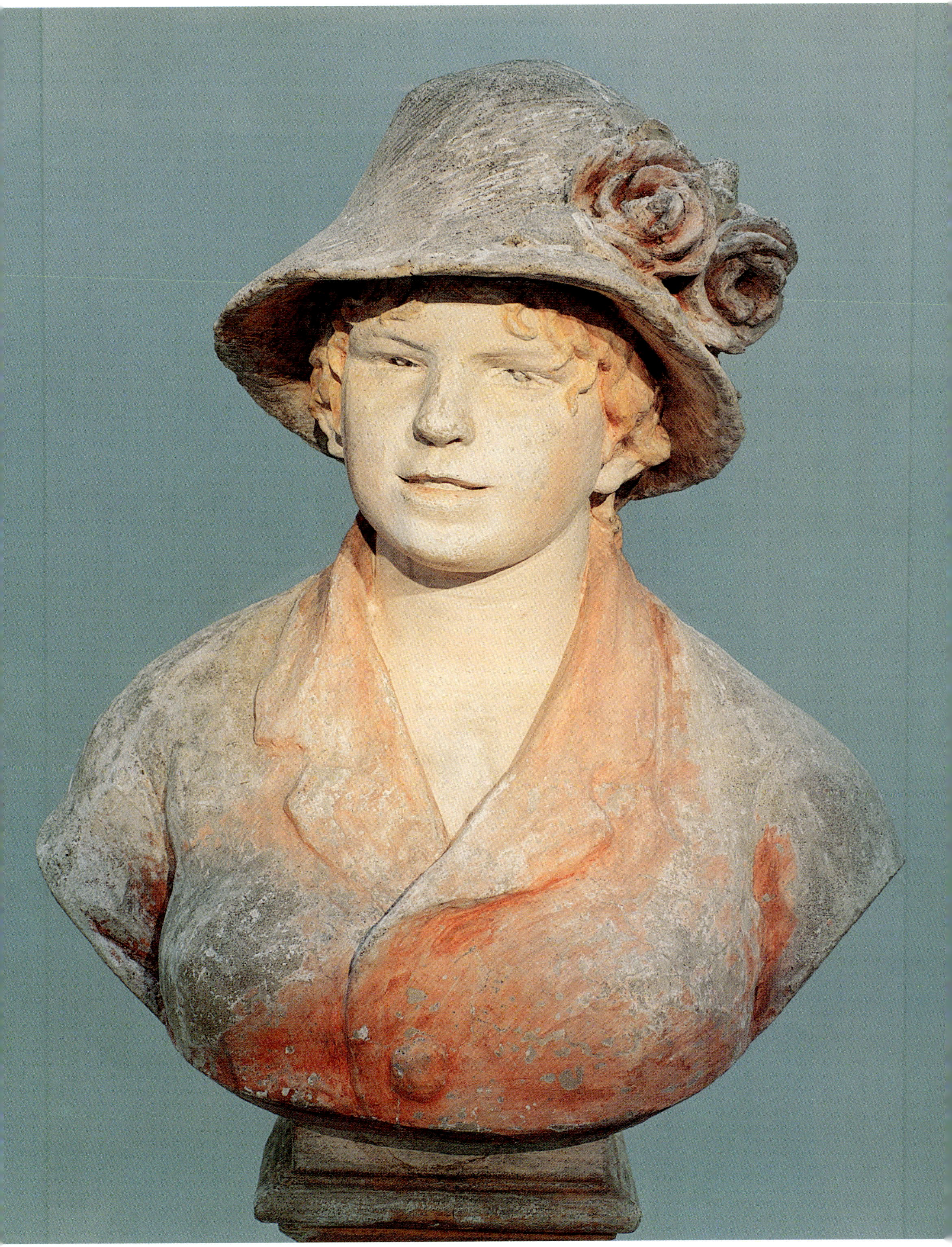

Pierre-Auguste Renoir
The Bathers, 1918–19

Musée d'Orsay, Paris. Courtesy of AKG London/Erich Lessing

THIS is Renoir's last painting of any size and he intended it as his final pictorial statement. In recognition of this, his sons made a gift of it to the state on his death.

This monumental painting is a summary of one of the most important themes of his career: nudes in a landscape – and a recapitulation of his *Bathers* (1887), which he painted in the 1880s in the same classical style as *Maternity* (1886) and *The Plait* (1884).

His allegiance to colour and his large, lushly painted female forms remind us of Titian and Rubens. He merges the figures, their clothes and the cushions with the vigorous landscape, each a part of the other. In 1918 Renoir told a friend, 'My landscape is only an accessory; at the moment I am trying to fuse it with my figures.'

Painted on a white primed canvas that increases the luminosity of the pigments, the colours sing, assembled 'like a musician who ceaselessly adds new elements to the orchestra'. His friend, the critic J. F. Schnerb, described his later works: 'M. Renoir loves his canvas being full and sonorous. He loathes empty spaces. Every corner in his landscapes offers a relationship of colours and values with a view to embellishment of the surface.' Renoir would not have disagreed. In 1908 he said, 'With all modesty, I consider not only that my art descends from a Watteau, a Fragonard … and also that I am one with them'.

Renoir received a medal from the Légion d'honneur before he died in 1919 in Cagnes, aged 78.

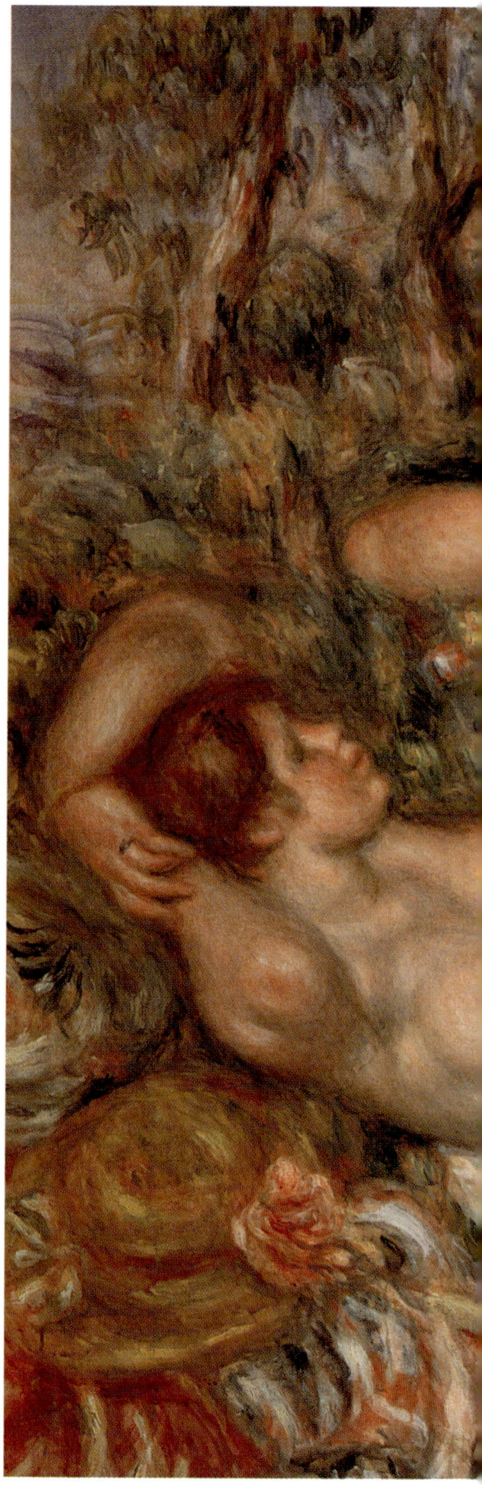

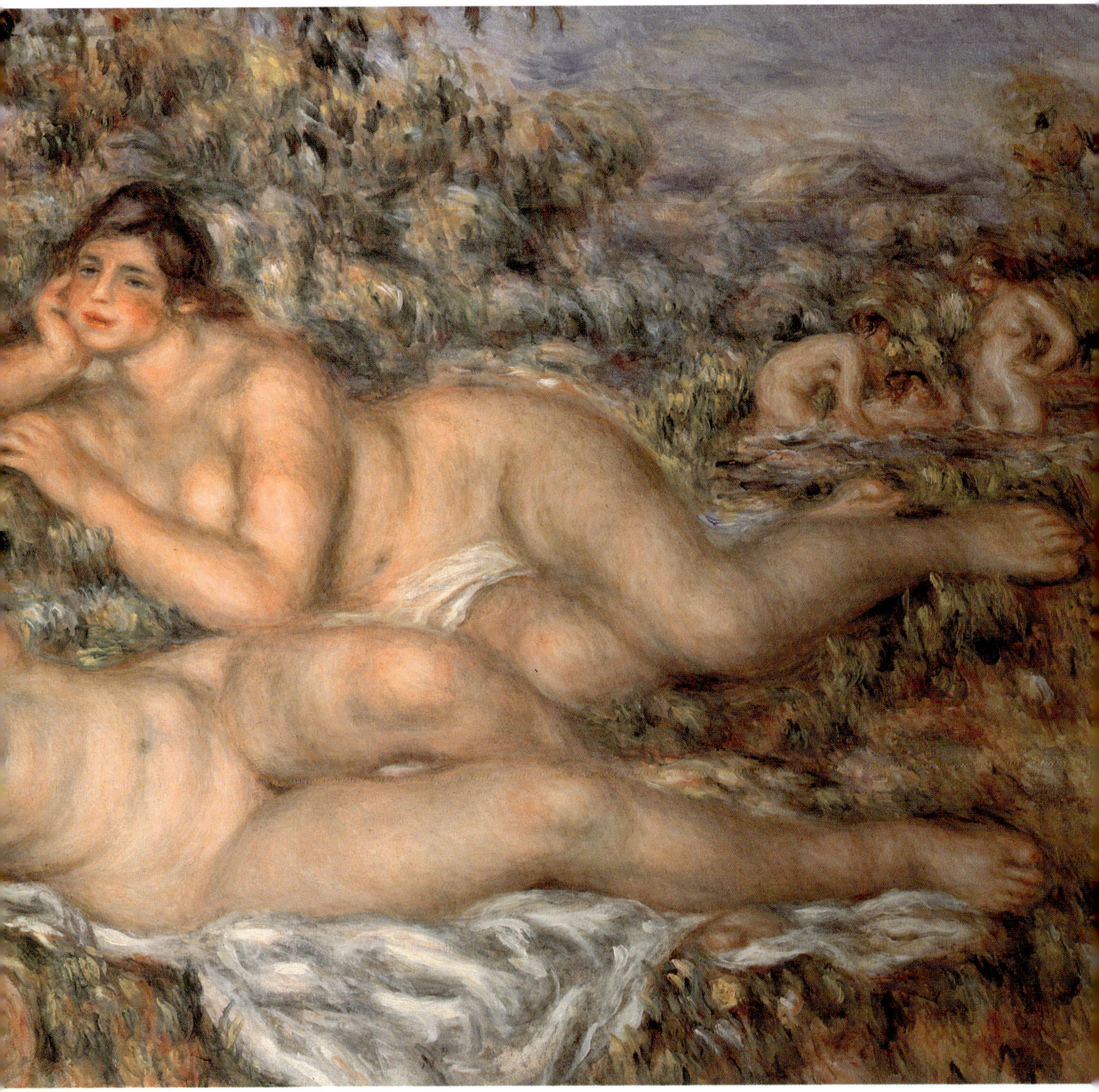

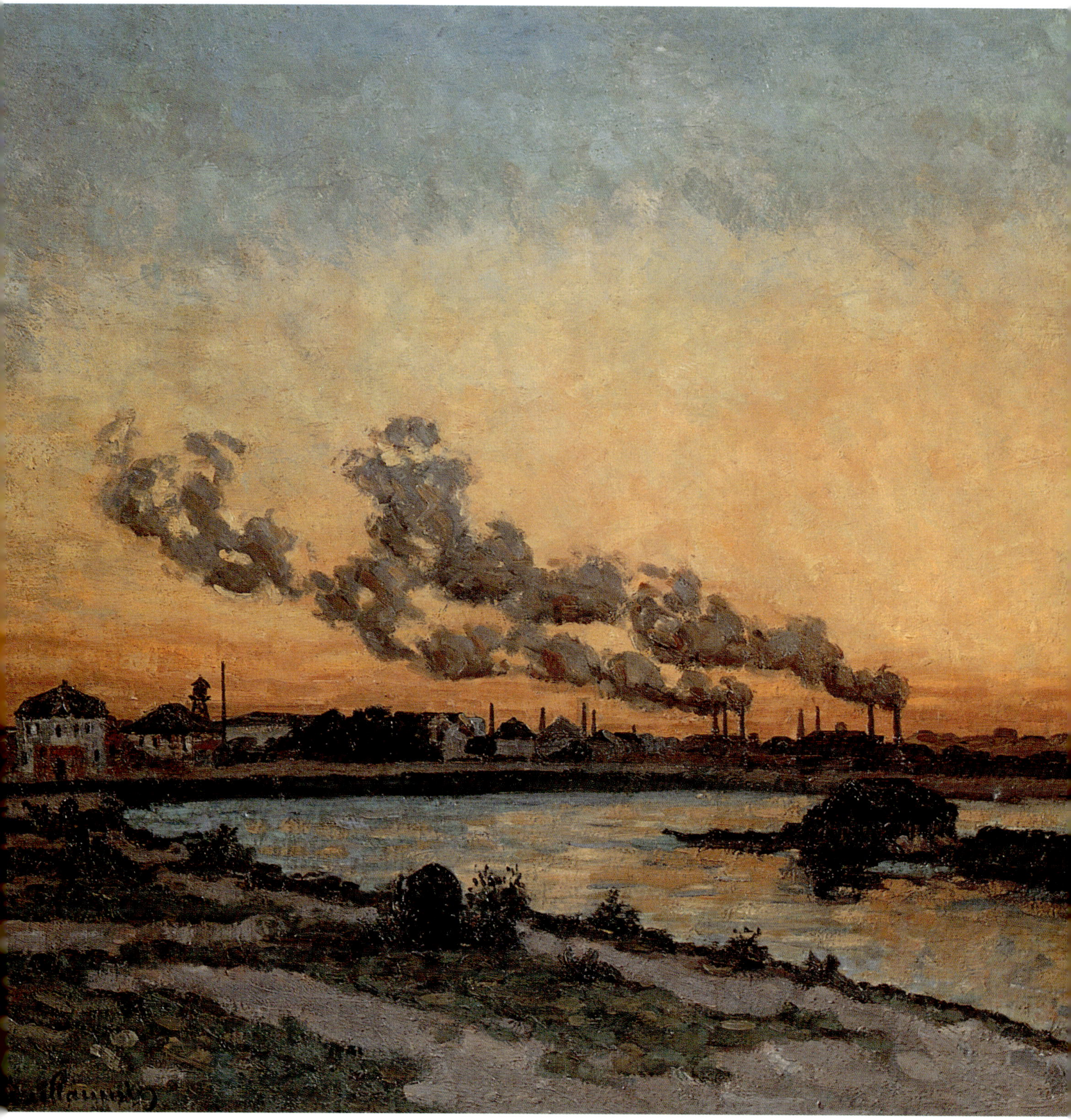

Armand Guillaumin (1841–1927)
Sunset at Ivry, 1874

Musée d'Orsay, Paris. Courtesy of AKG London/Erich Lessing

ARMAND GUILLAUMIN was working in his uncle's shop when he began to attend evening drawing classes at the age of 15. In 1861 he began to make use of the facilities at the Académie Suisse where, for a small fee, artists could paint nude models provided by the atelier. It was here that he met Pissarro and Cézanne.

Although he has never been regarded as a major Impressionist painter, Guillaumin was involved from the beginning when, like many of the group, he was rejected at the Salon of 1863 and exhibited at the Salon des Refusés.

Under the influence of Pissarro, Guillaumin, like Cézanne at this time, took up the Impressionist way of painting and often painted out-of-doors – often at Pontoise, where Pissarro lived. The three still remained friends and Cézanne once even copied a painting of Guillaumin's which showed workers shovelling sand.

A part-time artist, Guillaumin worked night shifts on the railway so that he could paint during the day. He is known for landscapes around Paris and along the Seine. This is a view of Ivry, an industrial suburb of Paris, in which he combines the glorious blue heights of the sky and the sun's golden rays with the factory chimneys billowing smoke.

Armand Guillaumin
The Creuse in Summer, 1895
Private Collection. Courtesy of AKG London

BY 1895 Guillaumin was a full-time painter, having given up his work with on railway after he won 100,000 francs in the national lottery in 1891. Until that time he concentrated on docklands and industrial landscapes. Thereafter he travelled extensively through France painting Impressionist motifs.

This is a painting of the river Creuse in the Massif Central, which Monet painted many times in 1889. Guillaumin takes a different view from Monet, who generally took a closer perspective with the bank on the left and the river disappearing to the right.

Guillaumin's image shows a wide expanse of river with the banks on either side overlapping as the river goes round the bend. The brushwork is formal, the colours pure and contrasting. Although he clearly shows an interest in the light falling on the landscape and river, the overall effect is not impressionistic. The colours are divided too clearly, as if an area has been allotted to each one and filled in. This is not a landscape under the fleeting effects of errant light, nor does it seek out the essence of a form like the compositions of Cézanne. Works of the 1890s, such as this, are often considered to anticipate the violent, vigorous brushstrokes and pure colour of Henri Matisse (1869–1954) and the Fauves.

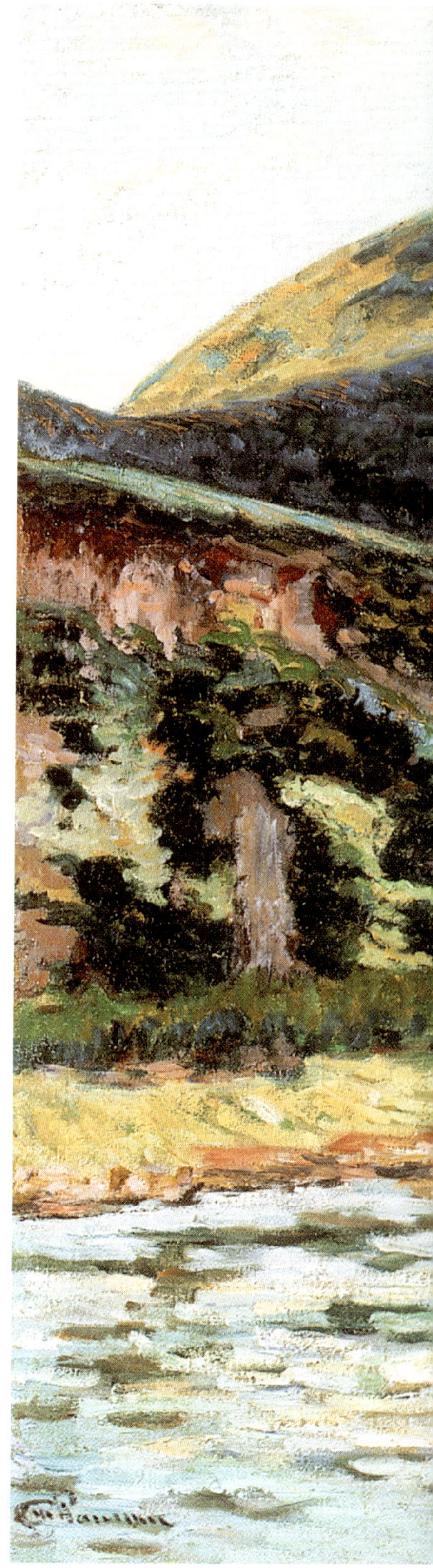

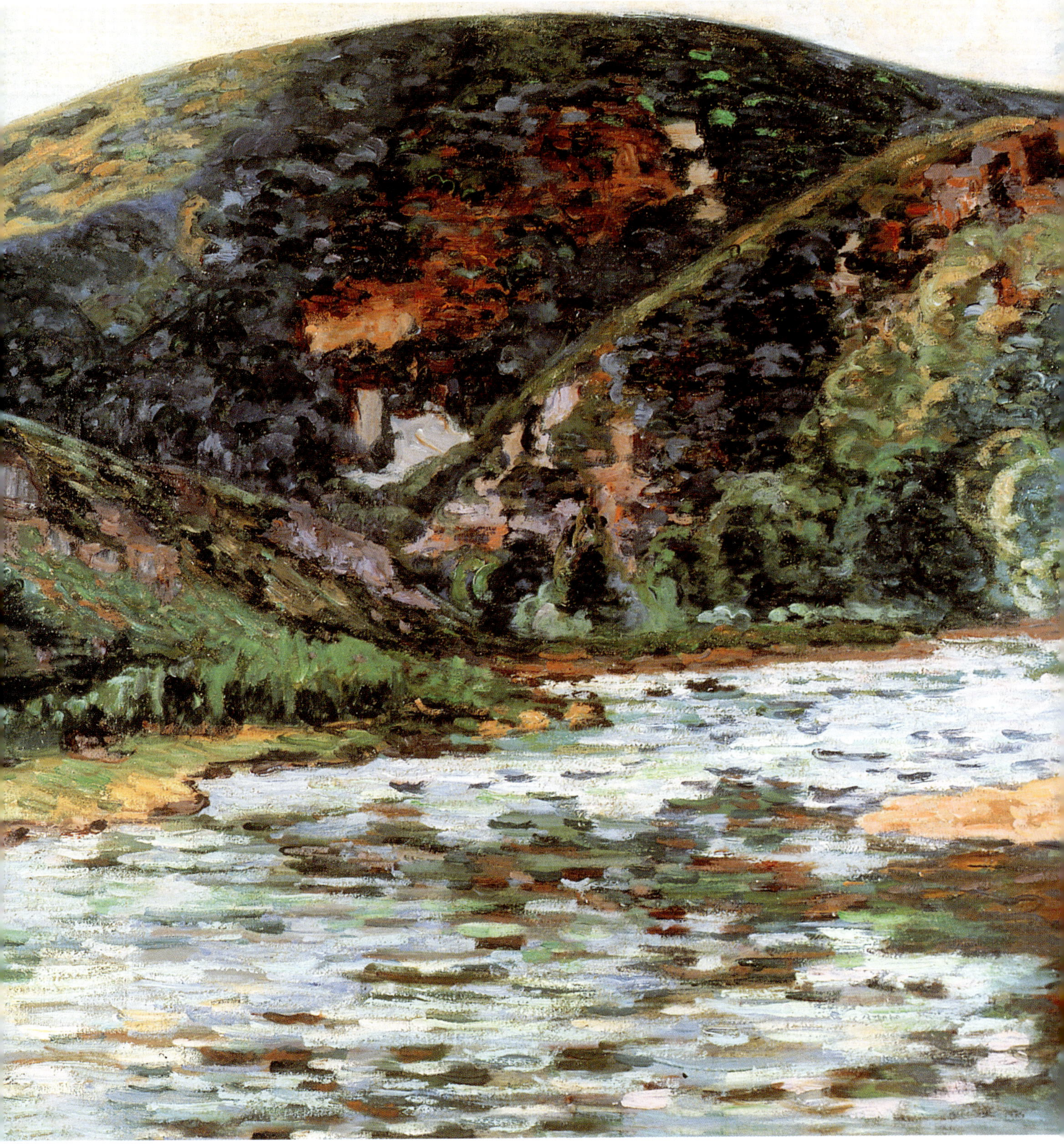

EDGAR DEGAS (1834–1917)
The Bellelli Family, 1858

Musée d'Orsay, Paris. Courtesy of AKG London/Erich Lessing

DEGAS came from a wealthy background and followed a traditional course of study at the Académie des Beaux-Arts. He also made several trips to Italy. In 1857 he stayed in Florence for several months with his uncle and aunt, the Baron and Madame Bellelli, when he painted this family portrait.

This is Degas' first large work, painted in oil on a non-standard size canvas – something more typical of great, heroic historical works – and therefore unusual. The portrait reveals, even at this early stage in his career, Degas' ability to arrange his compositions in such as way as to suggest the nature of the relationship between the sitters – creating a tension or a rapport between them. Here, the painting and the family are clearly divided in two – the strong triangle of the mother and two daughters in the light with the father separate in the shade on the right, his back to the viewer. The relationship between the baron and his wife is clearly strained. Contrast the black dresses blending together on the left, worn in mourning for Mme Bellelli's recently deceased father, whose portrait is on the wall and forms part of the female group, and the lighter, casual clothes of the father, and the alienation between the two groups is complete.

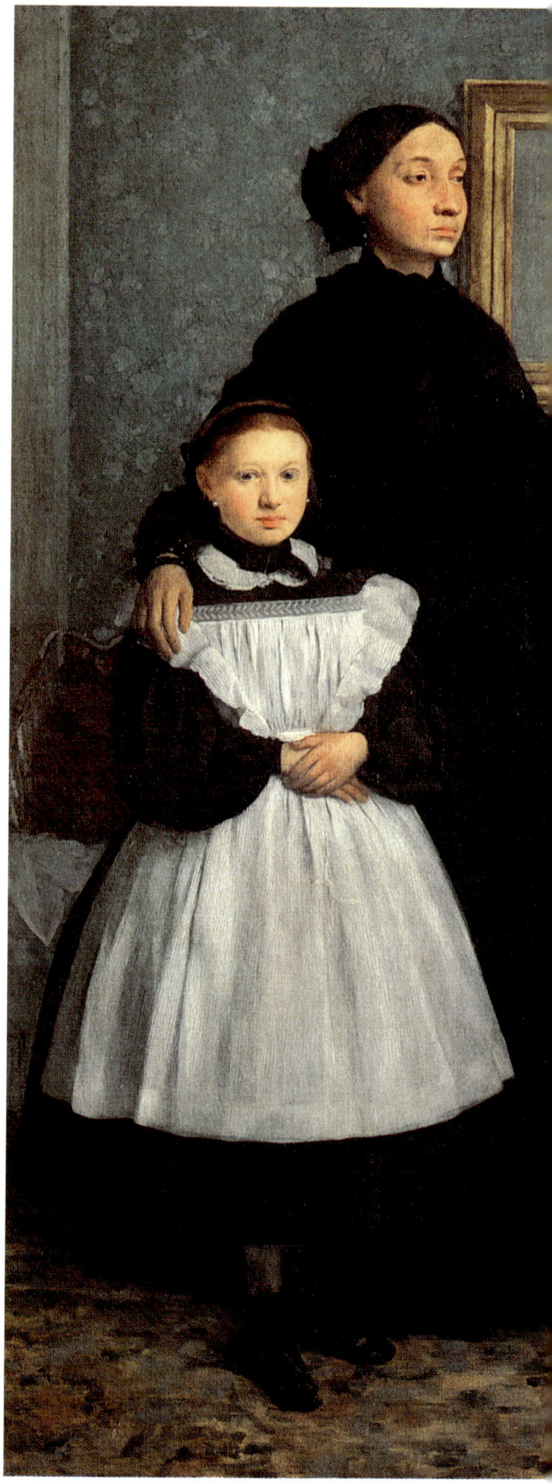

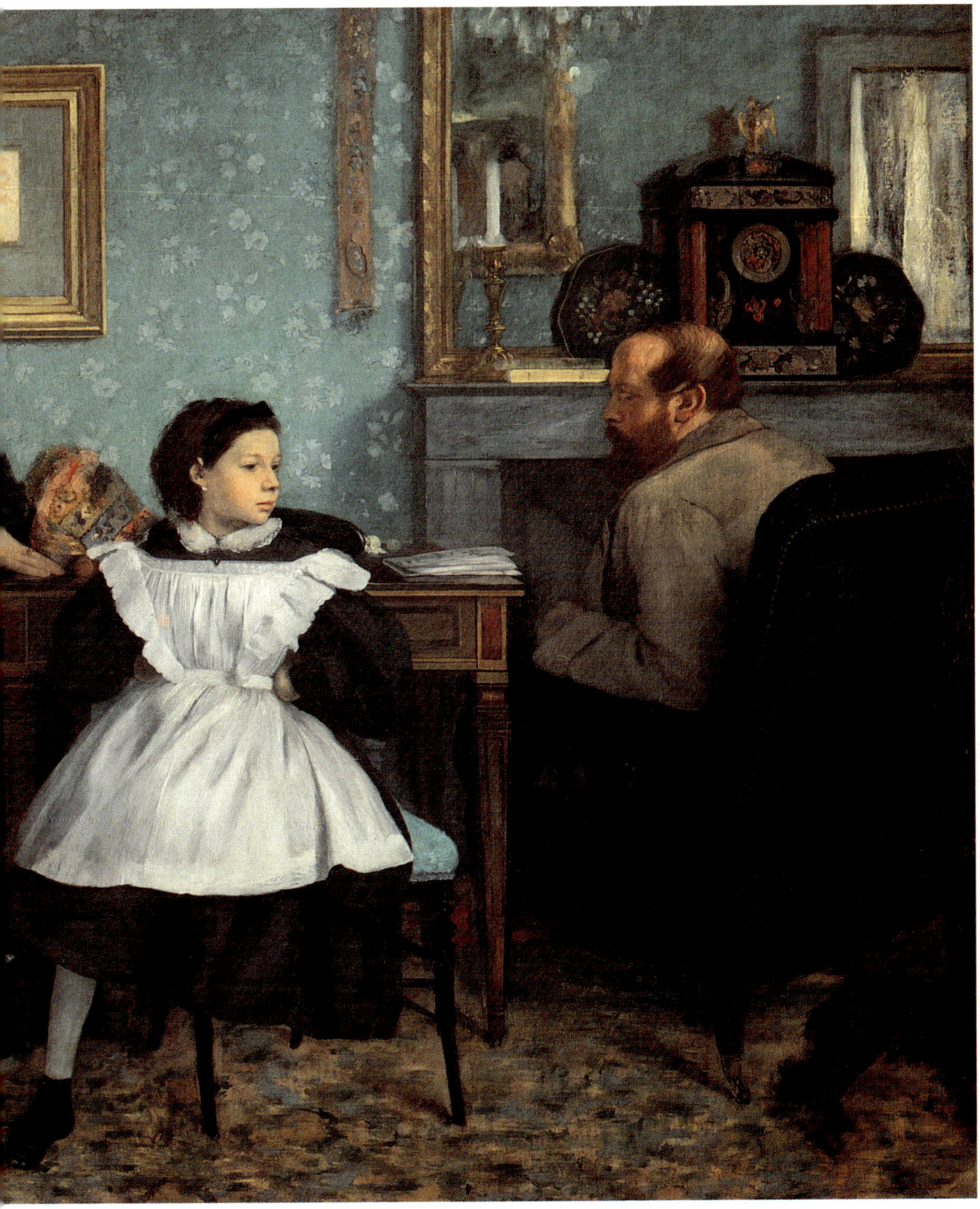

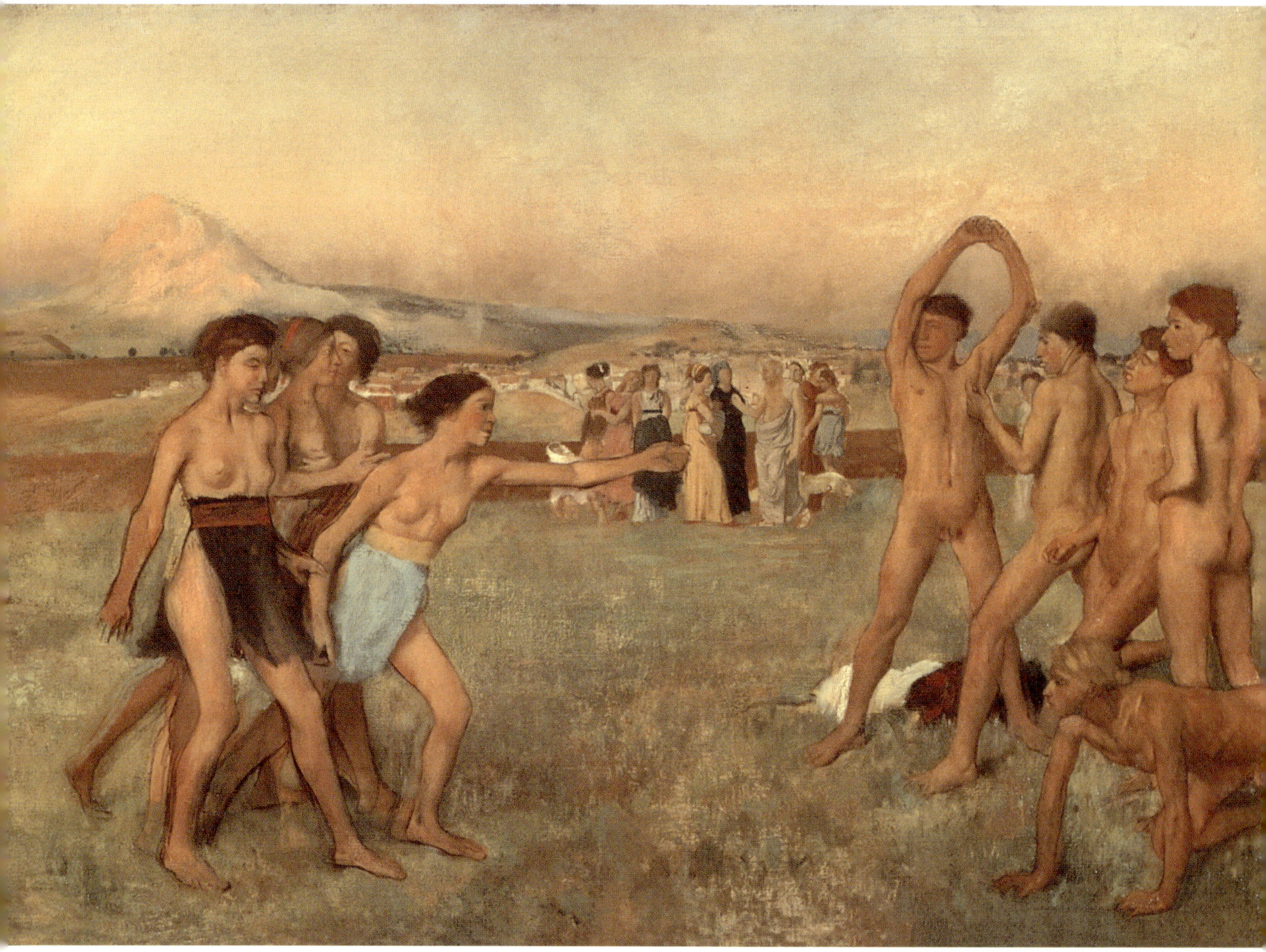

Edgar Degas

Young Spartan Girls Provoking the Boys, 1860

National Gallery, London. Courtesy of The Bridgeman Art Library

DEGAS' early work, of which this is an important example, is in the traditional, historical manner. Like so many artists before him, he copied Old Masters in the Louvre (notably Andrea del Mantegna's *Crucifixion* (1431–1506) and went to Rome to study ancient sculpture. It was his intention to become a history painter – the highest calling for an artist in 19th-century France.

But even here, in *Young Spartan Girls*, despite the apparent Classical subject-matter, the spirit of the work is revolutionary. What is the picture really about? Unlike traditional history painting, this painting has no story based on the writings of the Classical canon and is probably taken from a 17th-century source, *Voyage de Jeune Anarchiste en Grèce*, in which the Abbé Barthélemy describes the warlike upbringing of Spartan girls. This, as in so many of Degas' better-known, later paintings, is a description of life – the then-modern life of the Spartans – rather than a Classical conquest or mythical story.

Degas' style does not yet reach the heights of colour that he was to achieve later, nor is the broken brushwork typical of the Impressionists yet in evidence, but the independence for which he was renowned both as a man and an artist, is here in embryonic form.

Edgar Degas

At the Races, in Front of the Stands, c. 1866–68

Musée d'Orsay, Paris. Courtesy of AKG London/Erich Lessing

DEGAS first began to paint racehorses in 1861, but he continued to work on historical subjects as well until 1865, the year he met Monet and Renoir and became a frequent visitor at the Café Guerbois, where the group often gathered. There is some doubt as to the date of this particular painting; it has been suggested that it was painted in 1879.

This is one of many works of horses and jockeys on the racecourse, a theme he treated several times before 1872 (when he went on an extended trip to New Orleans to see his brothers) and one to which he returned in the 1880s.

This painting already shows many of Degas' typical artistic traits. It is cut off on the left to indicate greater space beyond the 'viewfinder' of the canvas; has a clearly thought out, almost geometric spatial design; shows an interest in contemporary Parisian life (the racecourse at Longchamps was new and very fashionable); makes an interesting use of colour (note the mix of gold, green and blue in the grass); and, something that was to become increasingly noticeable, it shows Degas' fascination with movement, clearly expressed in the horses and their shadows. Degas' racehorses prefigure his dancers and nude studies. They are also the only pictures that depict outdoor scenes but, contrary to the ideals of the Impressionists, they would have been painted in the studio from numerous notes and sketches.

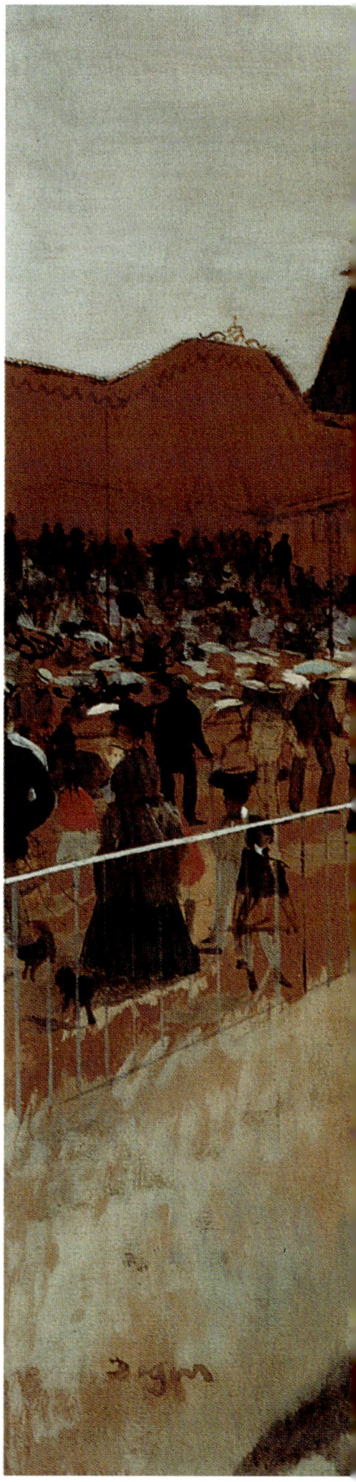

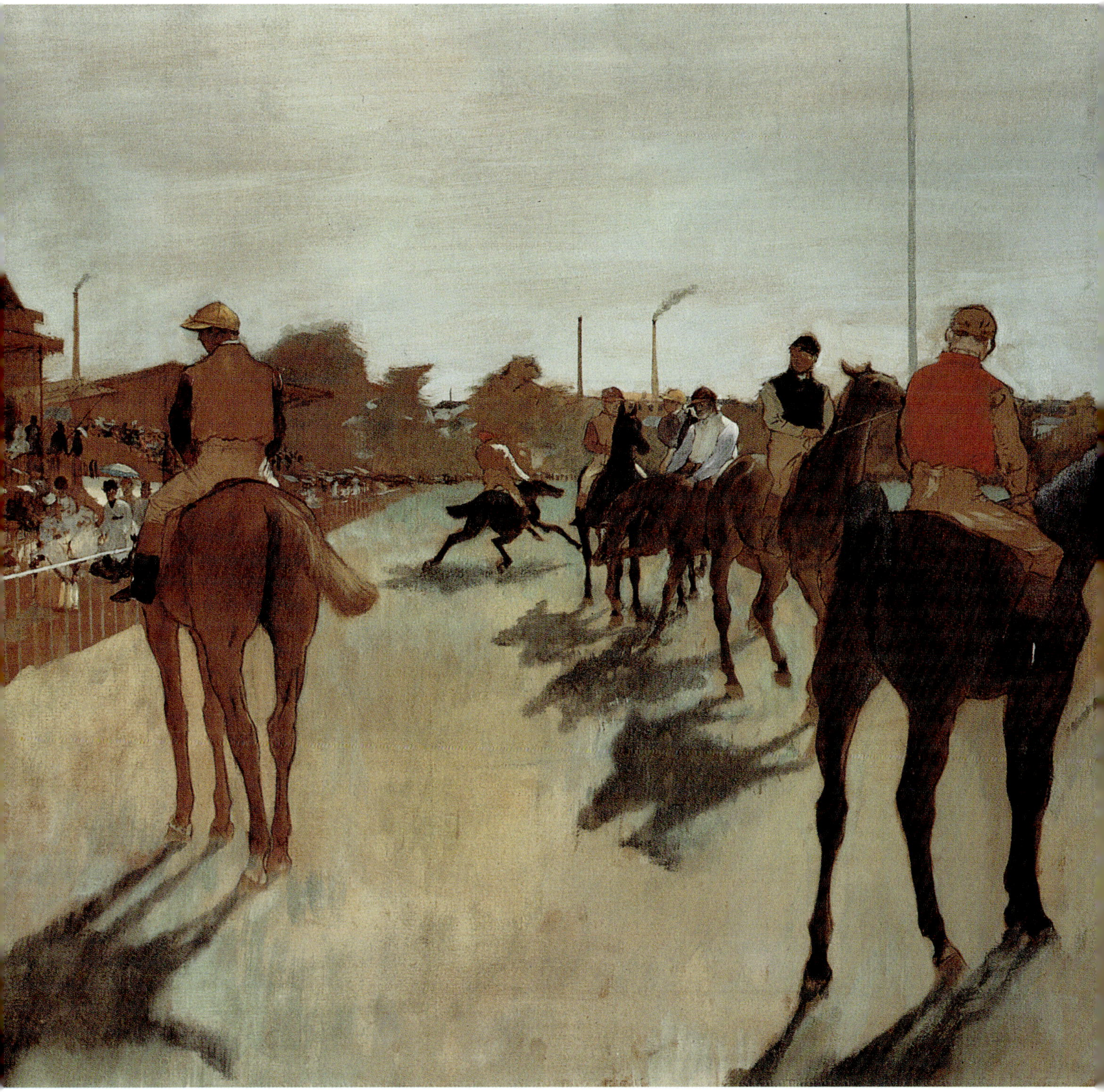

EDGAR DEGAS
The Orchestra at the Opera, 1868

Musée d'Orsay, Paris. Courtesy of London/Erich Lessing

ONE of Degas' many depictions of scenes from modern life, this painting shows an extraordinary composition, breaking all the rules of the traditional art establishment.

From a low viewpoint across the orchestra we see the skirts and legs of the dancers, lit up by the footlights and cut off at the ankle by the apron of the stage. The foreground, using a dark, Manet-like palette, shows the orchestra. Degas' friend, bassoonist Desiré Dihau, is slightly off-centre directly below the dancers. His right hand creates a patch of light amid the blacks and browns. The draughtsmanship is fine and the individuality of the faces pays tribute to Degas' portraiture skills – indeed, this is, in effect, a portrait of his friend in his working environment.

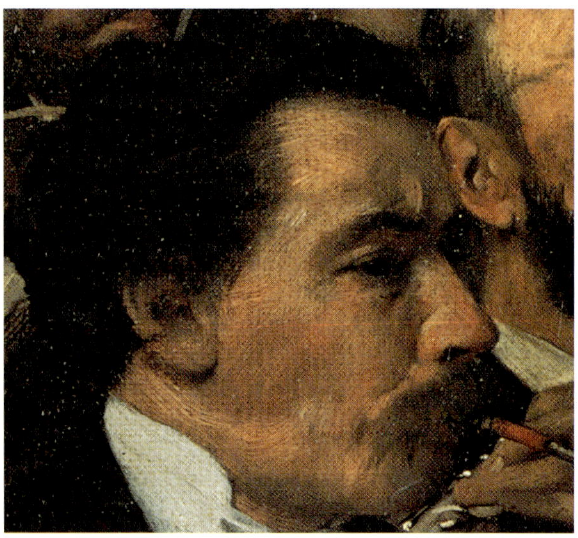

Degas' revolutionary compositional style, influenced by photography and the Japanese prints flooding into France at this time, is evident in the interplay of diagonal, horizontal and vertical lines that link the three pictorial planes and sometimes bind them together as if there were no distance between them at all – note the scroll of the double bass on the right. Nobody else at this time was as daring in compositions as Degas.

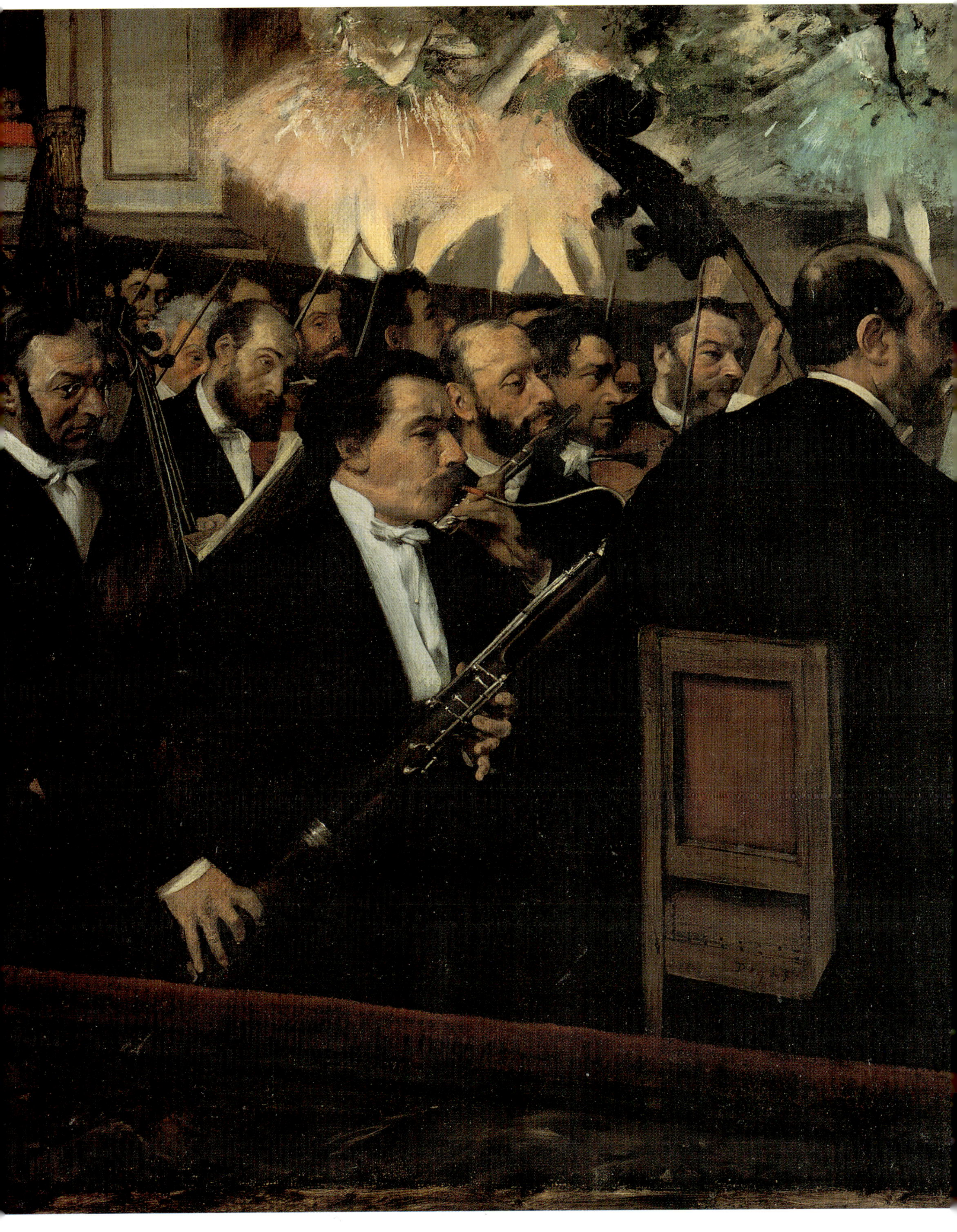

Edgar Degas
Ballet Rehearsal on the Stage, 1874

Musée d'Orsay, Paris. Courtesy of AKG London/Erich Lessing

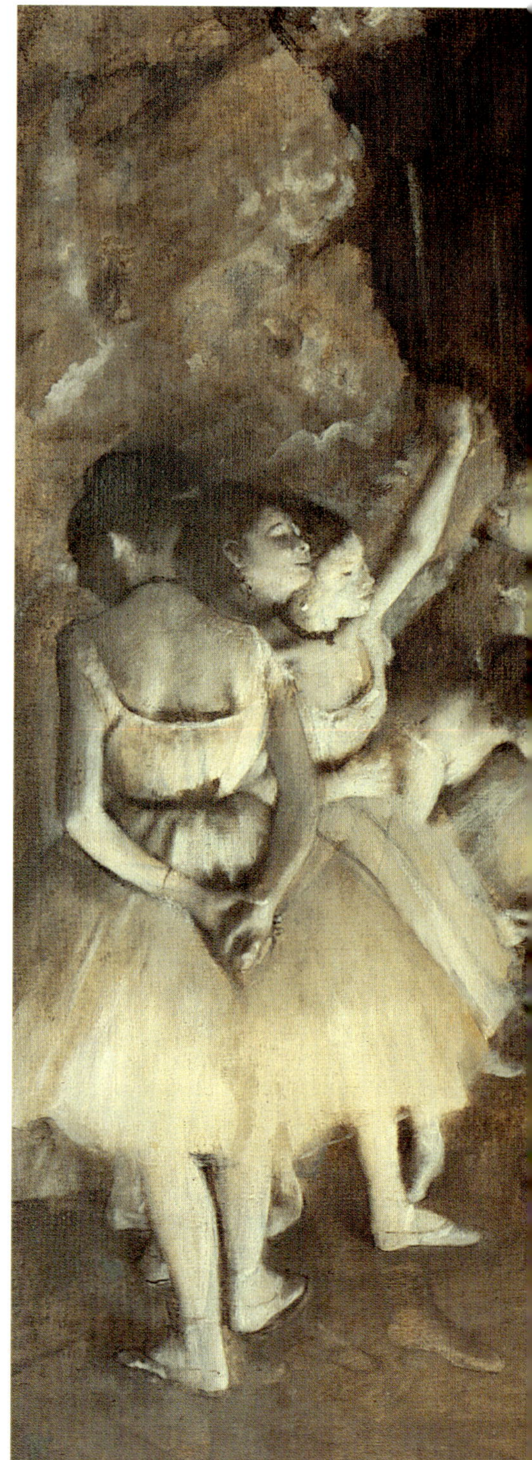

BY 1874, Degas had already begun to paint and draw scenes from the ballet, of which this is one of his most well-known. It is one of three paintings of the same subject painted that year, and was exhibited at the first Impressionist exhibition in 1874.

Degas, never an Impressionist in the same way as Monet, Renoir or even Manet in the 1870s, was instrumental in organising this event and exhibited in all eight shows, although he subscribed to few of the group's ideals, including landscape *plein-air* painting. What Degas shared with all these artists was a desire to be independent, to break away from, and be successful in spite of, the Salon – to pursue goals and present art in a way never seen before.

Degas never painted compositions from life. Although he created works that have a stunning immediacy, he built up his compositions using constant notes, sketches, workings and reworkings of his material – note the ghostly foot on the left side of this painting. As his eyesight began to deteriorate from the 1970s, memory also played a part.

This painting, in sepia tones like that of a photograph, presents an unusual perspective on an unusual scene, with the dancers glowing in the gloom of the stage. The poses often recur in his works and bear comparison with his nudes and women ironing, revealing his fascination with movement.

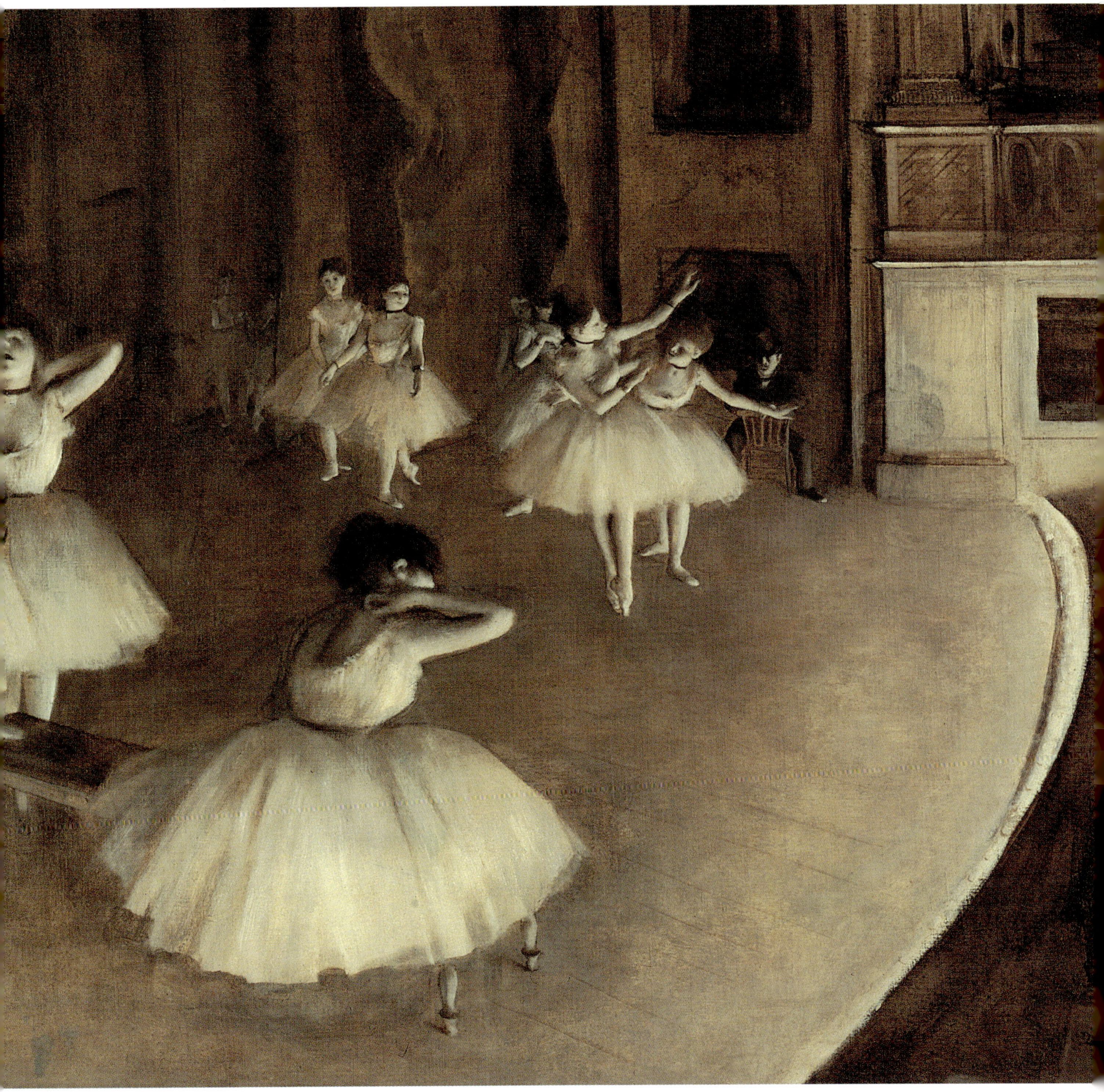

Edgar Degas
The Dance Class, 1873–76

Musée d'Orsay, Paris. Courtesy of AKG London/Erich Lessing

BEGUN in 1873, this is Degas' first large canvas of dancers. It was commissioned by the opera singer Jean-Baptiste Faure. However, Degas could not resolve the composition so, as Faure was insisting on receiving his canvas, Degas painted a similar work, *The Dance Exam* (1874), for him.

Lit by a large, unseen window on the right, the class is finishing. The dancers are tired and taking little notice of the teacher, Jules Perrot, whom Degas sketched in 1875 and added in his reworking of the composition. The dancers scratch their backs, stretch and adjust their clothing – a recurrent theme. Note the small details, such as the pink highlight on the calf of the standing dancer in the foreground, the dog and the watering can.

Painted from a low viewpoint, another Japanese influence, the composition works in several directions. In the middle ground, the eye focuses on Perrot. The empty expanse of floor diagonally to his right is typical of Degas' compositions. Perrot's upright figure is echoed in the standing dancer and strengthened further by the marble pilasters on the wall. A deeper diagonal runs from the two dancers in the foreground, following the floorboards and the wall to the dancer in the far corner – a quasi-mirror image of the girl perched on the piano.

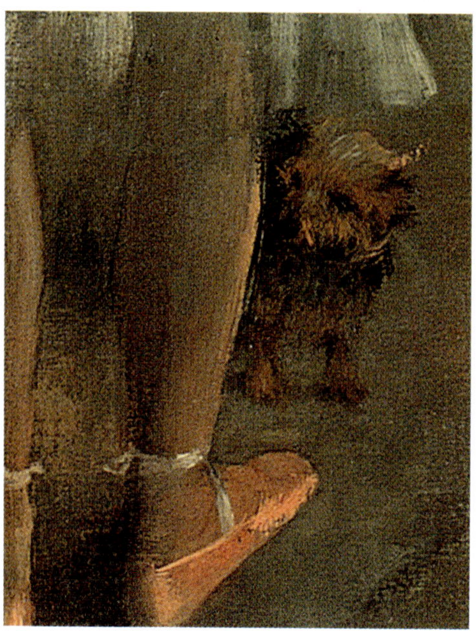

Like Manet, with whom he became friends in 1861, Degas uses a limited, though much lighter palette, with a lot of white interspersed with flashes of pure colour.

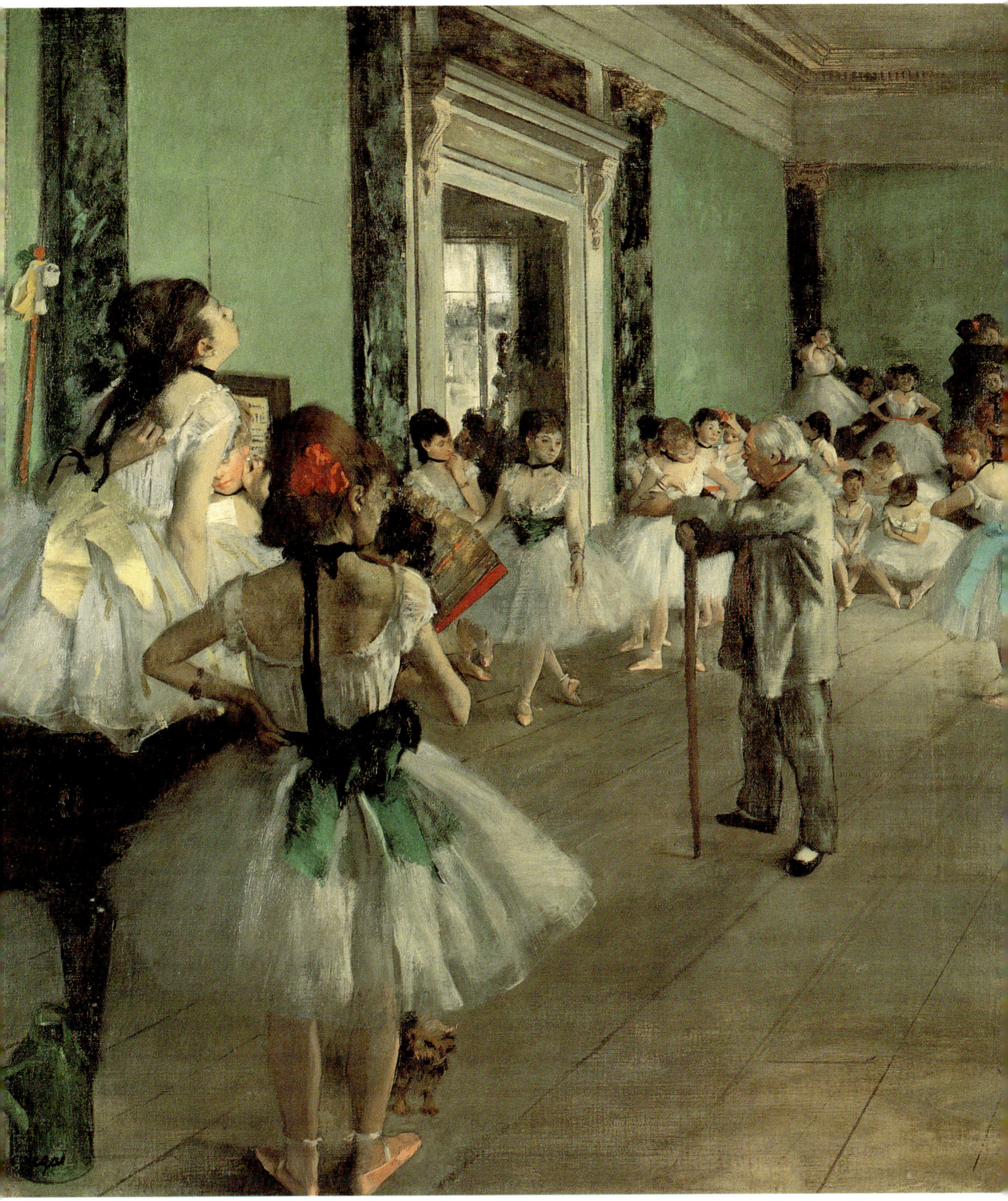

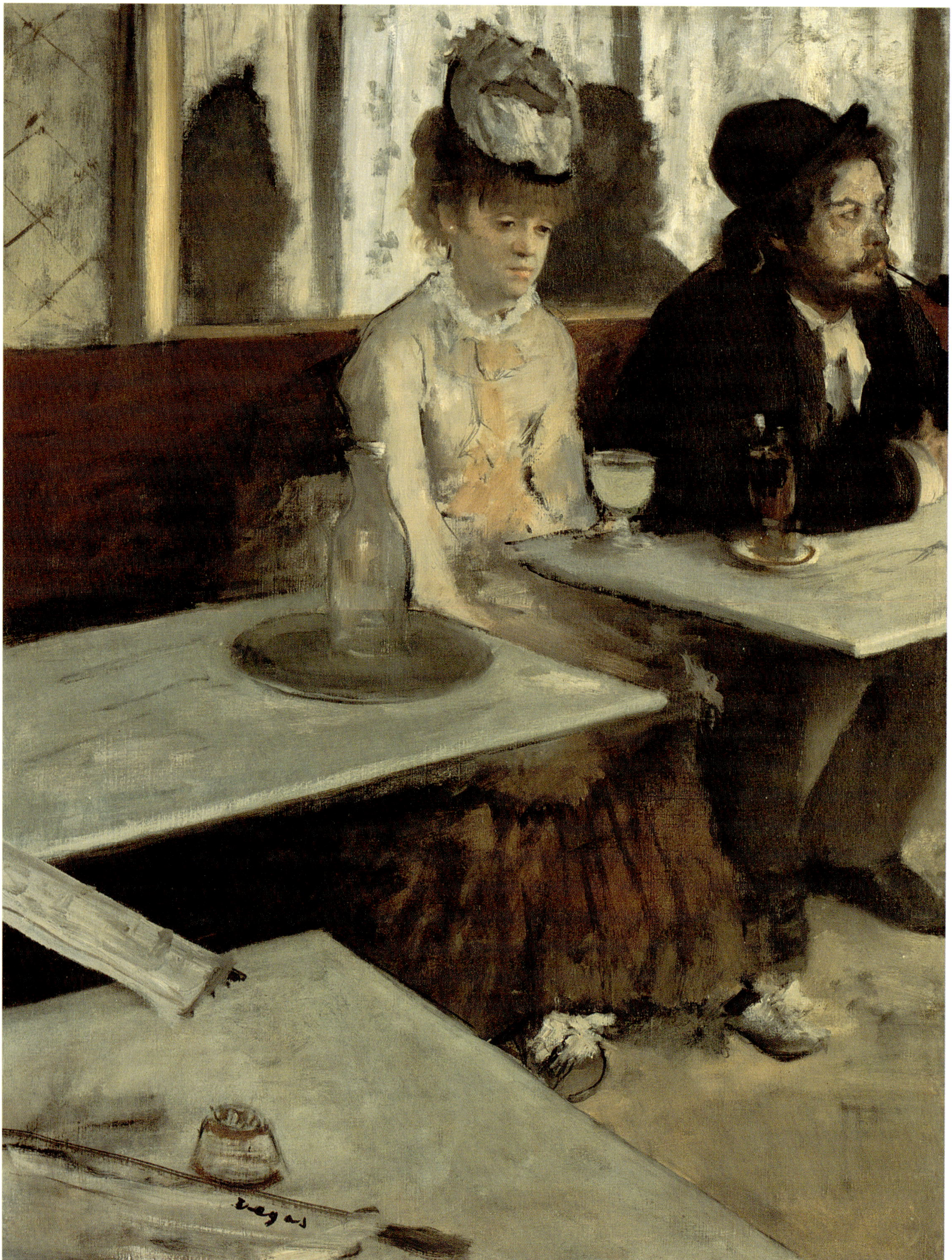
Degas

Edgar Degas
In the Café (Absinthe), 1875–76

Musée d'Orsay, Paris. Courtesy of AKG London. Erich Lessing

IN *the Café* is one of Degas' most depressing works. It shows a melancholic woman and her apparently dissolute male companion in a café on a sunny afternoon sitting side by side but in their own separate worlds. The woman has a glass of absinthe – a notoriously cheap alcoholic drink given to inducing hallucinations.

The models for the painting were Degas' friends the engraver Marcellin Desboutin (1823–1902), (who was teetotal), and the actress Ellen Andrée. The café is the Nouvelle Athènes one of the cafés where the Impressionists used to gather in Paris.

The painting caused a scandal in London, where it was sold, and in Paris, where it was shown at the Impressionists' third exhibition in 1877, because it appears to depict a down-at-heel prostitute.

Degas may have been inspired by Émile Zola's recent low-life novel *L'Assommoir* (1877). Both Manet and Degas produced paintings and pastels of prostitutes. Degas even made a series of 50 satirical monotypes depicting brothel scenes – many of these were destroyed by his family on his death in 1917.

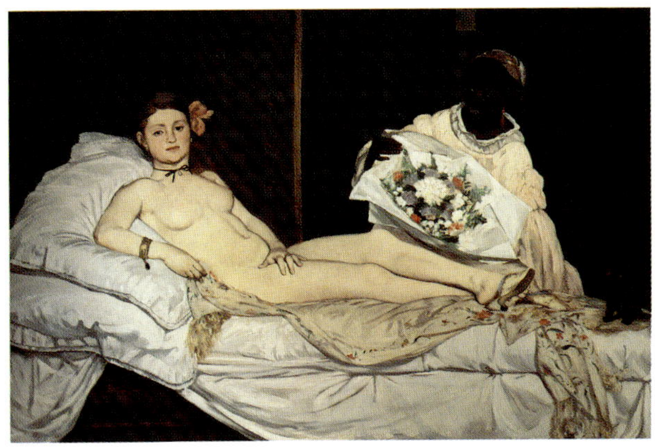

Edouard Manet
Olympia, 1877
Musée d'Orsay, Paris. Courtesy of AKG London/Erich Lessing. *(See p. 22)*

As ever, the composition and perspective are innovative. The scene is viewed from a nearby table, allowing a design of table-tops to enclose the figures. Degas makes use of one his favourite devices of placing figures slightly off-centre, with a large intervening space in the foreground. Unusually, on this occasion he may have painted from life without preparatory drawings, with a few areas, such as the slight blurring of the woman's face, being touched up afterwards.

EDGAR DEGAS
The Racecourse, 1877–80

Musée d'Orsay, Paris. Courtesy of AKG London/Erich Lessing

THIS marks Degas' return to painting racehorses in the 1880s. Unusually, it shows a landscape with a town in the background and a steam train rushing in from the left – the smoke from its funnel echoed in the white, cloudy sky above.

Both sides of the painting are cropped – on the left a jockey reins in a galloping horse. A clear comparison is being made between the horse and the train behind it. On the right, a woman in a carriage looks at the jockeys. A man with a cane, cut off on the right, comes into the foreground. Three jockeys on horses overlap in such as way as to suggest a composite animal. This patterning effect shows Japanese influences. The bottom-left quarter of the canvas is empty – another device borrowed from the Japanese and used in many of Degas' paintings.

According to critic Paul Valéry, who was a friend of Berthe Morisot's, Degas was 'one of the first to study the appearance of the noble animal by means of Major Muybridge's (1830–1904) instantaneous photographs'. He began to show the correct position of the running horse's legs after about 1880.

Racecourses appear in the work of both Degas and Manet and they certainly visited the racecourse together at least once. Ironically, despite the speed and the liveliness of the movement, all their works were painted in the studio from drawings.

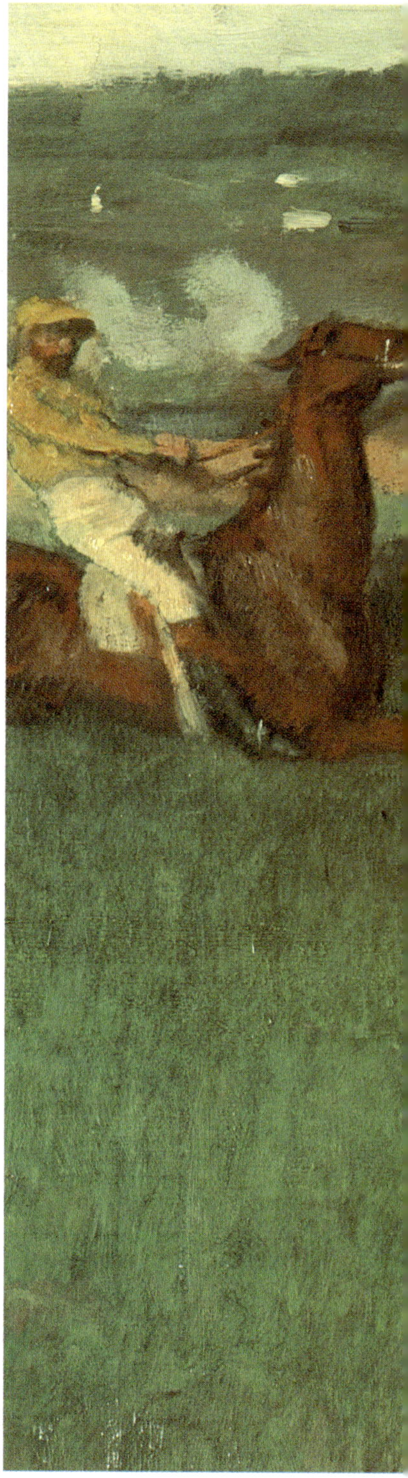

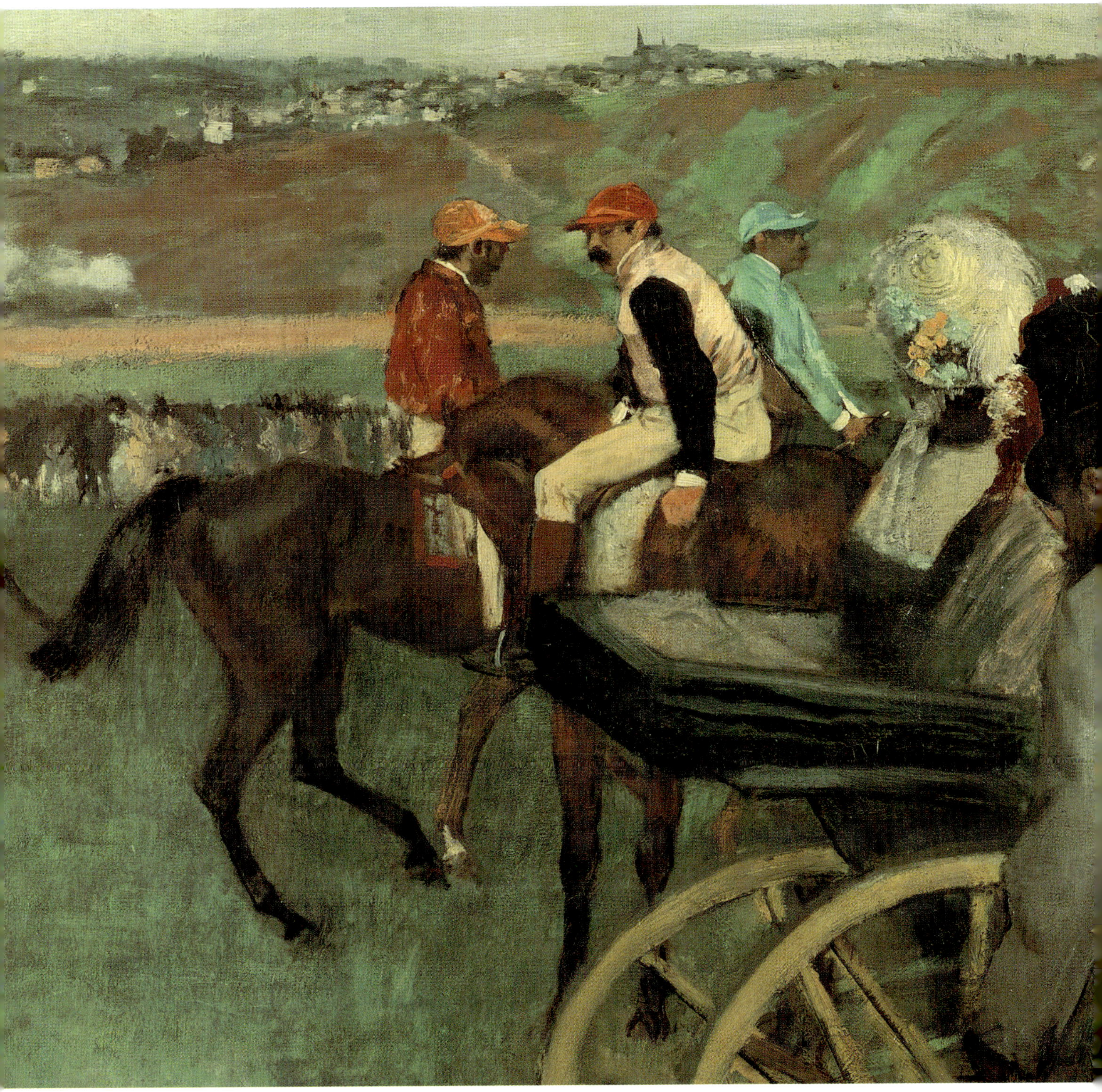

Edgar Degas
Portrait of Edmond Duranty, 1879

The Burrell Collection, Art Gallery and Museum, Glasgow. Courtesy of AKG London

THIS work shows the writer Edmond Duranty (1833–80) the year before he died. A friend of Degas and the Impressionists, Duranty wrote extensively about art and did much to promote the concept of realism. He was also the first to distinguish Manet and Degas as realist painters from the romanticism of the rest of the group. He often joined them in the Café Guerbois.

The portrait, in an unusual square format, shows Duranty surrounded by his books and papers. Viewed from across the desk, he is enclosed by the shelves that recede behind him diagonally to the left. Yet these shelves also act as a flat pattern – the third shelf up skimming his head. The flat, patterning effect is enhanced by colours echoing each other in the foreground and background. In general, the colours are bright and intuitive – note the bright blue defining line which shines down Duranty's fingers.

Between 1875 and 1885, Degas experimented prolifically with artistic techniques. Here, he uses a mixed medium - predominantly gouache, a matt, water-based paint, and pastel, a matt, powdery medium. The gouache is spread very thinly in places, such as across the papers and pipes. Pastel is applied over the top, notably on the face and hands, crosshatched in places and not always following the form it is describing, making the viewer aware of the techniques used and the patterns created. In places, the texture and colour of the light canvas beneath also shows through.

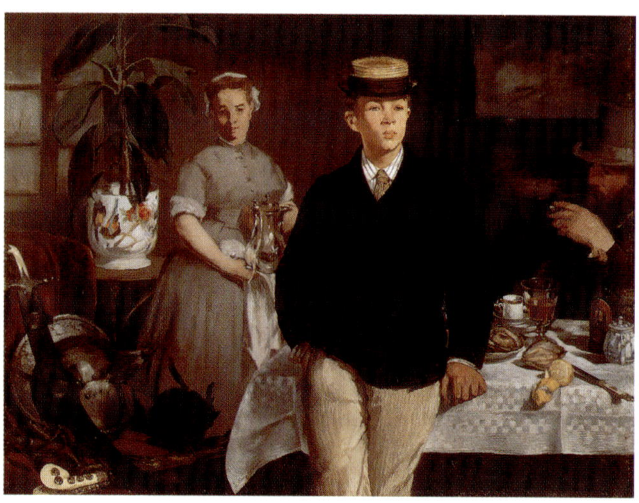

Edouard Manet
Lunch in the Studio, 1868
Neue Pinakothek, Munich. Courtesy of AKG London. *(See p. 26)*

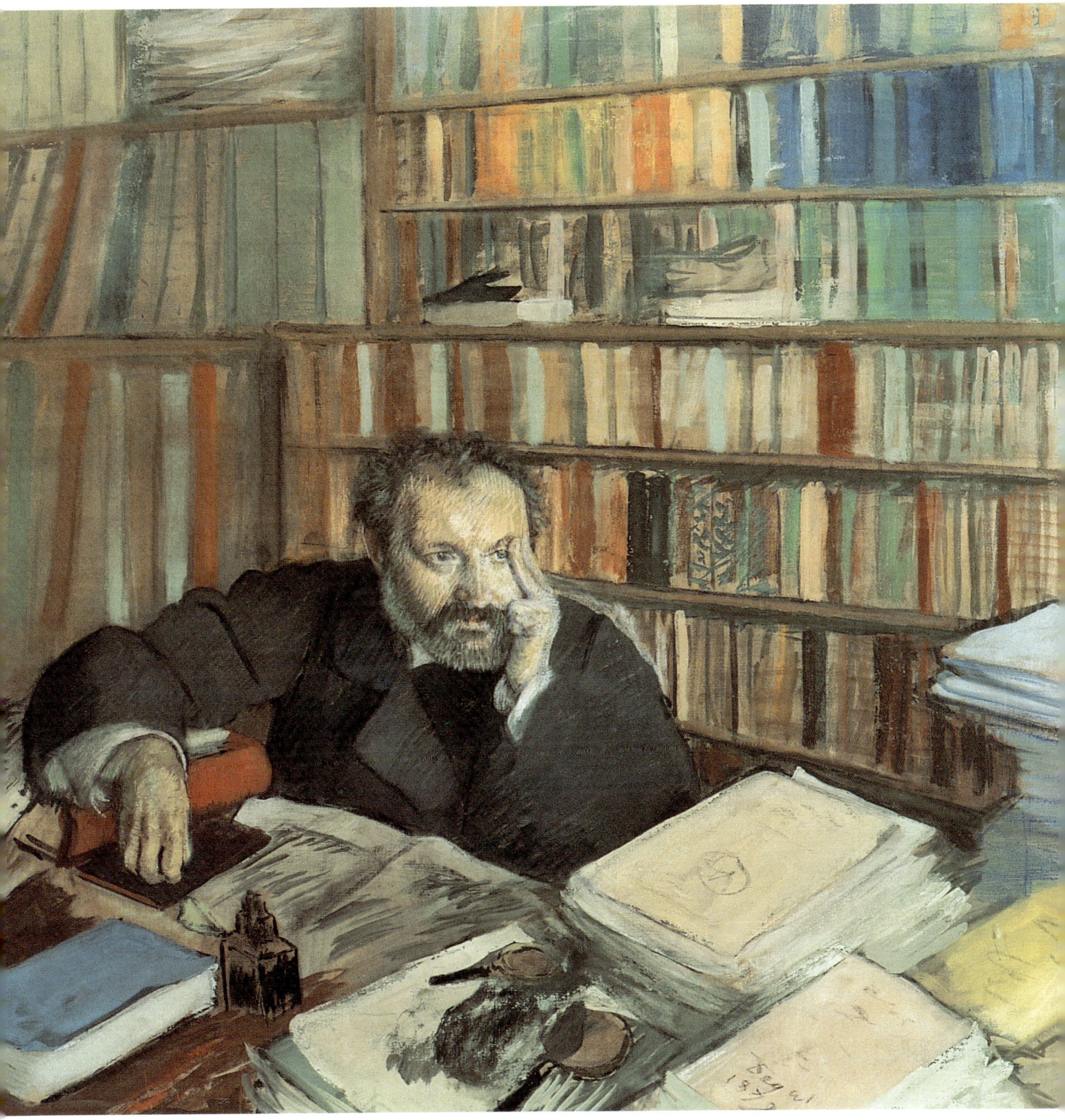

Edgar Degas
Green Dancers, c. 1880

Thyssen-Bornemisza Collection, Lugano. Courtesy of AKG London/Erich Lessing

THIS an early example of the pastel work that came to dominate Degas' later years. It is notable, above all, for its composition – three dancers in bright green seen from a plunging height as if from a box, cut off on the right and with only one whole dancer, the others simply a combination of legs and skirts. Dancers in orange strike casual poses in the background. In reality, they could not be seen by the audience, but their inclusion gives a sense of both the 'real' and the 'magical' aspects of the dancers. The customary empty space, in this case the stage, is tilted to an angle of 45 degrees, making the foreground seem yet more vertiginous.

This painting was very much admired and belonged to the English artist Walter Sickert (1860–1942). It shows Degas' lively analytical curiosity, his absolute fascination with how subjects can be ordered and presented in novel ways. Here, as in *In the Café* (1875–76), Degas' love of design comes to the fore – his dancers are almost abstract patterns on a page. The cut-off figures in the foreground also betray Degas' interest in photography, their portrayal is of three frames of the same dancer – something Degas had seen from the photographs of Eadweard Muybridge showing horses and people in motion.

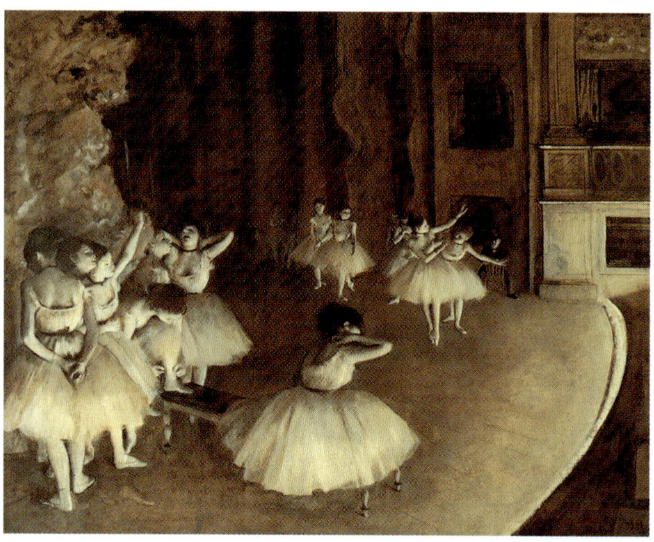

Edgar Degas
Ballet Rehearsal on the Stage, 1874
Musée d'Orsay. Courtesy of AKG London/Erich Lessing. *(See p. 166)*

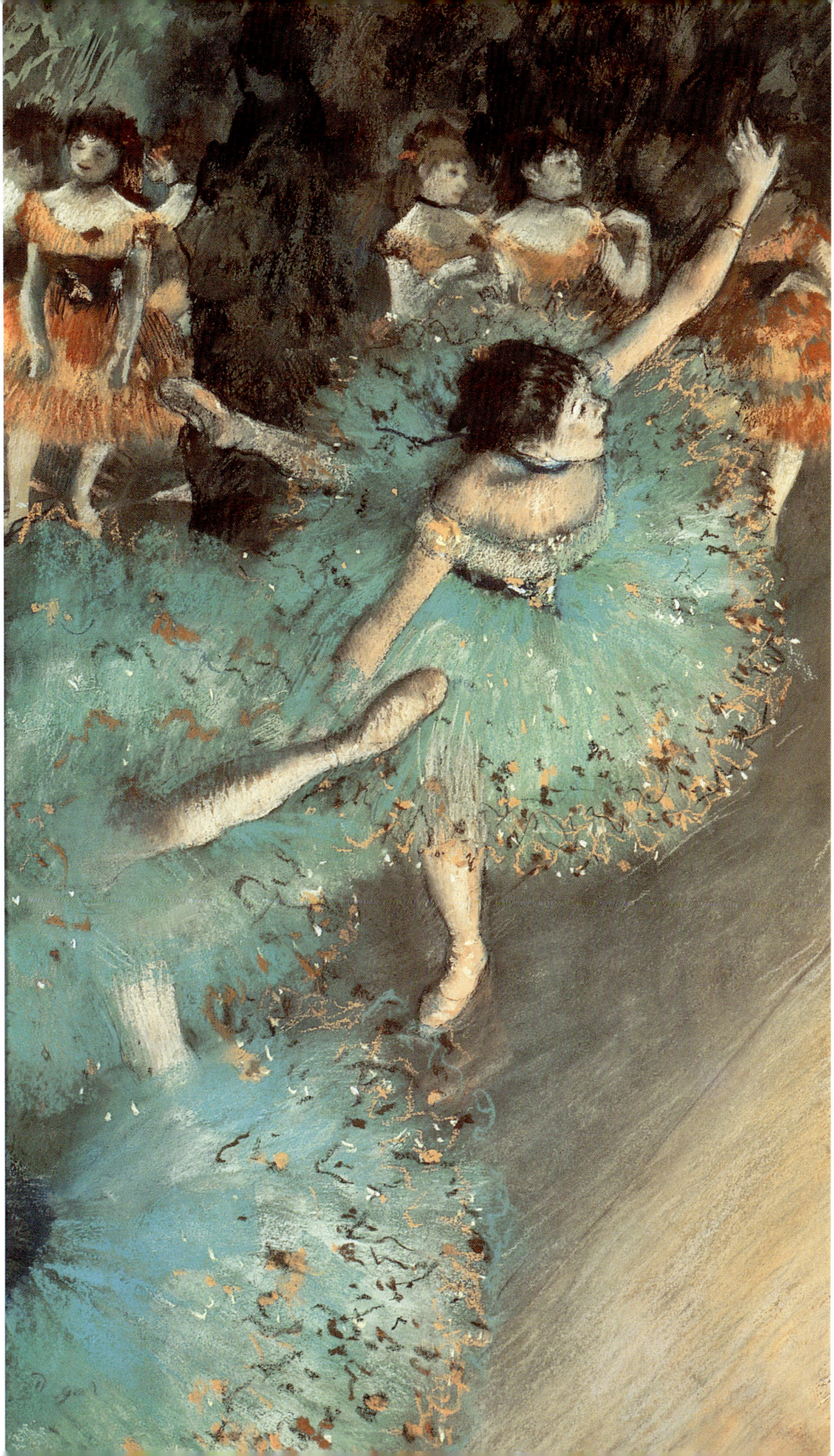

EDGAR DEGAS
Dancer, 1884

Musée d'Orsay, Paris. Courtesy of AKG London/Erich Lessing

DURING his working life Degas produced at least 500 models of horses, dancers and women at their toilette as part of the preparation for his paintings and pastels. Of these, 73 were cast in bronze by Degas' great friend Barthélemy towards the end of 1919, two years after Degas died, including the one shown here.

The only sculpture that Degas ever cast during his life was the *Fourteen-Year-Old Dancer* (1879). She was two-thirds life-size, dressed in real clothes and with a real ribbon in her hair. Degas exhibited her, after much hesitation, at the Impressionist exhibition of 1881. The bronzes cast after his death were shown in Paris in 1921 to such acclaim that another of the casters, Albino Palazzolo, received the Légion d'honneur – something of which Degas would not have approved.

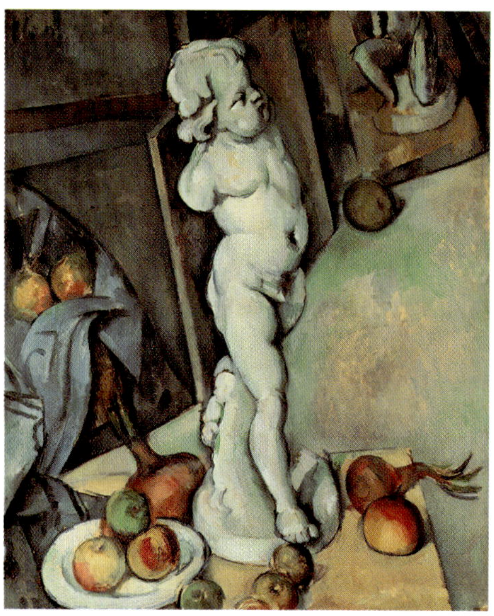

Paul Cézanne
Plaster Cupid, 1895
Courtauld Institute Galleries. Courtesy of AKG London. *(See p. 236)*

Many people saw Degas working on models in his studio, adding or subtracting wax, or giving up and starting again. They were a means of experimenting with movement and seeing all around his subject – an idea that the Cubists would embrace in years to come.

The English artist Walter Sickert describes how Degas, in 1910, 'showed me a little statuette of a dancer he had … and – it was night – he held up a candle and turned the statuette to show the succession of shadows cast by its silhouette on the sheet … .'

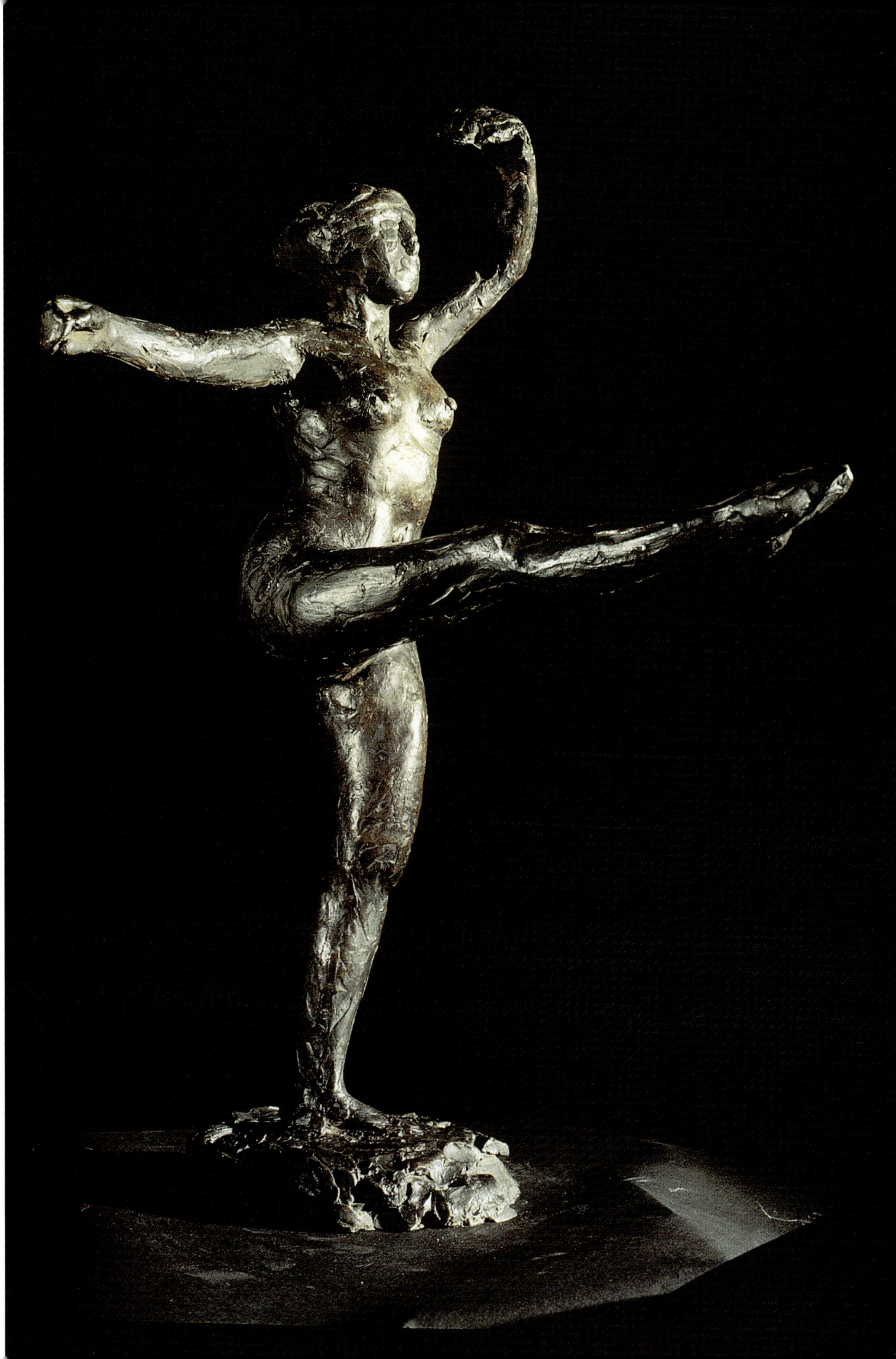

EDGAR DEGAS
Women Ironing, 1884

Musée du Louvre, Paris. Courtesy of AKG London/Erich Lessing

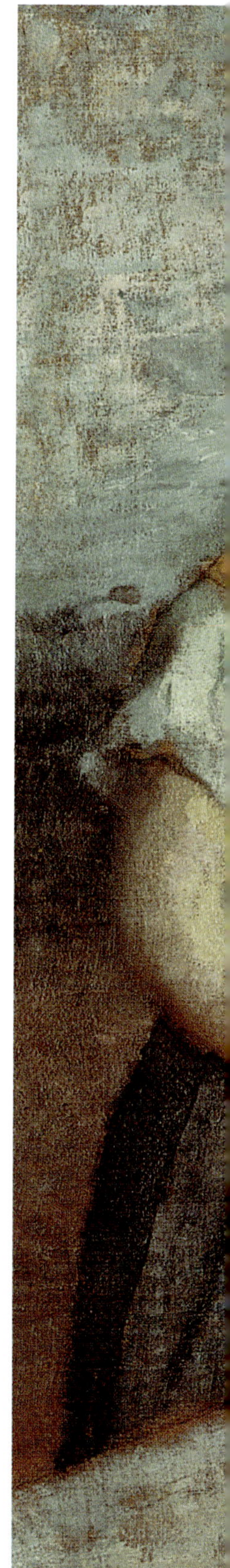

DEGAS had begun to portray women ironing as early as 1869. The weariness of the young girl is touching; so tired that she has to hold her head as she lifts her chin to yawn. Meanwhile, her colleague bears down on her iron with an exhausted weight. Degas, as in other works such as *Portrait of Edmond Duranty* (1879) or *In the Café (Absinthe)* (1875–76) views his subjects across a table that encloses them within their own space. The background, two strong verticals (one of them the stove) echoes the figures. The scraped and patchy oil paint and bare canvas in-between suggests the barrenness of the girls' lives in the sweatshop.

The round figures are heavy and the movements natural – as with Degas' women bathing, these two are unaware of the viewer, who glimpses a moment in their dreary lives. The realism of the textures – the arms, the wool, the glass bottle, are typical of some of Degas' work of the 1880s, especially those showing milliners' shops.

Women Ironing was not well received. The English critic George Moore explained, 'It is one thing to paint laundresses amid decorative shadows like Teniers [David the Younger, 1610–90] did; it is another to show these laundresses yawning above the work table, profiled in strong contrast against a dark background.'

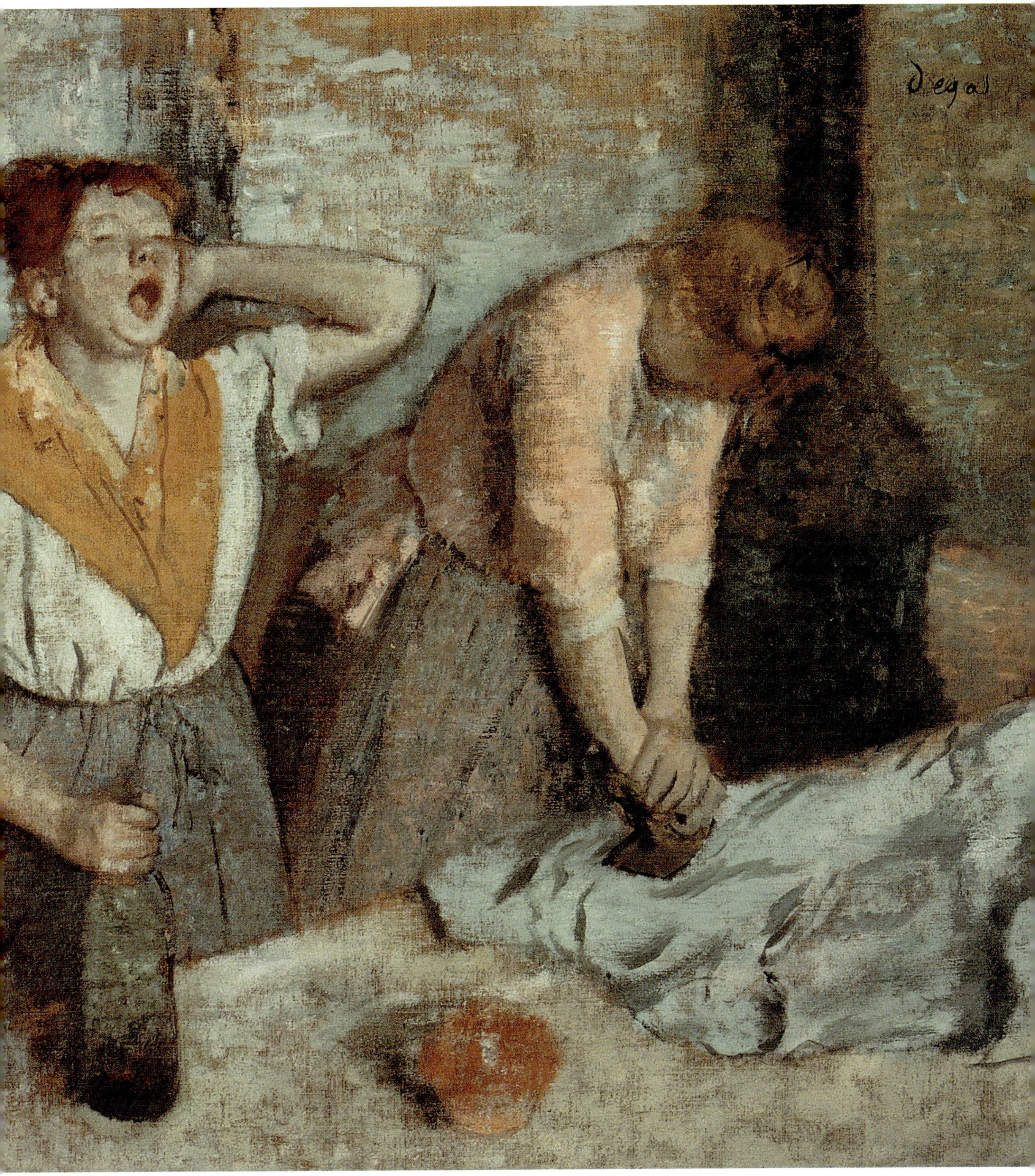
Degas

EDGAR DEGAS
Woman in a Tub, 1885

Courtesy of AKG London

THIS pastel may be one of the series of ten showing women at their toilette that Degas exhibited, to public horror, at the eighth Impressionist exhibition in 1886. In much the same way as Manet's *Olympia* (1863) and *The Lunch on the Grass* (1862–63) had caused shock in 1863, these nudes appaled the public because of their modern subject matter and their ability to make the viewers question their role in the visual process.

Degas' nudes are simple working girls, whom the public will have presumed to be prostitutes. Their portrayal was deemed offensive and the act of washing, particularly showing the postures and contortions required to wash effectively in a tin bath, thought to be degrading. In addition, these women are completely unaware of the viewer – apparently putting the viewer in the position of voyeur. The honesty of Degas' portrayal (which was motivated by considerations of form and movement as much as by anything else) was too much for the critics and the public.

The critic J.-K. Huysman spoke for the majority when he wrote, 'It seems as though [Degas] … has determined to retaliate and fling in the face of the century the worst insult he can devise, overturning that cherished idol, woman, degrading her by showing her actually in her bath in the humiliating postures of her toilette.'

It is interesting to note, however, that over half the nudes were sold before they even reached the exhibition.

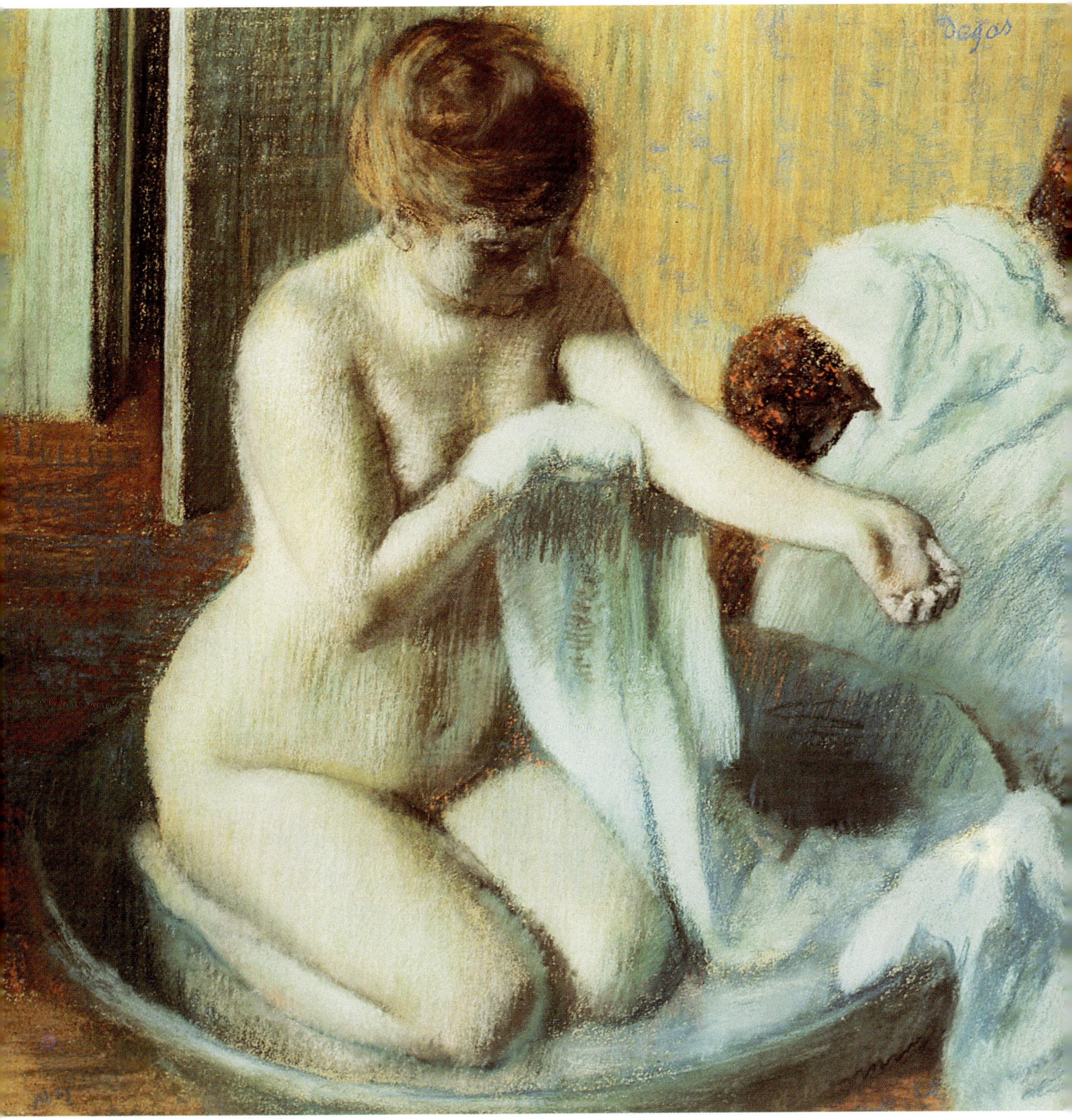
Degas

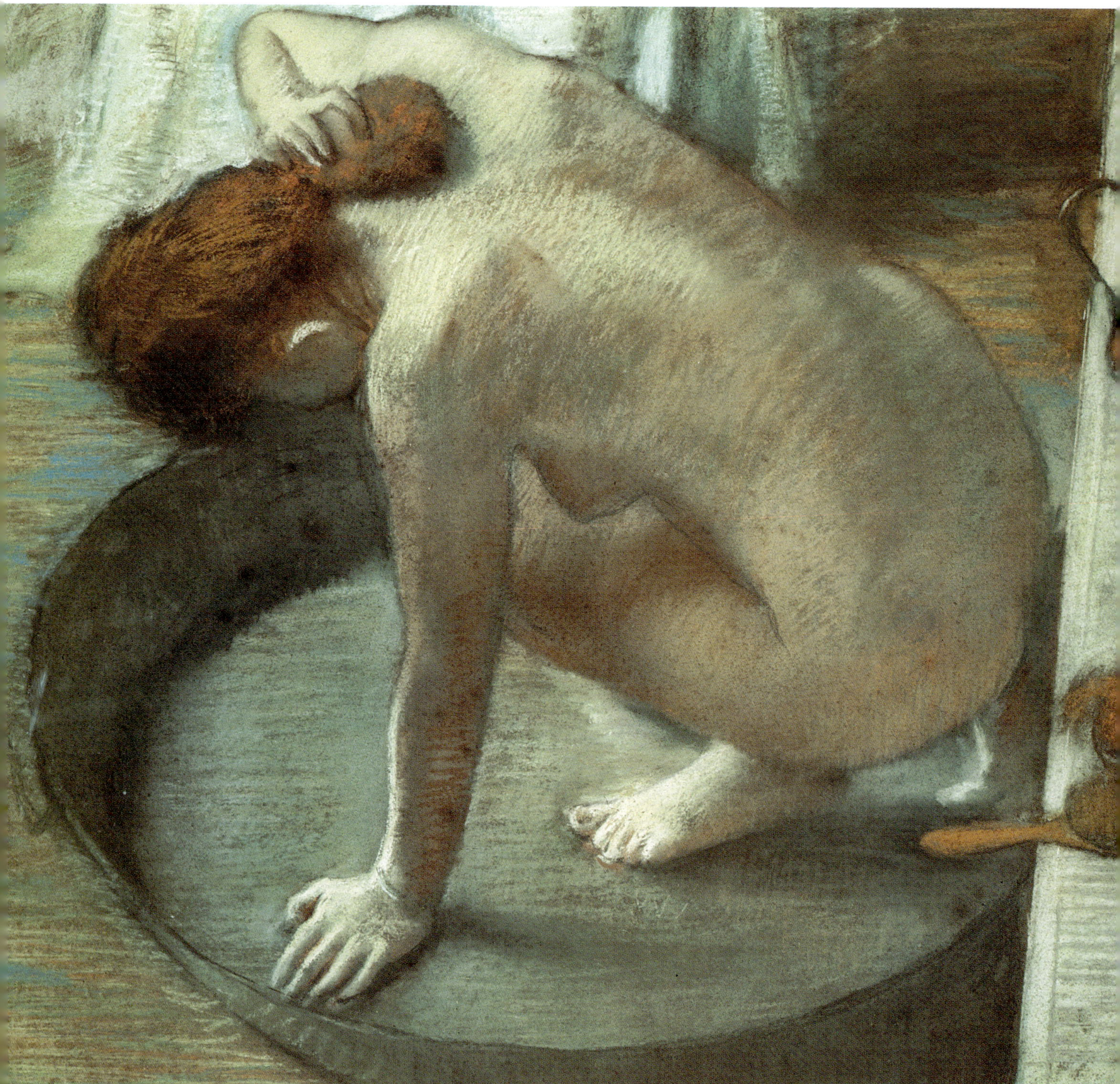

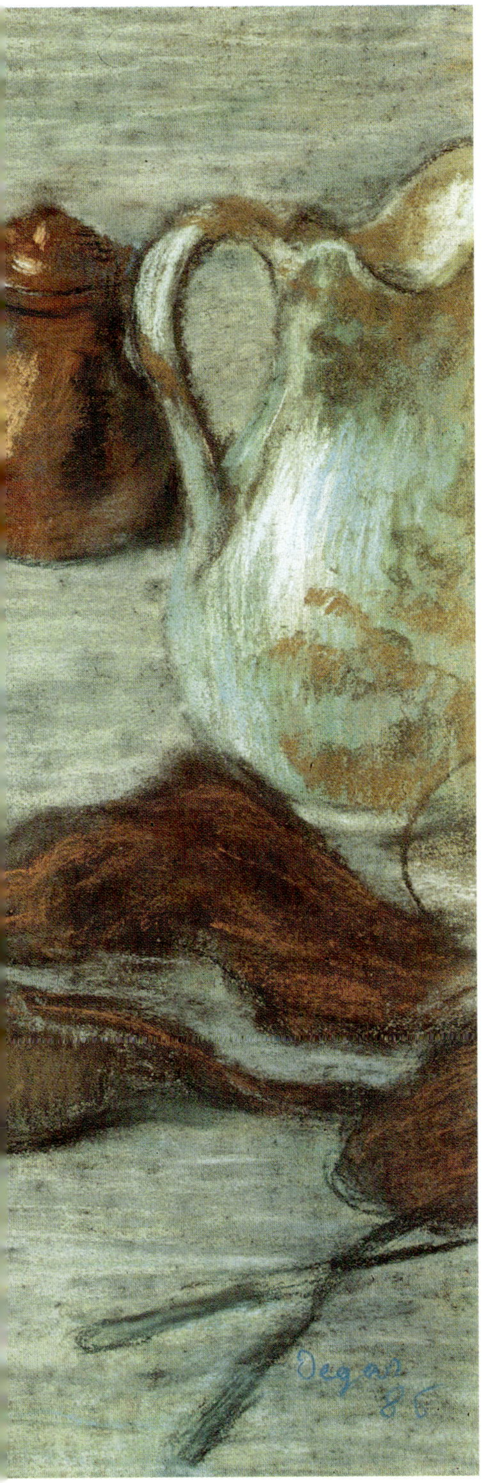

EDGAR DEGAS
The Tub, 1886

Musée d'Orsay, Paris. Courtesy of AKG London

THIS pastel was exhibited at the Impressionist exhibition of 1886. But, shocking though Degas' nudes were to the public, his main interest was in natural, innocent, untroubled form and movement. He once described woman as 'the human creature preoccupied with itself, a cat that licks itself', and also as seeing his nudes 'as if through a keyhole'. This comment has caused controversy over the years, suggesting a titillating voyeurism by catching these women unawares. But, from the works themselves, which show a curious lack of objectivity, and Degas' own comments, it is clear that he simply did not want the figures to be self-conscious. 'Perhaps I have treated women too much as animals,' he later said.

Degas' love of interesting compositions and viewpoints is clear. The overhead view indicates a Japanese influence, as does the cropping on the right side with a strong vertical (actually a receding table edge, only placed in 'real' space by the objects upon it). The pose of the nude also owes much to the flood of Japanese prints by artists such as Katsushika Hokusai (1760–1849) and Kitigawa Utamaro (1754–1806), that were coming into Europe for the first time.

Done as pastel on card, this work also shows Degas' fascination and increasing experimentation with colour, different media and new techniques such as crosshatching, which in some places is rubbed and blurred but elsewhere defining or flattering the form. His Classical concern for drawing (learnt from studying Ingres) is also clear.

Edgar Degas
Blue Dancers, c. 1893

Musée d'Orsay, Paris. Courtesy of AKG London/Erich Lessing

By 1893 Degas' eyesight, which had begun to trouble him in 1870, was beginning to deteriorate more rapidly. Increasingly, he had to rely on his memory rather than his sight in order to create the images that he wanted.

Here, in oils, he returns to his dancers – four girls in a circle, elbows and skirts sticking out, arranging themselves before they go on stage. The blue of their costumes and the flesh of their décolletage and arms create an almost abstract pattern. The two girls in the foreground are virtually mirror images of each other, viewed from different angles.

In the background Degas creates a Pointillist effect – dabs of pure colour side by side. But his aim is not a scientific one concerning the rendition of light. Rather, these marks create a pattern against which the shapes of the dancers stand out and suggests the decoration of the scenery on the stage.

As we look at the scene, a column blocks our view and creates a dramatic vertical element that recalls *The Tub* (1886). Dancers in the background merge with the overall pattern – the flash of orange complementing the peacock blue of the costumes.

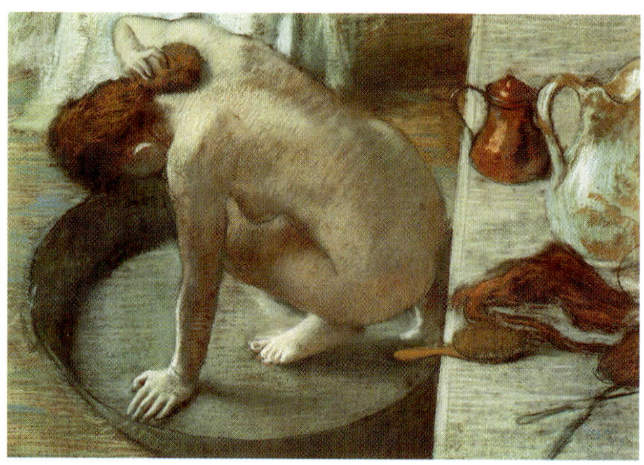

Edgar Degas
The Tub, 1886
Musée d'Orsay. Courtesy of AKG London. *(See p. 185)*

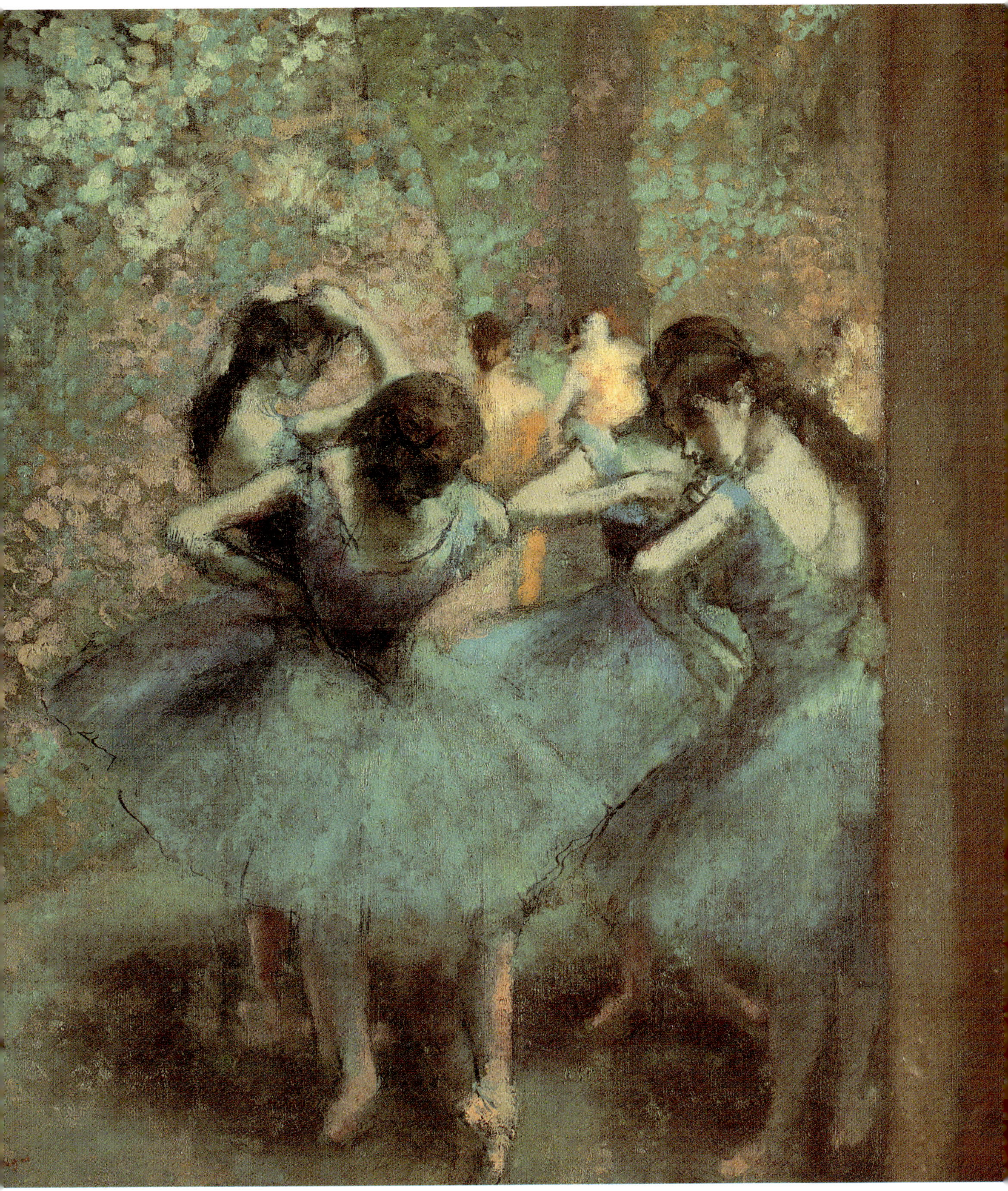

EDGAR DEGAS
Blue Dancers, 1897

Pushkin Museum, Moscow. Courtesy of AKG London

IN this pastel painted late in his career, Degas has begun to view his subjects from close up – perhaps because of his ailing eyesight or, possibly, in response to work by his contemporaries Cézanne, Gauguin and Van Gogh.

It shows four dancers, viewed from above, in similar poses – the two on the right practically identical except for the direction of their heads. Where they are in relation to the stage (although we presume they are in the wings) is not clear. These mirror images and more precise ones occur in many of Degas' paintings and the same poses are repeated many times.

This pastel, as with all the others, would have been created laboriously in the studio from memory, using a number of drawings and sketches – some of which Degas may have used before. He often created the 'mirror image' simply by tracing over and pressing paper over a charcoal sketch and reworking the reversed image. He may have worked with photographs – a picture exists of a dancer in this pose, her elbows sticking out, that Degas may have taken.

'Art is artifice,' he once said – completely at odds with his Impressionist friends – and, although he created some of the most fleeting-effect images of the entire group, his manner of working was laborious in the extreme.

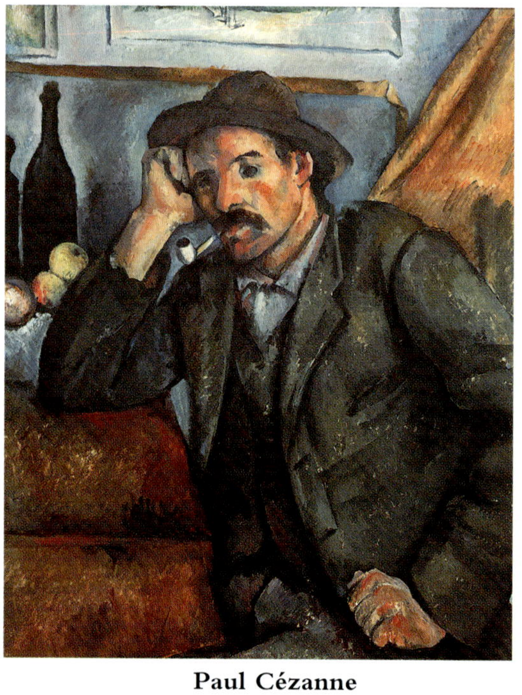

Paul Cézanne
Detail from *The Smoker, 1890–92*
Courtesy of AKG London. *(See p. 230)*

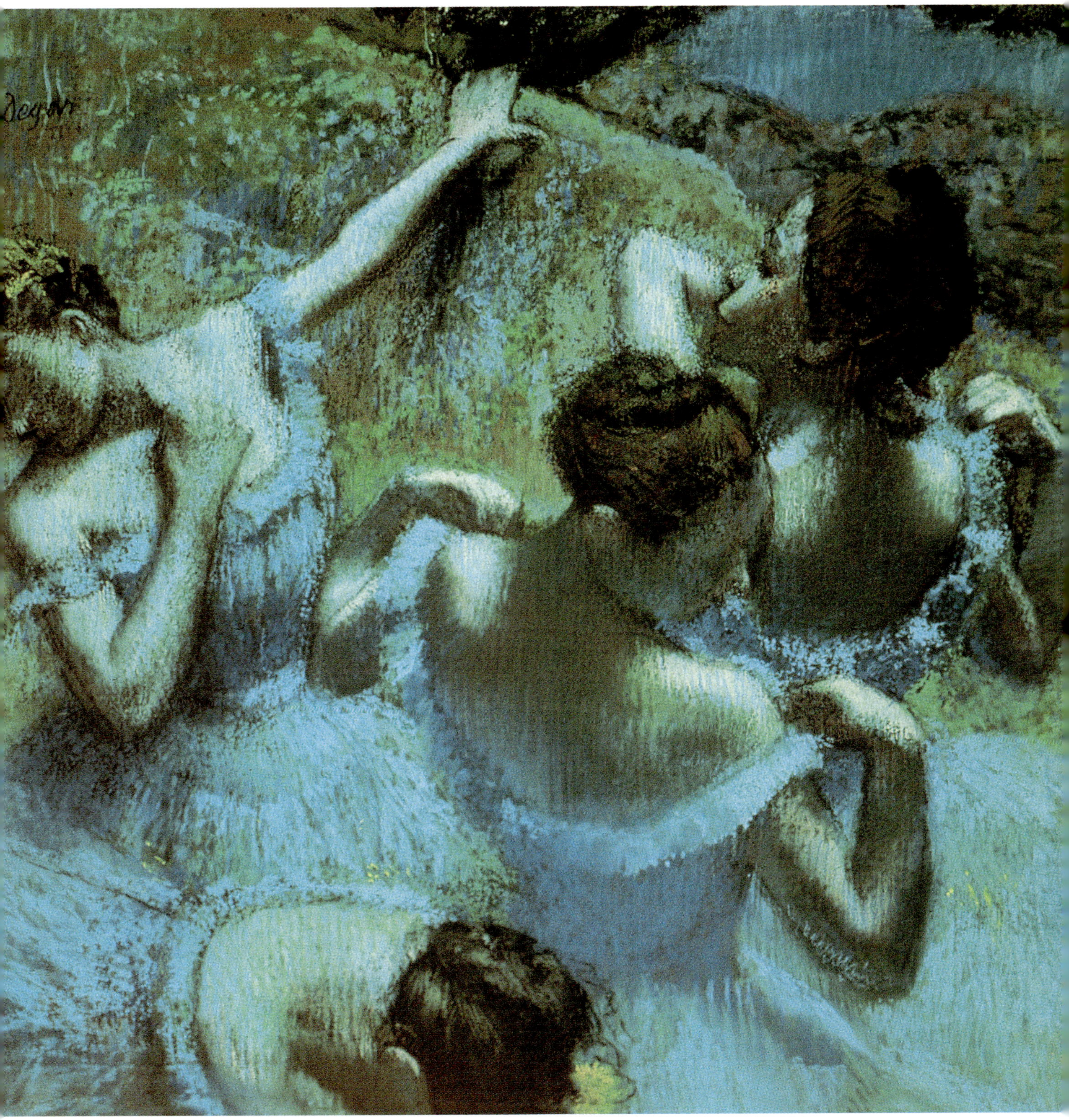
Degas

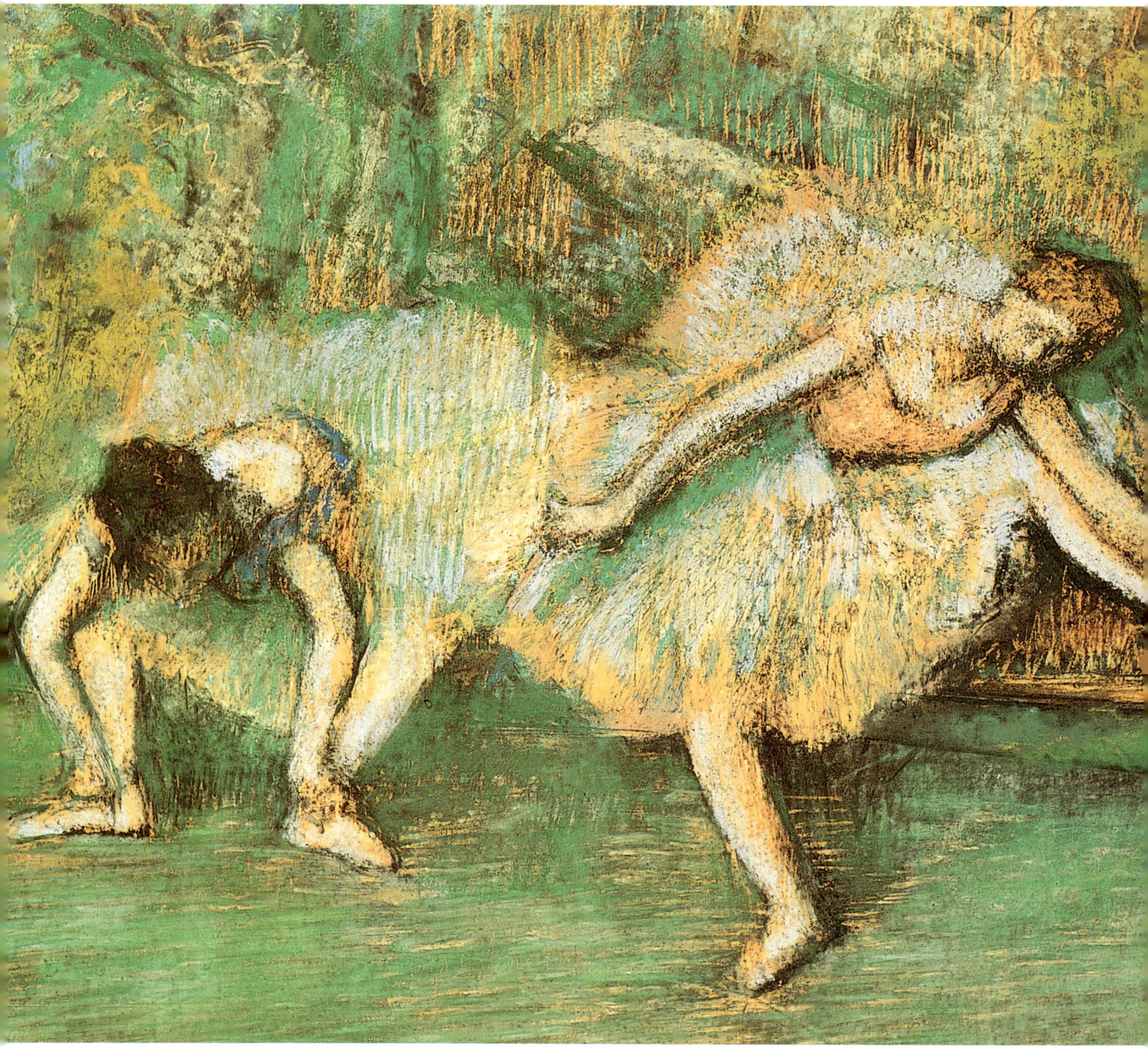

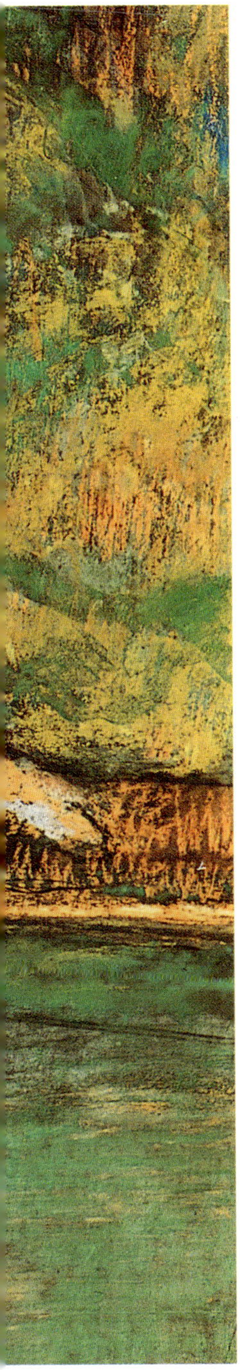

EDGAR DEGAS

Two Dancers on a Bench, c. 1900–05

Private Collection. Courtesy of AKG London

THIS is a late pastel, typical of those from the 1890s onwards that explode with colour and show an element of abstraction. Many pastels and drawings show these poses, including drawings of nude dancers – a natural progression of Degas' fascination with movement and his quest to find the best way to express it.

The two dancers, or 'horse-girls' as one critic has put it, stretch their backs and their legs – making apparent the wearisome reality behind the gauzy tutus and the bright lights. The abstraction of the picture is created by Degas' use of pastel, in which the vivid strokes of colour are separate, applied layer by layer, creating a filmy haze between the viewer and the dancers.

Degas has used various techniques, including both dry and wet pastel. He experimented constantly and his techniques included brushing applied pastel with water, burnishing it to create a cratered effect, wetting the end of the pastel stick and 'fixing' his pictures with steam. He referred to his techniques as his 'cooking' or 'recipes'.

Tragically, Degas' sight deteriorated so much that he was forced to stop working by the year 1912. In his last years he was almost blind. He died in 1917, aged 83.

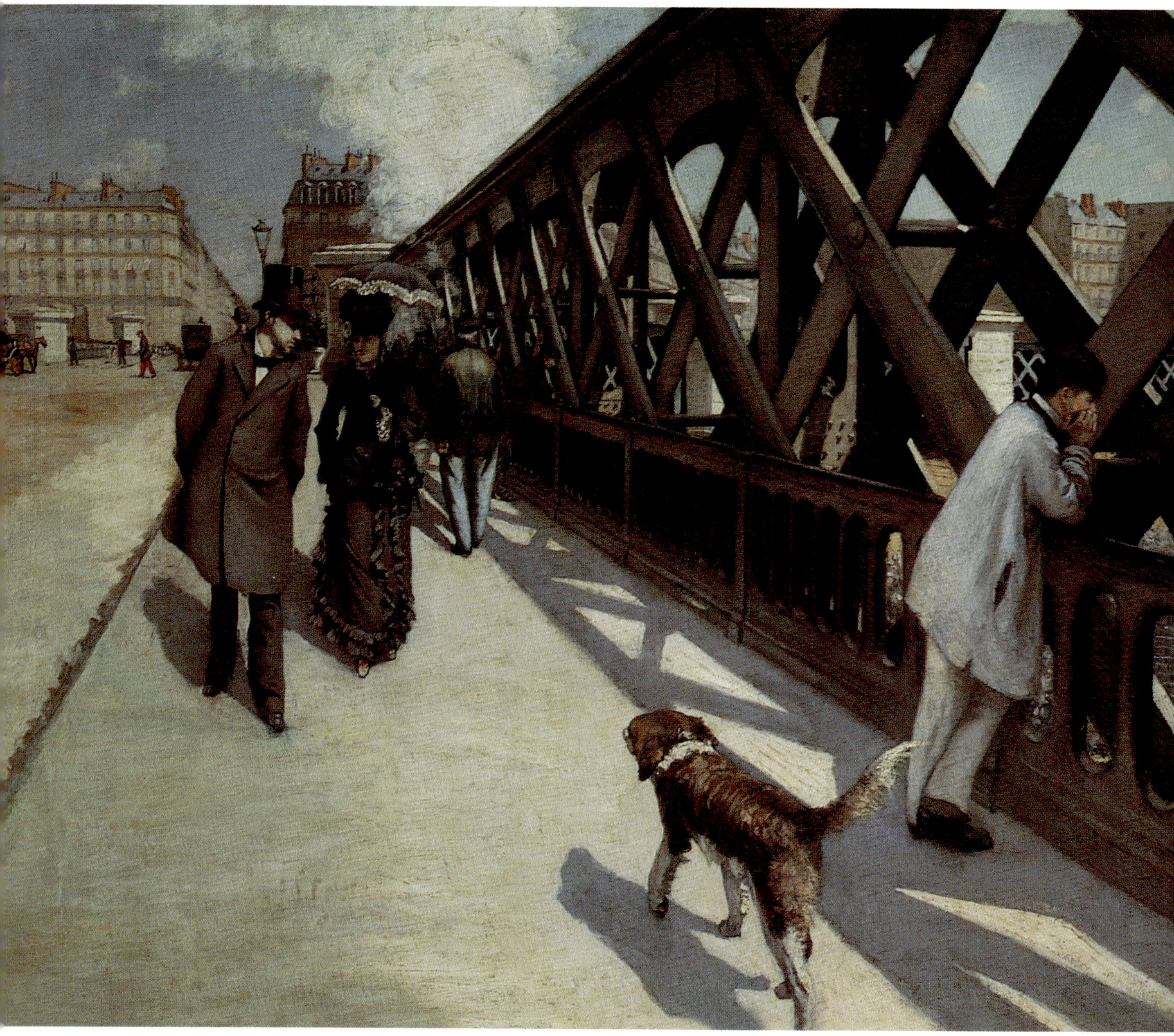

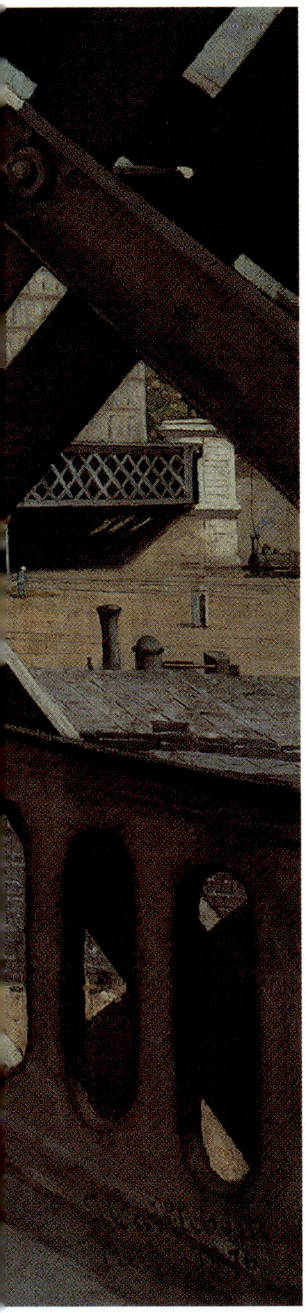

Gustave Caillebotte (1848–94)
Pont de L'Europe, 1876

Musée du Petit Palais, Geneva. Courtesy of AKG London/Erich Lessing

GUSTAVE CAILLEBOTTE, a naval engineer and amateur painter, studied under Léon Bonnat (1833–1922), the portraitist and historical painter. He met Degas, Renoir and other artists exhibiting at the Boulevard des Capucines in 1874.

His early work bears affinities with Manet and Degas, both realist painters of city life. Here, Caillebotte provides a fleeting moment on a sunny day on the new Pont de l'Europe in Paris. The viewers walk behind a dog and towards a couple walking and talking, who will pass out of the picture shortly. On the left, a man in a smock-type jacket leans over the bridge, gazing to the view beyond. The sun shines through the girders of the bridge, swallowing up the pavement and decorating it with purple shadows. The painting is overwhelmed by a glistening clarity and the background is not lost in an 'impressionistic' haze.

Like Manet, Caillebotte's figures are part of his modern setting and not simply a vehicle for the effects of light and colour. The draughtsmanship and the palette also reflect Manet and his delight in differentiating between shades of white.

The composition is made up of six triangles, which meet behind the heads of the couple. It is cut off as in a photograph. A large empty space takes up the left side of the painting and the girders of the bridge forge their way in diagonally and dominate the composition. To counter this inward movement, the couple walk towards us, out of the painting.

GUSTAVE CAILLEBOTTE
Street in Paris in the Rain, 1877

Chicago Art Institute. Courtesy of AKG London/Erich Lessing

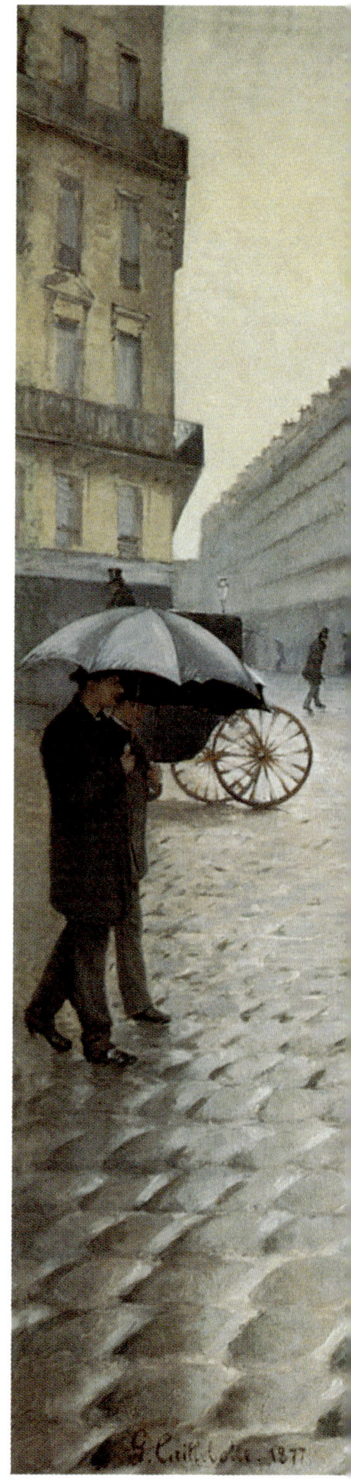

THIS is another street scene in which Caillebotte creates a sense of movement in and out of the canvas. It is a geometric design with an emphasis on the vertical. Horizontal movement is created by the people crossing the street. Open umbrellas prevent the design from becoming rigid.

Surprisingly, this is one of the few Impressionist works that depicts Paris in the rain, when the light becomes uniform without any direct sunlight to shine through the leaden sky. This may be because painting outside in the rain, as well as being uncomfortable, did not offer the contrasts of light and shade that lent themselves to the colourful palettes of artists such as Monet and Renoir. Caillebotte's palette is fairly muted although, when not using shades of black, grey and white, he uses complementary orange and green for the lamp-post and the wall on the right. He makes full use of the wet cobbles and pavement to create reflections and effects of glistening light.

The composition is unusual, with the edges 'cut off' and the viewpoint from the left, as if the viewer is walking along the pavement too. Borrowing from Japanese techniques, a lamp-post cuts the canvas in half and divides the close-up, cluttered view on the right from the long, relatively empty view on the left. These experiments in composition are reminiscent of Degas' work.

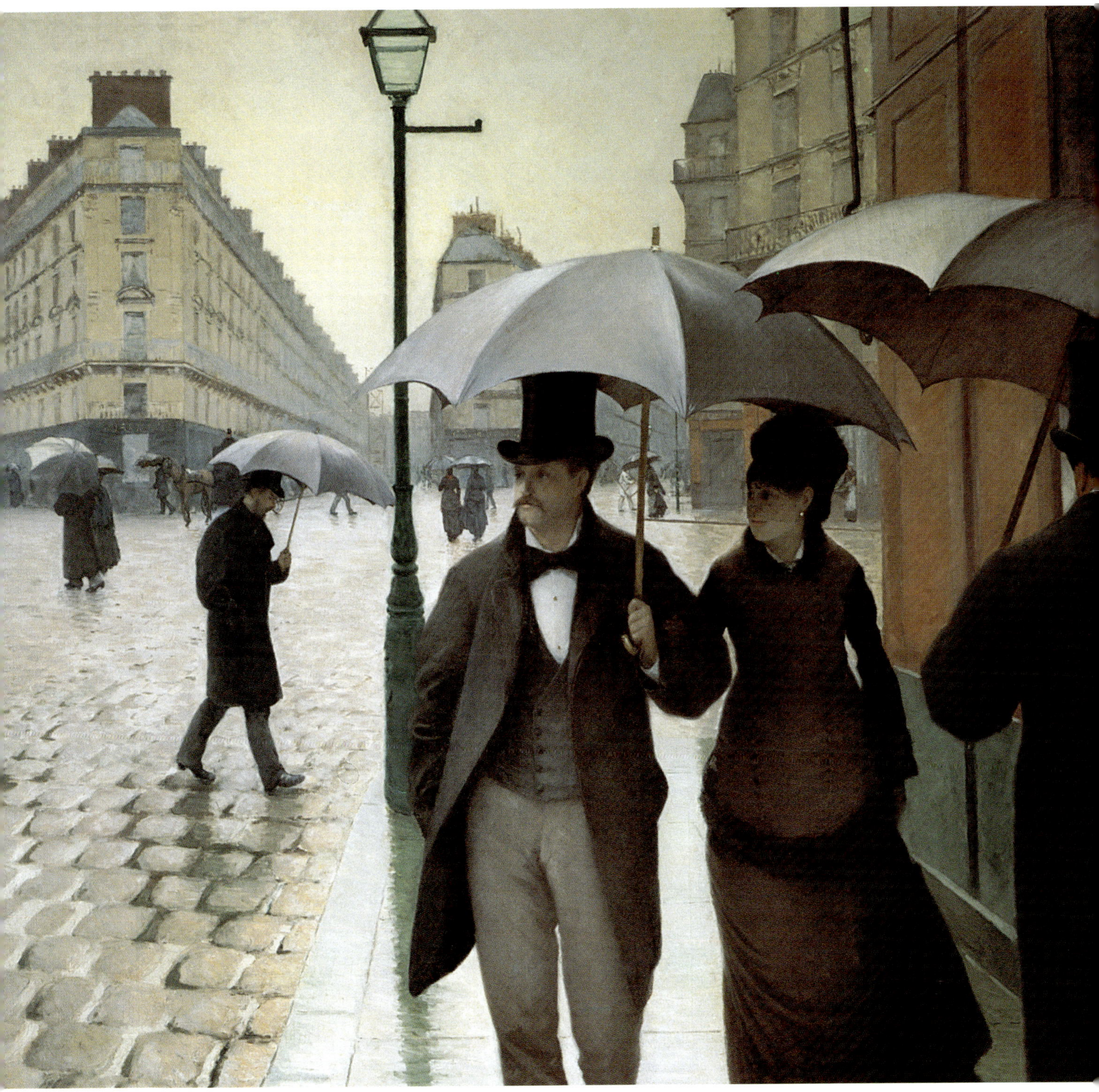

Gustave Caillebotte
Bathers, 1878

Private Collection, France. Courtesy of AKG London/Erich Lessing

By 1878, Caillebotte was increasingly using the Impressionist palette and painting naturally lit outdoor scenes. However, although his palette has lightened and his brushwork is more relaxed, he has not yet adopted a fragmentary or sketchy application of paint that might interrupt the contour or three-dimensional solidity of his figures.

This is one of several river scenes showing young men diving, rowing, swimming and climbing out of the water. The fact that it shows men bathing is quite unusual. Bazille painted his technicolour painting of young men bathing in 1869 and Seurat painted *Bathers at Asnières* in 1883, but virtually all other Impressionist bathing scenes show women and girls bathing.

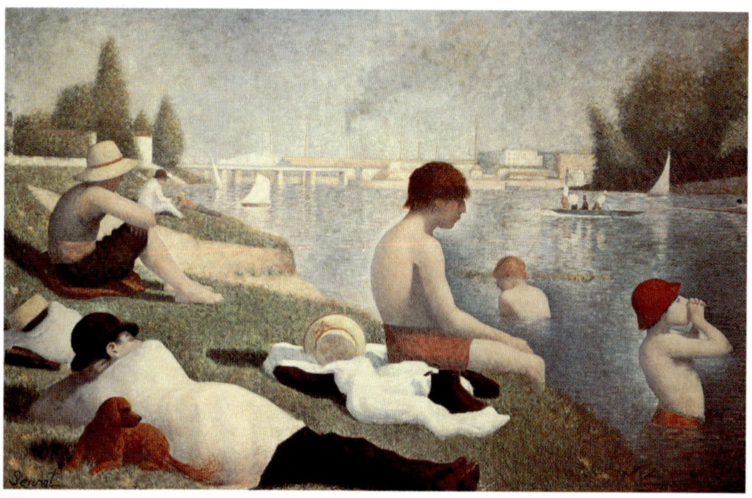

Georges Seurat
Bathing at Asnières, 1883–84
Tate Gallery, London. Courtesy of AKG London/Erich Lessing. *(See p. 253)*

This painting, along with *Pont de L'Europe* (1876) and *Street in Paris in the Rain* (1877) were exhibited at the fourth exhibition in 1879, which Gustave Caillebotte arranged. Although he was not one of the foremost Impressionists, he supported the group financially and built up a collection of their work. He died in 1894 and bequeathed his collection to the state of France which, typically, was unsure about accepting such an unorthodox collection. The bequest, now at the Musée d'Orsay in Paris, still caused controversy when it was shown in 1897.

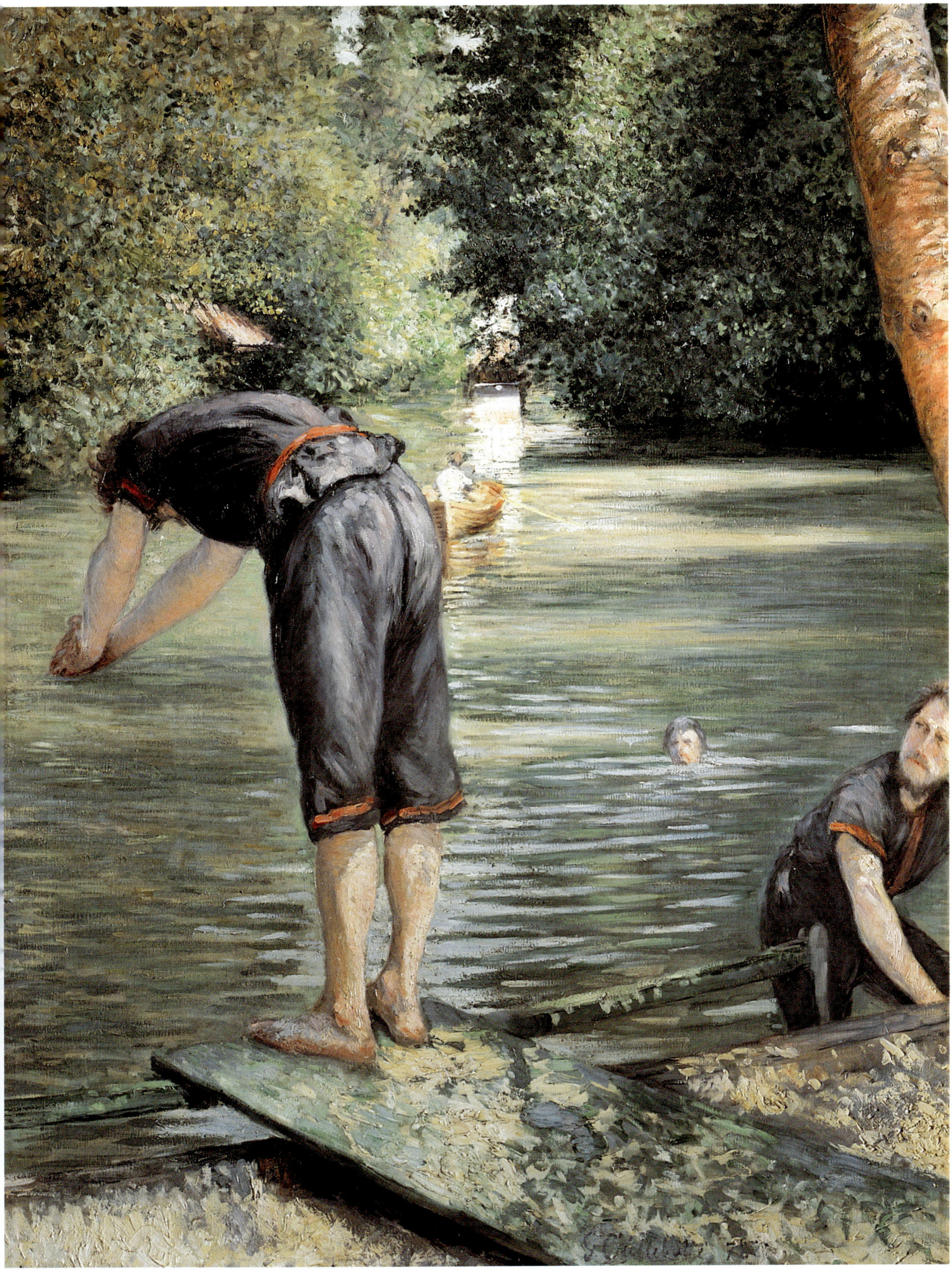

Berthe Morisot (1841–95)
The Mother and Sister of the Artist, 1869–70

Chester Dale Collection, National Gallery of Art Washington. Courtesy of AKG London

BERTHE MORISOT was the daughter of a top civil servant and the great-great-grand-niece of the painter Jean-Honoré Fragonard. Between 1860 and 1862, she was a pupil of Camille Corot, who advised her to paint out-of-doors. She came into contact with the Impressionists through Manet, whom she met in the Louvre with the artist Henri Fantin-Latour (1836–1904) in 1869. They became friends, and Morisot and her mother and sister used to visit Manet and his wife socially. Morisot modelled for several paintings, including *The Balcony* (1868–69).

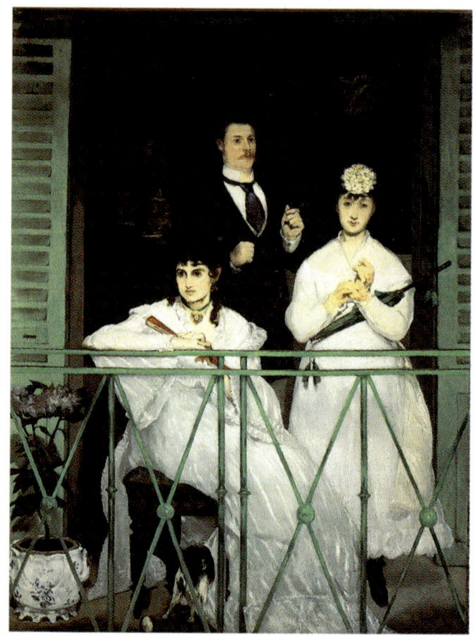

Edouard Manet
The Balcony, 1868–69
Courtesy of AKG London/Erich Lessing.
(See p. 28)

This painting shows Morisot's mother and pregnant sister Edma. Her mother, in black, takes up almost the whole of the bottom right of the picture. She is balanced by Edma in white on the other side, with a mirror above her head which reflects a window with open curtains and light streaming in.

This painting is the subject of the only documented source of friction between Manet and Morisot. Asking for advice, she was horrified when he took a paintbrush and worked on directly on to the canvas. Manet's work is evident in the heavier strokes around the eyes and mouth of Mme Morisot, in her fingers and in the broadly painted, thickly impastoed black dress. The composition is cut off and the mirror, a familiar image in many Impressionist interiors, is off-centre – the influence of both photography and Japanese prints. The painting was shown at the first Impressionist exhibition in 1874.

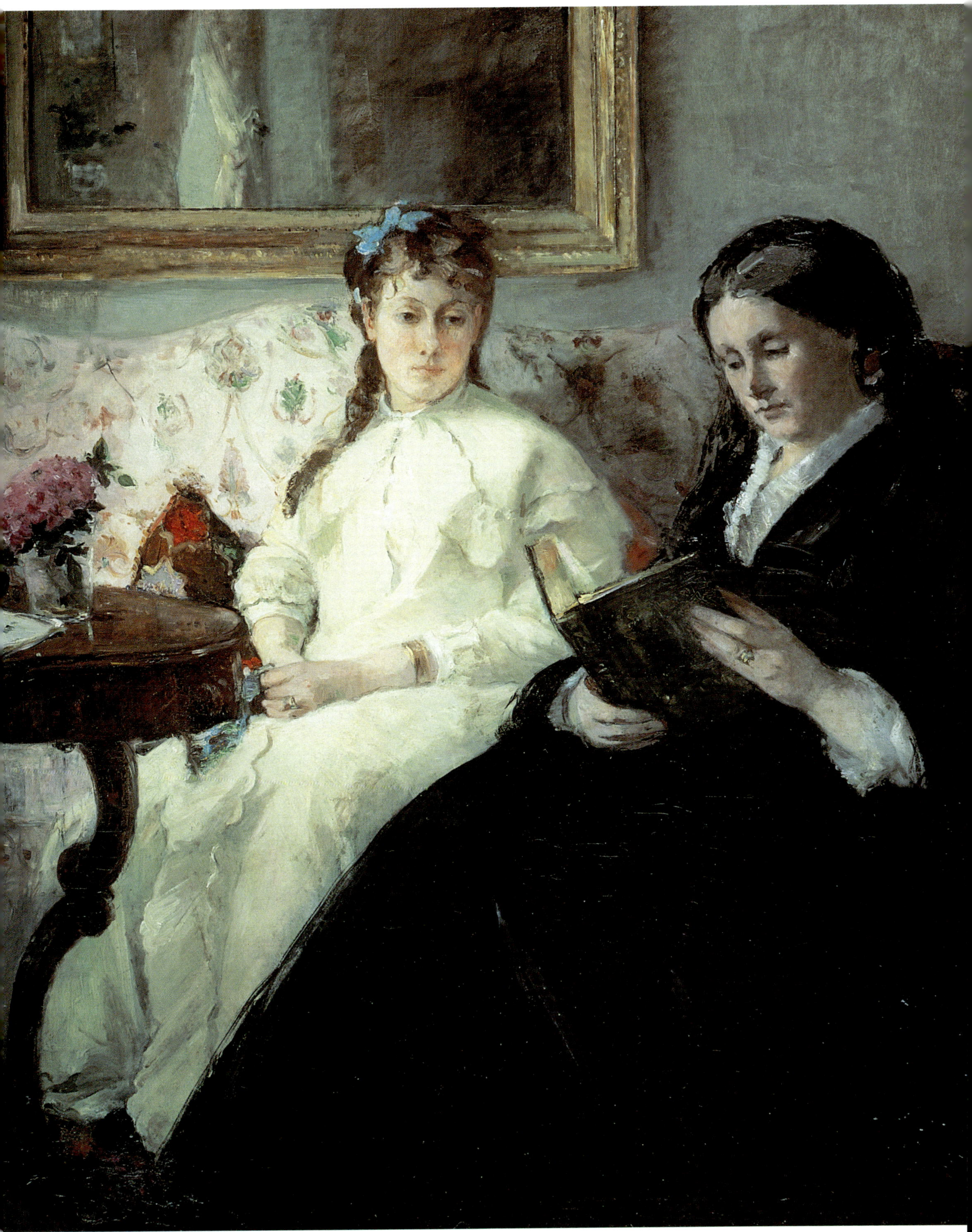

Berthe Morisot
In the Cornfield at Gennevilliers, 1875

Musée d'Orsay, Paris. Courtesy of AKG London/ Erich Lessing

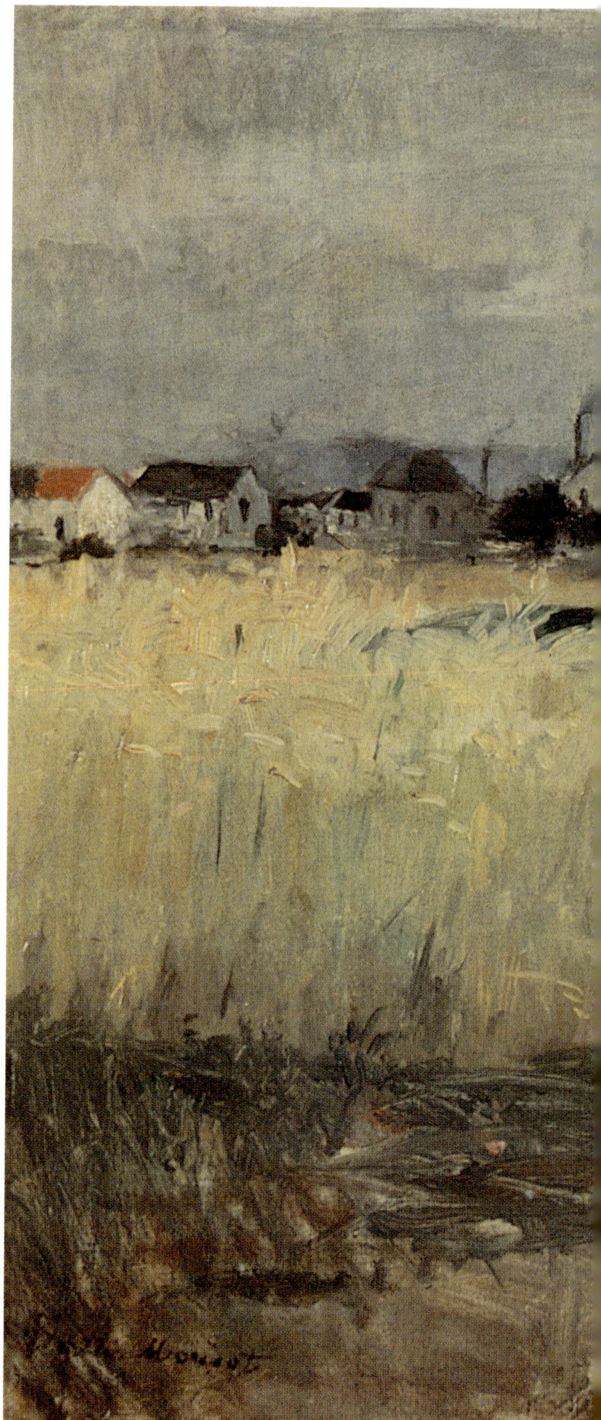

BY 1875, when this painting was completed, Morisot had married Manet's younger brother Eugène. She painted many landscapes as well as bourgeois women – rather like Renoir and Mary Cassatt (1845–1926). Here, she was painting at Gennevilliers, where Manet had a house. Painted in the open air, it shows a man standing on a path at the edge of a cornfield. In a typically Impressionist manner, she uses fleeting, dab-like strokes that many contemporary critics considered 'slapdash'. To others, such as the critic Paul Mantz, 'her freshness and improvisation' made her the 'only impressionist in the group'.

In this light-filled canvas, she is using a palette that hovers around yellow and blue, with very tiny touches of red in the roofs of two houses in the background. The emphasis is on the land and sky, a horizontal that Morisot does not interrupt. Even the man, painted in the same manner as the corn and landscape so that he blends in, is contained within the gold band of the cornfield. True to Impressionist theory, Morisot builds up her scene and the effects of light and the breeze by the way in which she applies the paint and juxtaposes colours. Draughtsmanship, edges and contours are not a priority.

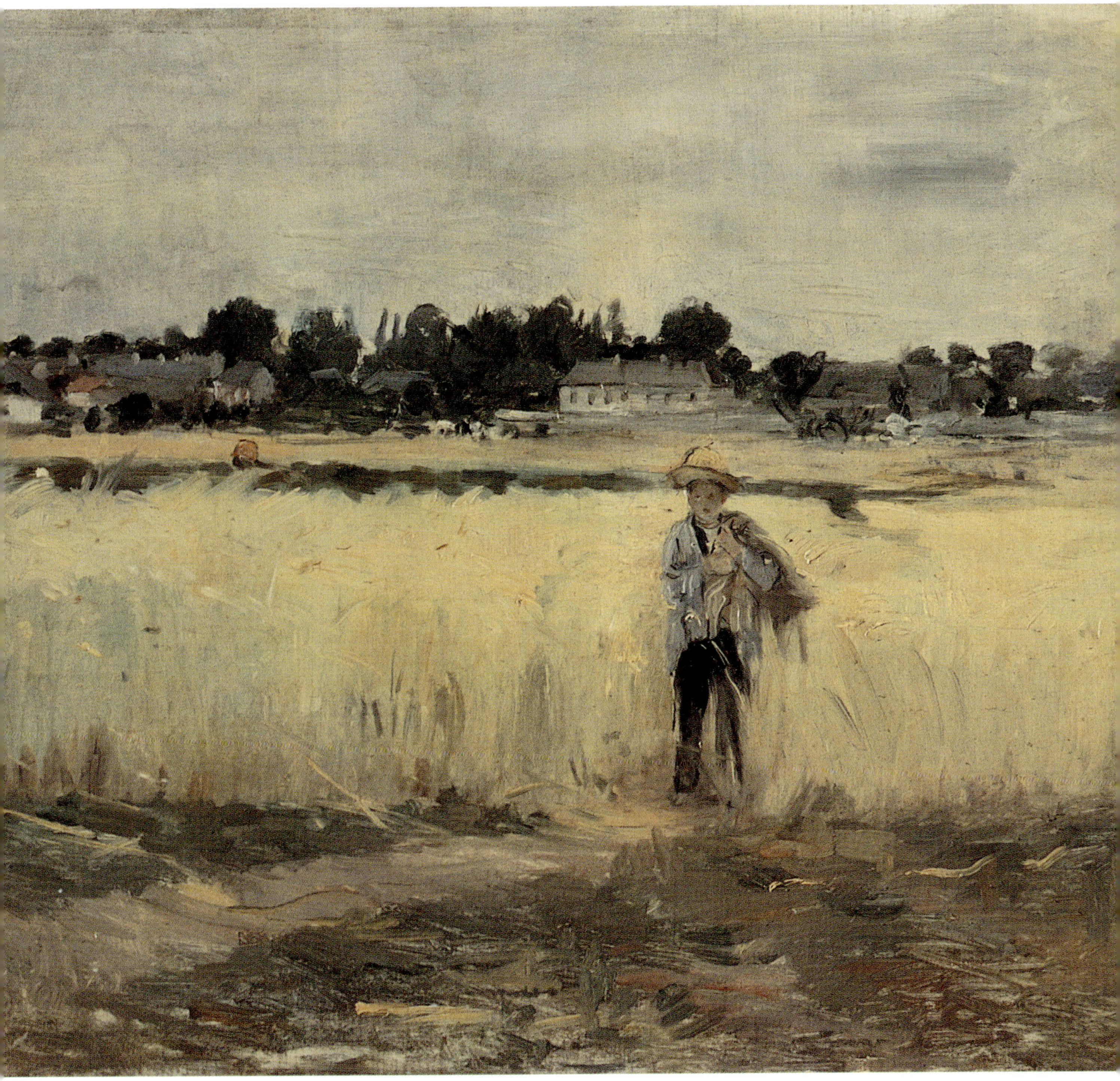

Berthe Morisot
Young Girl at the Ball, 1875

Musée Marmottan, Paris. Courtesy of AKG London

COMPLETED the same year as *In the Cornfield at Gennevilliers*, but in a more formal Impressionist style, *At the Ball* shows Morisot painting another of her favourite topics – bourgeois women. She painted many scenes of women dressed for a ball and provides a psychological insight into the moods of her models.

In this slightly asymmetrical composition, she makes fine use of colour, not dissimilar to Manet's before he embraced a lighter palette. It is at about this time, partly under her influence, that he, too, embraces the Impressionist way of painting. The young girl, her cheek on her fan, gazes to the left, her eyes caught by something or deeply intent on her own thoughts. She holds the fan gingerly, as if she has just been taught how to do so. This is a portrait of a girl in thought as much as a ball scene showing a young girl sitting out a dance. The composition is fairly straightforward but note how the right-hand side of the painting is unadorned and empty apart from the fan, while the left-hand side is busier, and the colours darker.

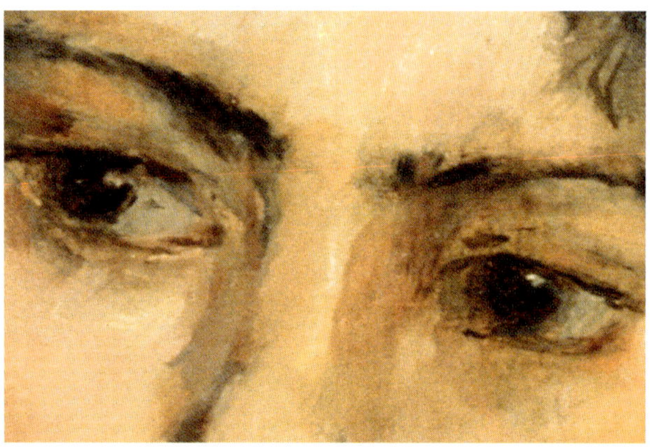

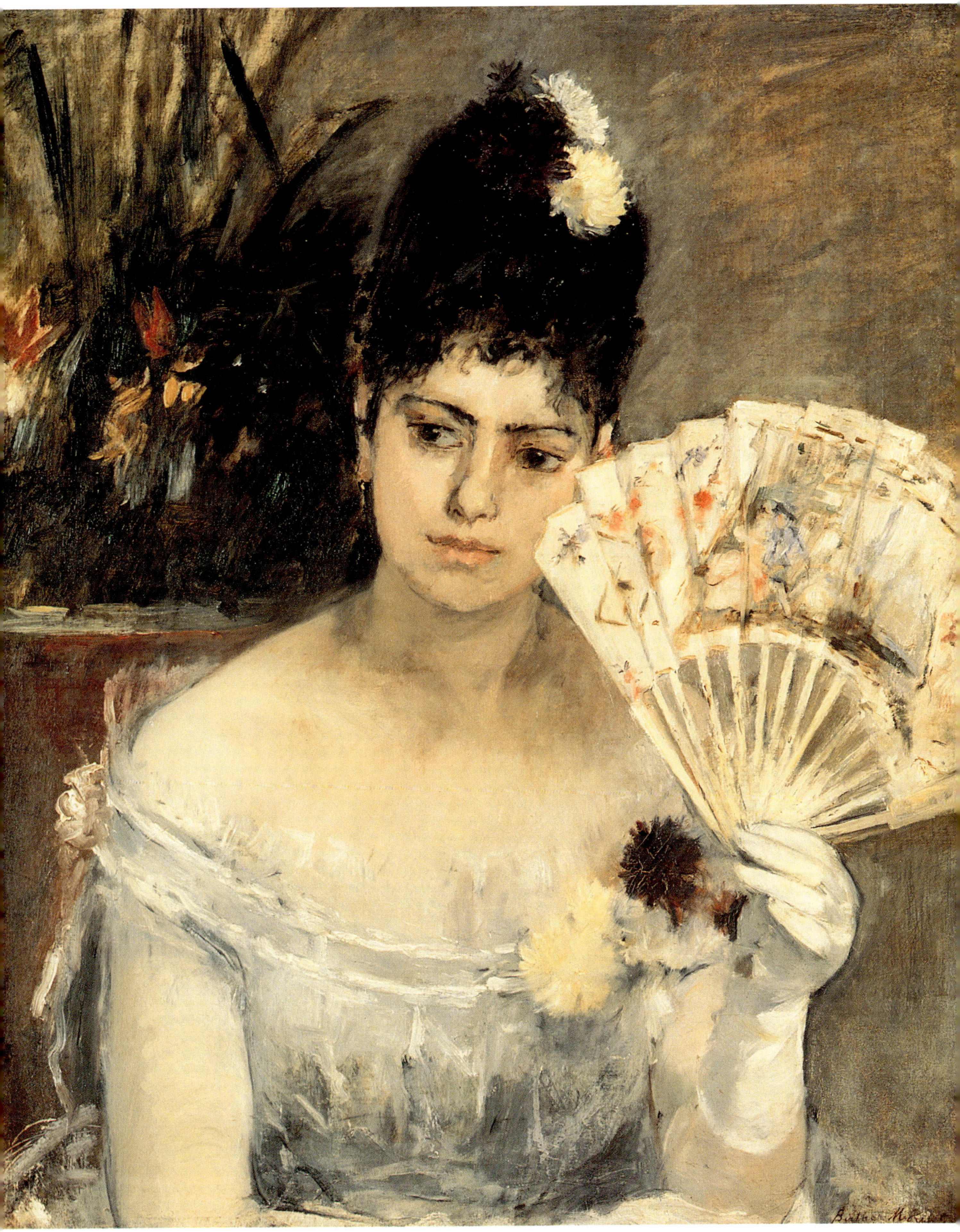

Berthe Morisot
Young Woman Powdering Herself, 1877

Musée d'Orsay, Paris. Courtesy of AKG London/Erich Lessing

LIKE Manet, Degas and Renoir, Morisot painted women at their toilette, but her women are bourgeois and her paintings show the intimate details of the daily ritual of women in a circle like her own. There is nothing remotely salacious about them. *Young Woman Powdering Herself* was painted the same year that Manet painted *Nana*, a young woman at her toilette. Both used a light palette, painted in the Impressionist style and showed women in front of their mirrors. But Manet's was shocking – his model, Henriette Hauser, was the mistress of the Prince of Orange and Nana was the name of the prostitute in Zola's novel, *L'Assommoir* (1877).

Morisot did not concern herself with 'unsuitable' subjects, which were in the male domain. As a bourgeois lady, she did not even join the rest of the Impressionist group at the cafés where they discussed art and literature. Morisot's is a private modern world; her women are usually dressed and not shown in situations that might be considered degrading. In addition, her models tend to be her friends and family – women posing for male artists, especially in an undressed state, were presumed to be immoral, simply because they posed in the first place. It was known that many of these models sold their sexual favours. For a woman painting women – dressed or not – none of these associations were relevant.

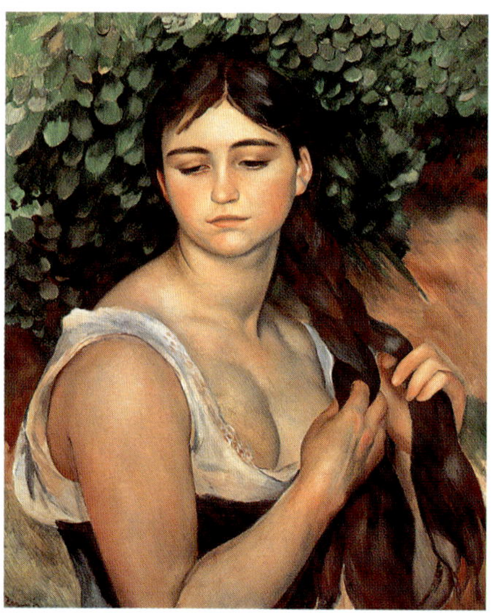

Pierre-Auguste Renoir
The Plait, 1884
Stiftong, Baden. Courtesy of AKG London. *(See p. 142)*

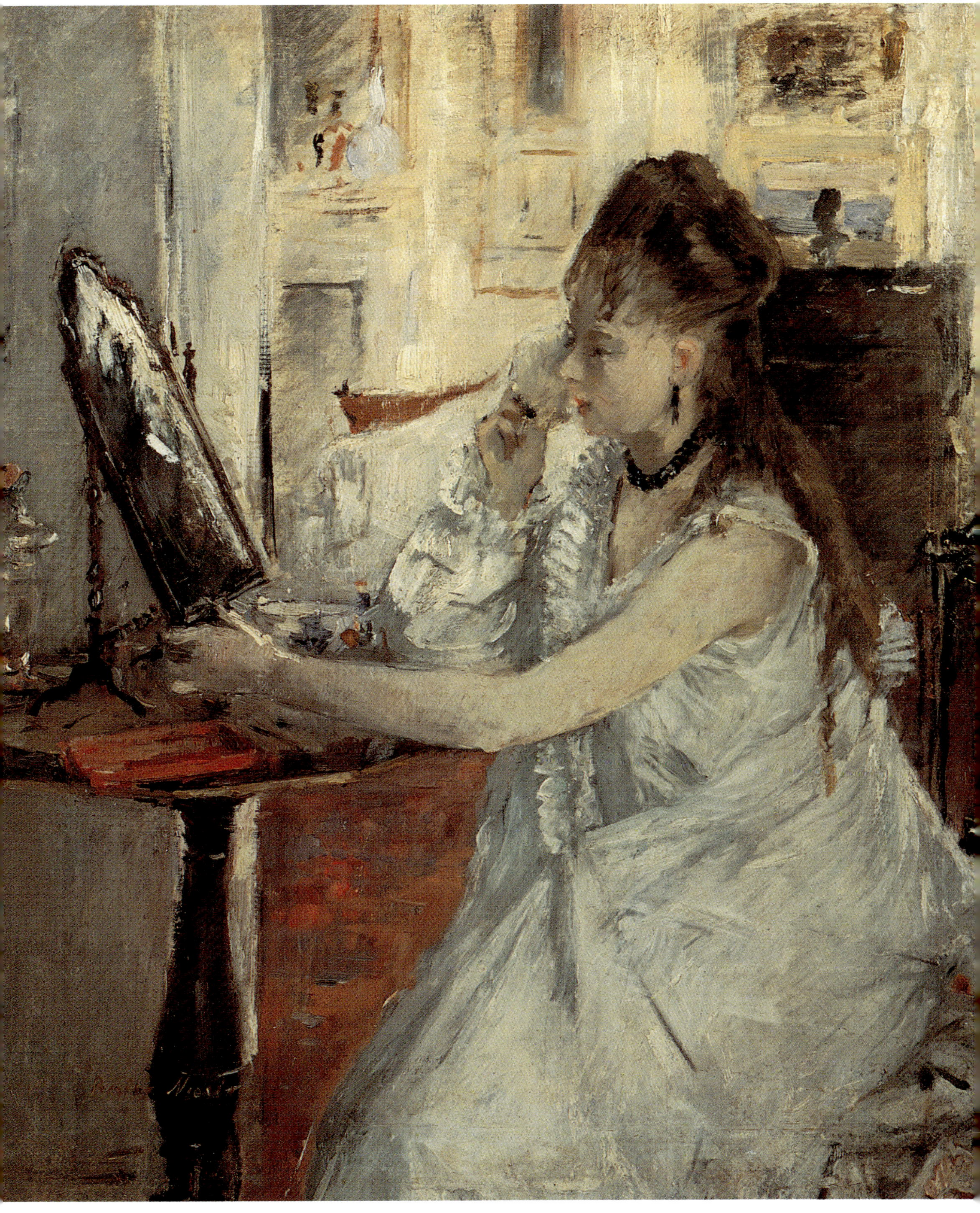

BERTHE MORISOT
Eugène Manet and his Daughter in the Garden at Bougival, 1881

Private Collection, Paris. Courtesy of AKG London

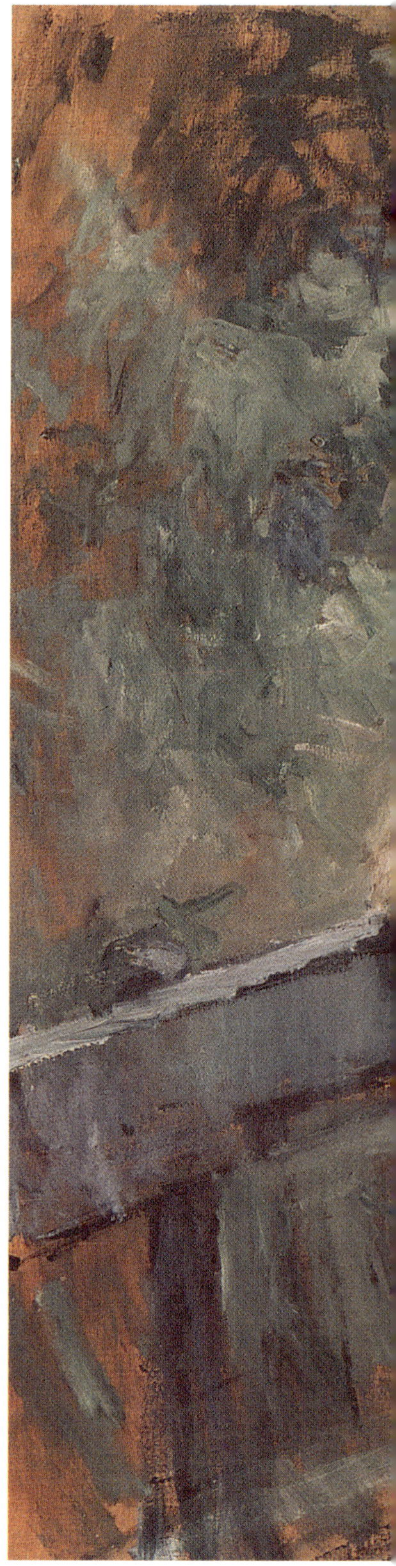

EARLY one summer or spring morning, Eugène Manet, Morisot's husband of seven years, sits in the garden with the couple's only child Julie. Sketchily painted in the Impressionist style with parts of the canvas showing through, Morisot has based her picture around greens and browns, with a lot of white to create a milky effect, and touches of pink and red to add warmth and so create complementary contrasts.

This is a charming, intimate picture showing a father and his young daughter. Julie has placed what seems to be some sort of model on her father's lap and is rearranging it intently; he seems to be concentrating as hard as she is.

As with most of Morisot's work, this presents a fresh, intimate insight into a personal, domestic world. But this is an unusual painting, probably intended only for the family, because it is a man who is playing with a child and not the traditional mother and child.

When the sixth Impressionist exhibition was held in 1881, thirteen artists were featured, including Morisot. The same year, she and her husband began to build a house in Paris. Finished in 1883, it became a meeting place every Thursday for painters and writers such as Degas, Caillebotte Monet, Pissarro, Renoir, Zola and Mallarmé (1842–98).

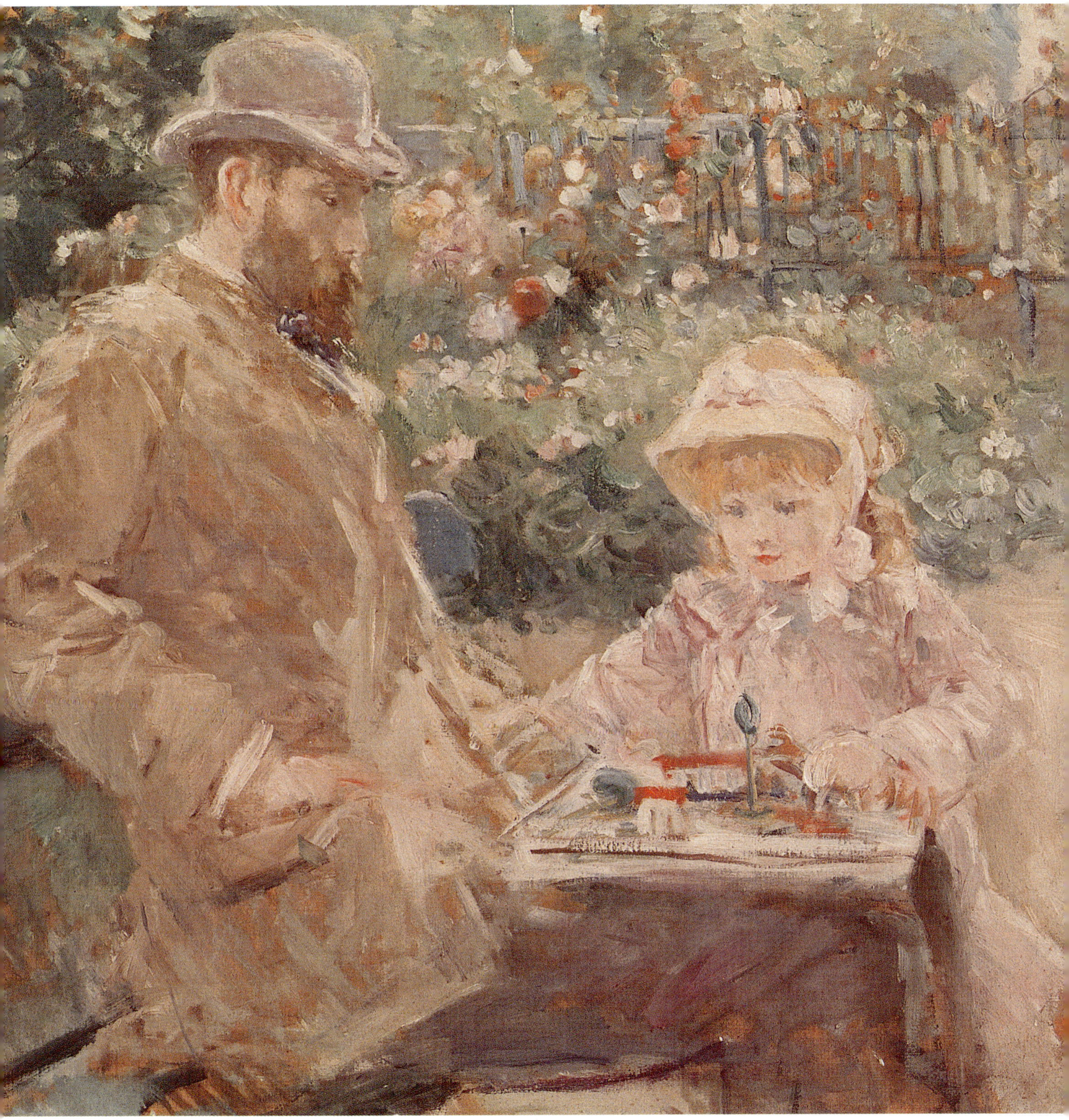

Berthe Morisot
Bildnis, A Young Lady, 1885

Musée d'Orsay, Paris. Courtesy of AKG London/Erich Lessing

PAINTED in 1885, this portrait clearly shows the influence of Renoir, with whom Morisot and her family were becoming friends. Indeed, Renoir looked upon Julie, Morisot's daughter, as the daughter he had never had and was a great comfort to her when Berthe Morisot died in 1895, as her father Eugène Manet died in 1892.

Painted in the loose, Impressionist style – and sketchily finished – the flesh is depicted in shades of pink, white and blue to indicate the hollows and shadows. But like Renoir at this time, Morisot is showing a concern for draughtsmanship – outlining the contours, arms and waist of her figure in a way that she has not done in her earlier works. The brilliance of her colours, especially the background behind her young model, reiterated in the lips, cheeks and the outlining of the arms in vermillion, are reminiscent of Renoir and recall the work of Eugène Delacroix.

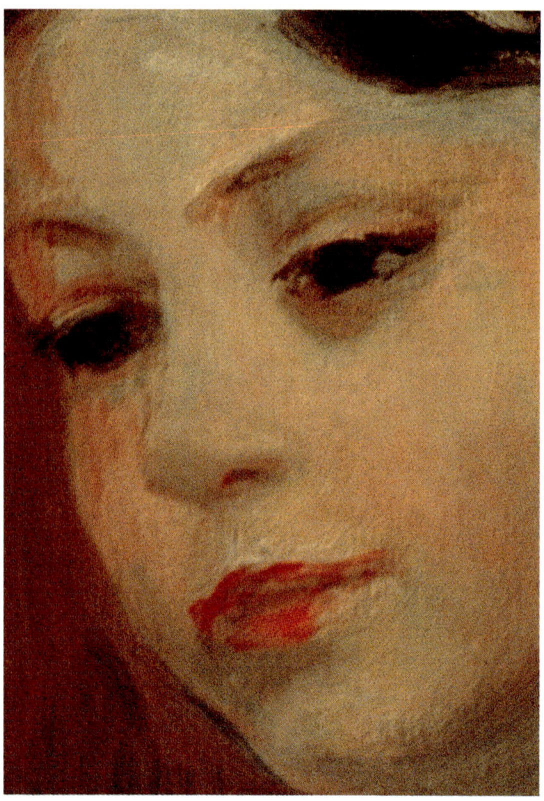

All the Impressionists revered Delacroix, but in the 1880s many of them, no longer working in the pure Impressionist style of the 1870s, were trying to reconcile his work with the draughtsmanship of artists such as Ingres. Renoir, in particular, was working by the mid-1880s in a linear style that Morisot very much admired, finding some of his drawings, 'as charming as the drawings of Ingres'. Much of Morisot's later work shows Renoir's influence either in terms of technique or subject matter.

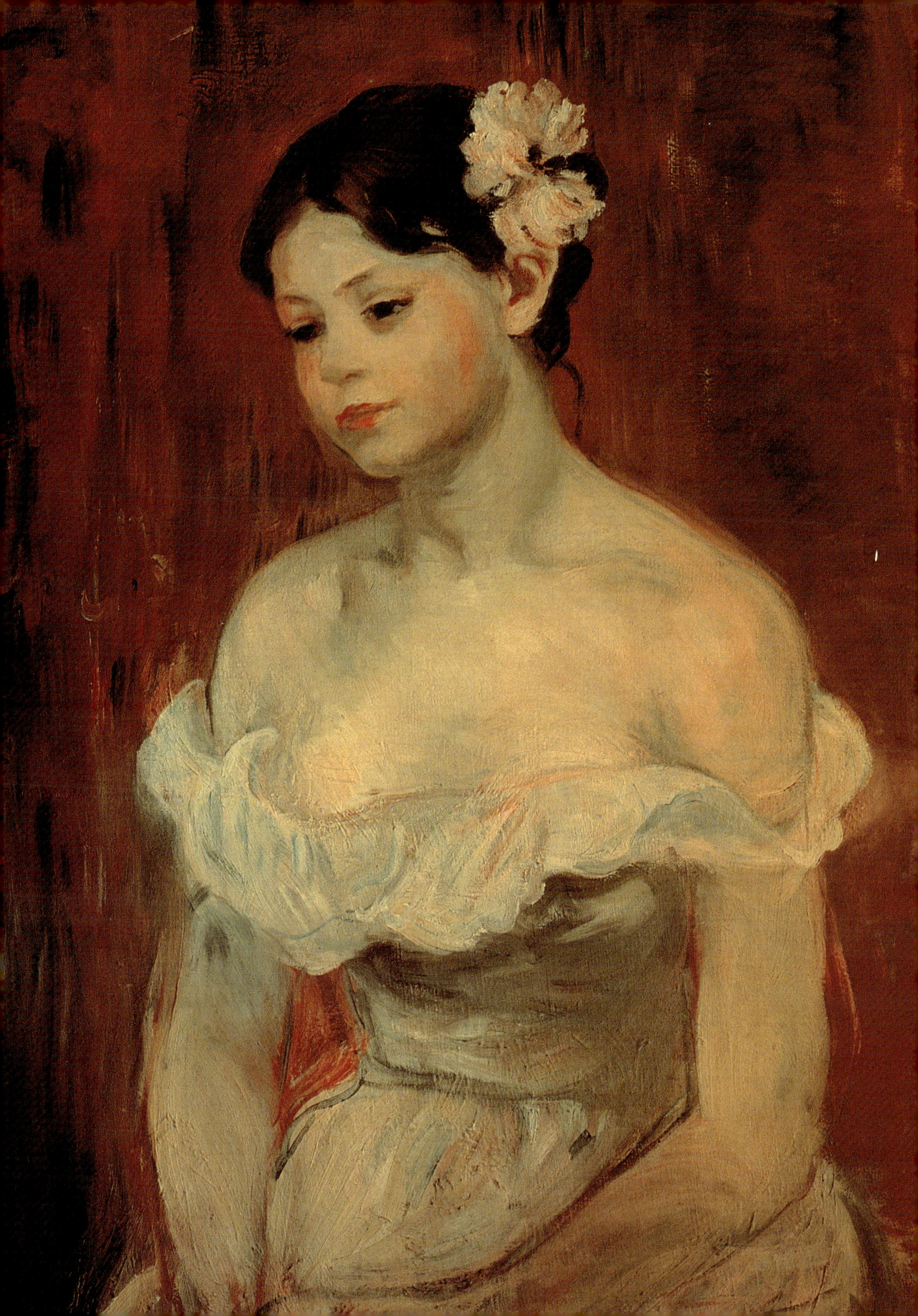

MARY CASSATT (1844–1926)

Lydia, c. 1878

Private Collection. Courtesy of AKG London

MARY CASSATT was a wealthy American who came to Europe in 1868 to study art. She lived alone until 1877, when her parents and her sister, Lydia, relocated to Paris. This was the same year that she met Degas, whose follower she became. They were both independently minded and, although they were friends for 40 years, they had many arguments. Through Degas, Cassatt became friendly with the Impressionists and their dealer Paul Durand-Ruel, and she was responsible for finding some wealthy Americans as buyers for their work – especially his.

She was a talented painter in the Impressionist style and an exceptional engraver – like Degas she chose to experiment with different media. A letter from Degas to Pissarro in 1880 mentions her: 'I congratulate you on your enthusiasm. I hurried to Mlle Cassatt with your parcel [of aquatints – an etching technique]. She congratulates you, as do I, in this matter.'

This portrait, showing her sister deep in a book, is painted in a typically Impressionist style, and the emphasis on white in the picture is very reminiscent of Manet. Cassatt, like Morisot, often painted portraits of society ladies, women and children and, under the influence of Degas, theatre scenes.

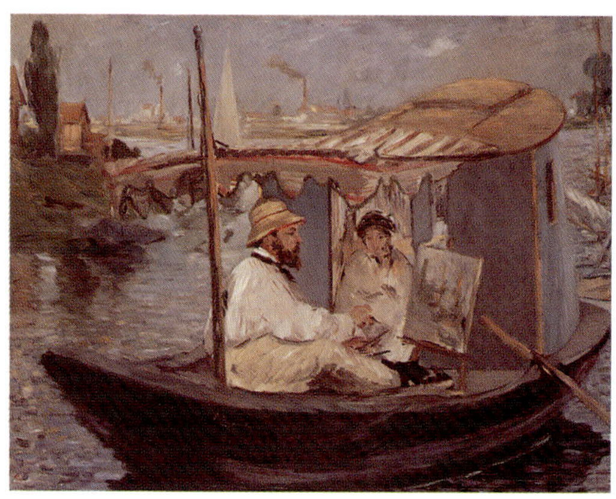

Edouard Manet
The Barge, 1874
Neue Pinakothek. Courtesy of AKG London. *(See p. 34)*

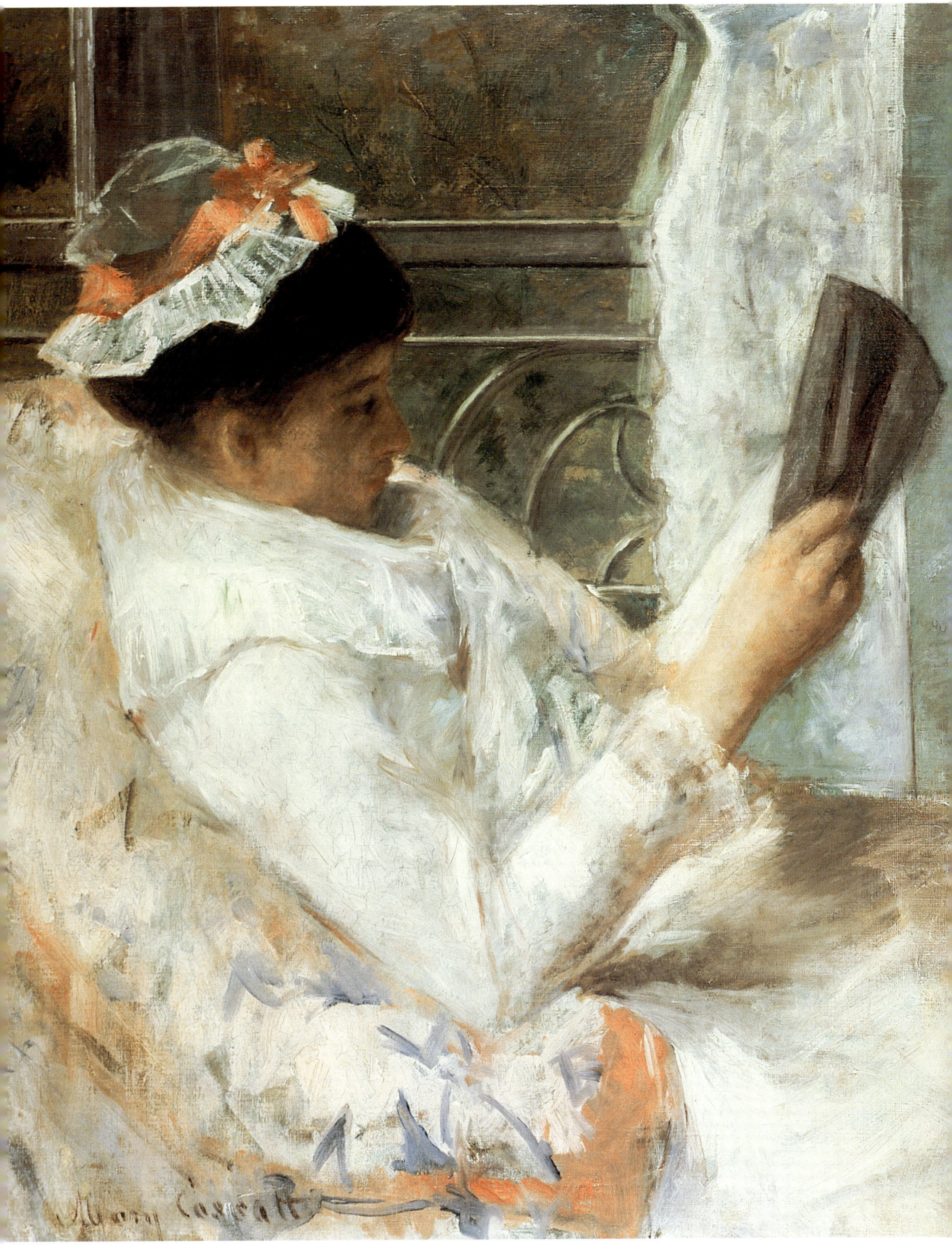
Mary Cassatt

Mary Cassatt
Girl in the Garden, c. 1880–82

Musée d'Orsay, Paris. Courtesy of AKG London/Erich Lessing

THIS is one of the many intimate scenes of daily life that Cassatt painted so well. Like Degas, whose art she compared favourably with the Old Masters and which she believed surpassed even that of Jan Vermeer (1632–75), her understanding of form and drawing are superior. By this time, the Impressionists were perceived to be in two groups, the 'Romantic Impressionists' – Monet and Pissarro, who painted out-of-doors and whose forms dissolved in a flood of light, and the 'Realist Impressionists', Degas and Manet, whose figures stood out from the backgrounds in their art and who showed a strong regard for line and drawing. Cassatt belonged with the latter.

Based around the colours white, red and green, this painting in Impressionist style, with its emphasis on sunlight and loose handling, is deceptively simple. The sketchy background and geraniums give the impression of a rich material. The red flowers punctuates the canvas, complementing the green and reflecting the rosy skin and bright lips of the girl who is so intent on her sewing. Look to the patterned background and you will see that this girl is sitting high up and the path, a horizontal stripe that cuts the painting in two, is far below her; the tree to the left and the hazy figures on a bench on the right indicate the height. Cassatt has combined two opposing Japanese effects – showing height but in such a way that the background seems like a flat, patterned backdrop.

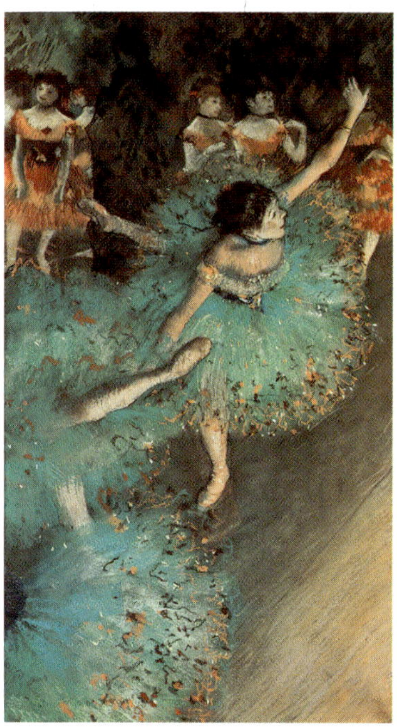

Edgar Degas
Green Dancers, 1880
Thyssen-Bornemisza Collection, Lugano. Courtesy of AKG London/Erich Lessing. *(See p. 176)*

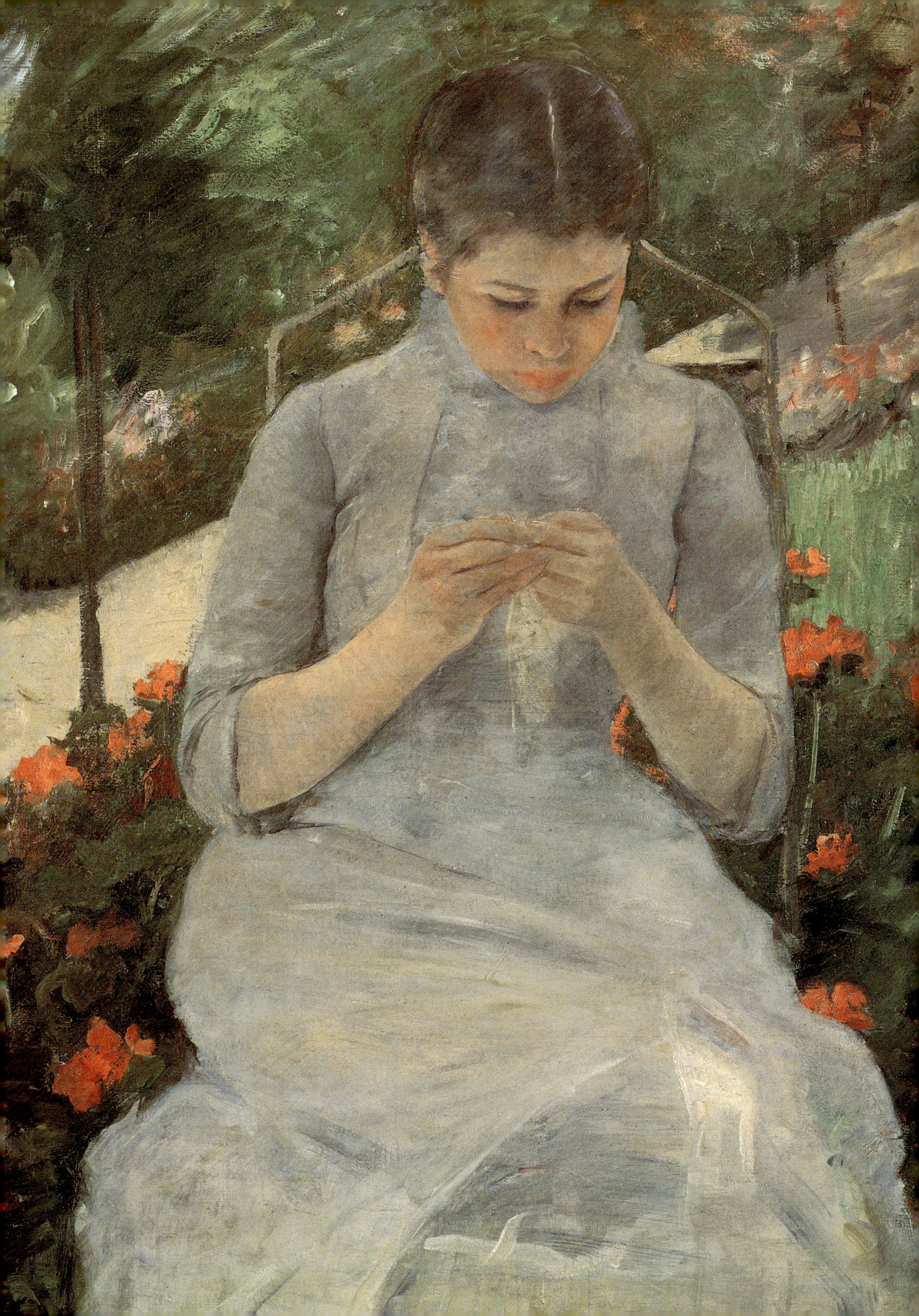

Mary Cassatt
Young Mother Sewing, c. 1890

H.O. Havemeyer Collection, Metropolitan Museum of Art, New York. Courtesy of AKG London/Erich Lessing

THIS charming scene shows a mother sewing while her little girl leans on her knee and looks out at the viewer – a way of involving the viewer that recalls work by Manet. It is a strong composition with the two figures creating a triangular effect in the centre, the vertical slats of the window frame on either side of the young mother's head reinforcing her shoulders and bringing the eye to her sensitive fingers, so intent on this delicate work. Her concentration is tangible. The little girl, whose diagonal figure also concentrates the gaze on her mother's fingers, seems faintly peeved that she is receiving no attention. They appear to be comfortably off – but note the blue apron around the mother's neck.

Cassatt's attention to the particular is clear in the background details in the garden – the trees echoing the vertical window frame and creating a link between the indoor and outdoor worlds. There is more refined detail in the light veil being sewn, the flowers in a vase, the handles on the chest of drawers and the tendrils of hair escaping at the woman's neck.

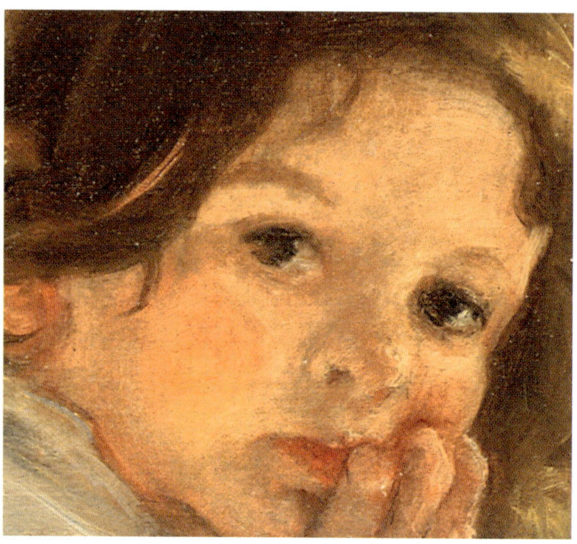

The colours are light and bright. Sunlight floods the scene, the skin of the child and mother glow in the light, and Cassatt's ability to create texture knows no bounds in the dress materials – especially the diaphanous veil upon which the young mother is working.

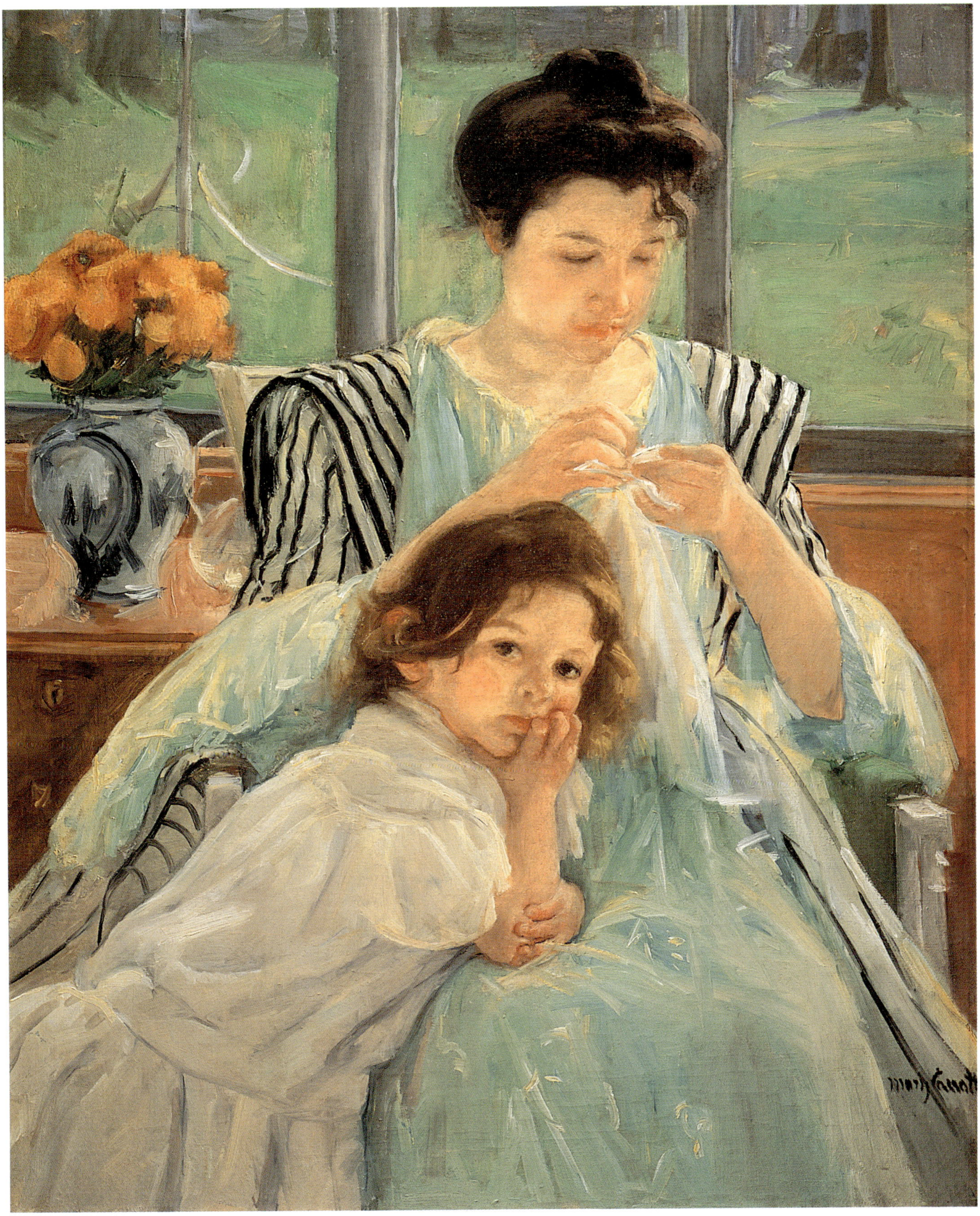

Mary Cassatt
Clarissa with a Fan, c. 1895

Private Collection. Courtesy of AKG London

C*LARISSA with a Fan* clearly shows Degas' influence on Cassatt's style. She is using pastel as a medium, as he was increasingly doing in the 1890s, and the long, individual strokes she uses are evident in much of Degas' work. Only in treating the face, arms and hands does she smudge the pastel to create a traditional smooth effect and a gradual merging of colours. But here, too, Degas' influence can be seen in the blue tones and the use of blue to delineate the fingers, as he does in his *Portrait of Edmond Duranty* (1879), for example. Also note that the figure is slightly off-centre and, although the chair that Clarissa is sitting on is visible in the bottom-left corner, this could be deemed to constitute an empty, triangular space in the foreground rather like those in many of Degas' works. The bent arm is also reminiscent of some of his dancers, although the bent fingers touching the ear are typical of Cassatt, who always shows a great concern for her treatment of hands.

The yellow fan is a Japanese touch, although the model does not show much interest in it or anything else as she looks off to the right. In terms of colour, the fan binds with the armchair opposite and complements the overall blues of the dress, the face and the background. As often in Impressionist works, the medium (card in this instance) is allowed to show through the paint.

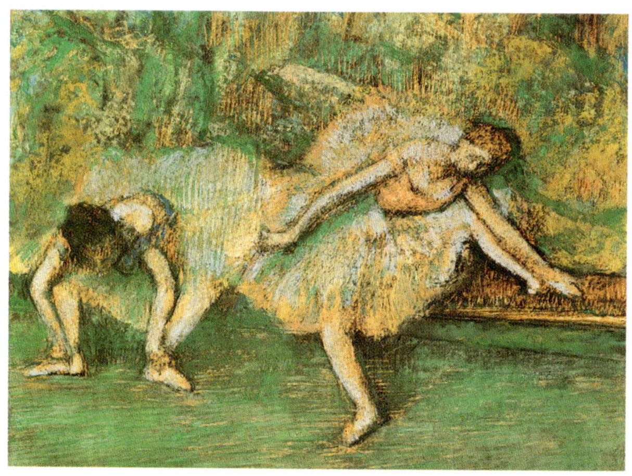

Edgar Degas
Two Dancers on a Bench, 1900–05
Private Collection. Courtesy of AKG London. *(See p. 191)*

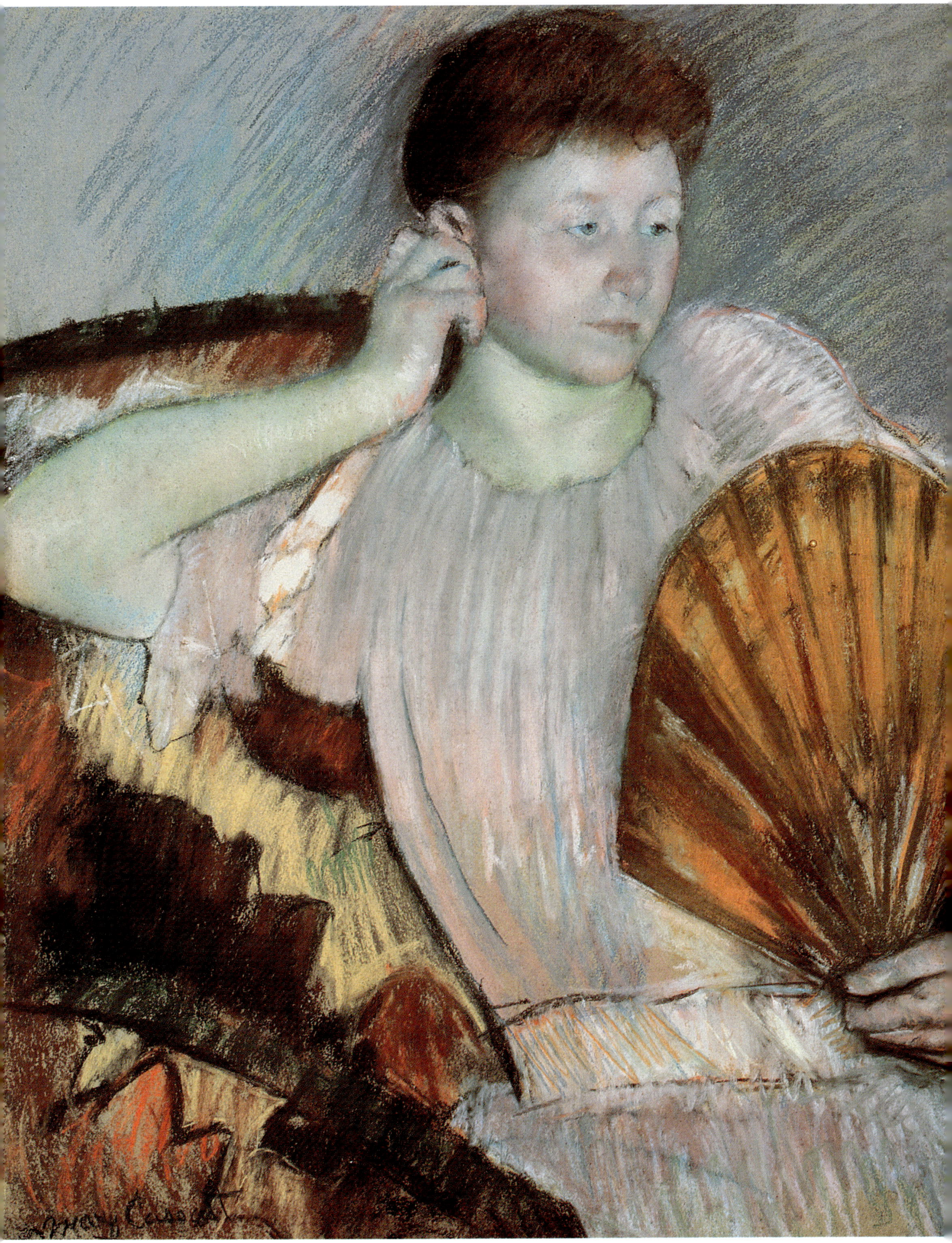

Mary Cassatt
Bathing, 1910

Musée du Petit Palais, Paris. Courtesy of AKG London

By 1910, most of the original Impressionist group were dead and a new, younger group of 'Post-Impressionists' came to the fore along with even more *avant-garde* groups such as the Fauves (literally 'Wild Beasts', a name given to the group by the critics). They used pure blocks of colour and did not concern themselves with natural light effects, taking a step on the path to abstraction. Although Cassatt's work is not Fauvist, she uses broad blocks of colour with very little interruption and chooses adjacent colours with great care. Note, for example, the pink peignoir that complements the virulent green of the water (which in turn shows the patchy reflection of trees – see the little area of blue sky bottom left), which extends beyond the figures.

This is a very peaceful painting, viewed from above and cut off at the bottom as if in a photograph. The figures are charming – the two women with their little girls, the central one wearing nothing but a pink headband. The well-defined figures stand out boldly from the background, clearly showing the drawing technique that once led Degas to exclaim somewhat peevishly, 'I will not admit a woman can draw like that.' Cassatt died in 1926, 16 years after she produced this painting, at the age of 82.

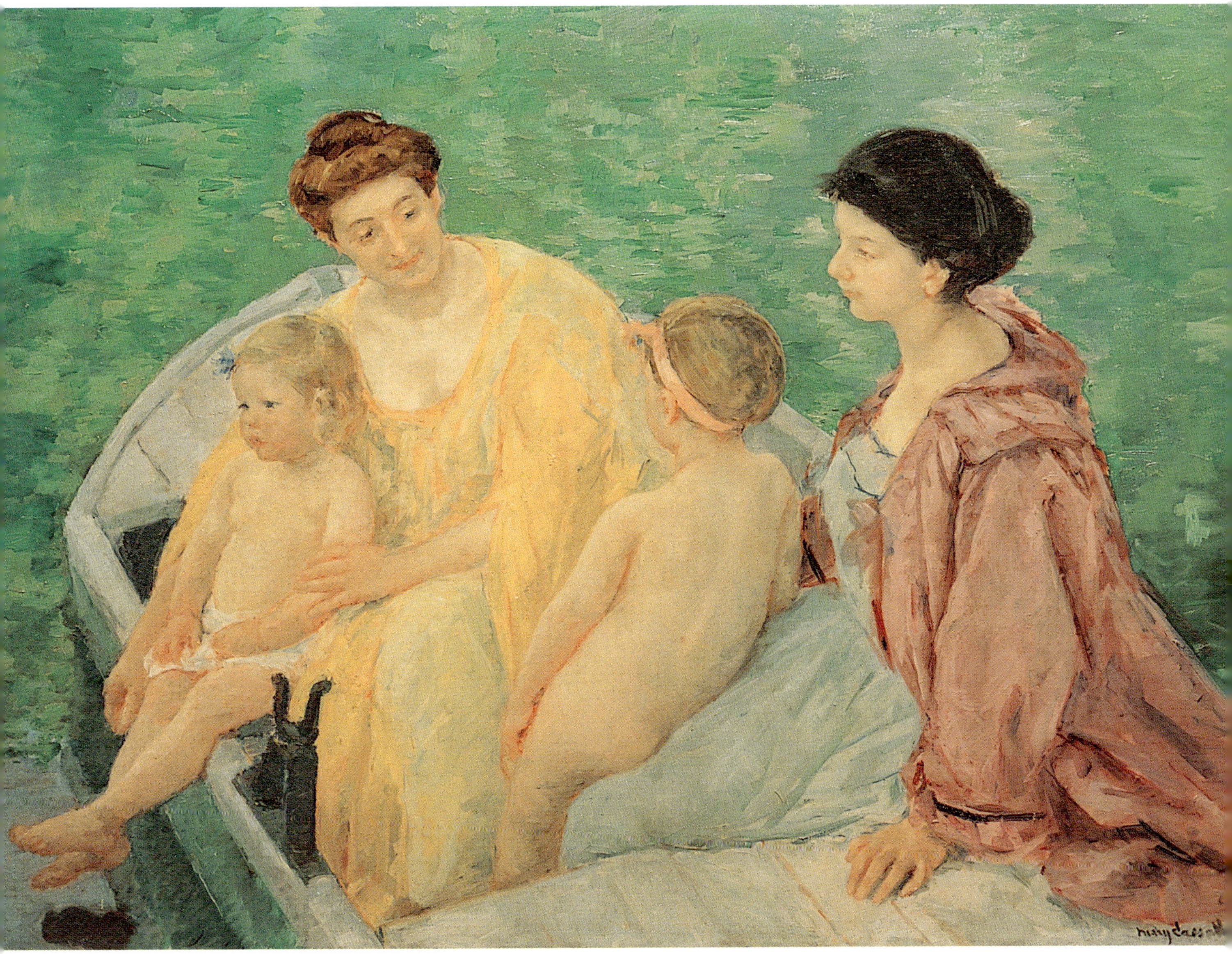

PAUL CÉZANNE (1839–1906)

Still Life with Bread and Eggs, 1865

Cincinnati Art Museum, Cincinnati. Courtesy of AKG London

IN 1865 Cézanne was living in Paris. Originally from Aix-en-Provence and destined by his family to be a lawyer, he pursued his art studies at the Académie Suisse from 1862. Here he met both Pissarro and Guillaumin. His work rejected at the Salon of 1863, he exhibited at the now-famous Salon des Refusés, where he came into contact with other artists who were unhappy with the Salon system.

Until about 1870, his work varied dramatically in style and motif. In some works he uses thick impasto and palette knife and in others, as here, traditional brushwork. He painted still lives, some portraits, and semi-historical and erotic subjects, all infused with an internal violence and frustration.

This still life, painted with a dark palette and influenced by 17th-century Spanish painting and the still lifes of Jean-Baptiste-Siméon Chardin (1699–1779), was refused at the Salon of 1865, where the judges did not appreciate the realism of the humble food and utensils of a poor artist living on a meagre income.

It is an interesting composition with the background and the table so dark that you cannot see where one ends and the other begins. It already shows Cézanne's interest in the balance of form and colour and the relationships between different planes.

Manet, who also used a dark palette at this time, saw several of Cézanne's still lifes in 1866 and, to the artist's pleasure, pronounced them 'powerfully treated'.

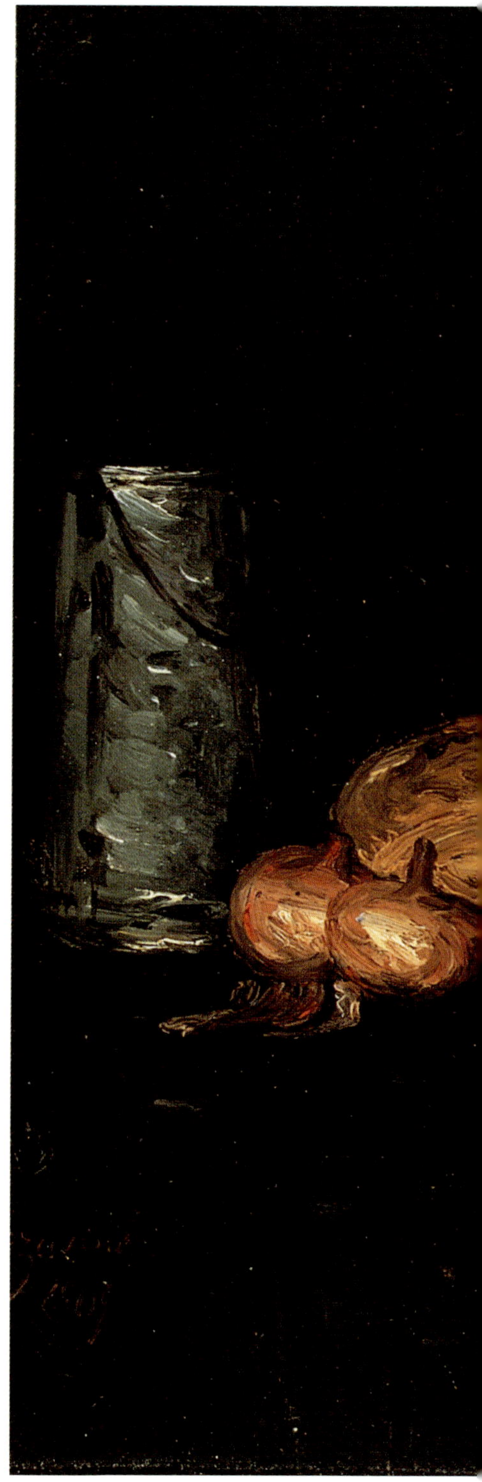

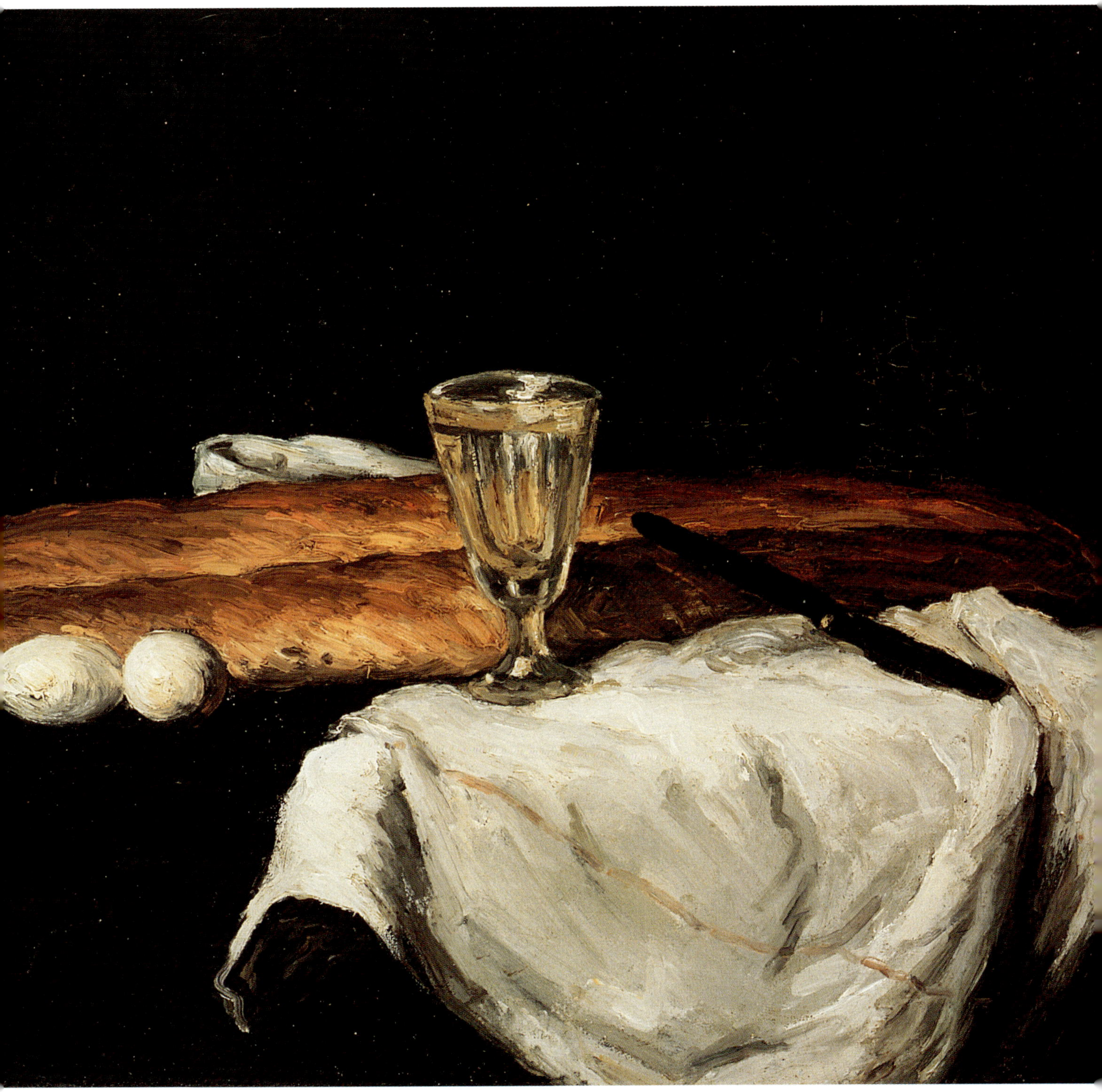

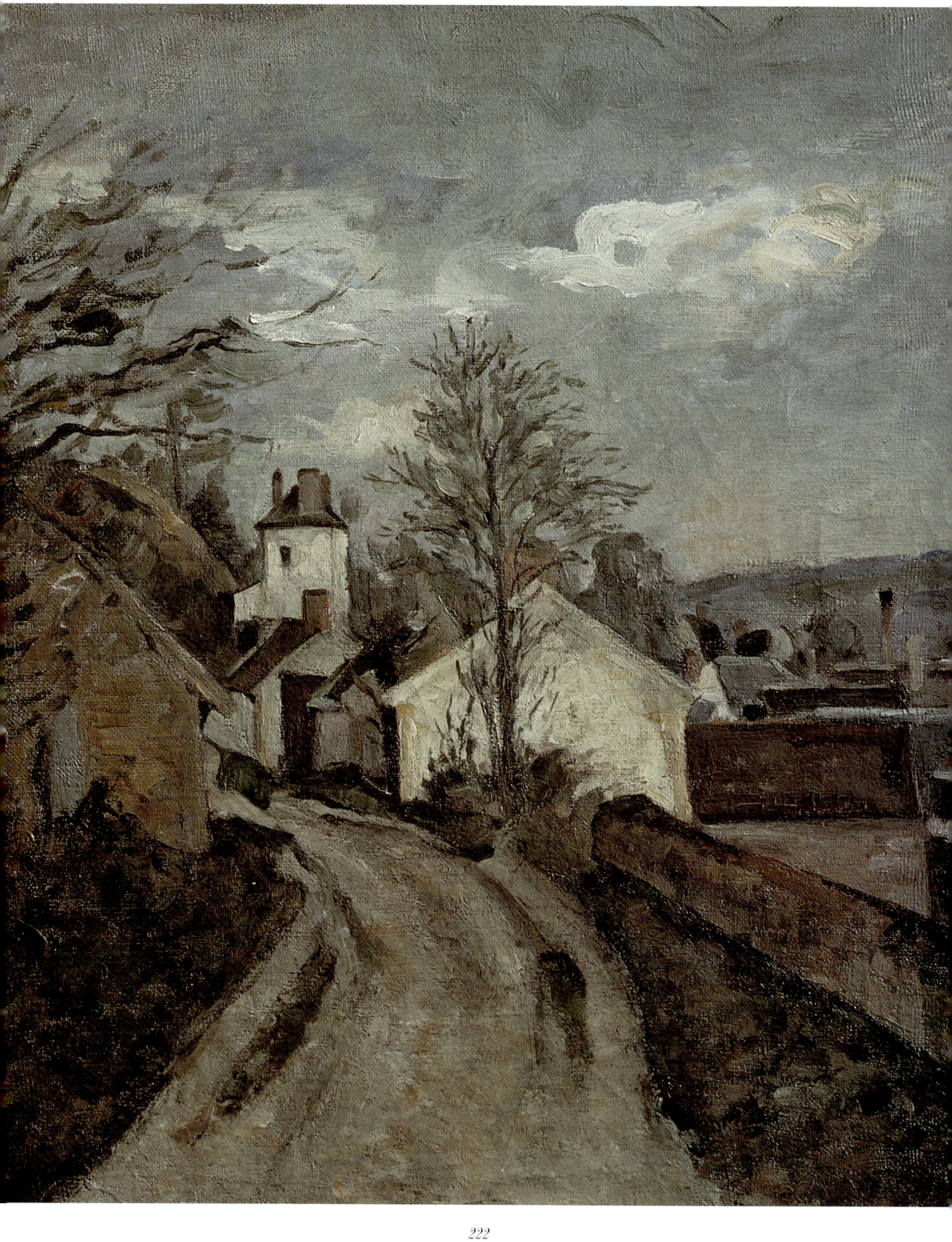

Paul Cézanne
The House of Dr Gachet at Auvers, 1872

Musée d'Orsay, Paris. Courtesy of AKG London/Erich Lessing

CÉZANNE was really not an Impressionist, although he had strong links with the group, particularly with Pissarro. As early as 1866 he had reflected, 'I shall make up my mind only to do things out-of-doors,' but it was not until about 1870 that his palette lightened and he began to show an interest in the reflections of light – ideas that had been current among the group for several years. This change may be due to the influence of Pissarro or perhaps related to time spent by the sea at L'Estaque, where he hid to avoid conscription to the army during the Franco-Prussian War.

In 1872 he went to live in Pontoise where he worked daily with Pissarro, whom he considered his mentor. In 1873 he moved to Auvers to be near Dr Gachet, a friend both of the Impressionists and Vincent van Gogh (1853–90). He was also a collector of Impressionist paintings and an amateur painter, and offered Cézanne lodging and the use of both a studio and an etching machine.

This painting shows Cézanne working in the Impressionist style. The composition and tendency towards browns and greys in the palette reflect the influence of Pissarro. Cézanne uses the Impressionist technique of cutting off the scene at the edges and creates a sense of movement and time by placing Dr Gachet's house at the end of the road down which the viewer has to travel.

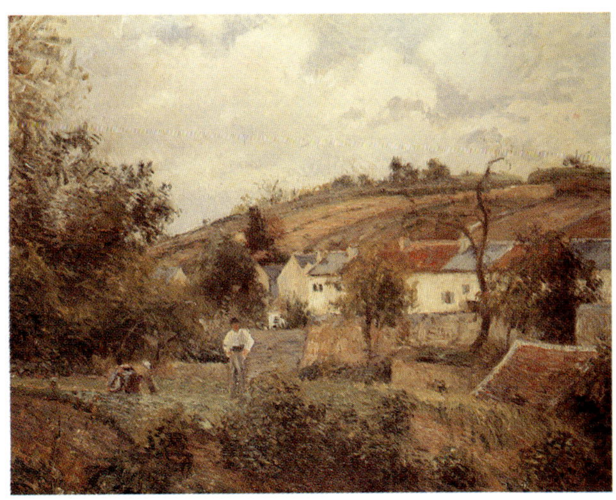

Camille Pissarro
Village near Pontoise, 1873
Offentliche Kuntsammlung. Courtesy of AKG London. *(See p. 103)*

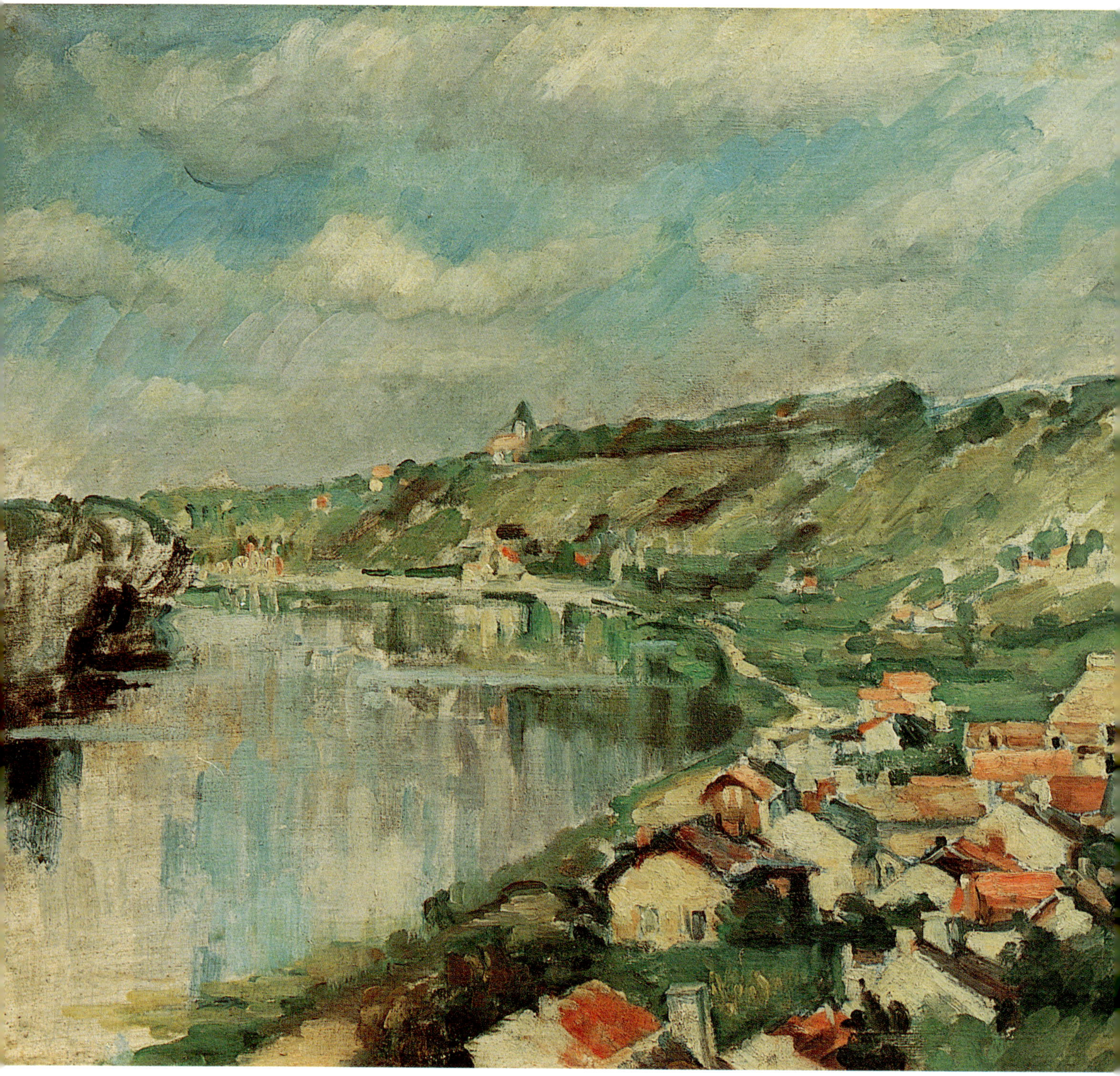

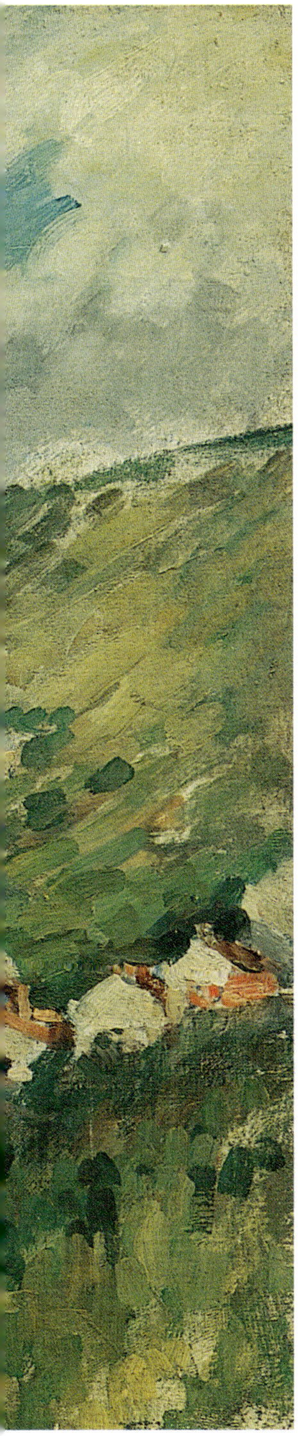

Paul Cézanne
Countryside by the River Oise, 1875

Musée du Petit Palais, Geneva. Courtesy of AKG London

THIS shows Cézanne still working in the Impressionist idiom, with an even lighter palette than before and a greater lightness of touch. The scene is bathed in a fresh, clear light, enhanced by the bright blue sky and the white clouds reflected in the water. Red roofs are scattered over the landscape. The brushstrokes are sketchy but mould the landscape, following the curve of the hills and indicating the depth as well as the surface of the river by using both vertical and horizontal strokes to show the reflections of the sky.

During the mid 1870s, Cézanne divided his time between Paris and Aix. He exhibited three paintings at the first independent exhibition of 1874 but refused to exhibit in 1876 because he was disgusted with the reaction of the critics. However, he participated in 1877 and exhibited 17 paintings, including a pastoral bathing scene and a portrait of his patron, Victor Chocquet, which showed the emerging monumentality of his work and his growing interest in building up form through the juxtaposition of patches of colour. This exhibition, although it had its detractors, found positive critics. Georges Rivière was especially interested in Cézanne's work and was later was to proclaim, 'The ignorant people who laugh at *The Bathers* (1902–06), for example, make me think of barbarians criticising the Parthenon.'

Paul Cézanne
Mont Sainte-Victoire, 1882–85

H.O. Havemeyer Collection, Metropolitan Museum of Art, New York.
Courtesy of AKG London/Erich Lessing

IN 1879 Cézanne wrote to his childhood friend, Émile Zola, 'I am using all my ingenuity to find my true path in painting.' His Impressionist phase was over, although he continued to paint out-of-doors and modify colour in relation to the light that was falling on it.

From about 1880, Cézanne developed a way of painting that he was to spend the rest of his life refining. The key was the way in which he began to apply paint in repeated parallel brushstrokes to produce a subtle patterned, almost woven, effect. His work took on an increasingly monumental and timeless quality.

This is the first in a series of paintings of Mont Sainte-Victoire, the mountain that dominated Cézanne's boyhood home and became his favourite motif.

The view is taken from a height, above a winding road where a small figure makes its way. An aqueduct runs in a pale straight line across the landscape in the same direction as the road and the curving trees on the top of the hill. The colour palette revolves around shades of green, blue and ochre until the eye reaches the pale, pinkish mountain. Patches of colour create form. The only visible outlines are up the trunk of the central tree. Although the distance is so clear, Cézanne is beginning to play with the dichotomy of three-dimensional illusion of the painting and its two-dimensional reality in that the patches of paint often overlap and emphasise the flat nature of the canvas.

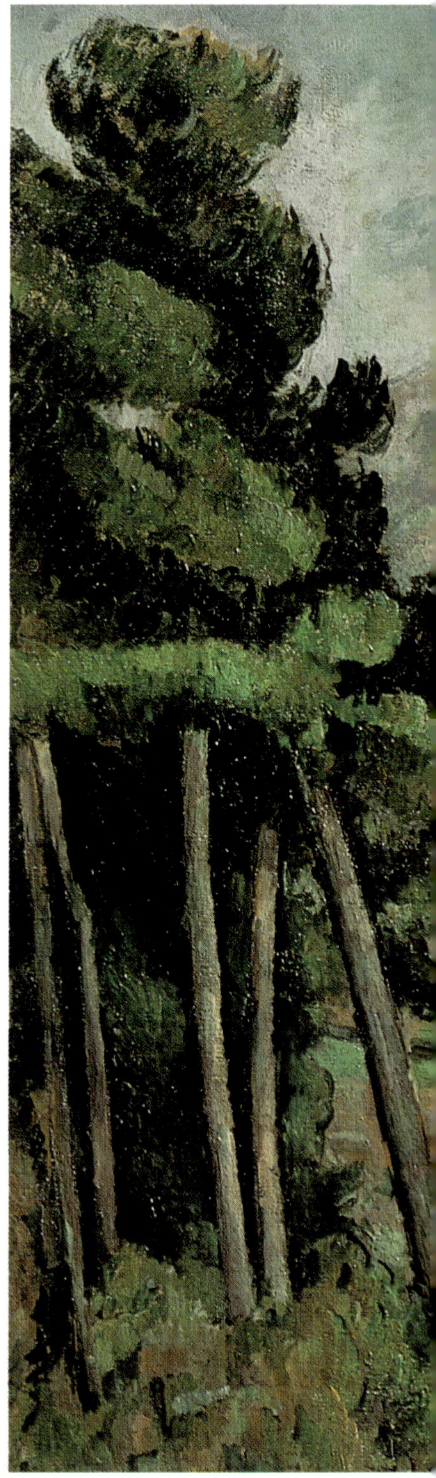

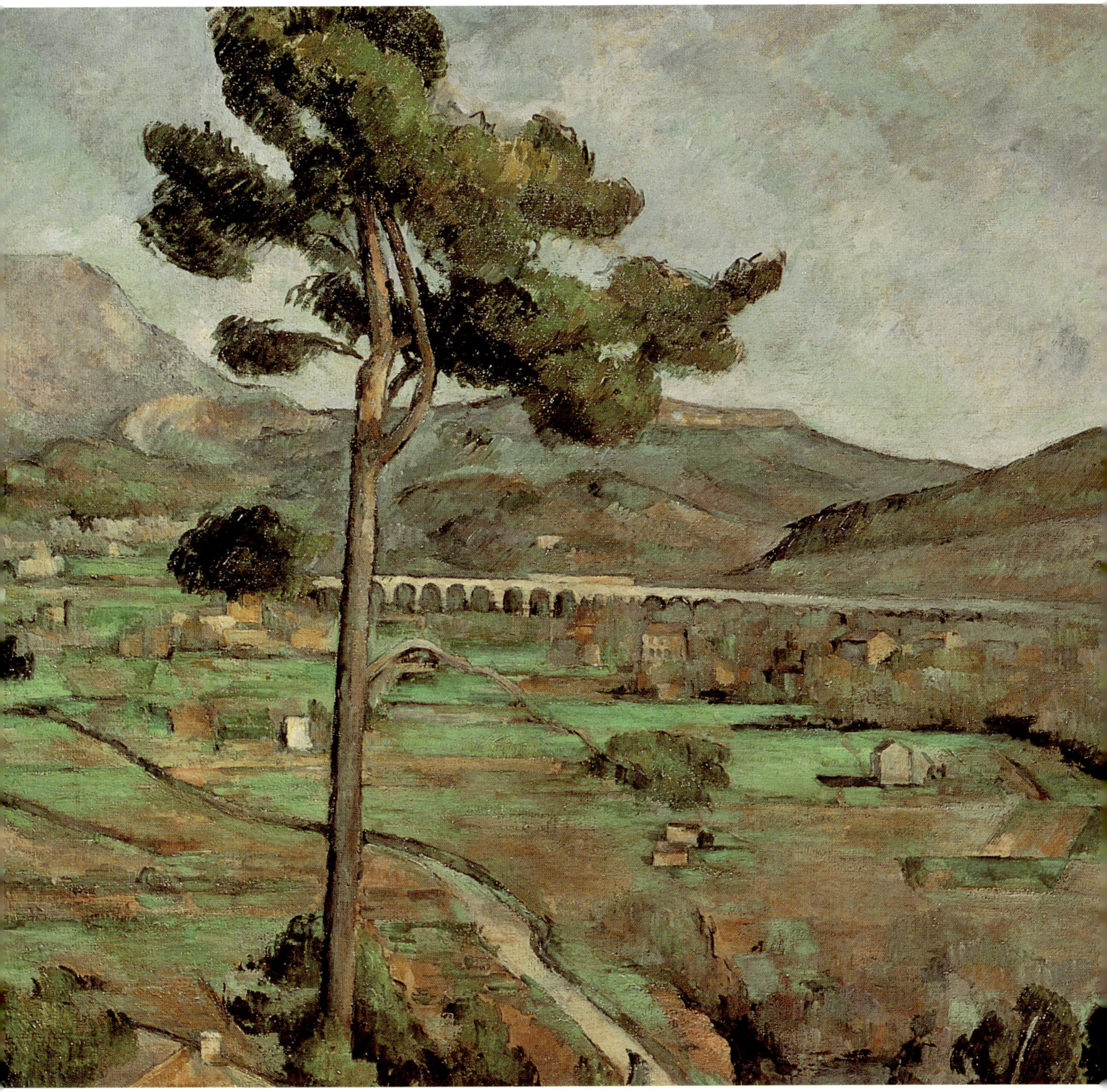

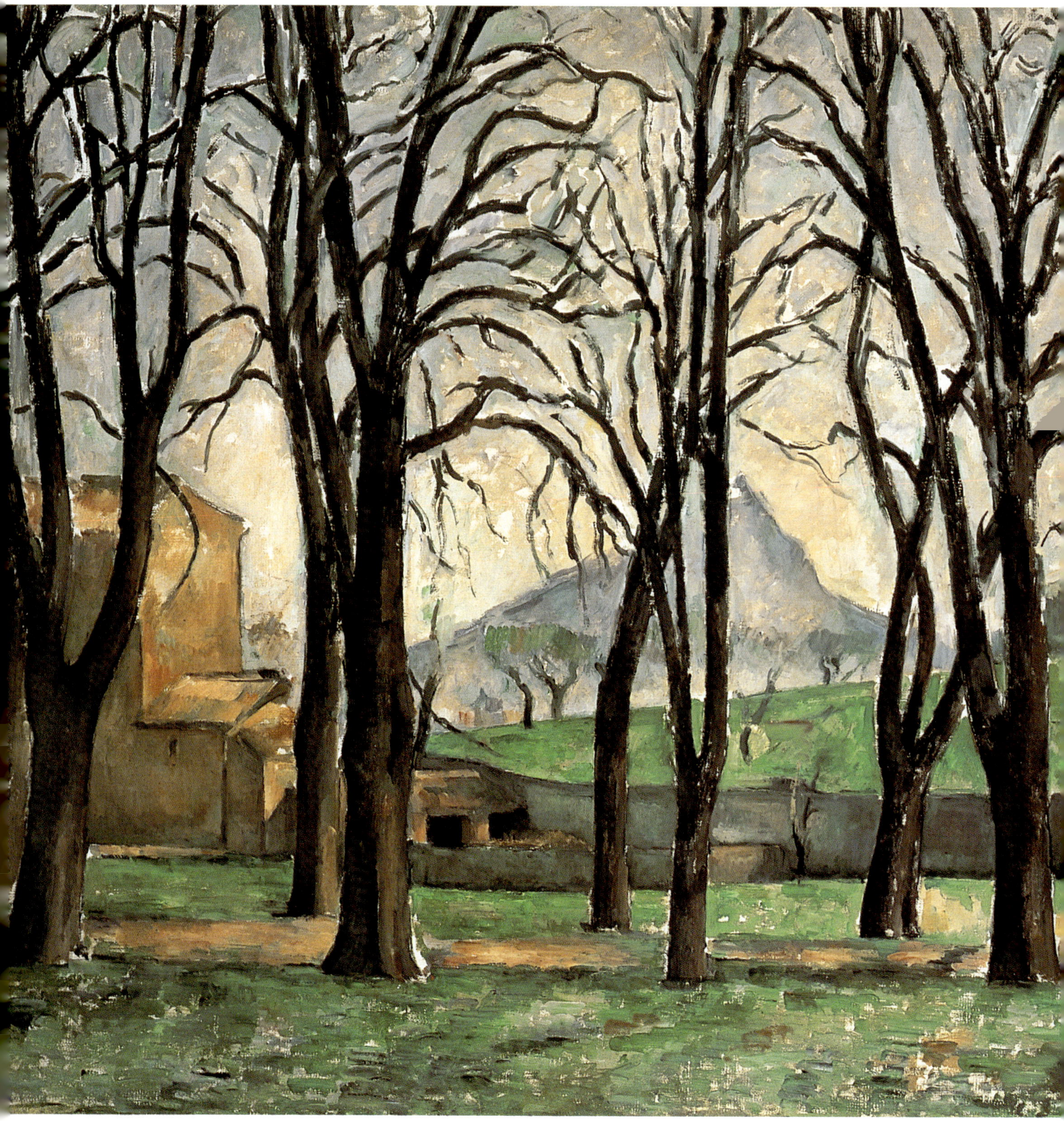

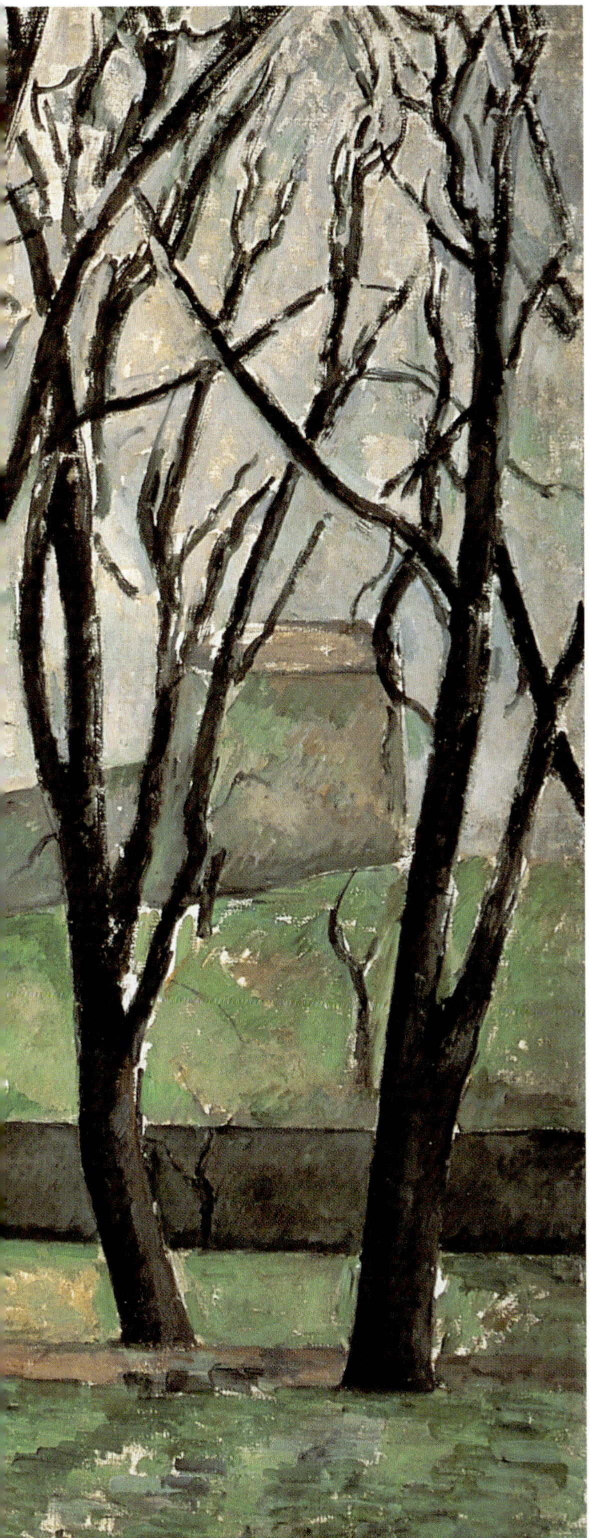

PAUL CÉZANNE

CHESTNUT TREES AT THE JAS DE BOUFFAN IN WINTER, 1885–86

Institute of Arts, Minneapolis. Courtesy of AKG London

JAS de Bouffan in Aix-en-Provence was the family property which Cézanne's father, a tradesman turned banker, had bought in 1859. When he died in 1886, leaving his son a fortune, Cézanne moved back to this property.

Mont Sainte-Victoire can be seen from the house but Cézanne has chosen not to paint it directly; instead he sees it through a decorative pattern of chestnut trees. The effect might be thought to relate to oriental art but there is no evidence that Cézanne was interested in the fashion for Japanese prints that appealed to many of his contemporaries. It is more likely to reflect the influence of Corot and Pissarro.

The trees provide depth as we look through to the mountain, but they also act as a patterned screen. The way in which Cézanne has painted the distant sky around the branches and twigs, using the lighter colour to define the darker edges, brings the sky forward, making the viewer more aware of the surface of the canvas.

Paul Cézanne
The Smoker, c. 1890–92

I. A. Morosov Collection, St Petersburg, State Hermitage. Courtesy of AKG London

THE model, Alex Paulin, who was Cézanne's gardener, also posed for the series of *The Card Players* which Cézanne began about this time. Cézanne uses the primary colours, red, yellow and blue, to great effect. The little patch of white in the clay pipe stands out all the more for its rarity. Viewed from close-up, the figure is weighty, and the patchy, rough treatment of the paint emphasises the rough skin and ruddy complexion of a working country labourer.

We presume that this man, leaning wearily on his elbow and perhaps a little bored, is in a café. However, close inspection reveals him to be in Cézanne's studio. The wine and the apples that appear to be on his table are part of a still-life canvas propped up against the wall, the curtain on the right a prop. These props are carefully chosen to complement the sitting figure, and create a horizontal with which to frame him and a diagonal that echoes his pose. Note also how the shadow of the bottle in the painting serves to place the sitter's wrist in relief.

Cézanne is again experimenting with the effect of overlapping planes. The blue shadow on the table by the man's elbow, for example, is almost an extension of the painted blue canvas behind him and the apples butt right up to his arms. The table on which he leans is tilted.

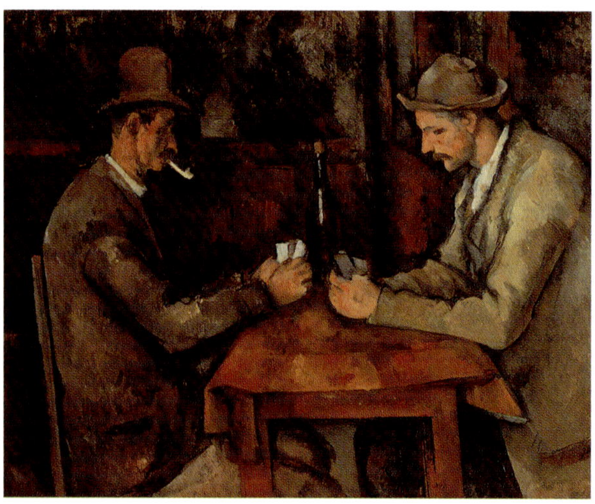

Paul Cézanne
***The Card Players* (1895)**
Musée d'Orsay, Paris. Courtesy of AKG London/Erich Lessing. *(See p. 234)*

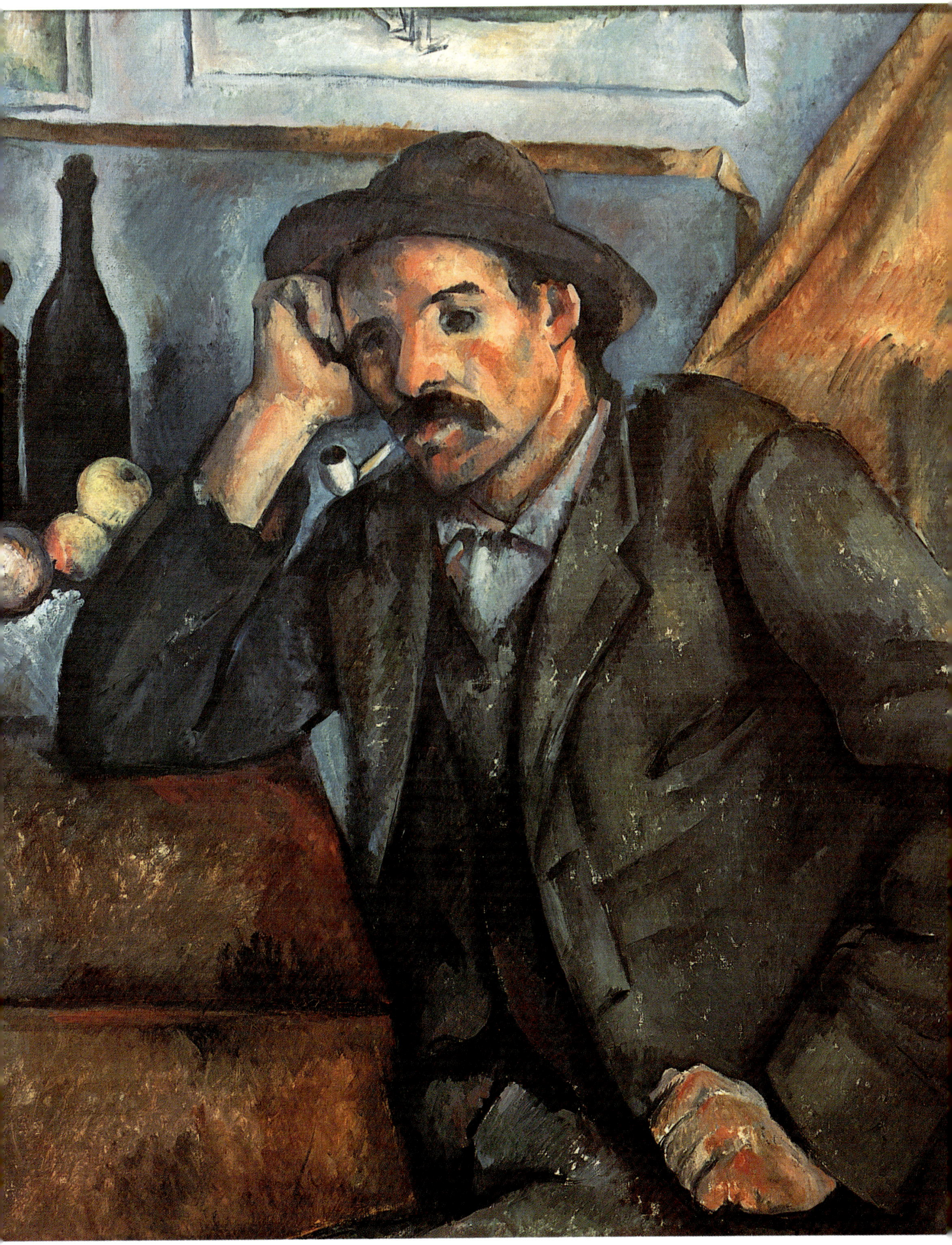

Paul Cézanne
Apples and Biscuits, c. 1880

Musée de l'Orangerie, Paris. Courtesy of The Bridgeman Art Library

UNLIKE many of the Impressionist group, such as Monet and Renoir, who only painted still lifes if the weather was too bad to paint outside, Cézanne did not regard them as a displacement activity and practised still-life painting throughout his career. Many only include apples, traditionally symbolic of love and for Cézanne, reminiscent of his childhood. Cézanne once wrote to Zola that he wanted 'to conquer Paris with an apple' – subject matter that was simple and everyday and yet full of symbolism.

This painting is typical of Cézanne's style. It shows three compositional, horizontal zones: the front of the chest, the top of the chest and the wall. One apple rises above the 'horizon'. The cut-off plate, the wallpaper and the lock provide the right amount of variation to animate the ponderous static objects that will not move unless pushed by an outside force.

In 1904, Cézanne tried to explain to painter Émile Bernard (1868–1941) how to perceive nature and thus create an effective unity: 'Treat … everything in perspective so that each side of an object or plane is directed towards a central point. Lines parallel to the horizon give breadth, that is a section of nature, or, if you prefer, of the spectacle that the *pater omnipotens aeterne deus* spreads before our eyes. Lines perpendicular to the horizon give depth.'

Cézanne's reference to God explains his religious feeling towards nature and art, which he expresses by the monumental solemnity and timeless quality of his compositions.

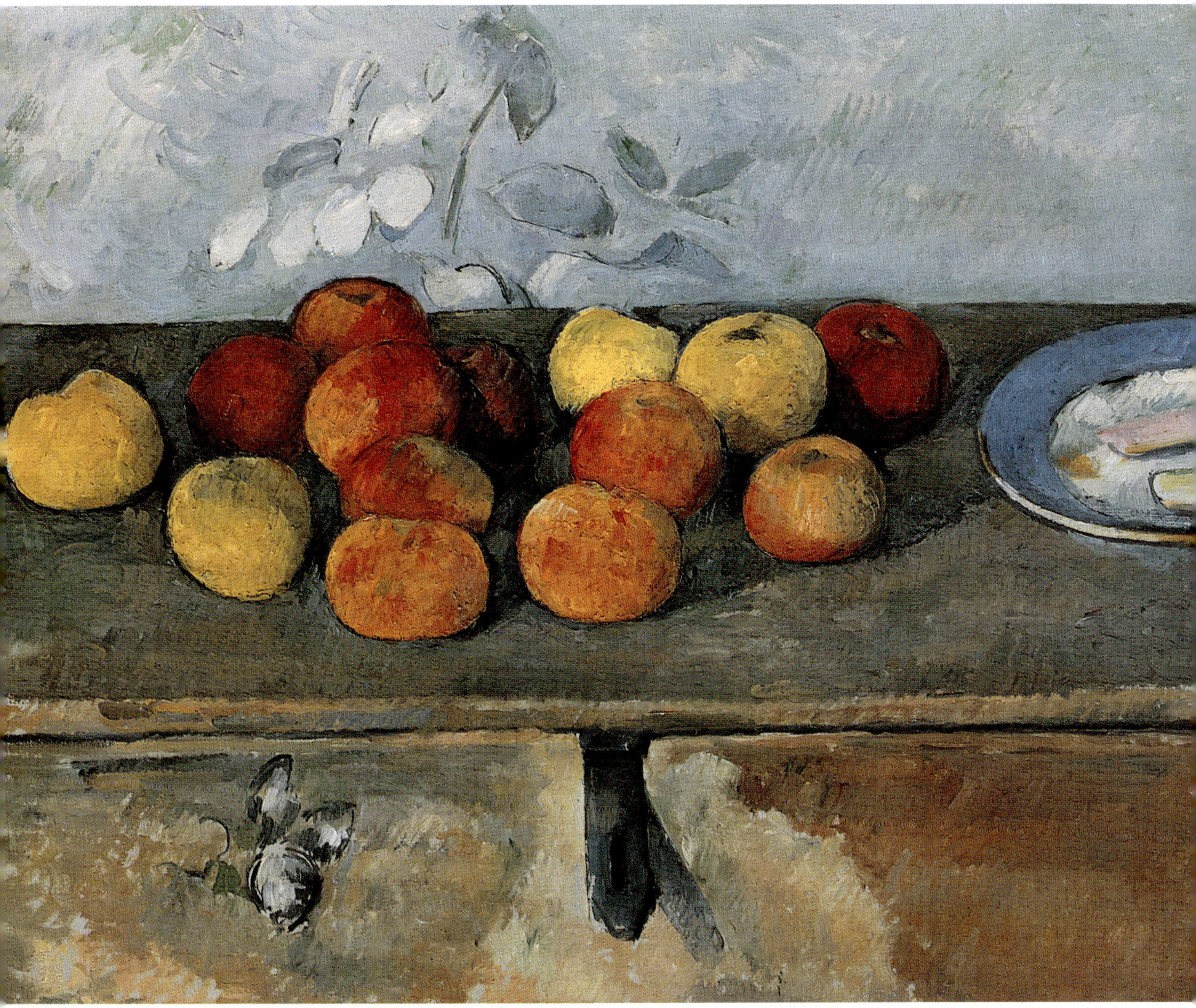

Paul Cézanne
The Card Players, c. 1895

Musée d'Orsay, Paris. Courtesy of AKG London/Erich Lessing

CÉZANNE produced several paintings of *The Card Players*; the first was probably in 1890, using his gardener Alex Paulin as a model. However, as he rarely signed and dated his work, an exact chronology of the paintings is difficult.

Cézanne's weighty style was now well-established and his 'card players' are as timeless as *Mont Sainte-Victoire* (1882–85) in their ponderous monumentality. They have been compared with the work of Giotto (c. 1267–1337) and Early Renaissance artists. There is no question of a fleeting Impressionist effect, rather an atmosphere of almost religious quiet as the players concentrate. The game has clearly been going on for some time.

The two men are almost mirror images of each other, sitting rocklike on either side of the table. The atmosphere is calm but the tension is palpable. One man is slightly more relaxed and leans forward, while the other is more upright, leaning against the rigid back of his chair, his hands closer to the edge of the table. A bottle, slightly off-centre, separates their hands on the table. The glinting bottleneck, the white clay pipe in the mouth of the man on the left and the two men's white shirt collars concentrate the gaze on the game in hand.

1886 was the year of the last Impressionist exhibition, although Cézanne had not exhibited with them since 1877. In 1895, the dealer Ambroise Vollard (1865–1939) organised Cézanne's first exhibition since then. In-between times his work could only be seen at the shop of Père Tanguy, a paint merchant based in Montmartre, who Van Gogh painted and whom Pissarro introduced to Cézanne in the early 1870s.

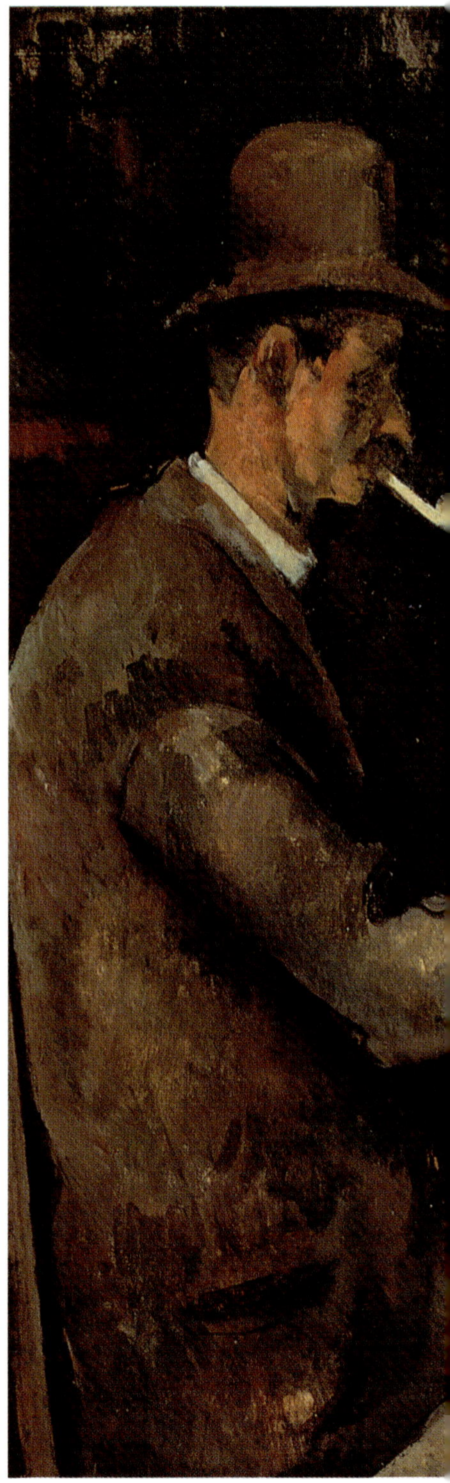

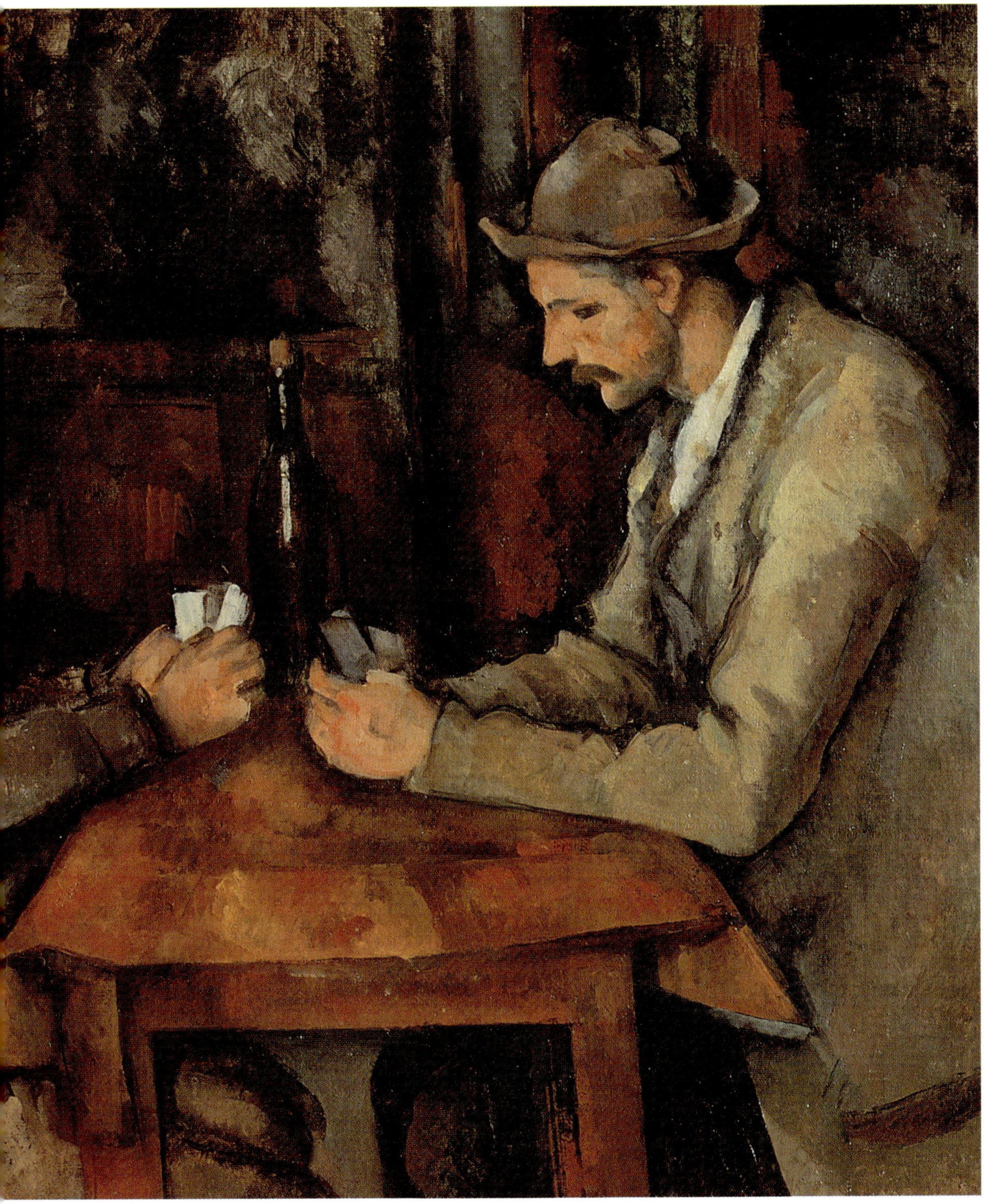

Paul Cézanne
Plaster Cupid, c. 1895

Courtauld Institute Galleries, London. Courtesy of AKG London

CÉZANNE'S vision at this time looks forward to the abstraction of the twentieth century without remotely losing sight of its subject matter. This large, extraordinary canvas is dominated by a small plaster cast of a truncated Cupid, thought to be by Nicolas Coustou (1658–1733) or François Desquesnoy (1594–1643).

The background is initially confusing, as everything is at different angles and from different viewpoints – something Cézanne began to investigate in the early 1890s. We see a Cupid placed on a table surrounded by apples and onions – rather an odd combination – and viewed from a slightly raised angle. The floor, on which a number of canvases are placed, recedes but not at the expected angle, as it is raised and tilted. An outsize apple in the corner of the room (but almost the middle of the canvas) seems ready to roll towards the Cupid as if it were a skittle. The kneeling sculpture, another painted still life that contrasts with the sculptural (but actually painted) Cupid, reinforces this idea, as do the diagonals of the table and canvas edges that enclose the Cupid and converge upon the apple.

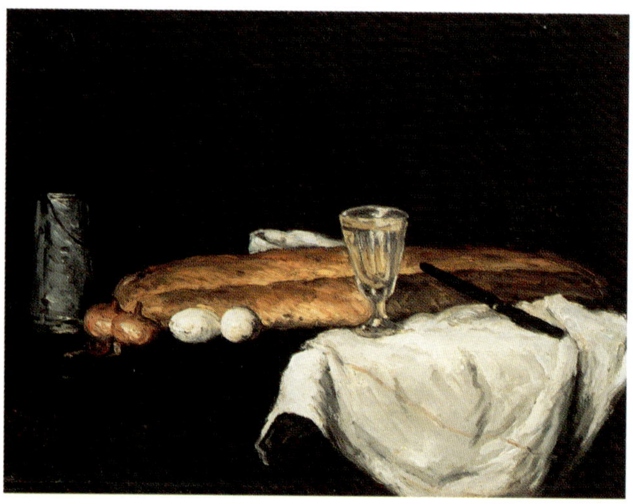

Paul Cézanne
Still Life with Bread and Eggs, 1865
Cincinnati Art Museum, Cincinnati. Courtesy of AKG London. *(See p. 220)*

The still-life canvas in the background confuses the sense of reality further in fusing with the 'real' still life in the foreground. The painted blue material combines with the 'real' blue material on the table and the painted fruits are as round, large and lush as their 'real' relations in the foreground.

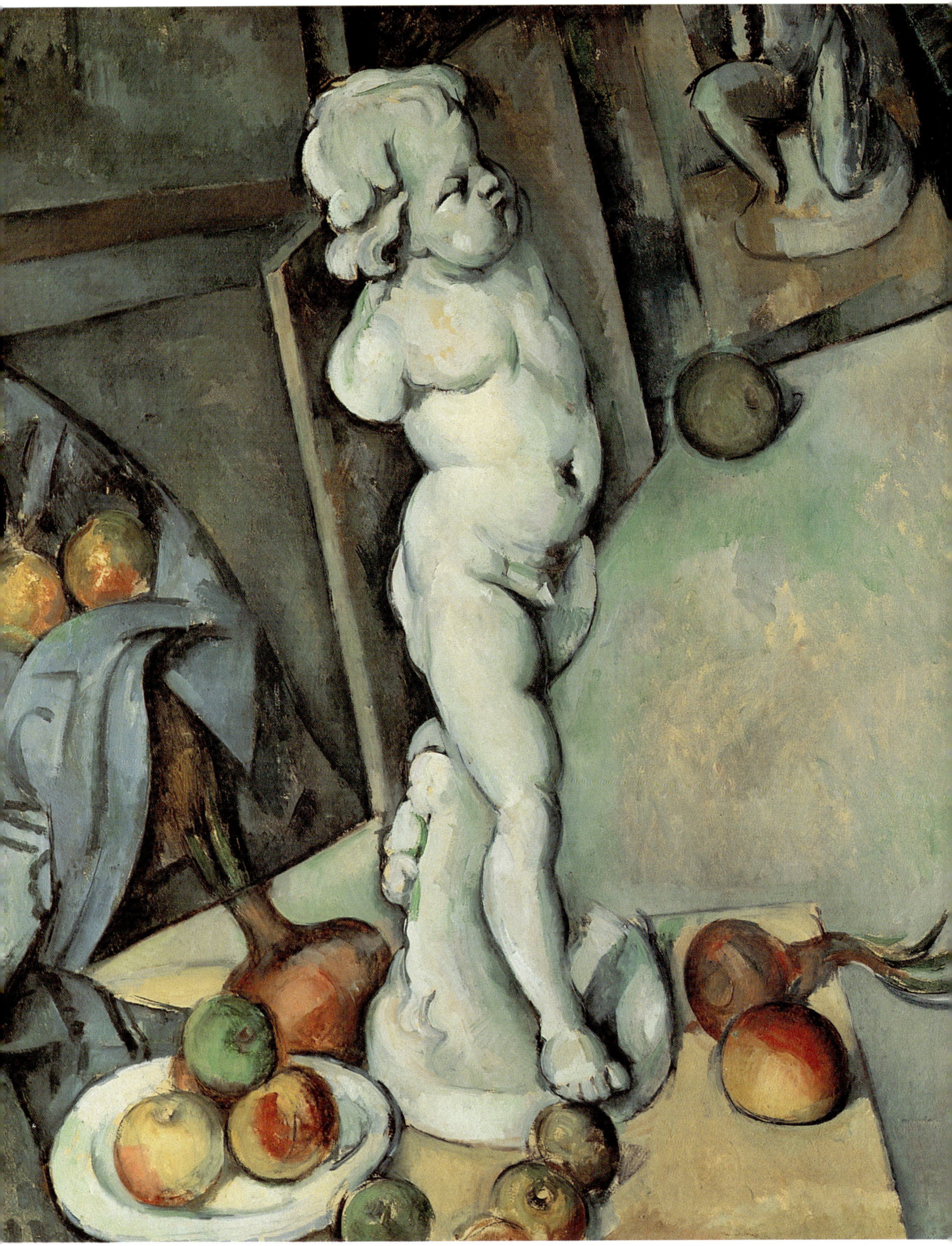

Paul Cézanne
Bridge Over the Pond, c. 1898

I.A. Morosoz Collection, Pushkin Museum, Moscow. Courtesy of AKG London

THIS picture was painted in 1898, the year that Monet was beginning to paint his Japanese bridge and the pond at Giverny. But the paintings could not be more different. Whereas Monet creates a sunlit, oriental, natural scene with fronds and reflections of nature mirrored in the water, Cézanne's scene is more like the darkened, hallowed interior of a Gothic cathedral with the trees on each side leaning inwards to converge, like a roof, at a point above the bridge, drawing us into the picture. The bridge, a short horizontal in the middle plane, almost like a rood screen in a cathedral, acts as a barrier to the vegetation beyond, which opens up to the glories of the sunlit sky.

It is a remarkably structured composition, painted almost entirely in shades of green. The water takes up the foreground in a broad horizontal swathe, the foliage reflected in solid blocks of colour made up of small strokes of paint side by side, almost like hatching. By placing the strokes at different angles Cézanne gives a form and shape to the real and reflected vegetation – flat in the water, but softer and more rounded in the trees. He achieves this either by overlapping the strokes in order not to create a sharp edge, or by leaving them surrounded by empty canvas, to give the impression of sun on the leaves.

'I paint as I see,' Cézanne once said, 'and I have very strong feelings.' He never stopped looking at nature and expressing himself in his landscapes, still lifes, portraits and compositions from his imagination.

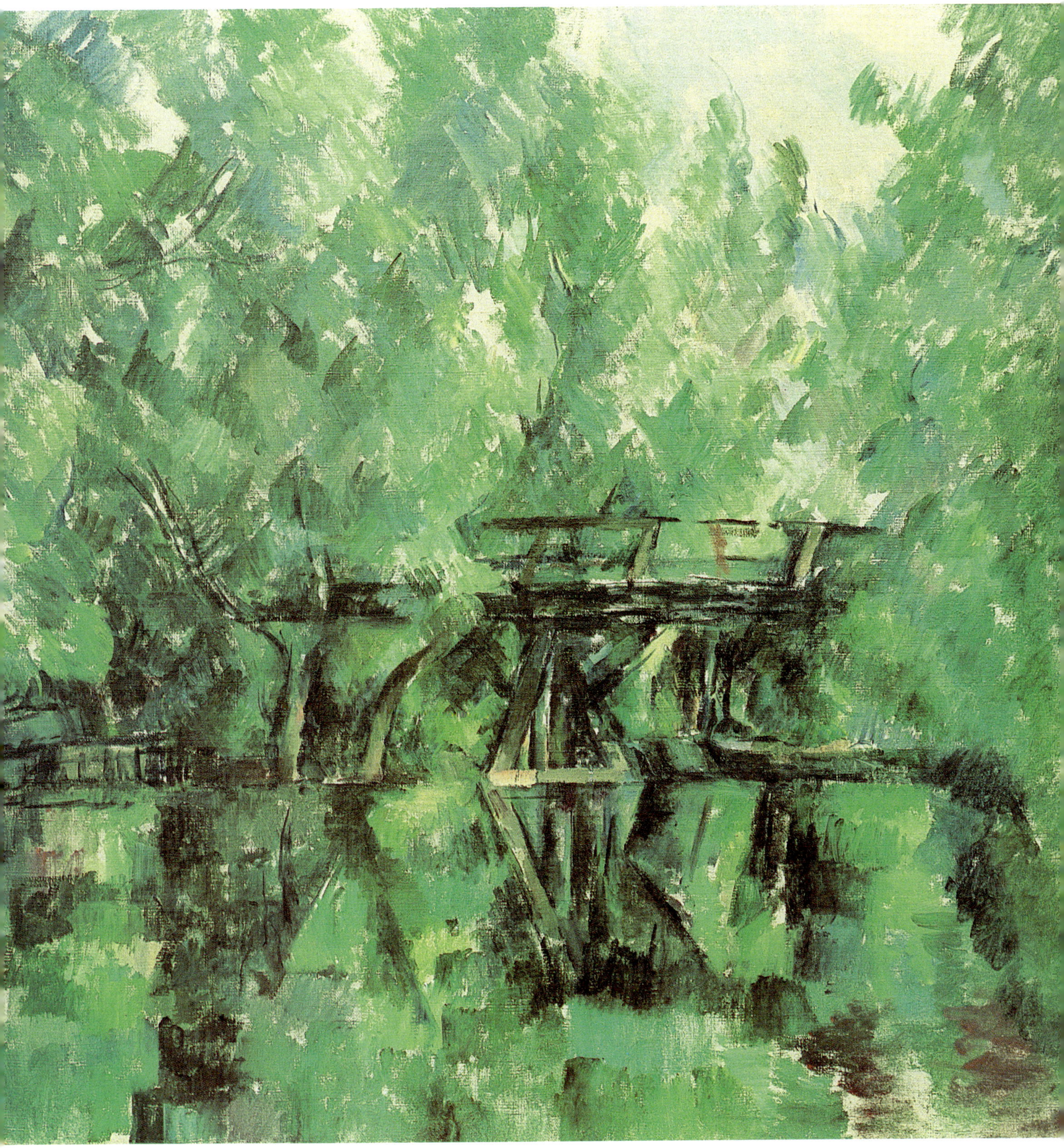

Paul Cézanne
The Quarry of Bibémus, 1898–1900

Museum Folkwang, Essen. Courtesy of AKG London/Erich Lessing

THE quarry of Bibémus lies on the western flank of Mont Sainte-Victoire, a strangely architectural place where stonecutters had been working since Roman times. Cézanne was drawn to this quiet, stately place and during the summer of 1897, he rented a cabin nearby where he could leave his painting materials and stay the night, if needed.

This painting expresses a great serenity, which Cézanne achieves by painting the rocks – a combination of soft shapes caused by erosion and harder, geometric shapes gouged out of the rock – and the sky and trees in such a way that, while completely separate, they seem to fuse in to one great still life. The consistency of the small, even brushstrokes helps to create this feeling.

Perhaps nowhere more than here can we see what Cézanne meant when he wrote to young painter and writer Émile Bernard in 1904: 'Treat nature by means of the cylinder, the sphere, the cone … .'

Although the geometry of this picture is natural to the quarry, it is not hard to see how Cézanne's ability to express the essence of what he saw before him appealed to the next generation of *avant-garde* painters. Max Weber (1881–1961), a pioneer of Fauvism, Expressionism and Cubism, wrote: 'When I saw the first ten pictures by this master … I said to myself as I gazed … "This is the way to paint. This is art and nature, reconstructed…".'

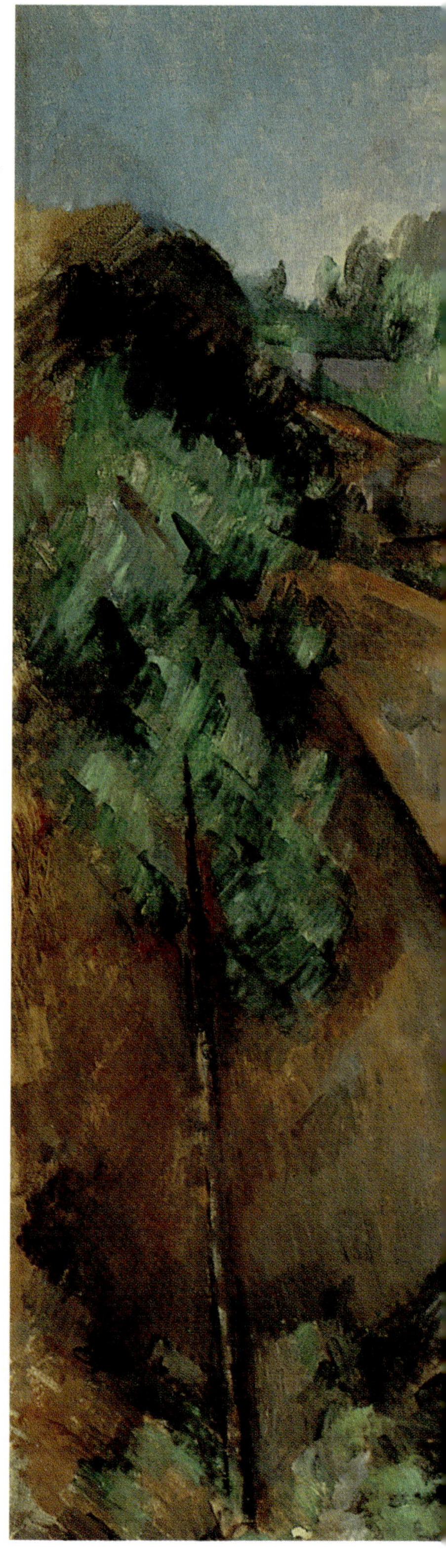

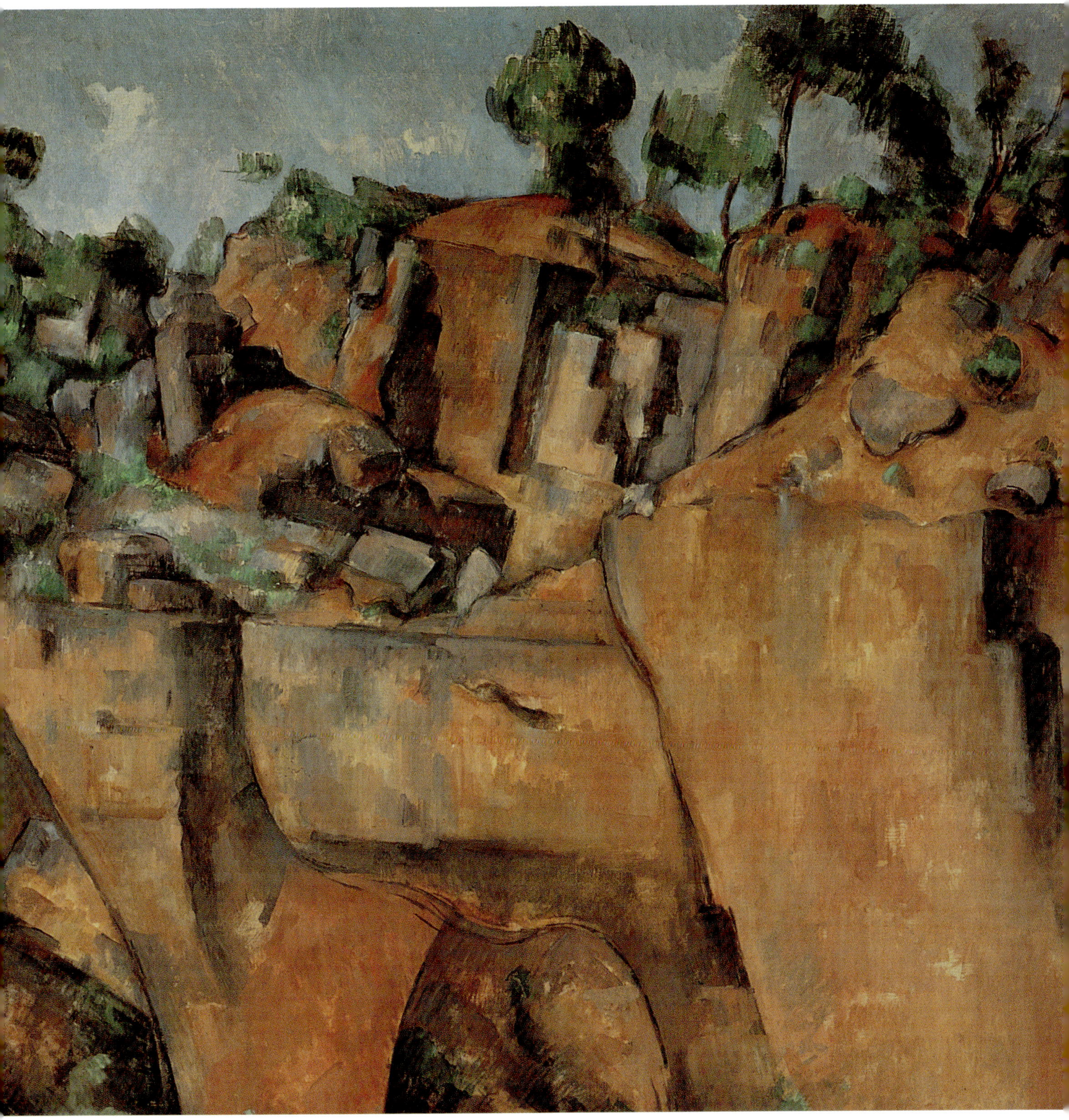

PAUL CÉZANNE
Apples and Oranges, c. 1898–99

Musée d'Orsay, Paris. Courtesy of AKG London

THIS is one of a series of still lifes that Cézanne painted in Paris, using similar, everyday objects. The chronology of the paintings is not confirmed but it seems likely that this is one of the last. Whereas spatial references can be relied upon in the other canvases – objects are where they appear to be – in this canvas, as in many of his later landscapes and portraits, the planes seem to overlap. Cézanne's art lies in creating pictures that work as an organic whole.

In this still life, each object is a definable entity and yet, together, they create a kind of landscape. The pyramidal structure of the fruit accentuates their volume and locks the objects together. The curtain, like a sun-dappled landscape, shields the still life like a mountain range. The colours of the fruit and also the pattern on the jug create a link with this patterned background. Yet the arrangement stands out, thrown into relief by the white tablecloth, plate and fruit dish. Secure spatial references cannot be relied upon here. Note also the table, the edge of which appears on the right but which, as you follow the diagonal left, runs into the scroll of an armchair.

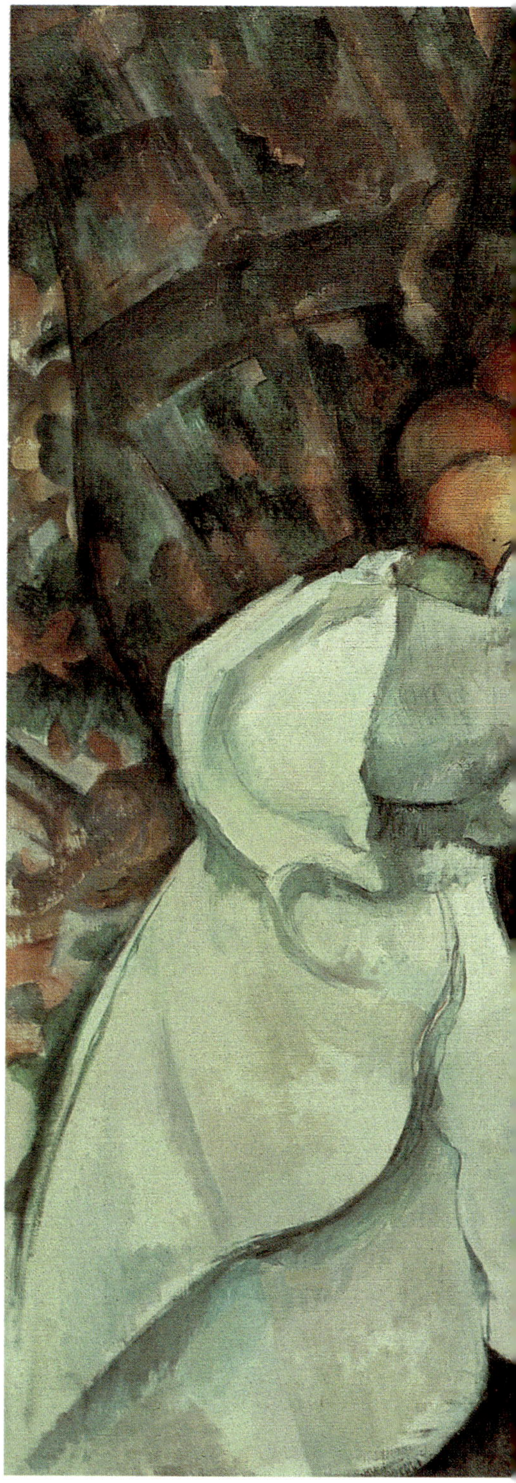

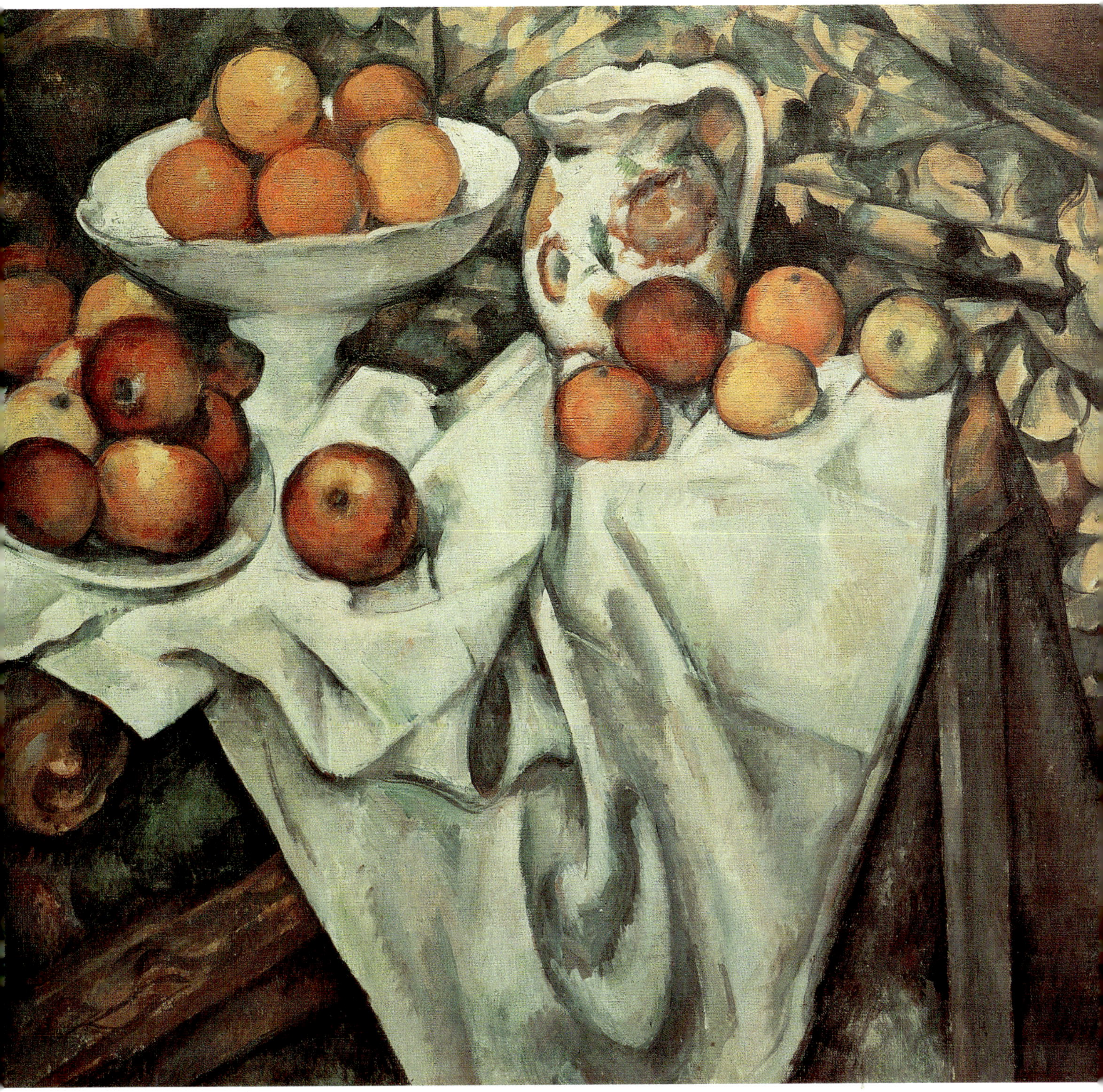

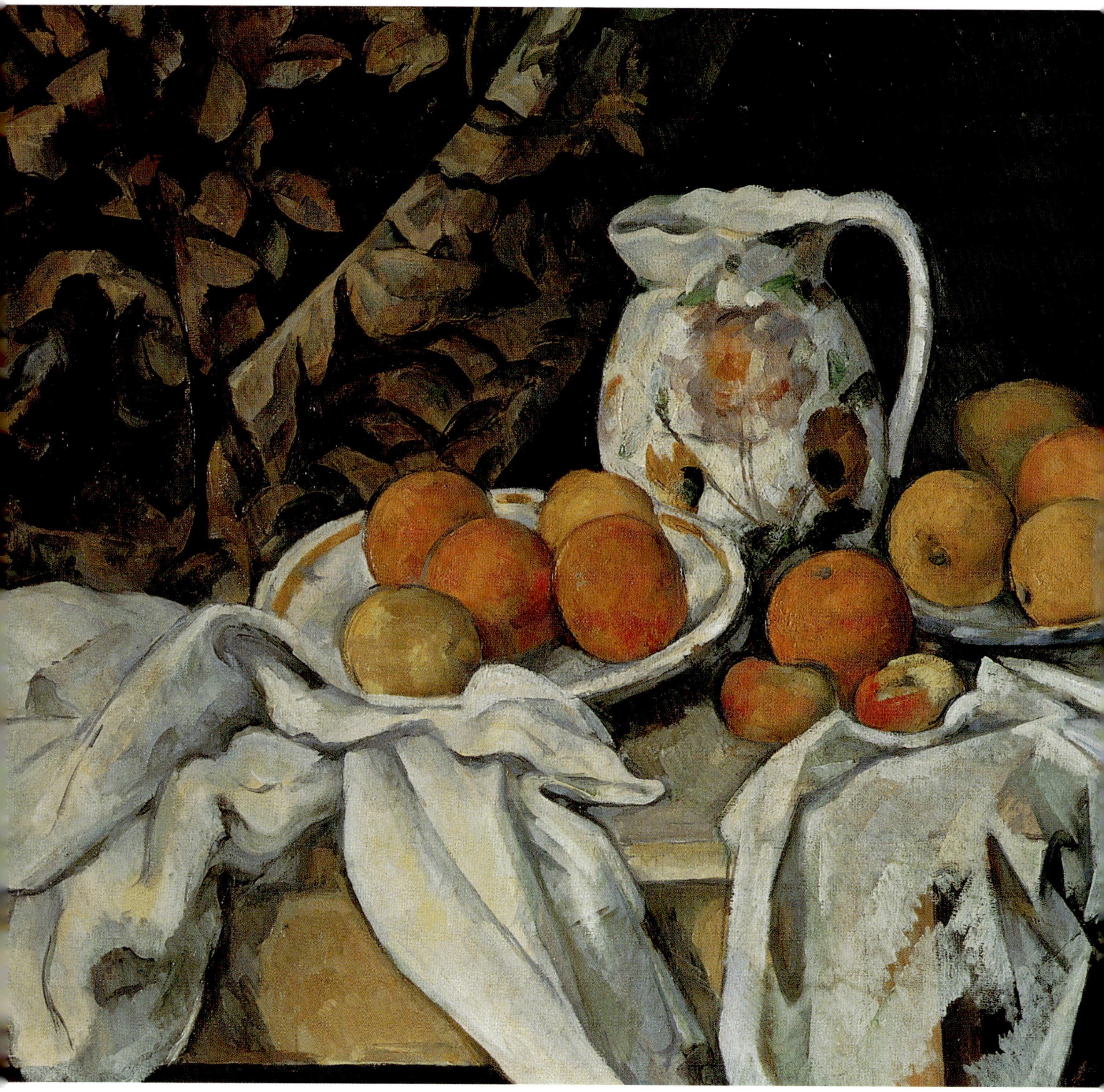

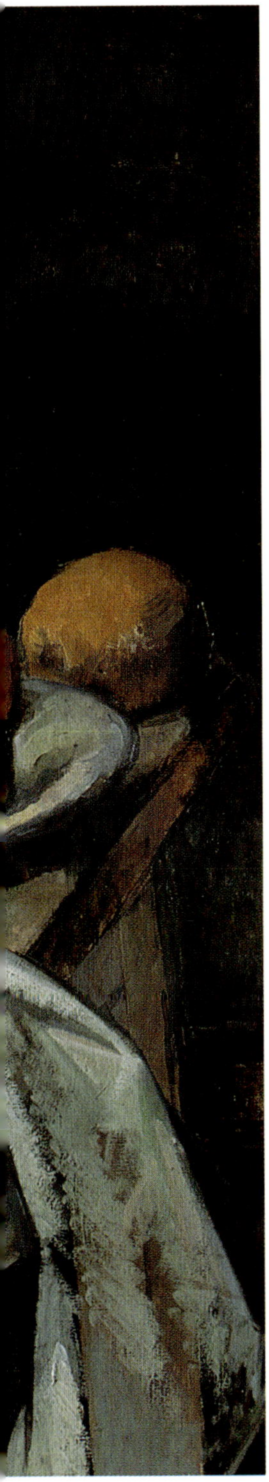

Paul Cézanne

Still Life with Curtain and Flowered Jug, c. *1898–99*

State Hermitage, St Petersburg. Courtesy of AKG London/Erich Lessing

THIS is another of the six canvases painted in Paris between 1898 and 1899 that all feature the same elements. Rather like Monet, whose series of Rouen paintings he greatly admired in 1897, Cézanne paints the same motifs several times. But, unlike Monet, his aim is not to see the effects of changing light but to understand the inner essence of an object and its relationship with the world around it.

Cézanne was very laborious in his painting. In 1914, the dealer Ambroise Vollard described how he had 115 sittings for his portrait in 1899, the year after Cézanne's exhibition in his gallery. He was just as meticulous in setting up and painting his still lifes. His friend, painter Louis le Bail, who worked with him in 1898, described how he arranged his compositions: 'The cloth was draped a little over the table with instructive taste; then Cézanne arranged the fruit, contrasting the tones against one another, making the complementaries vibrate, the greens against the reds, the yellows against the blues, fitting, turning, balancing the fruit as he wanted it to be, using coins of one or two *sous* for the purpose. He took the greatest care over the task and many precautions; one guessed that it was a feast for the eye for him.'

PAUL CÉZANNE
Seated Peasant, c. 1900–04

Private Collection. Courtesy of AKG London/Erich Lessing

THE sitter and the exact date of this portrait are unknown but the image is of such unabiding timelessness that it does not seem important. Cézanne creates a mountain of a man, centrally placed and looking forward. His head, arms and hands create a diamond-shaped composition that is only interrupted by the cane. This is a reference to the frailty of old age but actually enhances the upright, formal posture of the elderly man, whose huge hands are reddened from decades of outdoor work.

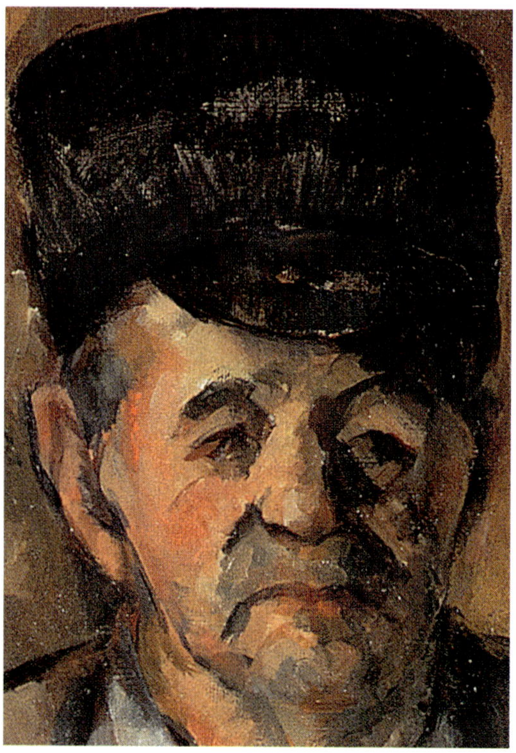

The symmetrical, central placing confers a certain grandeur on the massive figure. This is further enhanced by the way in which Cézanne has locked him into the surroundings over which he presides – his top half haloed by the upright pattern of the wallpaper behind him, his arms and legs the same colour as the skirting board and the floor. Although a spartan figure, he seems to be in his 'Sunday best', an idea emphasised by the formal pose and the crisp, white shirt that draws our attention to the centre of the canvas.

This figure brings to mind Cézanne's comment: 'I love, above all things, the aspect of people who've grown old without changing their ways, abandoning themselves to the jaws of time.'

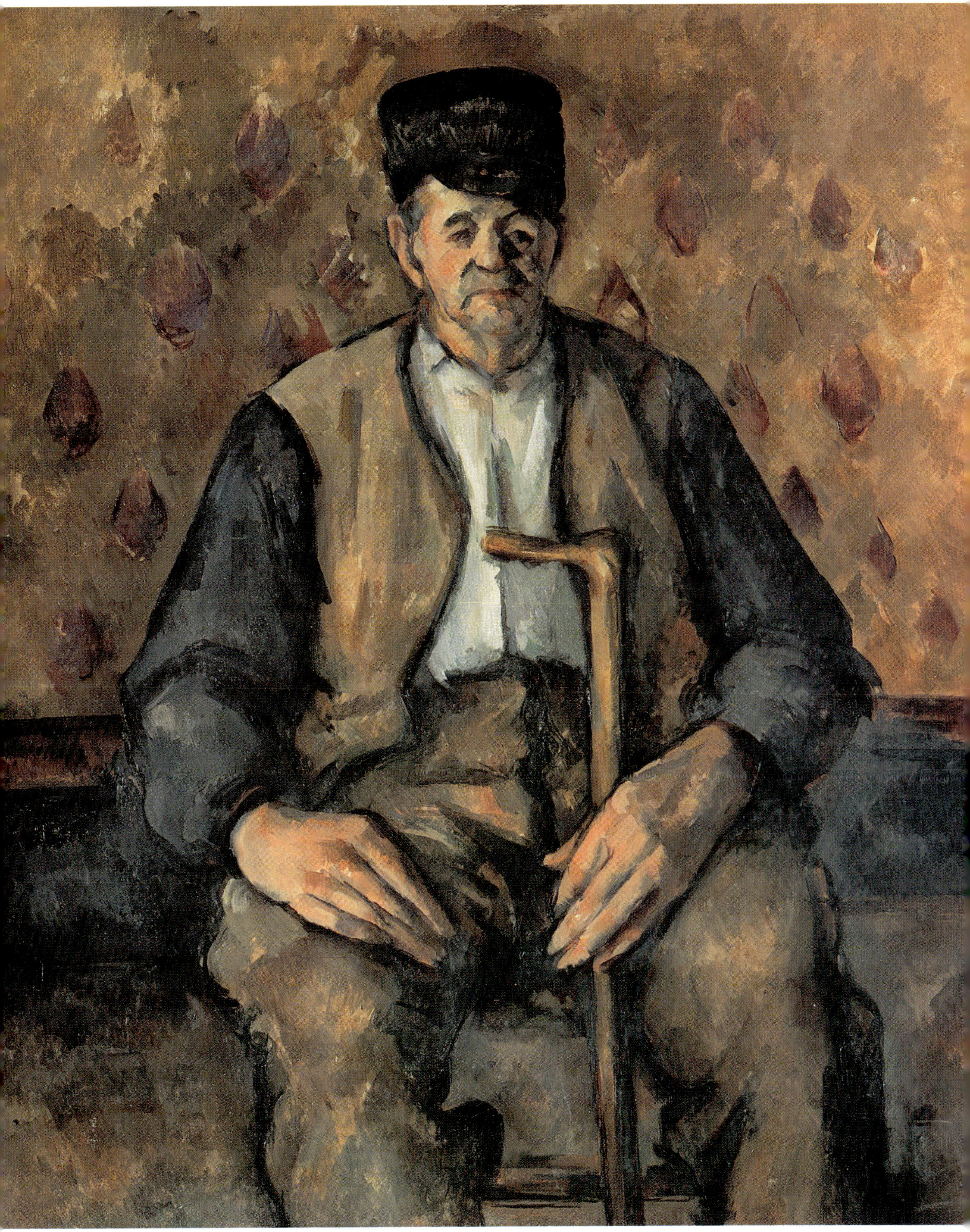

PAUL CÉZANNE
Mont Sainte-Victoire, 1902–06

I.S. Schtschukin Collection, Pushkin Museum, Moscow. Courtesy of AKG London

BETWEEN 1902 and 1906, Cézanne embarked on his last series of paintings of Mont Sainte-Victoire. There are 11 canvases and several watercolours. The size and angle of view vary slightly, although they are all painted from the same place east of the mountain, with the north-east plain below.

This is one of the smallest paintings of the series and one of the most heavily and intensely worked, in which Cézanne has created a highly charged landscape. As with most of his works, the canvas is divided into three horizontal bands: the slope below with a cyprus on the left and trees on the right; the patchwork, golden plane running to the base of the mountain; and the majestic, blue band of mountain and sky, separate and yet unified with each other.

The dramatic profile of the mountain and the heavy atmosphere of the sky is matched in the agitation and density of the brushstrokes in the foreground. The repeated green strokes through the golden middle ground, coupled with a sharp diagonal from the right, create a sense of depth. The sky is a backdrop to the mountain but it comes forward over the landscape, lowering as if a storm is about to break. However, a band of light breaks through to relieve the intensity and paint the right-hand slopes of the mountain in gentle shades of pink and lilac.

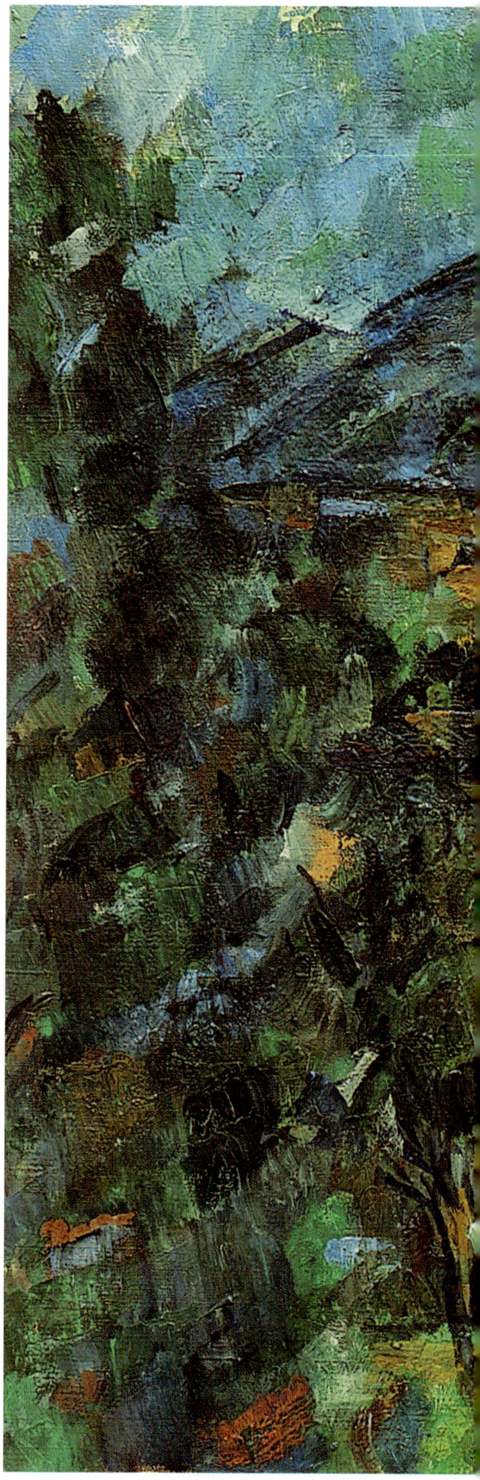

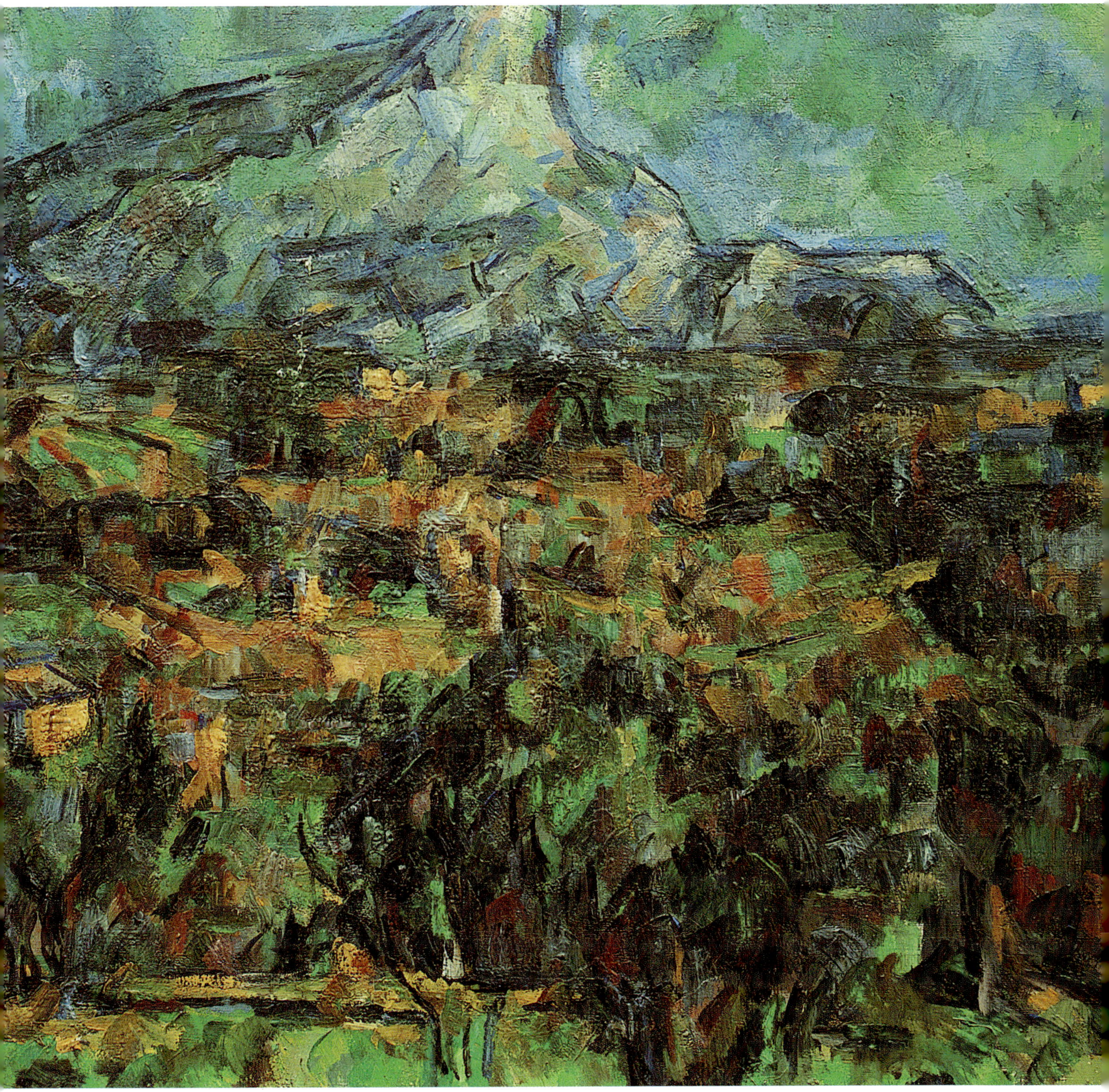

Paul Cézanne
Bathers, 1902–06

Private Collection. Courtesy of AKG London/Erich Lessing

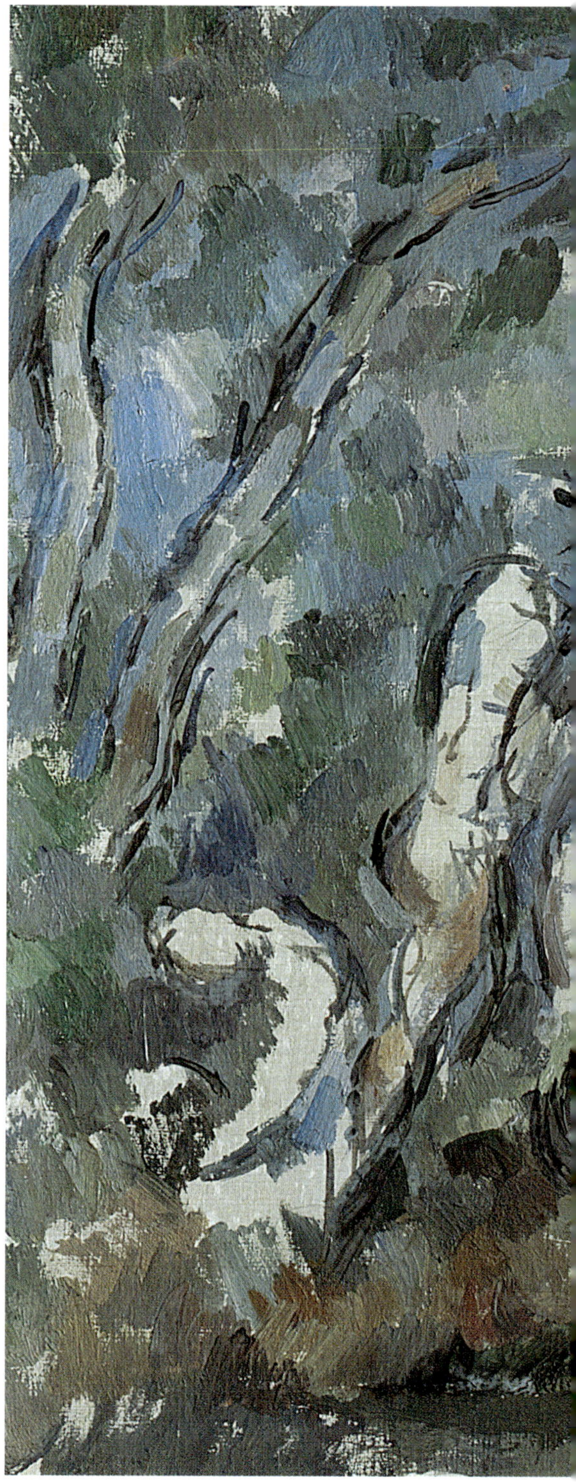

In the mid-1890s, Cézanne began work on a composition of female nudes beneath some trees. He had already painted male bathers in 1885 and 1890, but now, like Renoir, turned to this more Classical theme. Over the next ten years he made, at the very least, 30 small sketches in addition to two or three larger canvases.

This large oil sketch is not a preparatory study and is regarded as a substantial work in its own right. Cézanne painted the figures from life drawings that he made at the Académie Suisse and from his memories of the Old Masters – considering it inappropriate for a man of his age to ask a young woman to pose naked for him.

Cézanne places 11 bathers, engulfed in a milky-blue haze, on the banks of a river or lake. Placed in three triangular formations, they almost fill the width of the canvas. The lake, the bank on the other side and the blue-drenched hills open out into the distance. Once again, he creates a cathedral-like setting with the strong diagonals of the trees and figures creating height and depth, converging on a patch of green light in the sky. The rounded, organic bodies, and the caring way in which each group seems to tend to something, is suggestive of femininity.

This is one of Cézanne's last works. He died from pneumonia on 15 October 1906 – a week after he collapsed unconscious during a thunderstorm when out painting *en plein air*.

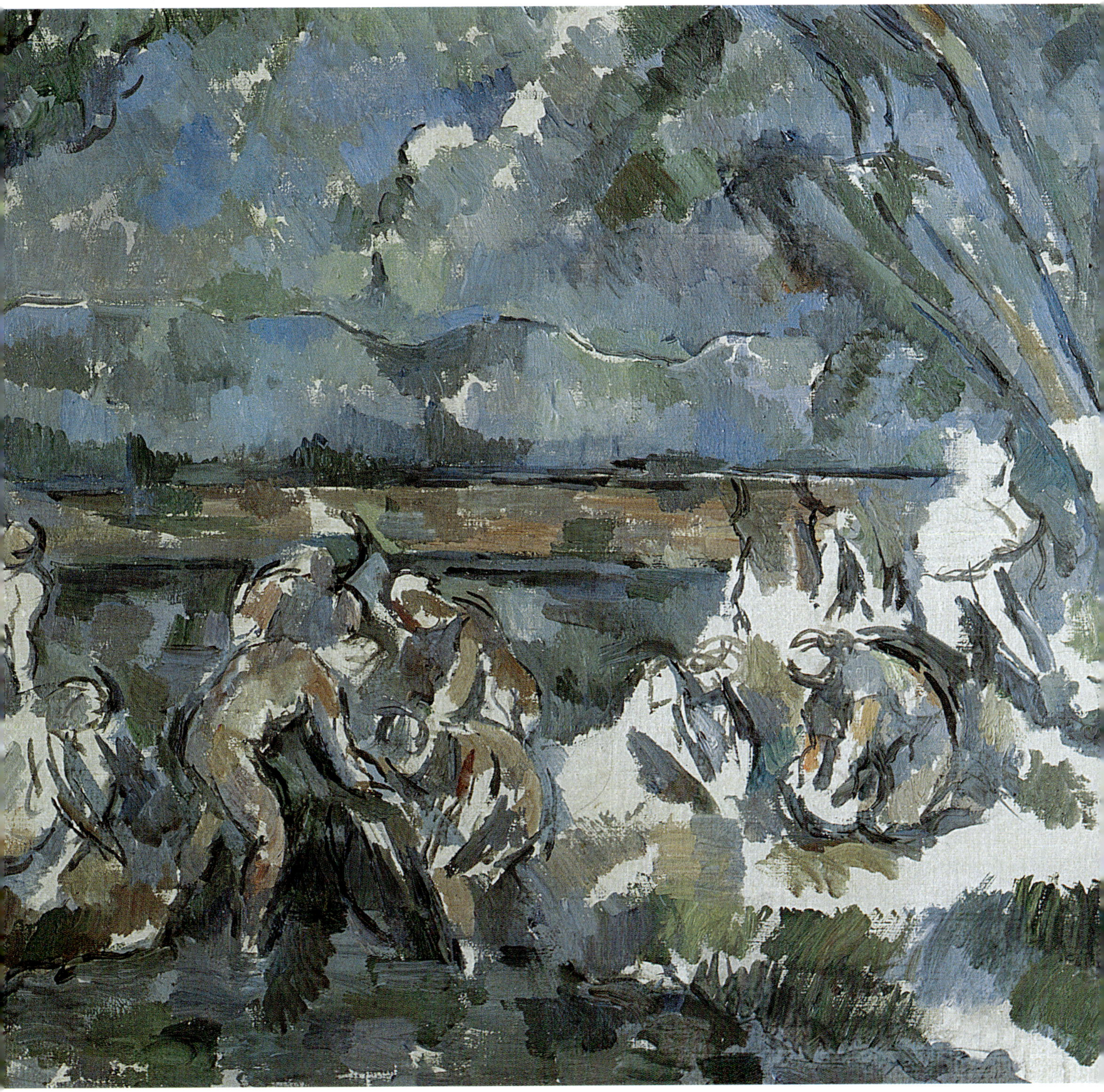

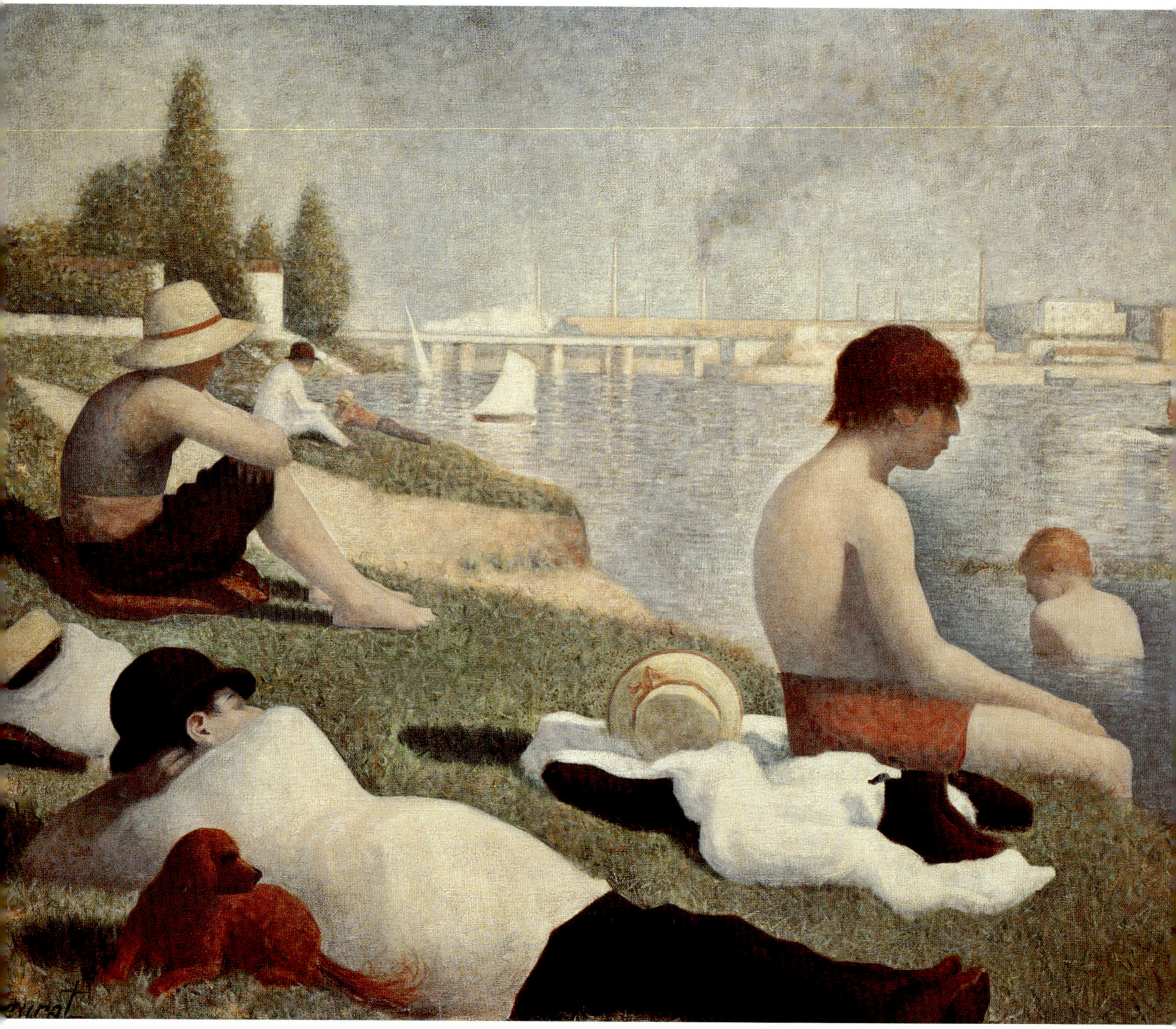

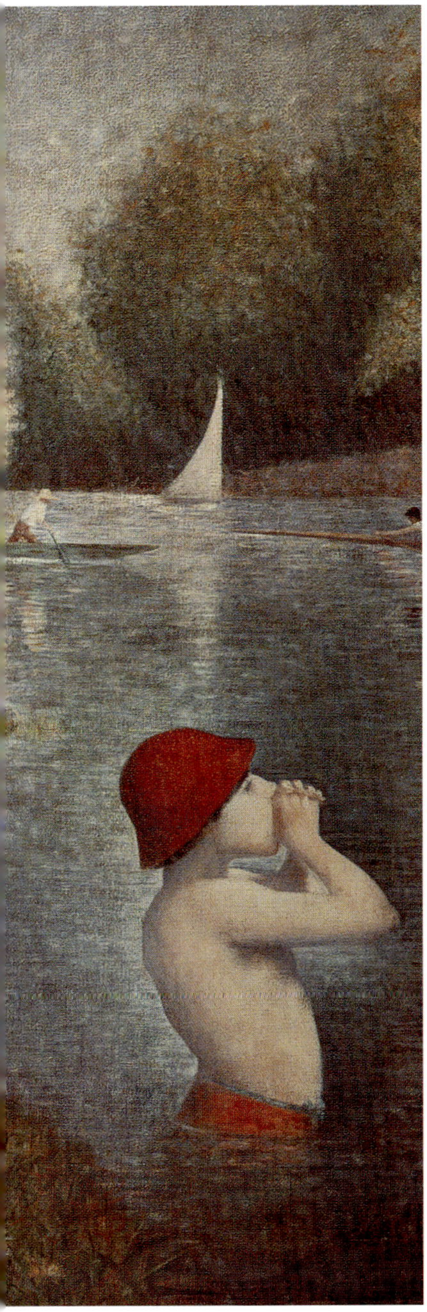

GEORGES SEURAT (1859–91)
Bathing at Asnières, 1883–84

Tate Gallery, London. Courtesy of AKG London/Erich Lessing

YOUNGER than the Impressionists, Georges Seurat started to paint in about 1881. He was not an Impressionist but knew their work from their fourth independent exhibition in 1879. He exhibited with them in 1886, with the support of Pissarro. Seurat, like many of the younger generation of painters, learnt from Impressionism but eventually moved on to other fields of experimentation and endeavour. This is his first large-scale composition; it was rejected at the Salon of 1884.

Asnières was an industrial suburb of Paris, and this work takes up the Impressionist ideal of painting modern, suburban life in much the same way as Monet and Renoir had both painted La Grenouillère in the early 1870s. But *Bathing at Asnières* has a static, monumental quality created by the massive canvas, the solidity of the figures and the quality of the brushwork that bears little resemblance to the work of the Impressionists. The light, bright palette is that of the Impressionists but the brushwork is tighter and less disordered. Seurat, in his own way, is every bit as concerned with light as the Impressionists, although he is not interested in its fleeting qualities. In this painting, he moves towards a studied approach to the painting of light, based on the science of the light spectrum and the way in which colours are perceived by the eye.

GEORGES SEURAT
The Circus, 1891

Musée d'Orsay, Paris. Courtesy of AKG London/Erich Lessing

THE innovation of Seurat's style can be clearly seen in this painting. He adopted a palette that used the pure colours of the spectrum, painting tiny dots on to a flat, coloured background. The intention was that these colours should become mixed in the eye of the viewer. Hence, the yellows and blues placed together would seem to be green when the viewer stood at the right distance from the canvas. This technique became known as Pointillism and was also propagated by Paul Signac.

Seurat, who came from a wealthy background, was a highly intelligent, methodical man with reformist political views. He studied colour theory as found in the work of Eugène Chevreul (1786–1889) and Charles Blanc (1813–82), which had so influenced the Impressionists, reinterpreting their findings in the light of *Modern Chromatics*, written by the American physicist Ogden Rood, which appeared in France in 1881. He sought to create an art that could be produced through the application of rules, free from messy or accidental improvisation, using colour and line in a prescribed form to create colour and light effects as well as certain emotional responses. Cheerfulness, for example, 'means a luminous dominant tone; in terms of colour, a warm dominant tone; in terms of line, lines above the horizontal.'

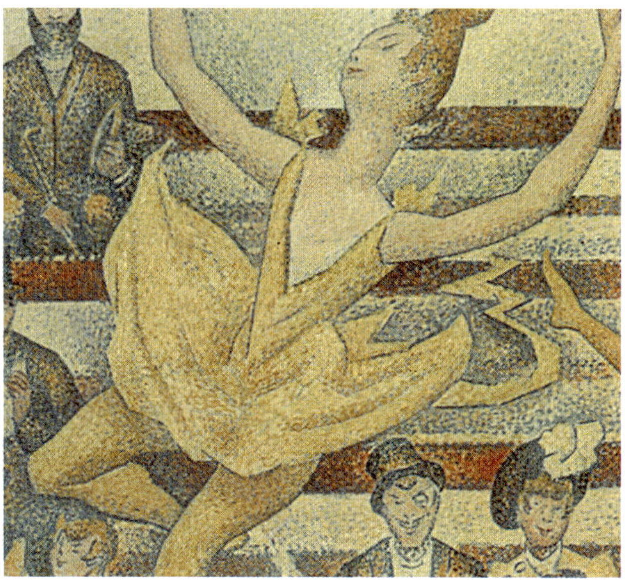

The Circus shows Seurat's pictorial science reproduced at an intense level, the extraordinary composition revealing his mastery of line. But, although it was exhibited in 1891, it was unfinished. Seurat died the same year.

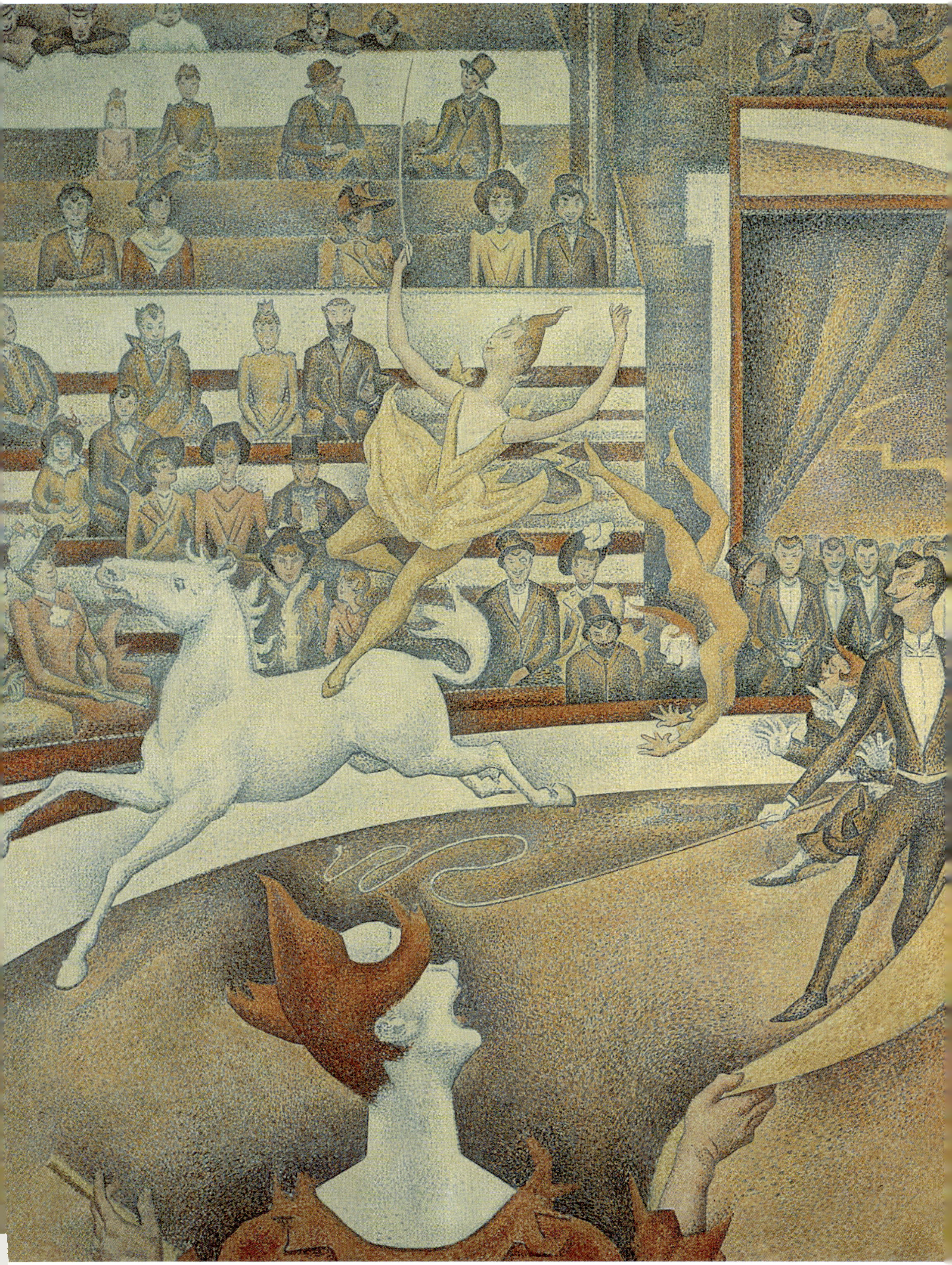

AUTHOR BIOGRAPHIES AND ACKNOWLEDGMENTS

For my parents and grandmother, with love.

Antonia Cunningham gained her degree in History of Art from Cambridge University in 1988, where she wrote her dissertation on Degas. She has taught art history to high-school level students and is now a writer and editor of both adult and children's books.

Karen Hurrell is Canadian-born and educated, and is the author of several art books, including works on Monet, Renoir, Turner and the Pre-Raphaelites. She lives in London with her two sons.

While every endeavour has been made to ensure the accuracy of the reproduction of the images in this book, we would be grateful to receive any comments or suggestions for inclusion in future reprints.

With thanks to AKG London and The Bridgeman Art Library for assistance with sourcing the pictures for this series of books. Grateful thanks also to Bridget Tily, Claire Dashwood and Karen Villabona.

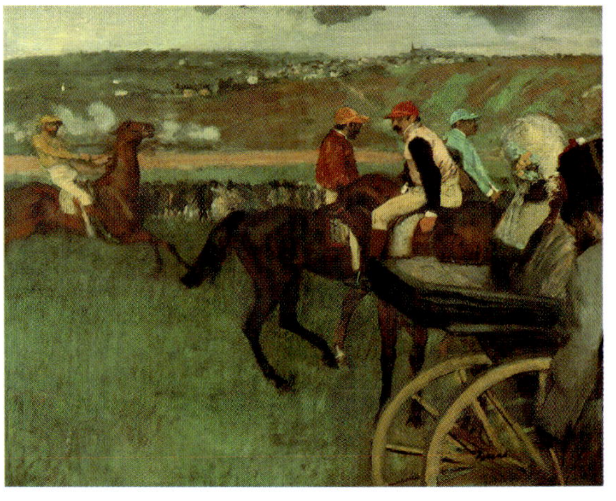